THE ENGLISH PSALTER

THE ENGLISH PSALTER

With a Devotional Commentary

BY

GEORGE D. CARLETON

A. R. MOWBRAY & Co. LIMITED
LONDON AND OXFORD
MOREHOUSE-GORHAM CO.
NEW YORK

THIS BOOK IS PRODUCED IN COMPLETE CONFORMITY WITH THE
AUTHORIZED ECONOMY STANDARDS

First published in 1945

PRINTED IN GREAT BRITAIN BY
A. R. MOWBRAY & CO. LIMITED, LONDON AND OXFORD
4544

PSALMORUM CLAVIS CHRISTI FIDES

PREFACE

THIS book, both in its plan and its substance, should be ascribed chiefly to my father, the Reverend James George Carleton, D.D., sometime Canon and Treasurer of S. Patrick's Cathedral, and Deputy Regius Professor of Divinity in the University of Dublin. He published in 1909, through the Cambridge University Press, a handbook of the Psalter, entitled *The Psalter of the Church*, which was 'designed to meet the case of the many Church people who would welcome help, if given in a concise and easily apprehended form, towards a better understanding' of the meaning of the psalms and of the use that can be made of them in the Church's ordered worship and in private meditation and prayer, but 'for whom the study of elaborate and diffuse commentaries is out of the question.'

The special feature of his book, and of this book of mine, is the printing of the text of the Psalter and the notes thereon in parallel columns. By this arrangement the notes have had to be limited to a number of words not greatly exceeding that of the words of the psalms, which is a feature not usual in commentaries; the reader also is enabled to take in the meaning of a passage at a glance, and the wearisomeness of carrying the eye to the foot of the page or of turning to the end of the volume for the commentary is avoided.

I have made several additions to, and a few excisions from, my father's notes. Chiefly I have amplified his references to the mystical interpretation of the psalms, the traditionally Christian method of interpretation, by which the Church has discerned Christ everywhere in the Psalter: but at the same time I have endeavoured to confine myself to giving general indications of the method, and to detailing only a sufficient number of examples to make clear to the reader how he may pursue this method of interpretation for himself. In general I have refrained from giving superfluous information, and have tried to give only such guidance as may help the unlearned worshipper to recite the Psalter with the mind of the Church, without saving him from the necessary work of doing his own thinking. Like my father, I have not dealt with questions of authorship and date, except in the few instances where their discussion was necessary for the elucidation of the meaning of a psalm. I have frequently stated readings of the Revised Version, as being nearer to the Hebrew than is the text of the Prayer Book Psalter; but in general I have been concerned to suggest interpretations consonant with Christian tradition of the phrases of the English Psalter given to us to use, rather than to set forth the original meaning of the Hebrew psalms.

I acknowledge gratefully the courtesy of the Syndics of the Cambridge University Press in permitting the publication of this book.

G. D. C.

CONTENTS

INTRODUCTORY NOTES

I

THE COMPILATION OF THE PSALTER

1. *The Hebrew Psalms*

IN the Hebrew Old Testament the psalms were arranged in five books: 1–41; 42–72; 73–89; 90–106; 107–150. These books are now indicated for English readers in the Revised Version. The end of each book is marked by a doxology; and the whole of the last psalm, 150, is a doxology.

An examination of the psalms leads to the conclusion that the Psalter was gradually compiled by the combination of several collections of psalms. The division into books is itself an indication of this; and also many of the psalms have titles which assign them to certain authors. The first book, in which nearly all the psalms are attributed to David, may reasonably be regarded as having once existed as a separate psalm-book, which was the nucleus of the future Psalter. Another collection of psalms is suggested by the title 'Of the Sons of Korah,' 42–49, 84–85, 87–88; another by that of 'Of Asaph,' 50, 73–83; another by 'A Song of Ascents,' 120–134; and yet another by 'Hallelujah' either at the beginning or the end of each psalm, 146–150.

The use of divine names also bears witness to the composite character of the Psalter. In the first book 'Jehovah' or 'Jahweh,' which is generally translated 'the LORD' in the English Versions, is almost exclusively employed. In the second and third books 'Elohim,' translated 'God,' is mainly used until Ps. 84, where 'Jehovah' again becomes prominent and so continues to Ps. 150. Another fact which points to the original independence of various parts of the Psalter is the repetition of psalms wholly or in part in different books. Thus Ps. 14 is repeated in 53, and 40. 16 ff. in 70, and 57. 8–12 with 60. 5–12 in 108. The frequent quotation of earlier in later psalms, and evident additions to psalms made in subsequent times, are significant in the same direction. Significant also is the grouping together of psalms which are akin in their subject-matter. The psalms of book i are of a personal character; they express the joys and sorrows and aspirations of individuals. In books ii and iii the national element is foremost; we find in them many prayers and thanksgivings which took their rise from public dangers and national deliverances. And in books iv and v the psalms are mostly of a liturgical character; they are specially suited for use in divine worship, and many of them were probably composed for that purpose.

2. *The Titles of the Psalms*

The titles of the Hebrew psalms were translated into our Authorized and Revised Versions, but not into the Psalter in the Book of Common Prayer. It is generally agreed among scholars that the ascription of several psalms to David or to other authors cannot be regarded as decisive of the question of authorship. Pss. 20, 21, 110, for instance, though entitled 'Of David,' are plainly addressed to a king, not written by a king; and Ps. 69, likewise attributed to David, has allusions which make it impossible to date it earlier than the Captivity. But we should not be justified in wholly disregarding the titles, as if they gave no guidance at all to the authorship. It would be difficult to account for the tradition which ascribes so many psalms to David—and it is with regard to David that the problem chiefly confronts us—if none or comparatively few were written by him. And we have independent witness to the truth of the title in one instance: Ps. 18 appears also in 2 Sam. 22, and is assigned to David both in the psalms and in the historical book. It seems probable that the first book originated in a collection of psalms composed by or closely connected with David, to which other psalms, not all by him, were subsequently added, and that the title 'Psalms of David' which belonged to the original collection was later prefixed in the singular to each psalm. When other books were added to the first, the general title 'Psalms of David' came naturally to be applied to the whole compilation.

In this commentary the titles and other historical references prefixed to the Hebrew psalms are quoted only in the few instances where they give help to the interpretation of the psalms. In most cases their interpretation as Christian hymns is not dependent upon questions of authorship or date.

3. *Hebrew Poetry*

The poetry of the Hebrews, in the opinion of many scholars, was written in metre based upon accent; but the rules of that metre are not easy to determine, and obviously the metre cannot be reproduced in a translation.

There is, however, a feature which is generally recognized as characterizing Hebrew poetry, namely, a system of parallelism which, as it belongs to the meaning and not to the mode of expression, retains its essence when translated. This system admits of much flexibility and assumes various forms, of which the two commonest are:

1. Synonymous parallelism, by which clauses correspond one with another in such a way that the second repeats the sense of the first in different terms. Thus in Ps. 15, 'LORD, who shall dwell in thy tabernacle: or who shall rest upon thy holy hill?' and in Ps. 21, 'The king shall rejoice in thy strength, O LORD: exceeding glad shall he be of thy salvation. Thou hast given him his heart's desire: and hast not denied him the request of his lips.'

2. Contrasted parallelism, by which two clauses are opposed one to another. Ps. 20: 'Some put their trust in chariots, and some in horses: but we will remember the Name of the LORD our God. They are brought down, and fallen: but we are risen, and stand upright.'

A characteristic of some psalms which cannot easily be preserved in a translation is the arrangement of the initial letters of the clauses or verses or pairs of verses, as the case may be, in the order of the Hebrew alphabet. This arrangement is as a rule found only in psalms of a special kind, those which give expression to thoughts more or less loosely strung together, bearing on a single topic and presenting them in various lights. The acrostic method supplied an artificial bond of connection which served as a help to the memory. The system is carried out in Ps. 119 with greater elaboration than elsewhere. The other alphabetical psalms are: 9, 10, 25, 34, 37, 111, 112, 145.

4. *The Vulgate Psalter*

A few words seem needed about the Vulgate Psalter, because from it our Prayer-Book Version of the Psalms in large measure derives its origin.

The Psalter in the Vulgate Latin Old Testament was the Psalter used in the Church Services in England up to the time of the Reformation; and the psalms being known by their first words in Latin, these words were retained as headings to the English psalms in the Prayer-Book, furnishing an evidence cognizable by all of the connection between the former and the latter.

The Psalter in the Vulgate, together with the rest of that Version, was the work of S. Jerome towards the end of the fourth century; but, unlike the other books, he did not translate it directly from the Hebrew original. His Psalter was a revision of the text which he found in older Latin manuscripts. This Old-Latin Psalter had become hallowed in people's minds by long use in private devotion and in public worship, and S. Jerome did not put another Psalter in its place. It had in early Christian times been translated from the Septuagint, the Greek Version of the Old Testament. Hence it arises that in most of the cases in which the English Prayer-Book Version agrees with the Vulgate against the Hebrew the rendering may ultimately be traced to the Septuagint. S. Jerome subsequently made a translation of the psalms from the Hebrew, but it was not admitted into the Vulgate, and the old familiar Version maintained its place in Church worship and in popular affection.

5. *The English Psalter*

The Version of the Psalms which finds place in the Book of Common Prayer is naturally the one which English Church people love best, both for meditation and for recitation, and with which from long use they are more familiar than with those of the Authorized or Revised Version.

This English Psalter in our Prayer-Book is practically the same as that in the First English Prayer-Book, 1549, which was taken from the accepted English Bible of that date, commonly called 'The Great Bible,' 1539.

In the Great Bible, although the other books had been translated from the original Hebrew or Greek, the book of the psalms was transferred, with some alterations, from Coverdale's Bible, 1535, which was a translation 'out of Douche [i.e. German] and Latyn into English,' as the title-page states. Hence it is that in many places the rendering of our Prayer-Book Psalter follows the Vulgate, the Latin Bible, where the Vulgate differs from the Hebrew.

In our Authorized Version, 1611, the psalms, like the other books, were translated directly from the Hebrew, and are on the whole more correctly rendered than in the Prayer-Book Version. It should, however, be noted that in several instances the scholars who gave us the Revised Version, 1885, have thought well to return to Prayer-Book renderings.

The Prayer-Book Version of the Psalter was maintained unchanged through all the revisions of the Book of Common Prayer, from the First Prayer-Book of 1549 to the last authoritative revision in 1662. The Epistles and Gospels were in 1662 conformed for the first time to the Authorized Version, but the old English Version of the psalms, having become familiar to the people (as had happened also in the case of the Old Latin Version), and being thought more rhythmical and better adapted for chanting than the new, was allowed still to retain its position. The same was the case also even in the proposed Prayer-Book of 1928; but a startling departure from Christian tradition was there suggested, by the marking of certain verses and groups of verses for omission 'at the discretion of the Minister,' as if they were judged to be unsuitable for recitation. The Church Catholic had always held that every part of the Psalter was capable of bearing a Christian meaning and was therefore suitable for use in divine worship; but this suggestion of optional omissions showed that among English people generally the key to the Christian interpretation of the psalms had been lost.

6. *The English of the Psalter*

Our Prayer-Book Psalter, being thus removed by so many steps from the original Hebrew, cannot claim to be a perfect translation; but still, in the main, it fairly represents the Hebrew; and, whatever inaccuracies it contains, we have means at hand for their correction in the Revised Version of the Bible. To a large extent the Psalter is its own interpreter; and it has instructed and cheered the hearts of thousands, who have sought no further guidance to its meaning than its own words afforded them. But, while this is undoubtedly the case, it is likewise true that the Prayer-Book Version is not in all parts easy to be understood. The meaning of many words has changed from that which they bore in the seventeenth century; and also, apart from that cause of ambiguity, we meet with passages here and there which lack any intelligible meaning. Some of these obscure places in the Prayer-Book Version are peculiar to itself; some it shares with the Authorized and even with the Revised Version: for it occasionally happens that the most accurate rendering of the original needs explanation before its meaning can be grasped.

If, then, the worshipper is not content to utter words which are without signification to him, if he is desirous of 'singing with the understanding' (1 *Cor.* 14. 15), it is necessary that he should seek external aid for the elucidation of the Psalter. One object of the present work is to render this aid to those who through want of time or opportunity are unable to consult more detailed commentaries, or even to check the Prayer-Book by the Revised Version. The other object in view is to supply the Christian interpretation of the psalms, whether simple or obscure. This suggests meanings which are sometimes far different from the primary sense of the words, but yet are profitable for edification and for the expression of Christian devotion.

7. *Some Words Explained*

There are some words of frequent occurrence in the English Psalter which may conveniently be considered here.

'Godly,' 'holy,' 'saint.' These words are used in many cases to translate a single Hebrew word, which in the opinion of many scholars should be explained according to the meaning given to it in the Revised Version margin of Ps. 4. 3, 'one that he [the LORD] favoureth,' the reference being primarily to the person's position of privilege as a member of the chosen race, or, by application, of the Church, rather than to his character.

'Soul.' The Hebrew word thus translated frequently means 'self' or 'life,' and should be so understood when the context requires either of these senses; cp. Ps. 3. 2 and 35. 4.

'Poor.' There is little difference in the Hebrew between the word thus rendered and another word which is translated 'meek,' 'lowly,' or 'humble': in fact the Hebrew margin frequently directs the one to be substituted for the other. The words therefore may be regarded as practically interchangeable, and each may be interpreted according to the requirements of the context. In the Christian interpretation all alike direct the thought to our Lord Jesus Christ. (Cp. II. 12, 13.)

'Hell,' 'the pit,' 'the grave.' These words represent the Hebrew word 'Sheol,' which is kept untranslated in the Revised Version. Sheol, like the Greek 'Hades,' signifies the abode of departed souls, and not a place of punishment as in the modern use of the word 'Hell.'

'LORD' when thus printed represents 'Jehovah' or 'Jahweh' in the original. The Jews from feelings of reverence shrank from pronouncing the Sacred Name, and substituted for it a word equivalent to the English 'Lord' (Elohim). Their example was followed by the translators of the Septuagint; and from it the usage found its way through the Vulgate into the English Bible. In a few passages 'Jehovah' is translated 'GOD.'

'The Name of the LORD' expresses the complex notion of God's person and character as he has revealed them to mankind (cp. *Exod.* 33. 19; 34. 5–7).

'Heard' is generally replaced by 'answered' in the Revised Version, when the reference is to prayer granted. Prayer heard by God is prayer answered.

'Save,' 'salvation,' 'redeem,' 'redemption.' These words as used by the psalmists referred to temporal deliverances personal or national: but when used by Christians they have been usually understood to refer to the saving work of Christ the Redeemer.

'People' frequently represents a Hebrew plural word meaning 'nations,' and in such cases the Revised Version makes the meaning clear by substituting 'peoples' (cp. *Ps.* 67. 3).

'Heathen.' This word, signifying in the Hebrew the non-Israelitish peoples, seems more expressive than the Revised Version's substitute 'nations.'

'Quicken.' The Hebrew word thus rendered varies in meaning between 'give new life to,' 'preserve alive,' and 'refresh.' Similarly the word 'quick' signifies 'alive.'

THE INTERPRETATION OF THE PSALTER

8. *The Christian Use of the Psalms*

THE fact that the psalms furnished words for the prayers of Christ on earth, and of the devotions of the Christians from the first dawn of the Gospel, cannot but give the greatest importance to the question which arises continually in our minds, as we recite the Psalter, 'Of whom speaketh the prophet this, of himself or of some other man?' (*Acts* 8. 34).

And further, we know that, following the custom of Judaism, the Church adopted the singing of the Psalter as the great medium of all her congregational worship. Wherever Christianity became established, there immediately were to be heard those solemn strains of joy, penitence, and petition, whereby the Church asserted her mystical identity with the chosen people of God, and in which she heard the voice and saw the features of her Lord.

The history of the use of the Psalter forms a large part of the history of the Church's worship. Even the division of that worship into the vigils and sacred hours taken over from those of the Temple services may be clearly traced to its origin in the New Testament. (Cp. *Acts* 3. 1, 5. 7, 10. 9, 12.12, 16. 25, 20. 7, 23. 11; 1 *Tim*. 5. 5.) That the Psalter in the earliest times was the basis of the Church-worship we know, not only from such definite notices as Acts 4. 24, 16. 25; Eph. 5. 19; Col. 3. 16; S. Jas. 5. 13; but also the whole tenour of the New Testament and of other Christian literature, compacted and interlaced with the phraseology of the psalms, makes us realize that from the beginning the words which were on Christian lips for argument, reproof, instruction, could not but have been also the natural songs of the Christian heart in praise and prayer. It was at once felt that what had been indispensable for the Redeemer must be also indispensable for the redeemed. That from which he proved the divinity of his mission and the age-long preparation for his coming (*S. Matt*. 21. 42, 22. 42; *S. John* 10. 34; etc.) must always have had a principal place in his Church's argument for faith in him. That which he used in devotion, in parables, in argument, in prophetic application, at the Passover feast (*S. John* 15. 25), in his high-priestly prayer (*S. John* 17. 12), on the Cross (*S. Matt*. 27. 46; *S. Luke* 23. 46), on the day of his Resurrection (*S. Luke* 24. 44), that which he had said would greet his advent (*S. Matt*. 23. 39), could not but be used also in the devout prayers of his mystical Body on earth.

And we have record that the Church did use the psalms both for doctrine and for worship (*Acts* 1. 20, 2. 25, 4. 25, etc.). The origin of Christian psalmody was contemporaneous with the birth of the Christian Church. As soon as we have clear testimony of history, we see that every nation, whether Greek or Barbarian, when brought within the pale of Christianity, set up together the divine service of the Psalter and the divine Liturgy. Such universality of use implies necessarily a general agreement about the suitability or adaptibility of the Psalter as the form of Christian worship; and this adaptibility of the Psalter to suit the different characteristics and circumstances of each different nation is one of the evidences of its inspiration.

But the point to be especially observed is this. It is not merely, as S. Ambrose has remarked, that the psalms, compared with other religious poetry, have the peculiarity that every one can use their words as if they were his own. Far more, the Psalter became, naturally and without artificial arrangement, the expression and medium of the formal and united worship of each Christian congregation in every land. They all had only this one hymn-book.

This universal liturgical use of the Psalter could not have been established unless there had been also a universal agreement as to the meanings to be put upon its words. That is to say, from the widespread use of the Psalter we can infer the existence of equally widespread agreement as to the broad lines of interpretation. And as the use of the Psalter can be traced back to the first age of the Church, the value and cogency of the Christian canons of interpretation are greatly increased. For we are led to believe that that system of interpretation which we see developed in the fourth century must have owed its origin to the teaching of the first evangelists, and that the germ of it is to be found in the infant Church in Jerusalem, and indeed in the teaching of the Lord himself. (Cp. *S. Luke* 24. 44: 'All things must needs be fulfilled which are written in the psalms concerning me.')

The same argument is evidenced also by two other salient points in the use of the Psalter. Following apostolic precedent the Church, spreading into the different nations, showed no desire to trace its way back, either for expression or for interpretation, to the original Hebrew. To the Church in the earliest days, the Greek Version was the Psalter, and its readings were the inspired Scripture. In the West, even after S. Jerome, the Latin Psalter stood without a rival, though it was but the version of a version. As if to make clear that the psalms, containing the essential spirit of the Old Dispensation, were now to be read in the new light of him who makes all things new, it was the providence of God to place Hebrew, the language of Judaism, outside the knowledge of the Church at large. The Lord's song was indeed still to be sung, and sung in strange lands, but no longer to the accompaniment of Jewish harps (*Ps.* 137. 2, 4).

Another characteristic of Christian psalmody was the custom of reciting the whole Psalter regularly in course, making no exception of any psalm. The details of arrangement differ considerably in various systems of recitation. The arrangement of the psalms for recitation in a month's regular succession from Ps. 1 to Ps. 150 is peculiar to English Church psalmody. But in every place, from the time when psalmody reached its development, the instinct of the Church established regular and complete recitation in one form or another. This was in marked contrast to the use of Judaism. It was agreed among Christians in all parts of the Church that Christ was to be found in the whole of the Psalter; and that belief is the basis of mystical (or, Christian) interpretation. The Psalter was the Church's lyrical complement to the great epic of redemption.

Also in every place there developed the use of 'proper' psalms for the feasts and holy seasons of the Church, and there was a tendency in every place to select the same psalms as proper to be used. Everywhere Ps. 19 was proper on Christmas Day, and Ps. 22 on Good Friday, etc. This shows that the same interpretation was put upon the psalms, and their Christian meaning was the same, in every part of the Church.

9. *The Life after Death*

The psalmists composed their psalms before Christ had 'abolished death, and brought life and incorruption to light through the Gospel' (2 *Tim.* 1. 10). Little had been revealed to them about the existence that survives death. Thus while they had a vivid realization of communion with the living God, and absolute trust in his mercy, they tended to write as those whose interests were confined to the present condition of things. When they referred to a future life, it was generally in gloomy terms, as a vague and shadowy state of being that hardly deserved the name of life when compared with the activity of 'the life that now is.' The dead are said to be 'in the darkness' (*Ps.* 143. 3); they are 'no more' (35. 15); they dwell 'in the land where all things are forgotten' (88. 12); they are 'cast off' by God, and 'remembered by him no more' (88. 4). 'The dust' cannot 'give thanks to God or declare his truth' (30. 10).

These despondent thoughts were the natural outcome of the teaching of the Law, which restricted the scope of its rewards and penalties to the present world. The devout Israelite who recognized his call as one of the chosen race to carry out God's will, to bear witness for him before the nations, and prepare the way for the ultimate triumph of righteousness, knew of no other sphere than the life in the flesh in which he could fulfil his divinely-appointed destiny.

It is worthy of note that this class of passages is not without parallel in the New Testament. Our Lord himself said, 'We must work the works of him that sent me, while it is day: the night cometh, when no man can work' (S. John 9. 4). And even though the Christian may feel assured of fuller life and higher service after death, yet he must recognize this world as the scene of the only kind of activity of which he has distinct knowledge.

The gloomiest psalms are such as Ps. 88, in which, as an old commentator has remarked, 'The psalmist did not, owing to the complaint and woe of his soul, unlit as it was by the light of the riven tomb, look beyond the present trouble to a better and more comfortable state. An eye bleared with present sorrow sees not so far, nor comprehends so much at one view, as it would at another time, or as it does presently when the tear is wiped out, and its own beams have cleared it up.' Even to the Christian such states of mind sometimes occur. Or else they are psalms written, like Ps. 6, under the stress of the sense of sin and of God's displeasure. To a man who is unforgiven, death is just what this psalm declares it to be: 'In death no man remembereth thee: and who will give thee thanks in the pit?'

In all these psalms, however, there is expressed an earnest solicitude for the glory of God. If death is deprecated, it is in order that the LORD may not lose his glory nor his Church the service which a prolonged life might furnish. In all the passages where the psalmists speak doubtfully of death, they do so in connection with the interest of God's cause on earth. 'I shall not die, but live: and declare the works of the LORD' (Ps. 118. 17).

But it would be incorrect to regard the psalms as devoid of all hope of a blissful immortality. We shall put an unnatural interpretation on the following passages, among others, if we fail to see this better hope more or less distinctly expressed in them: 'Thou shalt shew me the path of life; in thy presence is the fulness of joy: and at thy right hand there is pleasure for evermore' (Ps. 16. 12). 'As for me, I will behold thy presence in righteousness: and when I awake up after thy likeness, I shall be satisfied with it' (17. 16). 'God hath delivered my soul from the place of hell: for he shall receive me' (49. 15). 'Thou shalt guide me with thy counsel: and after that receive me with glory' (73. 23). The psalmists had now and again visions of the future life with God, which are irradiated with almost the brightness of the Christian revelation. And such words as 'O God, thou art my God' (63. 1), and 'God is my portion for ever' (73. 25), are premisses from which, as our Lord taught, the assurance of resurrection ought to be inferred. (Cp. *S. Mark* 12. 26 f.)

The psalms contained no clear statement, no prophecy, of the future life with God; but there was much that was patient of a new interpretation by the Church—an interpretation whose truth would depend not upon the meaning of the words as written by the psalmist, but upon the inspiration of Christian believers reading the psalms in the true light of Christ's Resurrection. The psalms were the hymns of Saul the Pharisee, and to him must have borne a sense at least not contradictory of the hope of a resurrection-life: they were the hymns of Paul the Christian, and therefore cannot be antagonistic to the Christian hope of glorious immortality. And so through the ages the Church has in her use of these doubting psalms followed the teaching of the first Christian interpreters (as found in the New Testament itself); and that Christian use cannot now be invalidated. Much that was conjectural to Jews is now read with the conviction which the Christian faith gives: much that was dubious has received direct affirmation from the truth of the Gospel. The revelation in Christ has been given, and its rays have pierced the old darkness. Christ has gone to the spirits in prison, he has 'opened the kingdom of heaven to all believers'; and the sad forebodings of the land of the shadow of death are now answered by the record of victory over death and hell, and become the songs of the ransomed led by Christ with joy and gladness to Sion. In union with the risen Lord the Church sings the Psalter, and its sorrow and sighing are fled away.

10. *Imprecatory Psalms*

We find in the psalms some prayers for vengeance upon wicked enemies, and expressions of exultation on their overthrow, which sound out of harmony with the spirit of Christianity. (See *Pss.* 35. 4–8, 40. 17–18, 58. 6–8, 59. 11–15, 69. 23–29, 109. 5–19, etc.) This language has been explained by attributing it to the imperfect standard of morality in Old Testament times, which our Lord, in the Sermon on the Mount and elsewhere, has contrasted with the higher requirements which he expects from his followers. But to leave the matter there would be to do an injustice to the psalmists. There are certain considerations to which we must give due weight before we can form a just estimate of these 'imprecatory psalms,' as they are generally called.

The imprecations were not prompted by feelings of mere irritation or desire for personal revenge. The appeal for vengeance was made to God, and judgement was left in his hands. Side by side too with the strongest denunciations we find sentiments of kindliness and goodwill towards the offender (cp. *Ps.* 35. 13–14, 109.

3–4). The motive of the psalmists' wrath was their zeal for God's righteousness, the triumph of which was delayed so long as wickedness had the upper hand. The psalmists had not the clear revelation, made to us, of an eternal state of retribution. They believed that punishment would overtake the ungodly in this life or not at all. Therefore when they saw might prevailing against right and the wicked persecuting the good, was it not, from their point of view, an imperative duty to implore God to vindicate his honour, and make manifest his righteous rule over the world, in the only way in which, according to their degree of knowledge, this could be effected, namely, by the overthrow and punishment of the wicked?

And this duty must have seemed all the plainer when the enemies who oppressed them were foreigners and heathen; for Israel was the people of God, and its foes were his foes. If the chosen race were subjected to the tyranny of strangers, it would appear that Jehovah was unable to protect his own; his promises would seem to have failed, and the cause of truth and righteousness to be in jeopardy.

Further, we have been taught more distinctly than those under the Old Covenant to distinguish between the wrong and the wrong-doer, to hate the sin but to love the sinner; and yet we are far from concluding that this duty forbids us in all cases to desire that the sinner may receive the due reward of his deeds openly before the world. The State enacts penalties against transgressors, the magistrate condemns not only crimes but criminals; and we approve. If we hear of some vile act of iniquity, we earnestly hope that justice will overtake the offender; we believe that it will be better even for his own sake that he suffer condign punishment, and we rejoice when the supremacy of the law is vindicated by the sentence pronounced upon him.

It should also be borne in mind that the unsettled state of society in which the psalmists lived prevented them from relying, as we can, on the orderly working of the law to bring criminals to account. And Israel was a small nation, unable to oppose their aggressive rivals with bigger battalions. They had to commit the maintenance of their just cause solely to God, the supreme Judge, and implore him to check the wicked in their career of violence. And if they prayed for the overthrow of their foreign oppressors, we should reflect that we also feel justified in praying that our king may 'vanquish and overcome all his enemies'; though we, unlike the psalmists, suppress all reference to the horrors which success in war implies.

Instead of apologizing for these psalms we should rather take to heart and profit by the practical lesson they have to teach us. By their righteous hatred of sin as an offence against God they impress upon Christians the truth to which the New Testament also distinctly testifies, that the stern side of religion is as real as the merciful; that God's compassion is not displayed in an indiscriminate benevolence; that the wicked are in rebellion against him, and unless they sue for peace a fearful retribution awaits them. These psalms are a standing protest, needful in all ages, against lack of moral earnestness, and a reminder of the danger of thinking lightly of sin.

At any rate these prayers which God of old made ready for the Church to offer under the inspiration of the Holy Spirit, and which have been offered without cessation by Christian saints, are not to be charged with any taint of mere vindictiveness or sinful passion. Their Christian use and the principles underlying that use, as evidenced in New Testament quotations (cp., for example, the quotations of *Ps.* 69 in *S. John* 2. 17, 19. 28, 15. 25; *S. Matt.* 27. 34; *Acts* 1. 16, 20; *Rom.* 11. 9–10, 15. 3), preclude them from being regarded, by those who admit that the Church has authority to interpret the Old Testament, as merely the expression of the lower code of Jewish legalism.

The specifically Christian interpretation may be considered under three heads. First, the allegorical, which disregarded the personality of those who were the objects of the writers' indignation, and gave the words no special reference to any person or persons, in the mouth of Christian worshippers. In singing of the destruction of sinners, they represented to themselves the sins rather than the persons who had committed the sins, or they thought of spiritual hosts of evil making war against the soul, and their passionate denunciations of the enemy became the cry for deliverance of hard-pressed Christian warriors.

Secondly, the imprecatory psalms were regarded, in accordance with the guidance of the New Testament, as being prophetical of Christ's passion under the hands of his fierce adversaries, and the recitation of them in Christian worship became a representation of that passion. Pss. 69 and 109 are so used explicitly in the New Testament, and the principle there exemplified was extended to other instances and applied in devotional use.

Thirdly, the Church identified her enemies with those of Christ, as the Jews had been wont to identify theirs with the enemies of Jehovah. But the Church had the greater justification in so doing, for she could identify herself with Christ her Head in a manner and degree and reality quite different from any identification that might be suggested between Jehovah and his ancient people. Christ on earth had used the words of the Psalter, and in using them had made them his own. Christ, then, was for the Church the speaker in the psalms: they were 'subjectively Messianic.' The denunciations in the Psalter were to be paralleled with Christ's proclamations of 'Woe unto thee' upon the sinful cities that rejected him. And in so far as the Church or an individual member of the Church could speak with the mind of Christ, in so far as their words were the words of Christ speaking in them, so far could the expressions of the Psalter be turned by them against the sinners as well as the sins that made havoc of the Church and sullied the beauty of the Body of Christ. And so we have the Christian imprecation of S. Paul's 'deliver unto Satan for the destruction of the flesh' (1 *Cor.* 5. 5), a succinct commentary on the Christian use of the imprecatory psalms. So we have Ps. 137 in a Christian form in Rev. 18. 2–6. So too we have the expression of them in act in the moral discipline of the Church upon wilful sinners. And the principle remains that in so far as any Christian person or congregation is united with Christ, to that degree they may without sin make, as he did, the imprecations of the psalms the prayers of their lips.

It is thus that we explain and justify the Christian use of the imprecatory psalms, contradictory though they seem at first hearing to the tone of the Gospel. That the contradiction can be only apparent is proved by the employment of the psalms without excisions in the Christian worship and teaching from the earliest times, for assuredly the immediate disciples of the Lord were not less but more conscious than we are of the apparent antagonism between the tone of the psalms (which in spite of this they loved to use) and the spirit of the Lord whom they knew in their intimate experience.

11. *Assertions of Righteousness*

Another feature in the psalms which sometimes causes perplexity is the presence in them of assertions of complete uprightness and perfect obedience to the commandments, with confident appeals to God to judge the hearts of the writers, which seem to savour of a self-righteousness incompatible with the spirit of Christianity. The chief passages of this kind are Pss. 7. 8, 17. 3–6, 18. 20–24, 26, 32. 7, 64. 4, 86. 2, 101. 3, 119. 101, 110, 128, 168.

In some cases where these sentiments occur the context proves that the psalmist is merely protesting his innocence of some specific charge brought against him (cp. *Ps.* 7. 3–4). And in general, before presuming to criticize the psalmists, we should make sure that we do not misinterpret or press beyond their due significance the moral terms that they apply to themselves. We have seen (cp. I. 7) that the word translated 'holy,' 'godly,' 'saint,' is now given by most scholars the meaning of 'one favoured by God.' Such epithets as 'righteous,' 'perfect,' 'clean,' 'innocent,' need not be taken as implying more than honesty of purpose, a right direction of the will, the character of a person who is sincerely desirous of serving God. They are declarations of integrity which may be paralleled by S. Paul's assertions, 'I have lived before God in all good conscience until this day' (*Acts* 23. 1), and 'I know nothing against myself' (1 *Cor.* 4. 4). They are Old Testament claims to the possession of the 'honest and good heart' of the parable of the Sower (*S. Luke* 8. 15). They are not meant to be declarations of total sinlessness: for the whole Psalter is pervaded by a sense of sin and of the need for pardon and renewal; and some of the psalms which contain these protestations of rectitude contain also humble prayers for mercy. 'But as for me, I will walk innocently: O deliver me, and be merciful unto me' (*Ps.* 26. 11). 'Preserve thou my soul, for I am holy: my God, save thy servant that putteth his trust in thee' (86. 2). And it is significant that the greatest psalm of righteousness, Ps. 119, ends with the verse, 'I have gone astray like a sheep that is lost: O seek thy servant, for I do not forget thy commandments.'

Nevertheless, it should not be forgotten that the psalmists, living before the Holy Ghost had come in his fullness to 'convict the world in respect of sin and of righteousness,' to enlighten the conscience and reveal the spiritual demand of God's law, found it easier than we should do to satisfy themselves that they had fulfilled all God's requirements. Thus we may shrink from employing, as our own, words of self-approval which they were able to use in all sincerity, and which from their standpoint betokened no lack of humility.

But we need not think that this impairs the value of these passages for us Christians or makes them less suited for our lips. The deepest consecration which the psalms possess for us is that they were used by Christ himself during his earthly life, that he made their words his own. Any difficulty we may have of interpreting them, any scruple about employing them in our worship, vanishes when we regard them as Christ's utterances. The more ample the assertions of innocence and integrity, the more worthy are they of the Perfect Man.

These verses, then, have come to their greatest validity in Christian use, inasmuch as it is union with the sinless Christ that gives their assertions the deepest significance. It is in so far as each person is in Christ that he can employ these words in their full sense; while at the same time finding the words of the penitential psalms equally suited to his lips, in so far as sin has shut him from that divine communion. The latter he can, so to speak, recite in his own person; the former, in that of Christ. Both kinds of psalms are to us also the actual words of Christ. The assertions

of innocence are the accents of the Sinless One: the confessions of
sin are those of him who bare the sins of all humanity, which he
has united with himself.

12. *Predictions of Christ*

Our Lord repeatedly appealed to the testimony of the psalms to
himself. (See, for example, *S. Luke* 24. 44.) And of all the books
of the Old Testament the Psalter is the most frequently quoted in
the New as having pointed forward to Christ and his Church.

The foreshadowing of Christ in the Psalter took, to speak generally, one of four forms. He was set forth as a King, as the Son of
Man, as a Sufferer, and as God, the supreme Judge of the world.

Christ as King: Pss. 2, 18, 20, 21, 45, 61, 72, 89, 110, 132. These
'Royal Psalms,' as they have been named, usually had for their
immediate object the reigning king, either David or one of his
successors, and they were called forth by some critical event in the
history of the kingdom. Their authors had before their minds the
divine promise made to David and his house through the prophet
Nathan: 'I took thee from the sheepcote, that thou shouldest be
prince over my people Israel. When thy days be fulfilled, and thou
shalt sleep with thy fathers, I will set up thy seed, and I will
establish the throne of the kingdom for ever. I will be his father,
and he shall be my son: if he commit iniquity, I will chasten him
with the rod of men; but my mercy shall not depart from him.
And thy house and thy kingdom shall be made sure for ever before
thee: thy throne shall be established for ever' (2 *Sam.* 7. 8–16).

This promise, this charter of the Davidic line, was developed
by the psalmists as circumstances prompted them. They dwelt
upon the predestined glories of the house of David, often sharply
contrasted with its actual abasement; they lamented the apparent
failure of the promise, and appealed to God to grant fulfilment of
it; they saw visions of a future period when the king of David's
line would reign victoriously over all the nations of the world.
Now, although the psalmists themselves may not have been conscious of it, we see that they claimed for David and his house such
powers and prerogatives, and for his kingdom such extent and
duration, as were destined to be realized only in the divine Son of
David and in his universal and everlasting dominion. In other
parts of the Psalter besides these royal psalms the kingdom of
Israel was identified with that of God, and the incorporation into it of
all the nations was predicted. There may be mentioned in particular
the series of triumphal psalms which read as if they had been
composed on the occasion of the overthrow of Sennacherib's hosts
in the reign of Hezekiah: Pss. 46, 47, 48, 66, 75, 76.

Christ as the Son of Man. Psalms which emphasize the dignity of man, and attribute to him universal dominion (*Ps.* 8); which delineate the perfect human character (15); which picture the ideal fellowship of man with God (16); which proffer on the part of man unreserved surrender to God's will (27): these are now seen to point forward for their adequate fulfilment to the Sinless Son of Man, who is one with the Father, the new Head of the human race, to whom all authority has been given in heaven and earth.

Christ as Sufferer. Passages from the following psalms are quoted in the New Testament as having been fulfilled in certain details of our Lord's sufferings: Pss. 22, 35, 41, 69, 109. These psalms bear in themselves plain evidences of having been written to describe the personal experiences of men passing through severe bodily and spiritual anguish. But these men were servants of God, unjustly afflicted; and being such, their afflictions, unknown to themselves, foreshadowed those of the great Servant of the Lord, the Man of Sorrows. And besides this, it was divinely ordered that certain features of their sufferings should prefigure some of the circumstances of Christ's passion, and even that what the psalmists evidently meant to be metaphorical descriptions of their trials should come literally true in the details of the Crucifixion. The words of the psalmists were thus, according to the New Testament phrase, 'fulfilled,' that is, filled full of a new and deeper meaning than the writers could have known.

Christ as God. In other psalms, chiefly Pss. 50, 68, 93, 95, 96–100, the visible appearance of Jehovah upon earth is announced, as a Conqueror to confound his enemies, as a Judge to vindicate the righteous, as a Saviour to deliver the oppressed. His reign of righteousness and joy is proclaimed. All peoples are bidden to worship and obey him. Here, as the Christian doctors have taught, we have witness borne to the advent of Christ under yet another aspect, the aspect that regards it as the coming of God himself in visible form. Whatever these visions of the psalmists meant to them, to Christians they speak plainly of the Incarnation of the Son of God.

13. *Mystical Interpretation*

In considering the testimony which the psalms bear to Christ, it would be unreasonable to confine our attention to the passages quoted in this sense in the New Testament. Our Lord said of the Old Testament Scriptures, 'These are they which bear witness of me' (*S. John* 5. 39; cp. *S. Luke* 24. 27); and his words authorize us to read those Scriptures with the conviction that he is to be found everywhere in them. Thus the references to the psalms which occur in the New Testament are to be regarded as only

B

specimens of the rich store of Messianic allusion which Christians may expect to find, and the Church has found, in the psalms.

And in making this use of the Psalter we are but continuing what has been the practice of Christians from the beginning. They have always followed the example set them by the New Testament writers in looking beyond the original purport of the psalms, and discerning in them a meaning fuller and more spiritual than the literal, a meaning which must have transcended the thoughts of the authors, because it needed the light of the Gospel for its elucidation.

It may indeed be truly said that the psalms were written rather for Christians than for God's ancient people. The Psalter passed as an inspired hymn-book from the Temple to the Church. Was not this divinely foreseen event providentially arranged for? Must we not believe that the psalmists were supernaturally guided to make their utterances such as would be patient of a higher interpretation than that of which they themselves were conscious; so that after the passing of the few centuries still allotted to the dispensation of 'Israel after the flesh,' those utterances might be fitted, throughout all subsequent ages, to express the devotional thoughts, the aspirations, the prayers, and the praises of the 'Israel of God'?

The Catholic Church is the successor of the Jewish, the inheritor of her privileges, traditions, and titles of honour. This fact gives the key to the Christian interpretation of the psalms. We see that the hopes which centred in David and his line received their fulfilment in his divine Son, the King of kings. We see that what is said of Israel or Jacob must be applied, on the principle of continuity, to the wider family into which Israel developed, to those who in Christ are 'Abraham's seed, heirs according to promise' (*Gal.* 3. 29). The names 'Sion' and 'Jerusalem' describe for us the Catholic Church in its militant and its triumphant states. 'Saints,' 'redemption,' 'salvation,' and many other terms, are glorified with their Gospel meaning. The undefined sense of fellowship with God is exalted into participation in the divine nature through membership of Christ.

The psalms were inspired in the first instance to be a manual of religious instruction and a hymnal of devotion for the people of Israel, but also and chiefly they were destined by God to be used in a different way under the Christian dispensation. And to that end they were originally written, selected, edited, translated, in such ways as to be patient of a new interpretation and application in the fulness of the times. Thus we can safeguard the real and original meaning of the psalms, as discerned by our critical commentators, which still remains true and valuable, and at the same time leave room for the complete change in use and interpretation, at once so revolutionary and so legitimate, that came with the dawning of Christianity. The validity of the Christian interpretation thus does not depend upon the inspiration of the psalms for their former purpose, nor on the presence in them through the centuries of an implicit meaning which awaited exposition. For us the validity of the Christian interpretation depends on the belief in the inspiration of the whole Church from Pentecost onwards as the teacher of divine truth and the authorized expounder of Holy Writ.

This, then, is what the Church did. Accepting the faith of Christ the Consummator, the Church has, from the standpoint of that faith and illumined by the Holy Spirit, read the Old Testament in the light of its knowledge, and interpreted the psalms in particular in its own way, making them the vehicle of her devotions, and expressing by her recitation of them those meanings of her own, which she obtained from her Catholic faith and not from the psalms, putting her own meaning upon their words rather than drawing it out of them. The truth of the Church's faith is the justification of her action.

The use to which the Church puts the Psalter in divine worship is the most prominent assertion of her right to understand the psalms mystically, that is, to interpret them from the viewpoint of her higher knowledge of spiritual things. The Church has claimed as her own these Hebrew poems, composed under the dim light of an imperfect revelation, and has made them her expression of public worship. The Church has ordered all the psalms to be used without making any exception; she has arranged for daily recitation from the Psalter every day of the year; and by appending the *Gloria Patri* to each psalm she has intimated the sense in which they are to be understood. And further, by the system of proper psalms for chief festivals and holy days, applied variously in every part of the Church Catholic, there has been given detailed guidance in spiritual interpretation; for, by assigning fixed psalms for use on the great days which commemorate the cardinal events of redemption, the Church testifies that these hymns of the ancient Church are now invested with special Christian meanings, that they proclaim truths which their authors desired to see but saw not.

So when we say that the Psalter, considered in relation to the Christian consummation, was inspired, we mean that it was so composed as to be capable of bearing new meanings (which meanings, however, it did not contain at the time of writing), in the light of the Christian faith. To take one illustration: the drama of Christ's sufferings and death is to be seen portrayed in Ps. 22, and it is for us the psalm proper on Good Friday; but not exactly because it was a direct prophetical delineation of that passion in its minute details. The psalm had its own occasion and purpose, unknown to us now. It has had multiform fulfilment in the sufferings of men and nation. But it is 'Messianic' because through the inspiration of God it was prepared as the material, as it were, of which the Church, also under the inspiration of God, should mould her crucifix. And so for us Christ's sufferings are told in the words of the psalm, not so much because the psalmist predicted them, as because the Church has known that all suffering and sacrifice have been perfected in the death of Christ. *Psalmorum clavis Christi fides.*

The thesis which we maintain is that the authority to which we bow in matters of faith, the authority of Incarnate God interpreted to us by his Spirit in the Church, is also ultimately the authority on which depends the whole system of Messianic and Christophorical exposition. In other words, the recognition of certain psalms as Messianic (and that some are Messianic is acknowledged in a sense by all critics), depends upon the inspiration of the Church Catholic rather than on the inspiration of the Bible, the inspiration of the interpreters rather than of the original writers. If this be so, it will follow that, at least in its broad lines, the whole system of mystical interpretation presses itself on our acceptance with as much cogency as the recognition of any specially selected 'Messianic' psalms. The Church has not made distinctions. The whole Psalter is redolent of the fragrance of Christ. So that, if it be true that it is the Church's authority that gives their real validity to our arguments for the Messianic import of some psalms, we may not consistently, against her authority, follow our own reasonings and reject that meaning in the case of other psalms or seek to excise them from the Christianized Psalter.

14. *The Christian Psalter*

By way of conclusion, to emphasize the chief points which have been here discussed, the author, or editor, of this book makes bold to quote some passages from his book, *The King's Highway*, pp. 169 ff.

From the beginning the Church has had two ways of worship. There was the holy sacrifice, which took the place and fulfilled the type of the old Jewish sacrifices. The other way of worship has been the divine office, that is, the divine duty, what is due to God. This was rendered to God, in praise and meditation and supplication, by the orderly recitation of the Psalter and the reading of Holy Scripture. The divine office, which grew out of the Jewish synagogue-worship, came to be regarded as the daily duty of the Church, and was divided into various numbers of offices in different places.

In the Western part of the Church there were established seven daily offices, in accordance with the words: 'Seven times a day will I praise thee' (*Ps.* 119. 164). Lauds was sung before dawn; Prime, Terce, Sext, Nones were intended for the first, third, sixth, and ninth hours; Vespers was the evening worship; and Compline, the night-prayers, completed the daily round. These offices were of obligation upon the clergy, but were shared in to a greater or less degree by the laity. Part of the night-time also was given to the night-office, called Nocturns or Mattins; even as it is written: 'At midnight I will rise to give thanks unto thee' (*Ps.* 119. 62).

In the Church of England since the Reformation the obligation has been reduced to two daily offices: Morning Prayer, which represented the older Mattins and Lauds; and Evening Prayer, which combined parts of Vespers and Compline. The language was changed from Latin to English, for the greater edification of the laity; and Holy Scripture was read more extensively than in the older offices.

In these daily offices, whether many or few, the main feature always has been the recitation of the Psalter in its entirety, either daily, or weekly, or once in a month.

The Psalter is the Church's hymn-book. The Jews had used psalms in their worship. Christ used them. The Church therefore adopted them from the beginning (cp. *Acts* 4. 23–28), claiming them as its own, and marking the Christian sense in which it understood them by the addition of the doxology: 'Glory be to the Father, and to the Son, and to the Holy Ghost; as it was in the beginning, is now, and ever shall be, world without end. Amen.'

Those Christians who know their Psalter well, and understand it, have little need of any other hymn-book. The production of many hymns, mostly of a personal sort suitable only for private use, marks a falling away from the sounder idea of corporate worship. It has arisen partly from the fact that the right interpretation and use of the Psalter have been to a great extent forgotten. Protestantism has always a tendency to depreciate the Psalter, to omit parts of it, and to substitute for it metrical versions or other hymns.

The key to the interpretation of the Church's hymn-book is that it is intended primarily for united use. The word 'I' in the Psalter does not mean the person who is reciting the words. It denotes our Lord himself, or the Church united with him; and if it is applicable to the individual worshipper, it applies to him only as a member of Christ and the Church. The worshippers are meant to use the words, not to express their own personal sentiments, but in order to enter into the mind of Christ and his Church. For example, such words as, 'I have refrained my feet from every evil way, that I may keep thy word' (*Ps.* 119. 101), are not an assertion of one's own self-righteousness, but of Christ's righteousness. The whole of Ps. 119 is a meditation on the perfect human nature and character of Christ. The Church contemplates him, while it repeats words which could be absolutely true only as spoken by Christ, and which, when spoken by the members of the Church, are true of them only in so far as they are in union with Christ and conformed by his grace to his likeness.

In the same way, the penitential psalms (*Pss.* 6, 32, 38, 51, 102, 130, 143) have their full meaning, not as expressions of the repentance of David or of any other repentant sinner, but as the words of him who bore for all men the burden of sin, and in union with whom alone men can truly repent.

The historical psalms (*Pss.* 44, 78, 95, 105, 106, 136, etc.) are used in Church worship, not simply as records of the events of Jewish history, but because that history is regarded as typical of the history of the Catholic Church throughout the ages: privileged, sinning, forgiven, punished. When we sing of Israel, Jacob, Sion, we mean the Church. (Cp. *Pss.* 48. 2, 85. 1, 114. 1, etc.)

Again, the imprecatory, or cursing, psalms (*Pss.* 55, 69, 83, 109, etc.) are by no means used by Christians as the expression of their own desire for God's vengeance upon their personal enemies. It is not likely that even the Jews in their worship so understood these psalms. Certainly to the instructed Christian they are lyrics of the passion of Christ, and of the vengeance of eternal righteousness upon wilful evil. They speak to us of Christ and Christ's enemies in every age. They lead us to look at his enemies from the point of view of the Cross, and show us the mystery of sin in its utmost malignity, and of sin's penalty in the just judgment of the God who died for love of sinners.

Thus the whole Psalter is full of Christ and the Church. A gospel could be compiled from the psalms. Indeed, if we put together only those phrases of the psalms which are directly applied to Christ in the New Testament, we get a fairly complete picture of him:

Christ is the Lord who in the beginning laid the foundations of the earth, and the heavens are the work of his hands (*Heb.* 1. 10). He is the Son of God (*Heb.* 1. 5, 5. 5). God prepared for him a body (*Heb.* 10. 5), and made him a little lower than the angels (*Heb.* 2. 7). He is the anointed Messiah (*Heb.* 1. 9), and David's Lord (*S. Matt.* 22. 24). He was the blessed one who came in the name of the Lord (*S. Matt.* 23. 39).

He declared God's Name unto men, his brethren (*Heb.* 2. 13). He opened his mouth in parables (*S. Matt.* 13. 35). God gave his angels charge concerning Christ (*S. Luke* 4. 10). God perfected his praise out of the mouths of babes and sucklings (*S. Matt.* 21. 16), but the reproaches of them that reproached God fell upon him (*Rom.* 15. 3). Judas, who ate Christ's bread, lifted up his heel against him (*S. John* 13. 18). Therefore the habitation of Judas was made desolate, and another took his office (*Acts* 1. 20). They parted Christ's garments among them, and upon his vesture did they cast lots (*S. John* 19. 24). They gave him gall and vinegar (*S. Matt.* 27. 34). He said, My God, my God, why hast thou forsaken me? (*S. Matt.* 27. 46) and, Into thy hands I commend my spirit (*S. Luke* 23. 46).

But he beheld the Lord always before him. God was on his right hand, that he should not be moved. Therefore his heart was glad, his flesh also rested in hope. God did not leave Christ's soul in hell, nor give his holy one to see corruption (*Acts* 2. 25–28, 13. 35). He was the Priest and Victim, and had come into the world to do the will of God, who had no pleasure in Jewish sacrifices for sin (*Heb.* 10. 5–7). And he is a priest for ever, after the order of Melchisedek (*Heb.* 5. 6). He was the stone which the builders rejected, but God made him the chief corner-stone of the Church (*S. Matt.* 21, 42; *Acts* 4. 11; *Eph.* 2. 20; 1 *S. Pet.* 2. 7). God said to the risen Christ, Thou art my Son, this day have I begotten thee (*Acts* 13. 33; *Rom.* 1. 4); sit thou on my right hand (*Acts* 2. 34).

Christ's throne is for ever and ever, and the sceptre of uprightness is the sceptre of his kingdom. He loved righteousness and hated iniquity. Therefore God anointed him with the oil of gladness above his fellows (*Heb.* 1. 8–9). God crowned him in his human nature with glory and honour, and put all things in subjection under his feet (*Heb.* 2. 7–8). So, when Christ ascended on high, he led captivity captive, and gave gifts unto men (*Eph.* 4. 8).

The sound of the Christian believers has gone out into all the earth, and their words unto the ends of the world (*Rom.* 10. 6). The eyes of the Jews were darkened, that they should not see (*Rom.* 11. 9–10); but the Gentiles praised the Lord, and all the peoples praised him (*Rom.* 15. 11). For Christ's sake Christians have been killed, and accounted as sheep for the slaughter (*Rom.* 8. 36): but it is they that shall enter into God's rest (*Heb.* 4. 3). Why did the nations rage, and the peoples imagine vain things, against the Lord and against his anointed one? (*Acts* 4. 25–26). God shall put all enemies under his feet (1 *Cor.* 15. 25).

The works of creation shall perish, but Christ continueth. They all shall wax old as doth a garment. Christ shall roll them up, and they shall be changed. But he is ever the same, and his years shall not fail (*Heb.* 1. 11–12).

This brief explanation of the Church's mind in the use of the Psalter may serve as a guide to its interpretation, for those who are willing to adapt their minds to the Church's mind. It is unfortunate that many, for lack of knowledge of this method of inter-pretation, persist in endeavouring to fit the words of the psalms only to themselves personally, an endeavour which means that they have no use for those parts which do not fit their experience or temperament, and at best endure the recitation of the whole Psalter for the sake of particular verses which appeal to them personally.

The principle here stated applies to the whole of the divine office. Always the words spoken by the congregation are the words of Christ or of the Church in union with him, which the con-gregation corporately repeat. A congregation is not a conglomera-tion of people praying privately and individually; it is a part of the Church exercising its share in the Godward attitude of the whole Church in Christ. This consideration alone can deliver many of the Church's prayers from the charge of unreality. Thus, when we say, 'We have erred and strayed from thy ways like lost sheep,' or 'The memory of our sins is grievous unto us, and the burden of them is intolerable,' we are not necessarily putting into words the sentiment of which at the moment each of us is conscious; but rather we are expressing together with the whole Church the only attitude of mind in which the Church can approach the holy God. The 'We' does not mean 'I': and the individual worshipper who does mean 'I' when he says 'We,' and thinks only of his own particular sins, may be making a good act of personal contrition, but has for the time let slip the idea of corporate worship. Simi-larly, when he says, 'We praise thee, O God; we acknowledge thee to be the Lord,' he is not making an act of personal faith, but stating the faith of the whole body of the Church. The first person singular rarely appears in the Church's forms of prayer. The most notable case is in the creeds: 'I believe in One God'; and in this case the Eastern use of 'We believe' is better than that of the Western Church.

The text of the Psalter is printed as it appears in the Book of Common Prayer, with these exceptions. 'LORD' or 'GOD' is printed in capitals where either word represents the Hebrew 'Jehovah' (cp. I. 7.). The Revised Version has also been followed in the removal of initial capitals in cases where they might mislead the reader. A few alterations have been made in punctuation, and parenthetic brackets and quotation-marks have been inserted where needed by the sense of the passage. Repeated phrases and refrains have been marked in small capital letters, and definite changes of subject within a psalm have been indicated by dividing lines.

ABBREVIATIONS

A.V.—Authorized Version.
R.V.—Revised Version.
A.R.V.—Authorized and Revised Versions.
O.T.—Old Testament.
N.T.—New Testament.
P.B.V.—Prayer-Book Version.
B.C.P.—Book of Common Prayer.
Sept.—Septuagint (the Greek Version).
Vulg.—Vulgate (the Latin Version).
mg.—margin.
cp.—compare.
i.e.—id est—that is.

THE PSALMS OF DAVID

BOOK ONE

THE FIRST DAY

MORNING PRAYER

PSALM 1. *Beatus vir, qui non abiit, etc.*

The contrast between the blessedness of the righteous and the misery of the wicked. Mystically, in the blessed man we can discern Christ himself in his perfect human nature, and in union with him all his Saints, and those who live by his grace, which is here symbolized by the water, v. 3; cp. 1 Cor. 12. 3; S. John 7. 37; Rev. 22. 1.

BLESSED is the man that hath not walked in the counsel of the ungodly, nor stood in the way of sinners : and hath not sat in the seat of the scornful.

A negative description of the righteous man: he avoids association with the wicked. The threefold parallelism : walk, stand, sit; and, counsel, way, seat; marks a steady progression in wickedness. The scornful are those who sin against God wilfully and care not.

2 But his delight is in the law of the LORD : and in his law will he exercise himself day and night.

The positive side of the righteous man's character: glad obedience to the law and continuous study of it.

A.R.V. in his law doth he meditate day and night.

3 And he shall be like a tree planted by the waterside : that will bring forth his fruit in due season.

The fruit of communion with Christ; cp. Jer. 17. 7–8; S. John 15. 4.

his: archaic for 'its.' *R.V. that bringeth forth its fruit in its season.*

4 His leaf also shall not wither : and look, whatsoever he doeth, it shall prosper.

27

5 As for the ungodly, it is not so with them : but they are like the chaff, which the wind scattereth away from the face of the earth.

The threshing floors of the East are on elevated places exposed to the wind which blows away the chaff when the winnower with his fan or shovel throws the grain into the air. Cp. S. Matt. 3. 12.

6 Therefore the ungodly shall not be able to stand in the judgement : neither the sinners in the congregation of the righteous.

The righteous here denote the ideal Israel which shall be manifested at the judgement, when the LORD'S people shall be all righteous; cp. Isa. 60. 21.

7 But the LORD knoweth the way of the righteous : and the way of the ungodly shall perish.

knoweth: i.e. regardeth with loving care.

PSALM 2. *Quare fremuerunt gentes?*

Vassal princes threaten a revolt, destined to result in their own utter discomfiture, against some king of David's line. Mystically the psalm points forward to the contest between the world and Christ, remarkably evidenced at his passion by the combination of Caiaphas and Pilate, Jews and Gentiles, against him; cp. Acts 4. 25–28. Vainly do men, however great they may be, oppose the reign of Christ. He is the universal king, appointed by God the Father, and all who would be saved must obey him. His triumph was declared by his resurrection. The psalm is proper on Easter Day.

WHY do the heathen so furiously rage together : and why do the people imagine a vain thing?
2 The kings of the earth stand up, and the rulers take counsel together : against the LORD, and against his Anointed.

Quoted by S. Peter in Acts 4. 25.

R.V. the peoples.

'his Anointed' denotes a king of David's line, the type of the coming Messiah or Christ (both words mean 'anointed'). From this verse and v. 7 were taken the two titles given by the Jews to the expected Deliverer, viz. 'Messiah' and 'Son of God'; cp. S. Matt. 26. 63; S. John 1. 49.

The rebel princes speak.

3 'Let us break their bonds asunder : and cast away their cords from us.'

their bonds . . . cords: i.e. the binding authority of the LORD and his Anointed over them.

4 He that dwelleth in heaven shall laugh them to scorn : the Lord shall have them in derision.

5 Then shall he speak unto them in his wrath : and vex them in his sore displeasure.

6 'Yet have I set my king : upon my holy hill of Sion.'

vex: *A.R.V.mg. trouble*.

The LORD speaks. Christ is the 'king'; and 'Sion' is to be interpreted, here and in most other passages, as meaning the Church on earth.

7 'I will preach the law, whereof the LORD hath said unto me : "Thou art my Son, this day have I begotten thee.

7–9. The king speaks, quoting the LORD'S promise to him. *R.V. I will tell of the decree : the LORD said unto me.* That is, I have declared thee my Son by placing thee on thy royal throne. The allusion is to God's promise to David and his heirs, 'I will be his father, and he shall be my son' (2 *Sam.* 7. 14.) These words received their complete fulfilment when Christ 'born of the seed of David was declared to be the Son of God with power by the resurrection of the dead.' (*Rom.* 1. 3–4; cp. *Acts* 13. 33; *Heb.* 1. 5; 5. 5.)

The LORD'S promise to the anointed Son.

8 "Desire of me, and I shall give thee the heathen for thine inheritance : and the utmost parts of the earth for thy possession.

9 "Thou shalt bruise them with a rod of iron : and break them in pieces like a potter's vessel." '

bruise: Sept. has 'rule,' which appears in Rev. 2. 27; 12. 5; 19. 9; cp. also 1 Cor. 15. 15.

10 Be wise now therefore, O ye kings : be learned, ye that are judges of the earth.

10–12. The psalmist speaks. He exhorts the insurgent rulers to show true wisdom by submitting to Jehovah in the person of his anointed Son.

learned: i.e. taught. *A.R.V. instructed*.

11 Serve the LORD in fear : and rejoice unto him with reverence.

12 Kiss the Son, lest he be angry, and so ye perish from the right way : if his wrath be kindled, (yea, but a little), blessed are all they that put their trust in him.

Give him the kiss of homage; cp. 1 Sam. 10. 1; 1 Kings 19. 18; Hos. 13. 2.

R.V. perish in the way (i.e. in your rebellious course), *for his wrath will soon be kindled.*

PSALM 3. *Domine, quid multiplicati?*

A psalm of David, when he fled from Absalom his son (Title). The morning prayer (see v. 5) of one who, in the midst of danger, put his trust in God. It is mystically fulfilled in Christ risen after his Passion, and in his Church triumphant. Christ is Victor in himself and in his Saints: but the attack continues upon his members here on earth, and victory still remains to be won by the Church militant. Proper on Easter Day.

LORD, how are they increased that trouble me : many are they that rise against me.

Cp. 2 Sam. 18. 31, 'The LORD hath avenged thee this day of all them that rose up against thee,' referring to David's victory over Absalom.

2 Many one there be that say of my soul : 'There is no help for him in his God.'

Many say that God as well as man has turned against him. Cp. Ps. 22. 8, 'He trusted in God, that he would deliver him : let him deliver him, if he will have him.'

3 But thou, O LORD, art my defender : thou art my worship, and the lifter up of my head.

R.V. art a shield about me. Cp. Gen. 15. 1.

my worship: *A.R.V. my glory.*

the lifter up of my head. Cp. Ps. 27. 5, 6.

4 I did call upon the LORD with my voice : and he heard me out of his holy hill.

his holy hill: see Ps. 2. 6, the hill of Sion where Jehovah specially manifested his presence: applicable to heaven, and to the Church.

5 I laid me down and slept : and rose up again : for the LORD sustained me.

Christ rose again after his Passion.

6 I will not be afraid for ten thousands of the people : that have set themselves against me round about.

7 Up, LORD, and help me, O my God : for thou smitest all mine enemies upon the cheek-bone; thou hast broken the teeth of the ungodly.

The hosts on the side of Absalom, and of the rebels against Christ in each age.

A.R.V. Arise, O LORD. The first words of the cry raised when the ark set forward in the wilderness (*Num.* 10. 35). They frequently occur in the Psalter. The complete formula appears in Ps. 68. 1.

Christ is Victor: see Ps. 2. 9. His enemies are like wild beasts made helpless by the breaking of the jaw.

8 Salvation belongeth unto the LORD : and thy blessing is upon thy people.

R.V. thy blessing be

PSALM 4. *Cum invocarem*

This psalm is an evening hymn (cp. v. 9). It is frequently sung in Compline. The voice of the Church is heard speaking.

HEAR me when I call, O God of my righteousness : thou hast set me at liberty when I was in trouble; have mercy upon me, and hearken unto my prayer.

2 O ye sons of men, how long will ye blaspheme mine honour : and have such pleasure in vanity, and seek after leasing?

God who knows my righteousness will vindicate it, as he is the cause of it. Former deliverances embolden me now to plead to him for help.

2–5 The Church addresses the world-powers.

Sons of men: the Hebrew phrase here means men of high rank. Cp. Ps. 49. 2; 62. 9.

R.V. how long shall my glory be turned into dishonour?
R.V. seek after falsehood?

3 Know this also, that the LORD hath chosen to himself the man that is godly : when I call upon the LORD, he will hear me.

4 Stand in awe, and sin not : commune with your own heart, and in your chamber, and be still.

godly : *R.V.mg. one that he favoureth:*

Stand in awe of God, and break away from your vain purposes. But R.V.mg. after Sept. has *Be ye angry and sin not.*

The verse is so quoted in Eph. 4. 26. With this rendering the primary meaning of the words is 'Be ye angry with my rule, if you must, but do not sin by rebelling against it.'

Commune and meditate on these thoughts in the silence of the night, and cease from your sinning.

5 Offer the sacrifice of right-eousness : and put your trust in the LORD.

A.R.V. sacrifices. Sacrifices of righteousness are those which are offered with a right dis-position (*Ps.* 51. 17, 19). Or, Offer righteous deeds as your sacrifices.

6 There be many that say : 'Who will shew us any good?'

The desponding words of David's faint-hearted adherents: they are answered in the next verse. Pessimism cannot stand in God's presence.

7 LORD, lift thou up : the light of thy countenance upon us.

God's countenance means God as showing his love to man (*Ps.* 89. 16). David's prayer combines two petitions of the priestly benediction: 'The LORD make his face to shine upon thee, the LORD lift up his countenance upon thee, and give thee peace' (see v. 9; *Num.* 6. 24).

8 Thou hast put gladness in my heart : since the time that their corn, and wine, and oil increased.

R.V. gladness in my heart, more than they have when their corn and their wine are increased. David's God-given gladness in this time of his trouble is great-er than that of his enemies in the time of their prosperity. The Church's enemies may have more of material goods, but she has the spiritual joys.

9 I will lay me down in peace, and take my rest : for it is thou, LORD, only, that mak-est me dwell in safety.

only : *R.V.mg. in solitude.*

PSALM 5. *Verba mea auribus*

A psalm of one who is in peril from treacherous foes; a suitable prayer of any one in the Church militant, amid the snares and deceits of spiritual evil, who would have recourse for safety to God's righteousness. It is a morning hymn (v. 3).

PONDER my words, O LORD : consider my meditation.

2 O hearken thou unto the voice of my calling, my King, and my God : for unto thee will I make my prayer.

3 My voice shalt thou hear betimes, O LORD : early in the morning will I direct my prayer unto thee, and will look up.

R.V. order my prayer. It is the word used of the priest's arranging the wood, etc., for the sacrifice (*Lev.* 1. 7). He compares his morning devotions to the daily morning offering.

R.V. and will keep watch for an answer to my prayer. See Hab. 2. 1.

4 For thou art the God that hast no pleasure in wickedness: neither shall any evil dwell with thee.

4-6 The wicked are excluded from God's presence, by reason of God's holiness.

5 Such as be foolish shall not stand in thy sight: for thou hatest all them that work vanity.

R.V. The arrogant shall not A.R.V. hatest all workers of iniquity.

6 Thou shalt destroy them that speak leasing : the LORD will abhor both the bloodthirsty and deceitful man.

R.V. speak lies:

7 But as for me, I will come into thine house, even upon the multitude of thy mercy : and in thy fear will I worship toward thy holy temple.

upon: i.e. relying upon.

Cp. 1 Kings 8. 29 f.; Dan. 6. 10.

8 Lead me, O LORD, in thy righteousness, because of mine enemies : make thy way plain before my face.

God's righteousness is pledged to protect his true worshippers.

thy way: i.e. the way thou hast appointed for me.

C

9 For there is no faithfulness in his mouth : their inward parts are very wickedness.

A.R.V. in their mouth.
very: i.e. veritable, actual.
Their deceitfulness spreads corruption. This verse is quoted by S. Paul in Rom. 3. 13.

10 Their throat is an open sepulchre : they flatter with their tongue.

11 Destroy thou them, O God; let them perish through their own imaginations : cast them out in the multitude of their ungodliness, for they have rebelled against thee.

R.V. Hold them guilty,
A.R.V.mg. let them fall from their own counsels:

12 And let all them that put their trust in thee rejoice : they shall ever be giving of thanks, because thou defendest them; they that love thy Name shall be joyful in thee.

A.R.V. let them ever shout for joy,
God's Name, Jehovah (LORD), here and elsewhere stands for God's character as he has revealed it to his people.

13 For thou, LORD, wilt give thy blessing unto the righteous : and with thy favourable kindness wilt thou defend him as with a shield.

EVENING PRAYER

PSALM 6. *Domine, ne in furore*

The psalmist is suffering through his sense of his sinfulness and through bodily sickness and the assaults of his enemies. Mystically the primary speaker in this psalm is our Lord speaking to the Father in his passion in which he bears the burden of the sinfulness of mankind and the assaults of evil spirits. This is the first of the seven psalms called The Penitential Psalms, viz. 6, 32, 38, 51, 102, 130, 143, and is used specially as an act of penance and a remedy for the sin of Anger. The Penitential Psalms are proper on Ash Wednesday and in any penitential season.

O LORD, rebuke me not in thine indignation : neither chasten me in thy displeasure.

He regards his sickness as a proof of God's anger. See Ps. 38. 1. Sin always merits the anger of God which sometimes is manifested in temporal chastisement (*S. John* 3. 36; 5. 14). Man's anger is rightly exercised only against sin.

2 Have mercy upon me, O LORD, for I am weak : O LORD, heal me, for my bones are vexed.

3 My soul also is sore troubled: but, LORD, how long wilt thou punish me?

4 Turn thee, O LORD, and deliver my soul : O save me for thy mercy's sake.

5 For in death no man remembereth thee : and who will give thee thanks in the pit?

6 I am weary of my groaning; every night wash I my bed : and water my couch with my tears.

7 My beauty is gone for very trouble : and worn away because of all mine enemies.

8 Away from me, all ye that work vanity : for the LORD hath heard the voice of my weeping.

But in wrath God remembers mercy (*Hab.* 3. 2).

R.V. for I am withered away: my bones are vexed: cp. Ps. 31. 10.

These words were used by our Lord on the eve of his passion, 'Now is my soul troubled' (*S. John* 12. 27; see *Ps.* 42. 6).

The general conception of death in the O.T. is as a cheerless existence cut off from communion with God; see Isa. 38. 18. Such a penalty for sin will be incurred, unless God in his mercy grant us penitence and deliverance.

R.V. in Sheol who will give thee thanks? Sheol: i.e. the world beyond the grave.

The pain of penance.

R.V. Mine eye is wasted away because of grief: See Isa. 53. 2, 'He hath no form nor comeliness; and when we see him, there is no beauty that we should desire him.'

and worn away: *A.R.V. it waxeth old.* Cp. Ps. 102. 26.

There is a sudden change of note from depression to exultation. His prayer is heard, his enemies will be discomfited. This change from the minor to the major occurs in nearly all the Penitential Psalms. True contrition wins acceptance with God.

A.R.V. Depart from me, all ye workers of iniquity: These words are appropriated by our Lord as his final sentence on the wicked (*S. Matt.* 7. 23).

9 The LORD hath heard my petition : the LORD will receive my prayer.

Cp. Heb. 5. 7, Christ 'in the days of his flesh, having offered up prayers and supplications with strong crying and tears unto him that was able to save him from death, and having been heard for his godly fear, though he was a Son, yet learned he obedience by the things which he suffered.'

10 All mine enemies shall be confounded, and sore vexed : they shall be turned back, and put to shame suddenly.

PSALM 7. *Domine, Deus meus*

According to tradition, this psalm was that which 'David sang unto the Lord concerning the words of Cush a Benjamite' (Title). In the figure of David pursued by his enemies, we may see Christ himself, who alone was truly the Innocent One suffering unjust and unmerited persecution at the hands of evil men and from the power of wicked spirits. The Church in some sort shares his experience, and can make his words her own. Otherwise, we may see Christ as the LORD who giveth just judgement upon evil, on whom the Church calls for justice. This psalm is specially suitable in the season of Advent.

O LORD, my God, in thee have I put my trust: save me from all them that persecute me, and deliver me;

R.V. that pursue me,

2 Lest he devour my soul, and tear it in pieces : while there is none to help.

he: i.e. Cush, or Saul, leading the enemies.

3 O LORD my God, if I have done any such thing : or if there be any wickedness in my hands;

Cp. David's words when he protests his innocence to Saul (1 *Sam.* 24. 11; 26. 18).

4 If I have rewarded evil unto him that dealt friendly with me : (yea, I have delivered him that without any cause is mine enemy;)

So far was David from wantonly injuring his friends, that he saved the life of Saul his enemy when it was in his power (1 *Sam.* 24. 4 ff.; 26. 8 ff.). And

'God commendeth his love toward us, in that, while we were sinners,' and therefore enemies, 'Christ died for us' (*Rom.* 5. 8); as he said, 'They hated me without a cause' (*S. John* 15. 25; cp. *Ps.* 35. 19; 69. 4).

R.V. pursue my soul,

5 Then let mine enemy persecute my soul, and take me : yea, let him tread my life down upon the earth, and lay mine honour in the dust.

mine honour: *R.V. my glory,* poetical for 'my soul,' as being the noblest part of man; cp. Gen. 46. 6; Ps. 16. 10.

David calls upon God to take his place as judge, and vindicate his innocence. So Christ 'committed himself to him that judgeth righteously (1 *S. Pet.* 2. 23).

6 Stand up, O LORD, in thy wrath, and lift up thyself, because of the indignation of mine enemies : arise up for me in the judgement that thou hast commanded.

7 And so shall the congregation of the people come about thee : for their sakes therefore lift up thyself again.

R.V. the peoples. In David's vision all nations will be gathered together (cp. *S. Matt.* 25. 32) to hear his acquittal pronounced. Or the meaning may be that all nations will come to worship the LORD when he manifests his just judgements (cp. *Ps.* 86. 7-10).

R.V. and over them return thou on high. I.e. after thy visit to earth to gather the peoples, take again the seat of judgement which thou hast seemed to abandon for a time.

8 The LORD shall judge the people; give sentence with me, O LORD : according to my righteousness, and according to the innocency that is in me.

R.V. the peoples;

Christians can claim righteousness only through Christ and in union with him.

9 O let the wickedness of the ungodly come to an end : but guide thou the just.

10 For the righteous God : trieth the very hearts and reins.

A.R.V. but establish

The heart in the O.T. is the seat of thought and determination; the reins, i.e. the kidneys, of the emotions.

11 My help cometh of God : who preserveth them that are true of heart.

12 God is a righteous Judge, strong and patient : and God is provoked every day.

strong and patient: these words do not occur in A.R.V., they are added in P.B.V. from Vulg.

provoked: i.e. by sinners.

13 If a man will not turn, he will whet his sword : he hath bent his bow, and made it ready.

he: i.e. God.

14 He hath prepared for him the instruments of death : he ordaineth his arrows against the persecutors.

R.V. he maketh his arrows fiery shafts, i.e. lightning-bolts.

15 Behold, he travaileth with mischief : he hath conceived sorrow, and brought forth ungodliness.

15-17. The wicked man brings destruction upon himself as the natural consequence of his own doings.

A.R.V. conceived mischief, and brought forth falsehood.

graven: cut through stone.

A.R.V. fallen into the ditch.

16 He hath graven and digged up a pit : and is fallen himself into the destruction that he made for other.

other: i.e. old plural for 'others.'

A.R.V. his mischief

17 For his travail shall come upon his own head : and his wickedness shall fall on his own pate.

18 I will give thanks unto the LORD, according to his righteousness : and I will praise the Name of the LORD most High.

David is sure that his prayer has been heard.

PSALM 8. *Domine, Dominus noster*

A psalm of David (Title), on the greatness of man as crown and lord of creation, which was fully realized when man in Christ was exalted to be Ruler of the universe. This psalm is proper for Ascensiontide, when we contemplate all power and authority given to Christ (*S. Matt.* 28. 18), in heaven and earth. We behold Jesus, who at his Incarnation was made a little lower than the angels, crowned with glory and honour (*Heb.* 2. 5-9).

O LORD OUR GOVERNOUR, HOW EXCELLENT IS THY NAME IN ALL THE WORLD : thou that hast set thy glory above the heavens!

excellent : formerly meant excelling, above all other. 'There is none like unto thee, O Lord' (*Ps.* 86. 8).

R.V. upon the heavens, cp. v. 3.

2 Out of the mouth of very babes and sucklings hast thou ordained strength, because of thine enemies : that thou mightest still the enemy and the avenger.

The glory of God is confessed by children whose lisping praises put to silence the hostility of the wicked. Our Lord quotes the words in accepting the Hosannas of the children in the temple (*S. Matt.* 21. 16; see *S. Matt.* 11. 25; 1 *Cor.* 1. 27). The English P.B. applies them to the Holy Innocents. For 'ordained strength' Sept. has *perfected praise;* so quoted in S. Matt. 21. 16.

avenger : i.e. revengeful (*Ps.* 44. 17).

3 For I will consider thy heavens, even the works of thy fingers : the moon and the stars, which thou hast ordained.

4 What is man, that thou art mindful of him : and the son of man, that thou visitest him?

visitest; i.e. with love and providential care.

A.V. a little lower than the angels. So Sept. Vulg. and Heb. 2. 7, where it is referred to Christ's humiliation in the Incarnation. But R.V. has *but little lower than God,* referring to the great dignity of mankind.

A.R.V. glory and honour.

5 Thou madest him lower than the angels : to crown him with glory and worship.

6 Thou makest him to have dominion of the works of thy hands : thou hast put all things in subjection under his feet;

'And God said, Let us make man in our own image, after our likeness: and let them have dominion over every thing upon the earth' (*Gen.* 1. 26). Man's dominion reached its climax in the universal rule of the ascended Son of Man. 'But now (i.e. as yet) we see not yet all things subjected to him (man). But we behold him who hath been made a little lower than the angels, even Jesus, crowned with glory and honour' (*Heb.* 2. 9).

7 All sheep and oxen : yea, and the beasts of the field;

8 The fowls of the air, and the fishes of the sea : and whatsoever walketh through the paths of the seas.

9 O LORD our GOVERNOUR : HOW EXCELLENT IS THY NAME IN ALL THE WORLD!

Many of the psalms have refrains.

THE SECOND DAY

MORNING PRAYER

PSALM 9. *Confitebor tibi*

A triumphant thanksgiving on the defeat of enemies. The psalm extolls the righteousness and power of God, the judge of the world. Each vindication and deliverance of Christ and his Church, or of any member of Christ, is an earnest of the final judgement. The psalmist here, as often, sees that end already accomplished. It is suitable in the season of Advent.

I WILL give thanks unto thee, O LORD, with my whole heart : I will speak of all thy marvellous works.

2 I will be glad and rejoice in thee : yea, my songs will I make of thy Name, O thou most Highest.

3 While mine enemies are driven back : they shall fall and perish at thy presence.

4 For thou hast maintained my right and my cause : thou art set in the throne that judgest right.

Cp. S. John 18. 6.

set : i.e. seated.
that: i.e. thou who.
'Righteousness and equity are the foundation of thy throne' (*Ps.* 89. 15).

5 Thou hast rebuked the heathen, and destroyed the ungodly : thou hast put out their name for ever and ever.

6 O thou enemy, destructions are come to a perpetual end : even as the cities which thou hast destroyed, their memorial is perished with them.

7 But the LORD shall endure for ever : he hath also prepared his seat for judgement.

8 For he shall judge the world in righteousness : and minister true judgement unto the people.

the heathen: *R.V. the nations.* And so also in vv. 15, 17, 19, 20. Cp. Ps. 2. 9.
R.V. The enemy are come to an end, they are desolate for ever : and the cities which thou hast overthrown, their very memorial is perished.
R.V. the LORD · *sitteth as king.*
A.R.V. his throne

A.R.V. the peoples. Cp. S. Matt. 25. 32.

9 The LORD also will be a defence for the oppressed : even a refuge in due time of trouble.

R.V. a high tower.
R.V. a high tower.
due time: i.e. a time when there is due cause for God's intervention.

10 And they that know thy Name will put their trust in thee: for thou, LORD, hast never failed them that seek thee.

11 O praise the LORD which dwelleth in Sion : shew the people of his doings.

Sion may usually be interpreted as meaning the Church, and Jerusalem as the Church triumphant in heaven. Cp. Ps. 46. 5 for God dwelling in the Church.
people: *R.V.mg. peoples,* i.e. the Gentile nations, and the heathen.

12 For, when he maketh inquisition for blood he remembereth them : and forgetteth not the complaint of the poor.

R.V. For he that maketh inquisition for blood (i.e. demandeth a reckoning for bloodshed) *remembereth them* (i.e. the poor). By the 'poor' here is meant the nation of Israel oppressed by foreign tyrants, and by application the Church poor, persecuted and patient; or Christ crucified himself; cf. Heb. 12. 24, 'the blood of sprinkling, that speaketh better things than that of Abel.'

13 Have mercy upon me, O LORD; consider the trouble which I suffer of them that hate me: thou that liftest me up from the gates of death;

The thanksgiving merges into supplication.
of: i.e. from.

gates: i.e. power, jurisdiction; the courts being held at the gates of a city. Cp. S. Matt. 16. 18.

14 That I may shew all thy praises within the ports of the daughter of Sion : I will rejoice in thy salvation.

ports: *A.R.V. gates*
daughter of Sion : i.e. Jerusalem personified, or the Church.
By faith he sees his prayer answered already.
Ps. 7. 26.

15 The heathen are sunk down in the pit that they made : in the same net which they hid privily, is their foot taken.

16 The LORD is known to execute judgement : the ungodly is trapped in the work of his own hands.

R.V. The LORD hath made himself known, he hath executed judgement:

17 The wicked shall be turned into hell : and all the people that forget God.

R.V. The wicked shall return to Sheol, the place of the dead; i.e. they shall die, perishing prematurely, and the godless nations shall come to an end. In the word *return* the allusion is to Gen. 3. 19, 'Dust thou art, and unto dust shalt thou return.' There is no reference here to hell, the place of torment, Gehenna. Be turned: i.e. turn; not, be caused to turn.

18 For the poor shall not alway be forgotten : the patient abiding of the meek shall not perish for ever.

19 Up, LORD, and let not man have the upper hand : let the heathen be judged in thy sight.

20 Put them in fear, O LORD : that the heathen may know themselves to be but men.

patient abiding: i.e. as *A.R.V.* *expectation.*

PSALM 10. *Confitebor tibi*

This Psalm forms a single psalm with the preceding in Sept. and Vulg. Each pair of verses in Ps. 9 begins with the earlier letters of the Hebrew alphabet in successive order; and the arrangement is continued irregularly in Ps. 10.

A plaintive appeal to Jehovah to assert himself and protect the nation from tyrants. The Church appeals to God against those powers of the world which afflict her and despise God. 'The Poor,' here as always in the Psalms, may be interpreted as meaning the suffering Christ and his persecuted Church. God seems to disregard his martyrs. This Psalm is a prayer for the establishment of social righteousness.

WHY standest thou so far off, O LORD : and hidest thy face in the needful time of trouble?

1-12. The complaint of the poor.

needful: i.e. when there seems to be need of God's intervention, cp. 'due,' with the same meaning, in Ps. 9. 9. Neither word is in A.R.V.; they were added in P.B. from Vulg.

2 The ungodly for his own lust doth persecute the poor : let them be taken in the crafty wiliness that they have imagined.

3 For the ungodly hath made boast of his own heart's desire : and speaketh good of the covetous, whom GOD abhorreth.

lust: i.e. strong and selfish desire. *R.V. In the pride of the wicked the poor is hotly pursued:*

R.V. and the covetous renounceth, yea, contemneth the LORD.

4 The ungodly is so proud, that he careth not for God : neither is God in all his thoughts.

R.V. *The wicked, in the pride of his countenance, saith, 'He will not require it': all his thoughts are, 'There is no God.'*

5 His ways are alway grievous : thy judgements are far above out of his sight, and therefore defieth he all his enemies.

R.V. *His ways are firm at all times:* i.e. not subject to fluctuations of fortune, but always prosperous.

far above: i.e. he thinks of God as so distant that he may safely be disregarded. ˙

6 For HE HATH SAID IN HIS HEART, 'TUSH, I shall never be cast down : there shall no harm happen unto me.'

7 His mouth is full of cursing, deceit, and fraud : under his tongue is ungodliness and vanity.

under his tongue: like a delicious morsel retained in his mouth; cp. Job 20. 12; Cant. 4. 11.

8 He sitteth lurking in the thievish corners of the streets: and privily in his lurking dens doth he murder the innocent; his eyes are set against the poor.

Such acts of brigandage have been common in all unsettled times; cp. Prov. 1. 10 ff.; Hos. 6. 9.

9 For he lieth waiting secretly, even as a lion lurketh he in his den: that he may ravish the poor.

The wicked man is compared to a lion (v. 9), a hunter (v. 10), and a lion again (v. 11).

ravish: i.e. seize with violence. A.R.V. *catch*

10 He doth ravish the poor : when he getteth him into his net.

11 He falleth down, and humbleth himself: that the congregation of the poor may fall into the hands of his captains.

R.V. *He croucheth, he boweth down* (like a lion in wait for his prey): *and the helpless fall by his strong ones* (i.e. his claws).

The three-fold 'Tush' expresses the scornful mind of the ungodly, repudiating God's judgement.

12 HE HATH SAID IN HIS HEART, 'TUSH, God hath forgotten: he hideth away his face, and he will never see it.'

13 Arise, O LORD God, and lift up thine hand : forget not the poor.

13-17. The Prayer.

14 Wherefore should the wicked blaspheme God : while HE DOTH SAY IN HIS HEART, 'TUSH, thou God carest not for it.'

A.R.V. contemn God:

A.R.V. thou wilt not require it.

15 Surely thou hast seen it : for thou beholdest ungodliness and wrong.

16 That thou mayest take the matter into thine hand : the poor committeth himself unto thee; for thou art the helper of the friendless;

Cp. S. Luke 23. 46, 'Father, into thy hands I commend my spirit.' 1 S. Pet. 2. 23, 'He committed himself to him that judgeth righteously.'
A.R.V. the fatherless.

17 Break thou the power of the ungodly and malicious : take away his ungodliness, and thou shalt find none.

A.R.V. seek out his wickedness till thou find none. I.e. make ungodliness ultimately to vanish. 'To seek and not to find' is a Biblical phrase for the entire disappearance of some object; see Ps. 37. 36; Isa. 41. 12; S. John 7. 34.

18 The LORD is King for ever and ever : and the heathen are perished out of the land.

18-20. The prayer answered. By faith the psalmist sees the deliverance for which he prays already accomplished.
A.R.V. out of his land: God's land, primarily Palestine, ultimately the whole world when it shall be subdued to him.

19 LORD, thou hast heard the desire of the poor : thou preparest their heart, and thine ear hearkeneth thereto;

Man's dispositions to prayer are directed by God who answers it.

20 To help the fatherless and poor unto their right : that the man of the earth be no more exalted against them.

R.V. may be terrible no more.

Psalm 11. *In Domino confido*

This is one of the psalms traditionally ascribed to David himself. We see him in danger of his life, and urged by his friends to seek safety in flight. And we can compare him with our blessed Lord similarly advised by his well-wishers: 'Get thee out, and go hence, for Herod will kill thee' (*S. Luke* 13. 31).

IN the LORD put I my trust : how say ye then to my soul, that she should flee as a bird unto the hill?

A.R.V. '*Flee as a bird to your mountain.*' The words of timid friends to David, continued in vv. 2-3. The hill-country was the natural place of refuge for those in danger; cp. Judg. 6. 2; 1 Sam. 23. 14; S. Matt. 24. 16.

2 For lo, the ungodly bend their bow, and make ready their arrows within the quiver : that they may privily shoot at them that are true of heart.

A.R.V. upon the strings:

3 For the foundations will be cast down : and what hath the righteous done?

A.R.V. If the foundations (of society) *be destroyed, what can the righteous do?*

4 The LORD is in his holy temple : the LORD'S seat is in heaven.

4-8. David's reply. The providence of the holy righteous God is over the faithful in their times of trial, and his approval rests upon them.

seat: *A.R.V. throne*

5 His eyes consider the poor : and his eye-lids try the children of men.

6 The LORD alloweth the righteous : but the ungodly, and him that delighteth in wickedness doth his soul abhor.

alloweth: used to have the meaning of 'approveth after trial'; cp. Rom. 14. 22. *A.R.V. trieth.*

his soul: i.e. God's soul abhors the ungodly; cp. Ps. 5. 5; Isa. 1. 14.

Vulg. The LORD trieth the righteous: but he who loveth wickedness abhorreth his own soul.

As he destroyed Sodom and Gomorrah (*Gen.* 19. 24).

7 Upon the ungodly he shall rain snares, fire and brimstone, storm and tempest: this shall be their portion to drink.

to drink: i.e. to experience; cp. Ps. 60. 3; 75. 8; S. Matt. 20. 22.

8 For the righteous LORD loveth righteousness : his countenance will behold the thing that is just.

behold: i.e. with approval. But R.V. has *the upright shall behold his face*, which is an anticipation of the Gospel revelation, 'we shall see him as he is' (1 *S. John* 3. 2; cp. *Rev.* 22. 4 and *Ps.* 17. 16).

EVENING PRAYER

PSALM 12. *Salvum me fac*

A prayer for help in a time of general corruption and hypocrisy.

HELP me, LORD, for there is not one godly man left : for the faithful are minished from among the children of men.

minished: i.e. diminished.

A.R.V. They speak vanity, i.e. falsehood.

2 They talk of vanity every one with his neighbour : they do but flatter with their lips, and dissemble in their double heart.

3 The LORD shall root out all deceitful lips : and the tongue that speaketh proud things;

4 Which have said, 'With our tongue will we prevail : we are they that ought to speak, who is lord over us?'

4. The words of the proud.

5 'Now for the comfortless troubles' sake of the needy : and because of the deep sighing of the poor,

5-6 The words of the LORD. comfortless: cp. Ps. 69. 21, 'neither found I any to comfort me.' Similarly other mentions of 'the poor' and 'the needy' in the Psalter are interpreted of Christ.

God will intervene to set things right. Cp. 'And shall not God avenge his own elect?' (*S. Luke* 18. 7).

6 'I will up,' saith the LORD : 'and will help every one from him that swelleth against him, and will set him at rest.'

7 The words of the LORD are pure words : even as the silver, which from the earth is tried, and purified seven times in the fire.

7-9. The words of the psalmist. Cp. Ps. 19. 8.

8 Thou shalt keep them, O Lord : thou shalt preserve him from this generation for ever.

them: i.e. the needy and poor, v. 5.

him: i.e. each sufferer.

9 The ungodly walk on every side : when they are exalted, the children of men are put to rebuke.

I.e. The ungodly arrogantly pursue their evil way without opposition.

the children of men: i.e. ordinary folk, as in *Ps.* 11. 5. The meaning of this verse is the same as that of *R.V. The wicked walk on every side; when vileness is exalted among the sons of men.*

PSALM 13. *Usque quo, Domine?*

The psalmist is passing through a prolonged period of extreme danger and perplexity, or it may be of temptation long continued by the spiritual enemy, while God seems to be afar off.

HOW long wilt thou forget me, O Lord, for ever : how long wilt thou hide thy face from me?

2 How long shall I seek counsel in my soul, and be so vexed in my heart : how long shall mine enemies triumph over me?

The confused question, 'How long . . . for ever?' indicates a state of mind wavering between hope and despair.

A.R.V. mine enemy as in v. 4; one foe in particular is before his mind.

3 Consider, and hear me, O Lord my God : lighten mine eyes, that I sleep not in death.

lighten mine eyes: i.e. revive my strength and spirits, and quicken my spiritual perception (cp. *Ps.* 19. 8; *Eph.* 5. 14); that I sleep not in spiritual death through sin or loss of faith. The eyes reflect the state of health (*Ps.* 38. 10; 1 *Sam.* 14. 27).

4 Lest mine enemy say, 'I have prevailed against him': for if I be cast down, they that trouble me will rejoice at it.

5 But my trust is in thy mercy : and my heart is joyful in thy salvation.

His appeal to God leads him to renewed faith and courage.

6 I will sing of the LORD, because he hath dealt so lovingly with me : yea, I will praise the Name of the LORD most Highest.

A.R.V. dealt bountifully with me. And so the psalm ends in A.R.V. The remaining words are added here from Vulg. which borrows them from Ps. 7. 18.

PSALM 14. *Dixit insipiens*

The psalmist looks out upon a world utterly godless and corrupt. The righteous few are the prey of the many wicked.

Vv. 5-7 do not occur in the Hebrew, and have no place in A.R.V. In Rom. 3. 10-12 S. Paul quotes vv. 2-4 from the Sept. and then adds citations from other parts of the O.T. This series of passages was transferred from the epistle to some MSS. of the Sept., whence it passed into the Vulg. and P.B.V.

This psalm is repeated in Ps.53.

THE fool hath said in his heart: 'There is no God.'

The fool: so the Bible describes the man who has forsaken the fear of God; cp. Ps. 84. 19, 23.

2 They are corrupt, and BECOME ABOMINABLE IN THEIR DOINGS: THERE IS NONE THAT DOETH GOOD, NO NOT ONE.

They, i.e. the fools.
Cp. Rom. 1. 28 ff.

3 The LORD looked down from heaven upon the children of men : to see if there were any that would understand, and seek after God.

See Ps. 11. 5; 102. 19; Gen. 11. 5; 18. 20.

4 But they are all gone out of the way, they are altogether BECOME ABOMINABLE : THERE IS NONE THAT DOETH GOOD, NO NOT ONE.

5 Their throat is an open sepulchre, with their tongues have they deceived : the poison of asps is under their lips.

Ps. 5. 10.

Ps. 140. 3.

6 Their mouth is full of cursing and bitterness: their feet are swift to shed blood.

Ps. 10. 7.

Isa. 59. 7.

D

7 Destruction and unhappiness is in their ways, and the way of peace have they not known : there is no fear of God before their eyes.

Isa. 59. 7, 8.

Ps. 36. 1.

8 'Have they no knowledge, that they are all such workers of mischief : eating up my people as it were bread, and call not upon the LORD?'

8. God speaks.

my people: i.e. God's faithful ones, called 'the generation of the righteous' in v. 9, and 'the poor' in v. 10.

brought in: i.e. brought into.

9 There were they brought in great fear, even where no fear was : for God is in the generation of the righteous.

The effect which God's words will have upon the wicked. Being alienated from God, they become victims of even groundless fears. (But 'even where no fear was' is not in A.R.V.; it was added here from Vulg., which borrows from the sister Ps. 53. 6).

10 As for you, ye have made a mock at the counsel of the poor : because he putteth his trust in the LORD.

11 Who shall give salvation unto Israel out of Sion? When the LORD turneth the captivity of his people : then shall Jacob rejoice, and Israel shall be right glad.

A.R.V. Oh that the salvation of Israel were come out of Zion where God dwells among men (*Ps.* 3. 4); i.e. the Church, through which comes salvation. Jacob and Israel also denote the Church, as the people of God; Jacob the Church militant, Israel the Church triumphant.

turneth the captivity: probably metaphorical for 'reverseth the misfortune,' as in Job 42. 10 and elsewhere.

THE THIRD DAY

MORNING PRAYER

PSALM 15. *Domine, quis habitabit?*

This psalm depicts the character of the servant of God worthy of being admitted to his presence, a character which has been realized perfectly only in the human nature and life of Christ, and is reproduced in his members only in so far as they are in union with him and live by his grace. Here we have in verse our Duty towards our Neighbour. The psalm is proper at Ascensiontide, and on Saints' Days.

LORD, who shall dwell in thy tabernacle : or who shall rest upon thy holy hill?

thy tabernacle: i.e. the tent of God's presence, as in the wilderness (*Exod.* 40. 34; *Ps.* 61. 4). God's holy hill of Sion, i.e. in Jerusalem, where was the Temple (*Ps.* 2. 6). This dwelling and resting is enjoyed now by holy communion and hereafter by the beatific vision in heaven.

2 Even he that leadeth an uncorrupt life: and doeth the thing which is right, and speaketh the truth from his heart.

3 He that hath used no deceit in his tongue, nor done evil to his neighbour : and hath not slandered his neighbour.

4 He that setteth not by himself, but is lowly in his own eyes: and maketh much of them that fear the LORD.

setteth not by: i.e. esteemeth not. But R.V. has *In whose eyes a reprobate is despised:*

5 He that sweareth unto his neighbour, and disappointeth him not : though it were to his own hindrance.

6 He that hath not given his money upon usury : nor taken reward against the innocent.

The taking of usury, or interest, was forbidden by the Law (*Lev.* 25. 35 ff.); and all such dealings as involve the taking advantage of another's poverty selfishly have likewise been forbidden to Christians.

7 Whoso doeth these things : shall never fall.

PSALM 16. *Conserva me, Domine*

'David, in distrust of merits, and hatred of idolatry, fleeth to God for preservation. He sheweth the hope of his calling, of the resurrection, and life everlasting' (A.V.). The LORD himself is the glorious inheritance and unfailing support of his people.

The use of v.11 by S. Peter, Acts 2 and 13, shews that this psalm is to be interpreted primarily of Christ. It is proper on Easter Eve.

PRESERVE me, O God : for in thee have I put my trust.

2 O my soul, thou hast said unto the LORD : Thou art my God, my goods are nothing unto thee.

Ps. 63. 1.

I.e. as Vulg.: *Thou hast no need of my goods*, i.e. I have no merit of my own in thy sight. *A.V. my goodness extendeth not unto thee*. But *R.V. I have no good beyond thee*, with which cp. Ps. 73. 24.

3 All my delight is upon the saints, that are in the earth : and upon such as excel in virtue.

the saints, i.e. the nation of Israel as set apart for God's service, and the faithful members of the Church on earth.

4 But they that run after another god : shall have great trouble.

I.e. the heathen nations and apostate Israelites, and unfaithful Christians.

5 Their drink-offerings of blood will I not offer : neither make mention of their names within my lips.

of blood: The meaning is doubtful; perhaps it alludes to human sacrifices offered to the false gods.

neither make mention: cp. Exod. 23. 13.

6 The LORD himself is the portion of mine inheritance and of my cup : thou shalt maintain my lot.

The allusion is to the promise made to the tribe of Levi: 'I am thy portion and thine inheritance' (*Num.* 18. 20), which promise was shared by the whole nation which was unto God 'a kingdom of priests' (*Exod.* 19. 6); and it finds its fulfilment in the Church (1 *S. Pet.* 2. 5; *Rev.* 1. 6).

my cup: the LORD in his spiritual sustenance, as the gifts consecrated to Jehovah were the food of the Levites (*Deut.* 18. 1). Cp. Ps. 23. 5; 116. 13. In the Church it is especially the Religious who enter into these promised privileges.

7 The lot is fallen unto me in a fair ground : yea, I have a goodly heritage.

A.R.V. The lines are fallen unto me in pleasant places: The allusion is to the measuring lines by which the plots of land were marked out.

8 I will thank the LORD for giving me warning : my reins also chasten me in the night season.

A.R.V. the Lord who hath given me counsel : yea, my reins instruct . . .The reins (kidneys) are put for man's emotional part, cp. Ps. 7. 10. The night season, cp. Ps. 17. 3; 42. 8, often interpreted as denoting those times in which God's light is not perceived nor God's love felt.

9 I have set God always before me : for he is on my right hand, therefore I shall not fall.
10 Wherefore my heart was glad, and my glory rejoiced : my flesh also shall rest in hope.

on my right hand: the position of a champion and defender.

my glory: i.e. my soul, so called as being the man's noblest part; cp. Ps. 7. 5; 30. 13.

R.V. my flesh also shall dwell in safety.

11 For why? thou shalt not leave my soul in hell : neither shalt thou suffer thy holy one to see corruption.

R.V. leave my soul to Sheol: i.e. thou wilt not give up my life to the unseen world.

holy one: *R.V.mg. godly one* or *beloved one.* It is the same word which in Ps. 4. 3 R.V.mg. is translated *one that he favoureth.* David's confident words that God would preserve him from the power of death were obviously not realized in his own case; they were fulfilled in the victory of the Son of David at his resurrection, which is the earnest and pledge of ours. See Acts 2. 25-31; 13. 25-37.

'Narrow is the way that leadeth unto life, and few there be that find it' (*S. Matt.* 7. 14).

12 Thou shalt shew me the path of life; in thy presence is the fulness of joy : and at thy right hand there is pleasure for evermore.

at thy right hand: i.e. among those that are saved (*S. Matt.* 25. 33). But *R.V. in thy right hand there are pleasures for evermore.* I.e. pleasures are evermore in God's possession and gift.

Psalm 17.   *Exaudi, Domine*

A cry to God for help, from a persecuted soul confident in his own integrity. Mystically, Jesus Christ the righteous is the speaker: he alone can stand in his own righteousness; we only in his, in union with whom we recite the psalm, cp. v. 5.

HEAR the right, O LORD, consider my complaint : and hearken unto my prayer, that goeth not out of feigned lips.

feigned: i.e. deceitful, hypocritical.

2 Let my sentence come forth from thy presence: and let thine eyes look upon the thing that is equal.

sentence: i.e. the declaration of my righteousness.
R.V. look upon equity.

3 Thou hast proved and visited mine heart in the night-season; thou hast tried me, and shalt find no wickedness in me : for I am utterly purposed that my mouth shall not offend.

He fearlessly offers his thoughts, words, and deeds (v. 4) to the test of God's scrutiny.
night-season: cp. Ps.16. 8.

4 Because of men's works, that are done against the words of thy lips : I have kept me from the ways of the destroyer.

R.V. As for the works of men, by the word of thy lips I have kept me from the ways of the violent. I.e. by making God's word my rule of conduct, I have avoided the lawless ways of worldly men.

5 O hold thou up my goings in thy paths: that my footsteps slip not.

R.V. My steps have held fast to thy paths, my feet have not slipped. P.B.V. follows Vulg. and its rendering is better suited to our lips.
thy paths: i.e. the ways which thou hast ordained for me to walk in unto salvation: the opposite of 'the ways of the destroyer' (v. 4).

6 I have called upon thee, O God, for thou shalt hear me : incline thine ear to me, and hearken unto my words.

7 Shew thy marvellous loving-kindness, thou that art the Saviour of them which put their trust in thee : from such as resist thy right hand.

8 Keep me as the apple of an eye : hide me under the shadow of thy wings.

I.e. God saves them who trust in him from such as resist him.

the apple of an eye: i.e. the pupil, called the 'apple' because of its apparent shape; symbolic of that which is cherished with the greatest regard; cp. Deut. 32. 10; Prov. 7. 2; Zech. 2. 8.

the shadow of thy wings: i.e. the shelter of the divine providence; cp. Ps. 36. 7; 57, 1; 61. 4; 91. 4.

9 From the ungodly that trouble me : mine enemies compass me round about to take away my soul.

10 They are inclosed in their own fat : and their mouth speaketh proud things.

11 They lie waiting in our way on every side : turning their eyes down to the ground;

12 Like as a lion that is greedy of his prey : and as it were a lion's whelp lurking in secret places.

13 Up, LORD, disappoint him, and cast him down : deliver my soul from the ungodly, which is a sword of thine;

soul: i.e. life. *R.V. my deadly enemies, that compass me about.*
Their worldly and luxurious life has made them arrogant and unfeeling.

R.V. they set their eyes to cast us down to the earth;

a sword of thine: i.e. God uses even the wicked to carry out his purposes; cp. Isa. 10. 5. But R.V. has *deliver my soul from the wicked by thy sword*, i.e. by thy vengeance upon my assailants.

men of thy hand: i.e. men whom thou makest thine agents, as in v. 13; but R.V. has *From men, by thy hand, O LORD, from men of the world.*

their portion: cp. S. Luke 16. 25,

14 From the men of thy hand, O LORD, from the men, I say, and from the evil world : which have their portion in this life, whose bellies thou fillest with thy hid treasure.

15 They have children at their desire : and leave the rest of their substance for their babes.

16 But as for me, I will behold thy presence in righteousness : and when I awake up after thy likeness, I shall be satisfied with it.

'Thou in thy lifetime receivedst thy good things.' But the LORD himself is the portion of the righteous, and in him alone is their true satisfaction and their hid treasure.

In their worldly prosperity and security they have plenty for themselves, and for many children after them.

thy presence: cp. v. 2. *A.R.V. thy face*, cp. Esther 1. 10; 2 Kings 25. 19.

after thy likeness: cp. 1 S.John 3. 2, 'We shall be like him, for we shall see him as he is.' *A.R.V. I shall be satisfied, when I awake, with thy likeness*, i.e. when I awake beyond this life, in the glory of the beatific vision of God, cp. Ps. 16. 12. God's 'likeness' is that which God is, and will then be seen to be.

EVENING PRAYER

PSALM 18. *Diligam te, Domine*

'A psalm of David . . . who spake unto the LORD the words of this song in the day that the LORD delivered him from the hand of all his enemies, and from the hand of Saul' (Title). These words appear also in 1 Sam. 22. 1, introducing the same psalm. It is a song of victory after battle. In reciting it we apply its words chiefly to the overcoming of spiritual enemies by the power of God. 'Much of it is suitable to Christ alone' (Vulg.)

I WILL love thee, O LORD, my strength; the LORD is my stony rock, and my defence : my Saviour, my God, and my might, in whom I will trust, my buckler, the horn also of my salvation, and my refuge.

The figures are suggested by the natural features of Palestine whose mountains and rocks had served David for strongholds when he was pursued by Saul.

my defence: *A.R.V. my fortress.* my might: *R.V. my strong rock.* my buckler: i.e. *R.V. my*

2 I will call upon the LORD, which is worthy to be praised : so shall I be safe from mine enemies.

3 The sorrows of death compassed me : and the overflowings of ungodliness made me afraid.

4 The pains of hell came about me : the snares of death overtook me.

5 In my trouble I will call upon the LORD : and complain unto my God.

6 So shall he hear my voice out of his holy temple : and my complaint shall come before him, it shall enter even into his ears.

7 The earth trembled and quaked : the very foundations also of the hills shook, and were removed, because he was wroth.

8 There went a smoke out in his presence : and a consuming fire out of his mouth, so that coals were kindled at it.

shield. the horn: cp. S. Luke 1. 69. my refuge: *A.R.V. my high tower.*

R.V. The cords of death. 2 Sam. 22. 5 has *The waves of death,* which agrees better with the parallel clause 'the overflowings (*A.R.V. floods*) of ungodliness.'
R.V. The cords of Sheol. Sheol and Death are likened to hunters snaring their prey.
R.V. of death came upon me.
Here and in many other verses of this psalm David is recounting his past experience; but P.B.V. has altered the past tense to the future, to make the words more suitable to our lips. *R.V. In my distress I called upon the LORD, and cried . . .*
A.R.V. He heard
his holy temple in heaven: cp. Ps. 11. 4.
R.V. and my cry before him came into his ears.

7-15. Jehovah intervened, manifesting his presence and power as by earthquake and thunder-storm. This is symbolic of the mighty overthrow of Satan and his angels by divine power, in the past, present, and future. Cp. Isa. 11. 4; 30. 28; 64. 1.
A.R.V. There went up a smoke out of his nostrils:
Fire is a frequently-used symbol of God's vengeance: cp. Deut. 4. 24; Ps. 21. 9; 2 Thess. 1. 8.

9 He bowed the heavens also, and came down : and it was dark under his feet.

Darkness is a symbol of God's presence: cp. Exod. 20. 21; Ps. 97. 2.

10 He rode upon the cherubims, and did fly : he came flying upon the wings of the wind.

Cp. Exod. 25. 19; 1 Kings 8. 7; Ps. 80. 1.

11 He made darkness his secret place : his pavilion round about him with dark water, and thick clouds to cover him.

R.V. his hiding place:

12 At the brightness of his presence his clouds removed : HAIL-STONES AND COALS OF FIRE.

Lightning, the reflection of his divine glory, divided the clouds.

13 The LORD also thundered out of heaven, and the Highest gave his thunder : HAIL-STONES AND COALS OF FIRE.

R.V. and the Most High uttered his voice: cp. Ps. 29. 3.

14 He sent out his arrows, and scattered them : he cast forth lightnings, and destroyed them.

15 The springs of water were seen, and the foundations of the round world were discovered: at thy chiding, O LORD : at the blasting of the breath of thy displeasure.

discovered: i.e. uncovered, R.V. laid bare.
A.R.V. of thy nostrils (Exod. 15. 8).

16 ff. David rejoices in his own personal experience of the mighty salvation of the LORD. In the future tense the words are equally applicable : for what God has done God will do.
A.R.V. He sent from on high, he took me : he drew

16 He shall send down from on high to fetch me : and shall take me out of many waters.

17 He shall deliver me from my strongest enemy, and from them which hate me : for they are too mighty for me.

A.R.V. He delivered
my strongest enemy: perhaps Saul is meant, and behind him Satan, cp. 1 S. Pet. 5. 8.
A.R.V. for they were

18 They prevented me in the day of my trouble : but the LORD was my upholder.

19 He brought me forth also into a place of liberty: he brought me forth, even because he had a favour unto me.

prevented: archaic for *R.V. came upon*

liberty: cp. Ps. 119. 45 and S. Jas. 1. 25. A place of liberty; *A.R.V. a large place,* where there is room for free action. Cp. v. 30; Ps. 31. 8; Job 36. 16; Ps. 118. 5.

favour: see Ps. 41. 11.

20 The LORD shall reward me after my righteous dealing : according to the cleanness of my hands shall he recompense me.

A.R.V. The LORD rewarded me according to

20 ff. Here is the confidence of the Saints in Christ, cp. 1 S. John 3. 21; 4. 17. But their righteousness is not their own, cp. v. 32.

A.R.V. hath he recompensed me.

21 Because I have kept the ways of the LORD : and have not forsaken my God, as the wicked doth.

22 For I have an eye unto all his laws : and will not cast out his commandments from me.

23 I was also uncorrupt before him : and eschewed mine own wickedness.

24 Therefore shall the LORD reward me after my righteous dealing : and according unto the cleanness of my hands in his eye-sight.

A.R.V. For all his judgements were before me : and I put not away

A.R.V. and I kept myself from mine iniquity.

A.R.V. Therefore hath the LORD recompensed me according to

25 With the holy thou shalt be holy : and with a perfect man thou shalt be perfect;

25 f. God deals with men according to their characters; see 1 Sam. 2. 30, 'them that honour me I will honour.'

A.R.V. With the merciful thou wilt shew thyself merciful: cp. S. Matt. 5. 7.

R.V. thou wilt shew thyself perfect.

26 With the clean thou shalt be clean : and with the froward thou shalt learn frowardness.

froward: i.e. *R.V. perverse.*
A.R.V. thou wilt shew thyself froward.

27 For thou shalt save the people that are in adversity : and shalt bring down the high looks of the proud.

28 Thou also shalt light my candle : the LORD my God shall make my darkness to be light.

The lighted lamp in a house is a symbol of the continued life and prosperity of the family: cp. 1 Kings 11. 36; Job 18. 6. Cp. 'Lighten our darkness' in the evening prayer, which is another application of these words.

David's physical strength is a gift to him from God. Perhaps there is a reference here to 2 Sam. 5. 6-9.

In v. 29 the thought changes from defensive to offensive war. The Christian must not only seek protection but strength to conquer. Each victory is the earnest of the next. These thoughts are developed in the following section.

Cp. Ps. 19. 9.

29 For in thee I shall discomfit an host of men: and with the help of my God I shall leap over the wall.

As metals are tried.

30 The way of God is an undefiled way : the word of the LORD also is tried in the fire; he is the defender of all them that put their trust in him.

31 For who is God, but the LORD : or who hath any strength, except our God?

A.R.V. who is a rock. Cp. Deut. 32. 4, 15, 18.

32 It is God, that girdeth me with strength of war : and maketh my way perfect.

33 He maketh my feet like harts' feet: and setteth me up on high.

A.R.V. upon my high places, i.e. Sion and other mountain fastnesses which came into David's possession.

34 He teacheth mine hands to fight : and mine arms shall break even a bow of steel.

35 Thou hast given me the defence of thy salvation : thy right hand also shall hold me up, and thy loving correction shall make me great.

36 Thou shalt make room enough under me for to go : that my foot - steps shall not slide.

37 I will follow upon mine enemies, and overtake them : neither will I turn again till I have destroyed them.

38 I will smite them, that they shall not be able to stand: but fall under my feet.

39 Thou hast girded me with strength unto the battle : thou shalt throw down mine enemies under me.

40 Thou hast made mine enemies also to turn their backs upon me : and I shall destroy them that hate me.

41 They shall cry, but there shall be none to help them : yea, even unto the LORD shall they cry, but he shall not hear them.

42 I will beat them as small as the dust before the wind : I will cast them out as the clay in the streets.

43 Thou shalt deliver me from the strivings of the people : and thou shalt make me the head of the heathen.

R.V. do bend
A.R.V. the shield
A.R.V. hath holden
R.V.mg. thy condescension; see Ps. 113. 5-7. *A.R.V. thy gentleness*
Cp. v. 19.

The Christian's conflict against sins must be to the death.

A.R.V. thou hast subdued

R.V. that I might cut off

A.R.V. They cried, but there was
A.R.V. unto the LORD, but he answered them not.

A.R.V. Then did I
A.R.V. I did

A.R.V. Thou hast delivered

A.R.V. thou hast made me
R.V. the nations. God had brought David safely through conflicts at home (the strivings of the people) in order to give him dominion over the neighbouring nations.

44 A people whom I have not known : shall serve me.

44-46. David's forecast of his future successes. As mystically Christ the Righteous is the speaker, these verses are a prediction of the victorious progress of his Church in the world.

45 As soon as they hear of me, they shall obey me : but the strange children shall dissemble with me.

R.V.mg. strangers (i.e. foreigners) *shall yield feigned obedience unto me. Heb. lie*, i.e. pay me the insincere allegiance of the vanquished (*Ps.* 66. 2; 81. 16).
A.R.V. The strangers shall fade away : and shall come trembling out of their close places.

46 The strange children shall fail : and be afraid out of their prisons.

47 The LORD liveth, and blessed be my strong helper: and praised be the God of my salvation;

A.R.V. my rock

48 Even the God that seeth that I be avenged: and subdueth the people unto me.

R.V. the peoples

49 It is he that delivereth me from my cruel enemies, and setteth me up above mine adversaries : thou shalt rid me from the wicked man.

R.V. thou deliverest. 'Rid' means 'rescue,' cp. Ps. 71. 1.

50 For this cause will I give thanks unto thee, O LORD, among the Gentiles : and sing praises unto thy Name.

Quoted in Rom. 15. 9 as proving that Christ's salvation includes the Gentiles as well as the Jews. David's rule over the nations prefigured the all-embracing kingdom of his Son.
Gentiles: *R.V. nations.*
An allusion to God's promise to David (2 *Sam.* 7. 12 ff.), which received its ultimate fulfilment in Christ.

51 Great prosperity giveth he unto his king : and sheweth loving-kindness unto David his anointed, and unto his seed for evermore.

THE FOURTH DAY

MORNING PRAYER

PSALM 19. *Coeli enarrant*

God's revelation of himself, in Nature and in his Law. The Incarnation is the crowning revelation of God, for which the earlier revelations were preparatory. The mystical interpretation sees Christ, the Incarnate Word of God, throughout the whole psalm. It is proper on Christmas Day, and on Feasts of the Apostles (cp. v. 4).

THE heavens declare the glory of God: and the firmament sheweth his handywork.

1-6. God's revelation of himself in Nature.

The firmament: the arched roof of the sky, which was thought to be solid, in which moved the sun and stars. Cp. Gen. 1. 6. The 'heavens' have the same meaning. For the works of creation as revealing God, cp. Rom. 1. 19 f.

2 One day telleth another : and one night certifieth another.

A.R.V. Day unto day uttereth speech : and night unto night sheweth knowledge. I.e. each day transmits its tidings to the next, and each night similarly. The day's testimony to God's glory is different from that of the night, and so day and night are mentioned separately.

3 There is neither speech nor language : but their voices are heard among them.

I.e. there is no speech or language in which the heavenly voices are not heard. (The same use of 'but' occurs again in Ps. 139. 3.) So *A.V. There is no speech nor language, where their voice is not heard.* This seems preferable to *R.V. There is no speech nor language; their voices are not heard,* i.e. the utterance of the heavens though so expressive is not audible.

4 Their sound is gone out into all lands : and their words into the ends of the world.

A.R.V. Their line. I.e. the measuring cord which marks boundaries. The meaning is that the revelations have been proclaimed everywhere. The word for 'line' may mean 'harp-string'; hence the P.B.V. which follows Vulg.

Verse 4 is quoted in Rom. 10. 18 as mystically referring to the spread of the Gospel through the preaching of the Apostles. Cp. 1 Thess. 1. 8. Christ is the 'Sun of righteousness,' cp. v. 5 and Mal. 4. 2; Ps. 84. 12, bestowing upon mankind the light of truth and the warmth of love; the Apostles are the stars, and S. Mary is represented by the moon.

5 In them hath he set a tabernacle for the sun : which cometh forth as a bridegroom out of his chamber, and rejoiceth as a giant to run his course.

5-6. The Christian interpretation is well given in the Christmas hymn: 'Forth from his chamber' (the womb of S. Mary in which he tabernacled) 'goeth he, That royal home of purity; A giant in twofold substance one, Rejoicing now his course to run. From God the Father he proceeds, To God the Father back he speeds; His course he runs to death and hell, Returning on God's throne to dwell.'

as a giant: *A.V. as a strong man*
tabernacle: i.e. tent.

6 It goeth forth from the uttermost part of the heaven, and runneth about unto the end of it again : and there is nothing hid from the heat thereof.

runneth about: *A.R.V. his circuit is*

7 The law of the LORD is an undefiled law, converting the soul: the testimony of the LORD is sure, and giveth wisdom unto the simple.

7-11. God's revelation of himself in his Law. This revelation being specially made to Israel, the covenant-name Jehovah, the LORD, is used. Jesus Christ is that LORD Incarnate. Grace and truth came by him. He is the Word of God.

R.V. The law of the LORD is perfect, restoring the soul:

8 The statutes of the LORD are right, and rejoice the heart : the commandment of the LORD is pure, and giveth light unto the eyes.

Cp. Ps. 13. 3.

9 The fear of the LORD is clean, and endureth for ever : the judgements of the LORD are true, and righteous altogether.

The 'fear of the LORD' is another name for the Law, regarded in its effect upon the heart; cp. Gen. 20. 11.

10 More to be desired are they than gold : yea, than much fine gold : sweeter also than honey, and the honey-comb.

Cp. Ps. 119. 103.

11 Moreover, by them is thy servant taught : and in keeping of them is great reward.

---

12 Who can tell how oft he offendeth : O cleanse thou me from my secret faults.

12-15. Man's need of making a sincere response to God's revelation.

R.V. Who can discern his errors? Clear thou me from hidden faults, i.e. from sins committed unwittingly (*Lev.* 4. 2 ff.; *Num.* 15. 28).

13 Keep thy servant also from presumptuous sins, lest they get the dominion over me : so shall I be undefiled, and innocent from the great offence.

presumptuous: i.e. done wilfully, with a high hand (*Num.* 15. 30).

the great offence: *R.V. great transgression,* i.e. mortal sin.

E

14 Let the words of my mouth, and the meditation of my heart: be alway acceptable in thy sight,

the words: like the voices of the heavens (v. 1).

acceptable: a sacrifice favourably received is said to be accepted before the LORD (*Lev*. 1. 3 f.). Prayer is a sacrifice of the heart (*Ps*. 141. 2; *Hos*. 14. 2).

15 O LORD : my strength, and my redeemer.

PSALM 20. *Exaudiat te Dominus*

A psalm designed to be sung at the sacrifice which the king offers before going to war. It speaks of the warfare of Christ the King.

THE LORD hear thee in the day of trouble : THE NAME OF THE GOD OF JACOB defend thee;

1-5. The supplication of the congregation for the king during the offering of the sacrifice. For us, the person addressed is Christ in himself or in any of his members fighting against evil (*Rev*. 19. 11). Also the sacrifice offered is Christ.

God of Jacob: perhaps an allusion to Jacob's words, 'God, who answered me in the day of my distress' (*Gen*. 35. 3). The Name: cp. vv. 5, 7.

2 Send thee help from the sanctuary : and strengthen thee out of Sion;

Sion: may be taken, as often, as meaning the Church on earth, cp. v. 6.

3 Remember all thy offerings: and accept thy burnt sacrifice;

offerings: i.e. the meal-offering which accompanied the burnt sacrifice of the victim. A portion of it was directed to be burnt as a memorial before God (*Lev*. 2. 1); hence the word 're-member' here.

4 Grant thee thy heart's desire : and fulfil all thy mind.
5 We will rejoice in THY SAL-VATION, and triumph in THE NAME OF THE LORD OUR GOD : the LORD perform all thy petitions.

thy salvation: i.e. the deliverance which the king would win for himself and for his people, cp. Ps. 21. 1, 5.

6 Now know I, that the LORD helpeth his anointed, and will hear him from his holy heaven: even with the wholesome strength of his right hand.

6-8. One of the priests or the king himself announces the acceptance of the sacrifice. For us, Christ in himself or in any of his members is now the speaker. All Christ's members are anointed to share his kingship and priesthood.

his anointed: cp. Ps. 45. 8, 84. 9, and 89. 38; Rev. 1. 6; etc.

his holy heaven: not only from his earthly sanctuary (v. 2).

wholesome: *A.R.V. saving.*

7 Some put their trust in chariots, and some in horses : but we will remember THE NAME OF THE LORD OUR GOD.

A.R.V. but we will make mention of

8 They are brought down, and fallen : but we are risen, and stand upright.

9 Save, LORD, and hear us, O King of heaven : when we call upon thee.

9. The concluding prayer of the congregation.

R.V.mg. O LORD, save the king : and answer us when we call, following Vulg. Hence the versicle and response: 'O Lord, save the king. And mercifully hear us when we call upon thee.'

PSALM 21. *Domine, in virtute tua*

A companion psalm to the preceding. After warfare, triumph. It is a thanksgiving on the king's return after victory. And Christ is King of kings and Lord of lords (*Rev.* 19. 16). In his human nature he has been crowned with glory and honour (v. 5; cp. *Heb.* 2. 9). The Church recites the psalm in union with Christ as an act of worship and of Christian hope. It is proper on Ascension Day.

THE king shall rejoice in thy strength, O LORD : exceeding glad shall he be of THY SALVATION.

1-7. The congregation praise Jehovah for the king's safety and victory.

thy salvation: i.e. the deliverance which thou hast vouchsafed to him and wrought through him (v. 5).

2 Thou hast given him his heart's desire : and hast not denied him the request of his lips.

3 For thou shalt prevent him with the blessings of goodness: and shalt set a crown of pure gold upon his head.

The prayer of the preceding psalm has been granted.

A.R.V. thou preventest, i.e. goest to meet. The future tenses used in P.B.V. are, however, more suitable, when the words are referred to the members of Christ who are still militant on earth.

goodness: i.e. good fortune.

shalt set: *A.R.V. settest*

set a crown: i.e. crown him again, renewing him in his kingdom. Cp. our Lord's words: 'All authority hath been given unto me in heaven and on earth' (*S. Matt.* 28. 18). And cp. 2 Tim. 2. 8; Rev. 3. 21; etc.

4 He asked life of thee, and thou gavest him a long life : even for ever and ever.

Cp. the usual salutation, 'Let the king live for ever' (1 *Kings* 1. 31; *Neh.* 2. 3). The words are applicable in the highest sense only to the Son of David, the eternal King.

5 His honour is great in THY SALVATION : glory and great worship shalt thou lay upon him.

thy salvation : cp. Ps. 20. 5, 21. 1.

R.V. honour and majesty dost thou lay upon him, i.e. bestow; cp. Ps. 89. 20.

6 For thou shalt give him everlasting felicity : and make him glad with the joy of thy countenance.

R.V. For thou makest him most blessed for ever: thou makest him glad with joy in thy presence. Cp. Ps. 4. 7, 16. 11, 45. 8.

7 And why? because the king putteth his trust in the LORD : and in the mercy of the most Highest he shall not miscarry.

8 All thine enemies shall feel thy hand : thy right hand shall find out them that hate thee.

9 Thou shalt make them like a fiery oven in time of thy wrath: the LORD shall destroy them in his displeasure, and the fire shall consume them.

8-12. The king himself is addressed.

Cp. Ps. 2. 9, 18. 8; Rev. 19. 5.

10 Their fruit shalt thou root out of the earth : and their seed from among the children of men.

11 For they intended mischief against thee : and imagined such a device as they are not able to perform.

12 Therefore shalt thou put them to flight : the strings of thy bow shalt thou make ready against the face of them.

13 Be thou exalted, LORD, in thine own strength : so will we sing, and praise thy power.

fruit, seed : i.e. offspring (*Ps.* 132. 12).

The concluding prayer of the congregation: parallel to Ps. 20. 9.

EVENING PRAYER

PSALM 22. *Deus, Deus meus*

An agonizing cry for succour by a servant of Jehovah, speaking as one who is undergoing inhuman persecution and suffering from bodily exhaustion, either in his own person or as representing the faithful and afflicted people of God. This is followed by a thanksgiving for deliverance and for the fruits of suffering. The words were divinely prepared to foreshadow the sufferings of Christ and of the faithful who have meritoriously suffered with him. It is he whom we now see and hear in this psalm. Proper on Good Friday.

As in Psalm 21 we can discern the victory of Christ the King, so in this psalm his passion, in Ps. 23 his death and descent into Hades, and in Ps. 24 his ascension into heaven.

MY God, my God, look upon me; why hast thou forsaken me : and art so far from my health, and from the words of my complaint?

Our Lord made these words his in his dereliction on the cross; and thereby authorized the Christian interpretation of the psalm.

from my health: i.e. from my welfare. *A.R.V. from helping me.*

2 O my God, I cry in the daytime, but thou hearest not : and in the night-season also I take no rest.

night-season: cp. Ps. 16. 8.

3 And thou continuest holy, O thou worship of Israel.

God's holiness is a pledge that he will be faithful to his own.

thou worship of Israel: i.e. thou whom Israel worships. *R.V.mg. But thou art holy, O thou that art enthroned upon the praises of Israel* : a spiritual form of the phrase 'that sittest upon the (worshipping) cherubim' (*Ps.* 80. 1, 99. 1).

4 Our fathers hoped in thee: they trusted in thee, and thou didst deliver them.

His faith in the holy God of Israel remains unshaken though God seems absent. That faith is confirmed by the previous experience by Israel of God's providence. Cp. Ps. 44. 1.

5 They called upon thee, and were holpen : they put their trust in thee, and were not confounded.

holpen: i.e. helped.

6 But as for me, I am a worm, and no man: a very scorn of men, and the outcast of the people.

7 All they that see me laugh me to scorn: they shoot out their lips, and shake their heads, saying,

Cp. the picture of the Suffering Servant (*Isa.* 53), 'He was despised and rejected of men.'

Cp. S. Luke 23. 35, 'The people stood beholding. And the rulers also scoffed at him.' S. Matt. 27. 39, 'They that passed by railed on him, wagging their heads.'

8 'He trusted in God, that he would deliver him : let him deliver him, if he will have him.'

Cp. S. Matt. 27. 43, R.V., 'He trusteth on God; let him deliver him, if he desireth him.'
R.V. deliver him, seeing he delighteth in him.

9 But thou art he that took me out of my mother's womb: thou wast my hope, when I hanged yet upon my mother's breasts.

His faith is further upheld by his own personal experience of God's providential care through his life.

10 I have been left unto thee ever since I was born : thou art my God, even from my mother's womb.

Cp. Ps. 71. 4 f. Some have discerned here a forecasting of the Virgin-Birth.

11 O go not from me, for trouble is hard at hand : and there is none to help me.

Cp. Isa. 63. 3.

12 Many oxen are come about me : fat bulls of Bashan close me in on every side.

about: i.e. around.

His enemies are likened to furious bulls. *A.R.V. strong bulls.* Bashan was a rich pasture-land (*Deut.* 32. 14; *Ezek.* 39. 18).

Cp. 1 S. Pet. 5. 8.

A.R.V. a ravening and

13 They gape upon me with their mouths : as it were a ramping and a roaring lion.

14 I am poured out like water, and all my bones are out of joint : my heart also in the midst of my body is even like melting wax.

15 My strength is dried up like a potsherd, and my tongue cleaveth to my gums : and thou shalt bring me into the dust of death.

Cp. S. John 19. 28, 'Jesus saith, I thirst.'

thou: The sufferer looks beyond his persecutors to God who uses their agency. Cp. Acts 2. 23, 'Being delivered up by the determinate counsel and knowledge of God, ye, by the hand of lawless men, did crucify and slay him.'

16 For many dogs are come about me : and the council of the wicked layeth siege against me.

The persecutors are likened to the fierce wild dogs of the east.

A.R.V. the assembly of evildoers have inclosed me.

17 They pierced my hands and my feet; I may tell all my bones : they stand staring and looking upon me.

17-18. The psalmist describes his sufferings in figurative or proverbial terms, which were literally fulfilled at our Lord's crucifixion.

tell: i.e. count; as in Ps. 48. 11, 56. 8, 139. 18, 147. 4.

they: i.e. my persecutors. Cp. S. Matt. 27. 36; S. Luke 23. 35; S. John 19. 37, 'Sitting down they watched him there. . . . And the people stood beholding. . . . They shall look upon him whom they pierced.'

18 They part my garments among them : and cast lots upon my vesture.

Cp. S. John 19. 24, 'They said therefore, Let us cast lots for it; that the scripture might be fulfilled.'

19 But be not thou far from me, O LORD : thou art my succour, haste thee to help me.

20 Deliver my soul from the sword : my darling from the power of the dog.

my darling: *A.R.V.mg. my only one*, i.e. as the parallel clause shows, my soul, or, my life; so called because one only is allotted to man. Cp. Ps. 35. 17.

lion's mouth: this phrase was used by S. Paul of his own deliverance from great peril (2 *Tim.* 4. 17).

unicorns: *R.V. the wild-oxen*, cp. v. 12.

21 Save me from the lion's mouth: thou hast heard me from among the horns of the unicorns.

22 I will declare thy Name unto my brethren: in the midst of the congregation will I praise thee.

22-26.   The psalmist's, or Christ's, thanksgiving for being supported through his trouble.

In Heb. 2. 12 this verse is quoted as an utterance of Christ's, avowing his kinship with his earthly brethren. 'He is not ashamed to 'call them brethren, saying,' etc.

All those who have been redeemed by the death of Christ, whether under trial here or in glory in heaven.

23 O praise the LORD, ye that fear him : magnify him, all ye of the seed of Jacob, and fear him, all ye seed of Israel;

24 For he hath not despised, nor abhorred, the low estate of the poor: he hath not hid his face from him, but when he called unto him, he heard him.

estate: i.e. state, condition.

the poor: i.e. Christ, and they that are Christ's. *A.R.V. the affliction of the afflicted*.

Cp. Heb. 5. 7, Christ, 'in the days of his flesh, having offered up prayers and supplications with strong crying and tears unto him that was able to save him from death, and having been heard for his godly fear,' etc.

25 My praise is of thee in the great congregation : my vows will I perform in the sight of them that fear him.

I.e. not merely, I praise thee, but, as *R.V. Of thee cometh my praise*, i.e. It is the LORD who giveth me cause for praise.

vows: i.e. the thank-offering which I vowed in my affliction.

The poor: *R.V. The meek*

The sacrifice of thanksgiving (v. 25) was eaten by the offerer (*Lev.* 7. 15 f.). Here the meek are invited to take part in the feast.

26 The poor shall eat, and be satisfied : they that seek after the LORD shall praise him; your heart shall live for ever.

R.V. Let your heart live for ever. The entertainer's blessing upon his guests.

27-32. Prediction of the future extension of God's kingdom: which is the fruit of Christ's passion.

In Ps. 9. 17 the nations are said to have forgotten God.

be turned: i.e. turn.

27 All the ends of the world shall remember themselves, and be turned to the LORD : and all the kindreds of the nations shall worship before him.

R.V. the ruler over the nations.

28 For the kingdom is the LORD'S : and he is the Governour among the people.

29 All such as be fat upon earth : have eaten, and worshipped.

A.R.V. shall eat and worship.

The guests at the eucharistic banquet are (1) the rich and powerful, such as be fat upon earth,

(2) the poor, they that through poverty and misery are ready to perish; as is explained by the parallel clause in *R.V.*: *even he that cannot keep his soul alive.*

30 All they that go down into the dust shall kneel before him: and no man hath quickened his own soul.

R.V. A seed shall serve him; it shall be told of the Lord unto the next generation, i.e. the knowledge of God's righteousness (v. 32), declared by his deliverance of his servant, will be handed down from father to son.

31 My seed shall serve him : they shall be counted unto the Lord for a generation.

32 They shall come, and the heavens shall declare his righteousness : unto a people that shall be born, whom the Lord hath made.

R.V. They shall come and shall declare his righteousness unto a people that shall be born, that he hath done it.

PSALM 23. *Dominus regit me*

'A Psalm of David' (Title). The shepherd king towards the close of his life reviews God's goodness to him in the past. Cp. also Ps. 78. 52; 80. 1; 96. 7; 100. 3; for the same image of a shepherd, which our Lord applies to himself in S. John 10. 11, 'I am the good shepherd,' etc. In this psalm Christ is mystically the speaker; or, the faithful are speaking to Christ.

THE LORD is my shepherd: therefore can I lack nothing.

2 He shall feed me in a green pasture: and lead me forth beside the waters of comfort.

3 He shall convert my soul : and bring me forth in the paths of righteousness, for his Name's sake.

1-4. The LORD the Good Shepherd.

A.R.V. He maketh me to lie down in a green pasture : he leadeth me beside the still waters.

A.R.V. He restoreth my soul.
R.V. He guideth me.

for his Name's sake: i.e. not for my worthiness, but as proving that he is merciful and gracious as his Name implies; cp. Exod. 34. 5 f.

4 Yea, though I walk through the valley of the shadow of death, I will fear no evil : for thou art with me; thy rod and thy staff comfort me.

the shadow of death: a figurative expression for *deep darkness* (R.V.mg.). The reference is not only to the hour of death, to which the words are most often applied, but to any time of trial and trouble. Cp. Job 3. 5; Isa. 9. 2.

rod and staff: the rod for correction, the staff for support. Some, however, interpret the rod as the 'rod of Jesse' (cp. Isa. 11. 1), and see a reference to the Incarnation; the staff being understood as denoting the cross of Christ.

5 Thou shalt prepare a table before me against them that trouble me : thou hast anointed my head with oil, and my cup shall be full.

5-6 The LORD is the Host at a Banquet; cp. Ps. 78. 20.

A.R.V. Thou preparest a table before me in the presence of mine enemies:

anointed with oil: as an honoured guest; cp. Ps. 45. 8; S. Luke 7. 46.

A.R.V. My cup runneth over.

6 But thy loving-kindness and mercy shall follow me all the days of my life: and I will dwell in the house of the LORD for ever.

for ever: *R.V.mg. for length of days.* The psalmist looks forward, it may be simply to a long life spent in communion with God. To the Christian his words speak also of eternal blessedness in the heavenly sanctuary.

THE FIFTH DAY

MORNING PRAYER

PSALM 24. *Domini est terra*

'A Psalm of David' (Title). It was perhaps composed on such an occasion as the removal of the ark to Mount Sion. We see the ascent of the LORD to his sanctuary: the character of the man who may ascend with him, which is first the character of Christ himself, the triumphant King.

The psalm is proper on Ascension Day, the 'holy place' (v. 3) being interpreted as heaven; and it is used at the consecration of a church or other holy place on earth. Also it is one of the psalms proper on feasts of S. Mary, in which case the 'everlasting doors' (vv. 7, 9) are taken as referring to the doors of her virginal womb ordained from all eternity to receive Christ the King (cp. *Job* 3. 10; *Ezek.* 44. 2). In many places in the Psalter Sion or Jerusalem has been interpreted as meaning not only the Church, but also the Blessed Virgin, as the Shrine in which God dwelt.

THE earth is the LORD's, and all that therein is : the compass of the world, and they that dwell therein.

1-2. Sung by the whole choir in procession.

the compass of the world: i.e. the whole extent of the world.

The world and its inhabitants

belong to the LORD, by virtue of creation by the Word (v. 2), and redemptive conquest of evil by that Word Incarnate, 'mighty in battle.' This verse is quoted in 1 Cor. 10. 26, to show the inherent cleanness of all foods.

2 For he hath founded it upon the seas : and prepared it upon the floods.

The earth rising above the waters is pictured as supported by them; cp. Gen. 1. 9.

A.R.V. and established it upon the floods.

floods: in the Psalter this word means not 'inundation' but 'flowing waters,' 'streams.'

3 'Who shall ascend into the hill of the LORD : or who shall rise up in his holy place?'

A single voice puts the question. Who shall enter with the King of glory into his palace? Which of earth's inhabitants is worthy?

rise up: *A.R.V. stand.*

Another voice replies.

4 'Even he that hath clean hands, and a pure heart : and that hath not lift up his mind unto vanity, nor sworn to deceive his neighbour.

pure in act and intention. He is worthy who has been made like to Christ; cp. Ps. 15. 1 ff.; S. Matt. 5. 8.

vanity: i.e. falsehood; here, whatever is opposed to the truth of God.

5 He shall receive the blessing from the LORD : and righteousness from the God of his salvation.

Even the pure and true receive righteousness, and do not create it. By grace we are saved, not by works.

6 This is the generation of them that seek him : even of them that seek thy face, O Jacob.'

O Jacob: i.e. as in *R.V. O God of Jacob.* The reference is perhaps to Jacob's words at Penial, 'I have seen God face to face'; cp. Gen. 32. 30.

7 'LIFT UP YOUR HEADS, O YE GATES, AND BE YE LIFT UP, YE EVERLASTING DOORS : AND THE KING OF GLORY SHALL COME IN.'

The summons of the choir as the procession reaches the city walls, or the temple, at Jerusalem; cp. v. 3.

everlasting: i.e. of hoary antiquity, in the primary meaning of the verse.

8 'WHO IS THE KING OF GLORY?' : 'IT IS THE LORD strong and mighty, even the LORD mighty in battle.'

Challenge of the priests and levites within the walls, and the reply of the choir.

9 'LIFT UP YOUR HEADS, O YE GATES, AND BE YE LIFT UP, YE EVERLASTING DOORS : AND THE KING OF GLORY SHALL COME IN.'

The summons, challenge, and reply, as before.

10 'WHO IS THE KING OF GLORY?' : 'EVEN THE LORD of hosts, he is the King of glory.'

the LORD of hosts: i.e. the LORD of the armies of heaven, the holy Angels. Cp. Rev. 19. 14. The LORD Christ is mighty upon earth (v. 8), and also in heaven (v. 10). Cp. S. Matt. 28. 18. First, Christ is called 'mighty in battle,' because his first ascension to heaven took place soon after his triumph over death and hell at his resurrection; secondly, he is called the 'LORD of hosts,' because his second and final ascension will be made together with the multitudes of the redeemed after his second coming.

PSALM 25. *Ad te, Domine, levavi*

The psalmist is passing through a time of trouble: he prays for instruction, pardon, and deliverance. The speaker is mystically the Church of earth, the Israel of God, as is shewn by v. 21.

UNTO thee, O LORD, will I lift up my soul; my God, I HAVE PUT MY TRUST IN THEE : O LET ME NOT BE CONFOUNDED, neither let mine enemies triumph over me.

Cp. 19, and the end of *Te Deum*: ' O Lord, in thee have I trusted : let me never be confounded.'

2 For all they that hope in thee shall not be ashamed : but such as transgress without a cause shall be put to confusion.

3 Shew me thy ways, O LORD : and teach me thy paths.

A.R.V. be ashamed.
This had been a prayer of Moses (*Exod.* 33. 13). Cp. Ps. 143. 8, 10, and many other places. Cp. Isa. 30. 21, 'Thine ears shall hear a word behind thee, saying, This is the way, walk ye in it, when ye turn to the right hand, and when ye turn to the left.'

learn: i.e. teach.

all the day long: of life on earth.

4 Lead me forth in thy truth, and learn me : for thou art the God of my salvation; in thee hath been my hope all the day long.

5 Call to remembrance, O Lord, thy tender mercies : and thy loving-kindnesses, which have been ever of old.

6 O remember not the sins and offences of my youth : but according to thy mercy think thou upon me, O LORD, for thy goodness.

A.R.V. the sins of my youth, nor my transgressions of later years.

7 Gracious and righteous is the LORD : therefore will he teach sinners in the way.

8 Them that are meek shall he guide in judgement : and such as are gentle, them shall he learn his way.

9 All the paths of the LORD are mercy and truth : unto such as keep his covenant, and his testimonies.

the way: cp. Ps. 119. 1.

judgement: i.e. the right rule of conduct; cp. Prov. 1. 3.

10 For thy Name's sake, O LORD : be merciful unto my sin, for it is great.

The LORD who had proclaimed his Name as a God full of compassion and gracious, slow to anger (*Exod.* 34. 6).

11 What man is he, that feareth the LORD : him shall he teach in the way that he shall choose.

I.e. in the way that the LORD shall choose for him.

12 His soul shall dwell at ease: and his seed shall inherit the land.

13 The secret of the LORD is among them that fear him : and he will shew them his covenant.

They shall be admitted to God's inner counsels and to his confidential communion; cp. Prov. 3. 32; Amos 3. 7.

14 Mine eyes are ever looking unto the LORD : for he shall pluck my feet out of the net.

the net: i.e. the snares of the evil one.

15 Turn thee unto me, and have mercy upon me : for I am desolate, and in misery.

16 The sorrows of my heart are enlarged : O bring thou me out of my troubles.

R.V.mg. The troubles of my heart relieve thou, and bring

17 Look upon my adversity and misery : and forgive me all my sins.

18 Consider mine enemies, how many they are : and they bear a tyrannous hate against me.

19 O keep my soul, and deliver me : LET ME NOT BE CONFOUNDED, FOR I HAVE PUT MY TRUST IN THEE.

20 Let perfectness and righteous dealing wait upon me : for my hope hath been in thee.

21 Deliver Israel, O God: out of all his troubles.

Cp. v. 1.
A.R.V. Let integrity and uprightness preserve me : for I put my trust in thee.

A concluding prayer for the whole people of God. It may have been added when the psalm was appointed for use in public worship. Note that 'God' (Elohim) occurs here, but elsewhere in the psalm 'LORD' (Jehovah).

Israel: because when delivered Jacob had been renamed Israel.

This prayer for Israel becomes on our lips a prayer for the whole Church suffering but patient and destined for glory; and so a prayer for ourselves as members of it. But Vulg. reads *Deliver me, O God of Israel, out of all my troubles.*

PSALM 26. *Judica me, Domine*

The psalmist pleads his uprightness and zeal for God's House, and prays that he may not share the fate of the wicked. This psalm is an expression of the integrity, innocence, and righteousness requisite in Christians, and especially in the priestly ministers to God. We hear in it the voice of Christ the Priest and of his saints in union with him; cp. S. Paul's confidence in Phil. 3.9 and 2 Tim. 4. 8. Of ourselves we can use its words only imperfectly and by way of aspiration, for we have no righteousness of our own.

BE thou my Judge, O LORD, for I have walked innocently: my trust hath been also in the LORD, therefore shall I not fall.

R.V. in the LORD without wavering.

2 Examine me, O LORD, and prove me : try out my reins and my heart.

The reins, i.e. kidneys, were regarded as the seat of the affections; the heart, of the thought and will. Combined they sum up the whole inner man.

3 For thy loving-kindness is ever before mine eyes : and I will walk in thy truth.

A.R.V. and I have walked

4 I have not dwelt with vain persons : neither will I have fellowship with the deceitful.

5 I have hated the congregation of the wicked : and will not sit among the ungodly.

Cp. Ps. 1. 1.

6 I will wash my hands in innocency, O LORD : and so will I go to thine altar;

As the priests did in symbolic act before ministering (*Exod.* 30. 17-21). Hence vv. 6-12 of this psalm are appointed to be said by the Christian priest at the *Lavabo* in the Mass.

7 That I may shew the voice of thanksgiving : and tell of all thy wondrous works.

thanksgiving: particularly in the offering of the Eucharist. The word Eucharist means Thanksgiving.

Cp. v. 5, 'I have hated the congregation of the wicked.'

8 LORD, I have loved the habitation of thy house : and the place where thine honour dwelleth.

R.V.mg. and the place of the tabernacle of thy glory. The reference is to the Ark of God, cp. Ps. 78. 62. We apply it to the Altar and the Tabernacle.

9 O shut not up my soul with the sinners : nor my life with the blood-thirsty.

I.e. include me not with the wicked in their fate.

10 In whose hands is wickedness : and their right hand is full of gifts.

gifts: i.e. as *A.R.V.* *bribes.*

11 But as for me, I will walk innocently : O deliver me, and be merciful unto me.

12 My foot standeth right : I will praise the LORD in the congregation.

A.R.V. standeth in an even place: i.e. on the level open plain, in security. In the full assurance of faith, the psalmist regards his prayer as already granted; and the Christian may have even greater confidence in union with Christ.

EVENING PRAYER

PSALM 27. *Dominus illuminatio*

The first part, vv. 1-7, is a confident assertion of unfailing trust in God who has saved and will save from enemies. The second, vv. 8-16, is an earnest entreaty for help in a time of gloom and extremity. The whole is eminently suited to Religious.

THE LORD is my light, and my salvation; whom then shall I fear : the LORD is the strength of my life; of whom then shall I be afraid?

my light: this name is applied to God here only in the O.T.

God is to me the source of truth (my light) and grace (my salvation) and power (the strength of my life).

2 When the wicked, even mine enemies, and my foes, came upon me to eat up my flesh : they stumbled and fell.

Mine enemies are as savage as wild beasts.

3 Though an host of men were laid against me, yet shall not my heart be afraid : and though there rose up war against me, yet will I put my trust in him.

F

4 One thing have I desired of the LORD, which I will require : even that I may dwell in the house of the LORD all the days of my life, to behold the fair beauty of the LORD, and to visit his temple.

require : i.e. as *A.R.V. seek after,* not, demand.

the fair beauty (*R.V.mg. pleasantness*) of the LORD: i.e. not merely the outward beauty of the sanctuary and its worship, but also the gracious character of him who is worshipped.
to visit: *A.R.V. to inquire in,* i.e. to meditate and pray in.
tabernacle: *A.R.V. pavilion.*
Courage is found through communion with God.
Cp. Ps. 26. 8; 31. 22; 91. 1.
Cp. Ps. 40. 2.

5 For in the time of trouble he shall hide me in his tabernacle : yea, in the secret place of his dwelling shall he hide me, and set me up upon a rock of stone.
6 And now shall he lift up mine head : above mine enemies round about me.
7 Therefore will I offer in his dwelling an oblation with great gladness : I will sing, and speak praises unto the LORD.

an oblation: i.e. an offered sacrifice.

8 Hearken unto my voice, O LORD, when I cry unto thee : have mercy upon me, and hear me.
9 My heart hath talked of thee, 'Seek ye my face' : 'Thy face, LORD, will I seek.'

hear me: *A.R.V. answer me.*

A.R.V. When thou saidst, 'Seek ye my face': my heart said unto thee, 'Thy face, LORD, will I seek.'

10 O hide not thou thy face from me : nor cast thy servant away in displeasure.
11 Thou hast been my succour : leave me not, neither forsake me, O God of my salvation.
12 When my father and my mother forsake me : the LORD taketh me up.
13 Teach me thy way, O LORD : and lead me in the right way, because of mine enemies.

A proverbial way of expressing extreme desolation.

A.R.V. and lead me in a plain path: i.e. level and free from obstruction.

14 Deliver me not over into the will of mine adversaries : for there are false witnesses risen up against me, and such as speak wrong.

false witnesses: as against Christ (*Ps.* 35. 11; *S. Matt.* 26. 29).

A.R.V. and such as breathe out cruelty.

15 I should utterly have fainted : but that I believe verily to see the goodness of the LORD in the land of the living.

16 'O tarry thou the LORD's leisure : be strong, and he shall comfort thine heart; and put thou thy trust in the LORD.'

The psalmist hears a voice encouraging him. Comfort: i.e. strengthen.

R.V. 'Wait on the LORD: be strong, and let thine heart take courage; yea, wait thou upon the LORD.'

PSALM 28. *Ad te, Domine*

A cry to God for help against enemies, vv. 1-6, and a thanksgiving for anticipated deliverance, vv. 7-10.

UNTO thee will I cry, O LORD MY STRENGTH : think no scorn of me; lest, if thou make as though thou hearest not, I become like them that go down into the pit.

strength: *A.R.V. rock*

R.V. be not thou deaf unto me; lest, if thou be silent unto me,

the pit: i.e. the grave, or Sheol; cp. Ps. 88. 4 ff. Frequently in O.T. the dead are spoken of as if apart from God's presence and favour.

2 Hear the voice of my humble petitions, when I cry unto thee : when I hold up my hands towards the mercy-seat of thy holy temple.

hold up my hands: the gesture of prayer (*Ps.* 44. 21, 63. 5; 1 *Tim.* 2. 8).

The mercy-seat, which was upon the Ark, was the shrine of the divine presence (*Exod.* 22.1). *A.R.V. towards thy holy oracle.* Cp. Ps. 26. 9.

3 O pluck me not away, neither destroy me with the ungodly and wicked doers : which speak friendly to their neighbours, but imagine mischief in their hearts.

4 Reward them according to their deeds : and according to the wickedness of their own inventions.

5 Recompense them after the work of their hands : pay them that they have deserved.

6 For they regard not in their mind the works of the LORD, nor the operations of his hands : therefore shall he break them down, and not build them up.

7 Praised be the LORD : for he hath heard the voice of my humble petitions.

8 THE LORD IS MY STRENGTH, and my shield; my heart hath trusted in him, and I am helped : therefore my heart danceth for joy and in my song will I praise him.

9 THE LORD IS MY STRENGTH : and he is the wholesome defence of his Anointed.

10 O save thy people, and give thy blessing unto thine inheritance : feed them, and set them up for ever.

4–5. We may lawfully desire that the divine retribution may fall upon sinners, for the vindication of God's righteousness, for the deliverance of God's people from injury and oppression, and for the ultimate benefit of the sinners; but not for the gratification of personal revenge.

The faith of the psalmist assures him that his prayer has been heard.

A.R.V. their strength: i.e. the strength of the people mentioned in v. 10.

the wholesome defence: i.e. as *R.V. a strong hold of salvation to* The LORD's Anointed: i.e. the king, and especially the Messiah. The title Messiah in Hebrew, like that of Christ in Greek, means Anointed.

thine inheritance: cp. 'O Lord, save thy people : and bless thine heritage' (*Te Deum* and Versicles, B.C.P.). God became the inheritor, or possessor by right, of his people, by his redemption of them. Cp. Deut. 9. 29; 1 Kings 8. 51; Ps. 2. 8, 74. 2, 3; etc. The thought of possession by succession from another is not present.

PSALM 29. *Afferte Domino*

Jehovah who manifests himself in the terrors of the thunderstorm speaks peace to his people. This psalm is in some places used as proper on Trinity Sunday. 'The LORD' occurs fifteen times, and 'The Voice of the LORD' seven times.

BRING unto the LORD, O ye mighty, bring young rams unto the LORD : ascribe unto the LORD worship and strength.

R.V. Give unto the LORD, O ye sons of the mighty, give unto the LORD glory and strength. The sons of the mighty (or, *sons of God, R.V.mg.*) are the angels (see *Ps.* 89. 7) who are called upon to praise Jehovah for the manifestation of his glory in the thunder-storm. See Ps. 104. 4: 'He maketh his angels spirits (*R.V. winds his messengers*) and his ministers a flaming fire.' See also Ps. 18. 10. The P.B.V. comes from the Vulg. : it must be understood as a call to the great ones of this world to worship the LORD with sacrifices.

2 Give the LORD the honour due unto his Name : worship the LORD with holy worship.

A.R.V. worship the LORD in the beauty of holiness. R.V.mg. in holy array. The angels are regarded as vested like the priests in an earthly temple; see Ps. 96. 9.

A.R.V. The voice of the LORD is upon the waters : the God of glory thundereth. The voice of the LORD seven times repeated indicates successive peals of thunder; cp. the 'seven thunders' (*Rev.* 10. 3 ff.).

3 IT IS THE LORD, THAT COMMANDETH the waters : it is the glorious God, that maketh the thunder.

4 It is the LORD, that ruleth the sea; THE VOICE OF THE LORD is mighty in operation: THE VOICE OF THE LORD is a glorious voice.

R.V. even the LORD upon many waters. The waters are the sea, or the rain-charged clouds; or perhaps the waters above the firmament (*Gen.* 1. 6, 7; cp. v. 9).

A.R.V. the voice of the LORD is full of majesty.

5 THE VOICE OF THE LORD breaketh the cedar-trees : yea, the LORD breaketh the cedars of Libanus.

6 He maketh them also to skip like a calf : Libanus also, and Sirion, like a young unicorn.

Sirion was another name for Hermon (*Deut.* 3. 9). Mts. Lebanon and Hermon are in the north of Palestine; Cades, i.e. Kadesh (v.7), in the south. The storm is seen sweeping through the whole land.

R.V. like a young wild-ox.

7 THE VOICE OF THE LORD divideth the flames of fire; THE VOICE OF THE LORD shaketh the wilderness : yea, the LORD shaketh the wilderness of Cades.

the lighting-flashes.

the rolling thunder.

8 THE VOICE OF THE LORD maketh the hinds to bring forth young, and discovereth the thick bushes : in his temple doth every man speak of his honour.

discovereth: archaic for 'uncovereth.' *R.V. strippeth the forests bare:*

R.V. in his temple every thing saith, Glory. The angelic worshippers respond to the call of the psalmist in vv. 1, 2.

9 The LORD sitteth above the water-flood : and the LORD remaineth a King for ever.

R.V. The LORD sat as king at the Flood: yea, the LORD sitteth as king for ever, i.e. he who of old presided over the Deluge (*Gen.* 6. 17), still rules and controls the convulsions of nature.

Peace follows upon the storm.

10 The LORD shall give strength unto his people : the LORD shall give his people the blessing of peace.

A portion of the priestly blessing (*Num.* 6. 26). Cp. Ps. 4. 7, 31. 18.

THE SIXTH DAY
MORNING PRAYER

PSALM 30. *Exaltabo te, Domine*

A thanksgiving after recovery from sickness. It may be applied to thanksgiving for deliverance from sin and spiritual evil. Mystically the speaker is Christ speaking to the Father who 'was able to save him out of death (*Heb.* 4. 7). Hence, like Ps. 16, it is specially suitable in Eastertide.

I WILL magnify thee, O LORD, for thou hast set me up : and not made my foes to triumph over me.

. *R.V. thou hast raised me up:* His enemies would have exulted had his illness proved fatal.

2 O LORD my God, I cried unto thee : and thou hast healed me.

3 Thou, LORD, hast brought my soul out of hell : thou hast kept my life from them that go down to the pit.

hell: *R.V. Sheol.* I.e. thou hast preserved me when in great peril of death; see parallel clause and cp. Ps. 16. 11, 'Thou shalt not leave my soul in hell: neither shalt thou suffer thy holy one to see corruption.'

4 Sing praises unto the LORD, O ye saints of his : and give thanks unto him for a remembrance of his holiness.

R.V. give thanks to his holy name (*R.V.mg. memorial*). God's Name (Jehovah) is his memorial, because it sets forth his character as he has revealed it (*Exod.* 3. 15, 34. 5–7).

R.V. For his anger is but for a moment; in his favour is life: i.e. 'life which is life indeed' (1 *Tim.* 6. 19). But *R.V.mg. His favour is for a life time* may give the true meaning.

R.V. weeping may tarry for the night (*R.V.mg. weeping may come in to lodge at even*).

joy cometh: cp. Ps. 16. 10, 'My heart was glad, and my glory rejoiced.'

5 For his wrath endureth but the twinkling of an eye, and in his pleasure is life : heaviness may endure for a night, but joy cometh in the morning.

6 And in my prosperity I said, 'I shall never be removed : thou, LORD, hast made my hill so strong.'

7 Thou didst turn thy face from me : and I was troubled.

8 Then cried I unto thee, O LORD : and gat me to my LORD right humbly.

9 'What profit is there in my blood : when I go down to the pit?

10 Shall the dust give thanks unto thee : or shall it declare thy truth?

11 Hear, O LORD, and have mercy upon me : LORD, be thou my helper.'

12 Thou hast turned my heaviness into joy: thou hast put off my sackcloth, and girded me with gladness :

13 Therefore shall every good man sing of thy praise without ceasing : O my God, I will give thanks unto thee for ever.

my hill: the stronghold of Sion is a symbol of security (2 *Sam.* 5. 9).
A.R.V. didst hide

Cp. Heb. 5. 7.
gat me: i.e. got me, I went.

9–11. The psalmist's expostulation and prayer. He regards death as a state which allows no scope for active service to God; and such is death for those who are not united with Christ. Cp. Ps. 6. 5, 28. 1; Isa. 38. 18.

12–13. His prayer is granted.
joy: cp. v. 5.

A.R.V. To the end that my glory (i.e. my soul, cp. *Ps.* 7. 5, 16. 10) *may sing praises to thee, and not be silent.*
O my God: *A.R.V. O LORD my God.*

PSALM 31. *In te, Domine, speravi*

The psalmist passing through sore persecution is sustained by his trust in God. Our Lord has made this psalm his own, v. 6.

IN thee, O LORD, have I put my trust : let me never be put to confusion, deliver me in thy righteousness.

1–4 are almost identical with 71. 1–2; and with 'O LORD, in thee have I trusted; let me never be confounded' (*Te Deum*).

God's righteousness is a pledge that he will succour his servant, and is the first ground of that servant's trust in him.

2 Bow down thine ear to me :
make haste to deliver me.

3 And be thou my strong
rock, and house of defence : that
thou mayest save me.

4 For thou art my strong rock,
and my castle : be thou also my
guide, and lead me for thy
Name's sake.

5 Draw me out of the net,
that they have laid privily for
me : for thou art my strength.

6 Into thy hands I commend
my spirit : for thou hast redeemed me, O LORD, thou God
of truth.

7 I have hated them that hold
of superstitious vanities : and
my trust hath been in the LORD.

8 I will be glad, and rejoice
in thy mercy : for thou hast
considered my trouble, and hast
known my soul in adversities.

Shew thyself to be that which
I know thou art (v. 4).

A second ground of trust:
God's strong protection heretofore.

My guide: for the faithful
need not only to flee to God for
protection, but also to make
progress,

and (with another change of
the metaphor) to be disentangled
from the snares of evil.

strength: *R.V. strong hold.*

I.e. Into thy hands I entrust
myself for safety. Our Lord
gave to these words a higher
sense, when he used them to
express the surrender of his
human life to God (*S. Luke*
23. 46).

redeemed: i.e. preserved me
amid temporal troubles; cp. 2
Sam. 4. 9. In the N.T. the word
is sanctified to a deeper meaning,
as in 1 S. Pet. 1. 18, 'Ye were
redeemed with precious blood.'
Christ, true Man, could himself
so speak, for human nature was
redeemed first in Christ himself.

*R.V. I hate them that regard
lying vanities*: i.e. false gods and
other worthless objects of trust,
as compared with the God of
truth (v. 6). Cp. Jonah 2. 8.

A third ground of trust: God's
loving compassion and comfort
in times of trouble.

considered . . . known: i.e. regarded with loving care; cp. Ps.
1. 7, 37. 18.

9 Thou hast not shut me up into the hand of the enemy : but hast set my feet in a large room.

R.V. in a large place: i.e. thou hast in the past given me freedom and security; cp. Ps. 18, 19, 36.

---

10 Have mercy upon me, O LORD, for I am in trouble : and mine eye is consumed for very heaviness; yea, my soul and my body.

10–20. An interlude in the minor key. We hear Christ speaking in his Passion, as he suffered for the sins of the world which he has taken as his own.

mine eye: the eye reveals the ravages of disease; cp. Ps. 6. 7, 13. 3; 38. 10.

waxen: i.e. grown.

11 For my life is waxen old with heaviness : and my years with mourning.
12 My strength faileth me, because of mine iniquity : and my bones are consumed.
13 I became a reproof among all mine enemies, but especially among my neighbours : and they of mine acquaintance were afraid of me; and they that did see me without conveyed themselves from me.
14 I am clean forgotten, as a dead man out of mind : I am become like a broken vessel.

The penitent sees his sins as the root of his troubles.

R.V. Because of all mine adversaries I am become a reproach,

a broken vessel, thrown away and forgotten, useless.
R.V. the defaming of many: Cp. Jer. 20.10.

15 For I have heard the blasphemy of the multitude : and fear is on every side, while they conspire together against me, and take their counsel to take away my life.
16 But my hope hath been in thee, O LORD: I have said, 'Thou art my God.'
17 My time is in thy hand; deliver me from the hand of mine enemies : and from them that persecute me.

The theme of v. 1 is resumed.

A.R.V. my times are

18 Shew thy servant the light of thy countenance : and save me for thy mercy's sake.

A.R.V. Make thy face to shine upon thy servant: a part of the priestly blessing (*Num.* 6. 25; *Ps.* 4. 7, 29. 10).

19 Let me not be confounded, O LORD, for I have called upon thee : let the ungodly be put to confusion, and be put to silence in the grave.

R.V. in Sheol.

20 Let the lying lips be put to silence : which cruelly, disdainfully, and despitefully, speak against the righteous.

---

21 O how plentiful is thy goodness, which thou hast laid up for them that fear thee : and that thou hast prepared for them that love thee, even before the sons of men.

21–27. Thanksgiving for prayer answered.

22 Thou shalt hide them privily by thine own presence from the provoking of all men : thou shalt keep them secretly in thy tabernacle from the strife of tongues.

I.e. even in the presence of hostile worldlings. Cp. Ps. 23. 5.
R.V. In the covert of thy presence shalt thou hide them from the plottings of man:
in thy tabernacle: *A.R.V. in a pavilion*, i.e. of booths. The Hebrew word means 'booth.' Cp. Ps. 27. 5.

23 Thanks be to the LORD : for he hath shewed me marvellous great kindness in a strong city.

marvellous: adverb, marvellously; cp. Ps. 145. 31.
Perhaps a reference to 1 Sam. 23. 7. Or the sense may be, His protection encompasseth me like a fortified city.

24 And when I made haste, I said : 'I am cast out of the sight of thine eyes.'

R.V. As for me, I said in my haste, I am cut off from before thine eyes. A recollection of former impatience. Cp. Ps. 116. 11.

25 Nevertheless, thou heardest the voice of my prayer : when I cried unto thee.

26 O love the LORD, all ye his saints : for the LORD preserveth them that are faithful, and plenteously rewardeth the proud doer.

27 Be strong, and he shall establish your heart : all ye that put your trust in the LORD.

rewardeth, i.e. requiteth, giveth him his deserts.

R.V. and let your heart take courage:

Cp. Ps. 27. 16.

EVENING PRAYER

PSALM 32. *Beati, quorum*

'A Psalm of David' (Title). David, penitent after his great sin, records the relief which his confession of it brought to his soul, and his joy at being forgiven by God. In the Hebrew of vv. 1–2 three words are used for misdoing: breaking loose from God (transgression), falling short of the mark (sin), perversion of the soul (iniquity). Also the divine pardon is expressed in three ways: taking away (forgiven), covering, not imputing or reckoning. In this P.B.V., by the use of the future tense for the past, the psalm appears as a preparation for confession rather than a rejoicing after it. This is the second of the Penitential Psalms, and it is directed especially against the sin of Pride. Proper on Ash Wednesday, and as an act of contrition at any time.

BLESSED is he whose unrighteousness is forgiven : and whose sin is covered.

Contrast the blessedness of the righteous man (*Ps.* 1. 1) with that of this unrighteous man forgiven.

unrighteousness: *A.R.V. transgression*

covered: cp. Ps. 85. 2; S. Jas. 5. 20.

2 Blessed is the man unto whom the LORD imputeth no sin : and in whose spirit there is no guile.

Note that vv. 1–2 are quoted by S. Paul in Rom. 4. 7 f. to express the blessedness of the Christian's state of justification.

A.R.V. imputeth not iniquity. Cp. 2 Cor. 5. 19.

guile: i.e. deceitfulness. God's forgiveness can reach the sinner only when his repentance is sincere. Cp. S. John 1. 47.

3 For while I held my tongue: my bones consumed away through my daily complaining.

3–4. David's suffering, in which he recognizes God's hand, before he confessed his sin. Cp. Ps. 31. 12. Suffering is sometimes, but not always, caused by personal sinfulness.

held my tongue: i.e. proudly kept silence as to my sin.

A.R.V. through my roaring all the day.

4 For thy hand is heavy upon me day and night : and my moisture is like the drought in summer.

A.R.V. was heavy

moisture: figurative for bodily vigour (Ps. 22. 15). *R.V. my moisture was changed as with the drought of summer.*

Confession is the renunciation of pride.

5 I will acknowledge my sin unto thee : and mine unrighteousness have I not hid.

A.R.V. I acknowledged my sin

Confession is of sins in the plural; but forgiveness is of sin as a whole.

6 I said, 'I will confess my sins unto the LORD' : and so thou forgavest the wickedness of my sin.

Cp. Ps. 38. 18, 51. 3; and 1 S. John 1. 9: 'If we say that we have no sin, we deceive ourselves, and the truth is not in us. If we confess our sins, he is faithful and just to forgive us our sins, and to cleanse us from all unrighteousness.'

Cp. Isa. 55. 6: 'Seek the LORD, while he may be found . . . our God will abundantly pardon.'

7 For this shall every one that is godly make his prayer unto thee, in a time when thou mayest be found : but in the great water-floods they shall not come nigh him.

but in, etc.: R.V. gives the meaning accurately: *Surely when the great waters* (i.e. the overwhelming onset of divine judgements) *overflow, they shall not reach unto him* (i.e. unto the godly and the penitent).

8 Thou art a place to hide me in, thou shalt preserve me from trouble : thou shalt compass me about with songs of deliverance.

Cp. Ps. 27. 5, 31.20, 91. 1; and Col. 3. 3: 'Your life is hid with Christ in God.'

9 'I will inform thee, and teach thee in the way wherein thou shalt go : and I will guide thee with mine eye.'

10 Be ye not like to horse and mule, which have no understanding : whose mouths must be held with bit and bridle, lest they fall upon thee.

11 Great plagues remain for the ungodly : but whoso putteth his trust in the Lord, mercy embraceth him on every side.

12 Be glad, O ye righteous, and rejoice in the Lord : and be joyful, all ye that are true of heart.

9. The response of God.
A.R.V. I will instruct thee
R.V. I will counsel thee with mine eye upon thee.
10-12. David, penitent and pardoned, out of his own experience proceeds to instruct others.
Use your free-will; do not yield only to compulsion. Obstinacy is pride.
R.V. else they will not come near thee.
A.R.V. Many sorrows shall be to the wicked:
The psalm, like all the penitential psalms, ends on a cheerful note.

true of heart: and without guile (v. 2).

Psalm 33. *Exultate, justi*

The providence of God is extended over the world which he has made. The Christian interpretation also discerns in this psalm a manifestation of the Most Holy Trinity, Father, Word, and Holy Spirit.

REJOICE in the Lord, O ye righteous : for it becometh well the just to be thankful.

2 Praise the Lord with harp : sing praises unto him with the lute, and instrument of ten strings.

3 Sing unto the Lord a new song : sing praises lustily unto him with a good courage.

Cp. Ps. 32. 12, 89. 16, 147. 1.

R.V. with the psaltery of ten strings.
a new song: The occasion calls for a fresh expression of thanksgiving. But also cp. Ps. 40. 3, 96. 1; Isa. 42. 10. To Christians the phrase suggests the new song of the redeemed, who worship Incarnate God the Redeemer (*Rev.* 5. 9, 14. 3).
A.R.V. play skilfully with a loud noise.

4 For the word of the LORD is true : and all his works are faithful.

5 He loveth righteousness and judgement : the earth is full of the goodness of the LORD.

6 By the word of the LORD were the heavens made : and all the hosts of them by the breath of his mouth.

7 He gathered the waters of the sea together, as it were upon an heap : and layeth up the deep, as in a treasure-house.

8 Let all the earth fear the LORD : stand in awe of him, all that dwell in the world.

9 For he spake, and it was done : he commanded, and it stood fast.

10 The LORD bringeth the counsels of the heathen to nought : and maketh the devices of the people to be of none effect, and casteth out the counsels of princes.

R.V. are done in faithfulness.

4–5. The LORD is praised on account of his moral attributes. The Word of the LORD is to Christians the Word Incarnate, the Revelation of God, through whom all things were made. Cp. S. John 1. 1, 3, 18.

6–9. Jehovah is praised on account of his creative acts.

the word: the fiat of creation, again referred to in v. 9. 'And God said, Let there be,' etc. (*Gen.* 1. 3).

the hosts of them: i.e. the sun, moon, and stars (*Gen.* 2. 1).

The Church has seen in this verse the Three Persons of the Holy Trinity: the Father who made all things, the Word through whom all things were made, and the Holy Spirit who is the Breath of God and Life-Giver (*Gen.* 1. 2, 2.7).

Gen. 1. 9.

God requires man's fear as well as his love.

Ps. 148. 5, 6.

10–18. Jehovah is praised on account of his providential rule over the world, and especially (vv. 12, 17, 18) for his care of his chosen people.

R.V. the counsel of the nations . . . the thoughts of the peoples. *A.R.V.* have not the words, 'and casteth,' etc.

11 The counsel of the LORD shall endure for ever : and the thoughts of his heart from generation to generation.

endure for ever: in contrast with the counsel and thoughts of the heathen peoples which the LORD bringeth to nought.

his heart: the eternal purpose of love in the mind of God has been made plain to us in the Sacred Heart of Jesus (*S. John* 1. 18).

12 Blessed are the people, whose God is the LORD Jehovah : and blessed are the folk, that he hath chosen to him to be his inheritance.

the people: now especially the new Israel of God, the Church (1 *S. Pet.* 2. 9; *Ps.* 144. 15).

inheritance: cp. Ps. 28. 10.
A.R.V. The LORD *looketh . . . beholdeth*

13 The LORD looked down from heaven, and beheld all the children of men : from the habitation of his dwelling he considereth all them that dwell on the earth.

Ps. 11. 4, 5.

14 He fashioneth all the hearts of them : and understandeth all their works.

15 There is no king that can be saved by the multitude of an host : neither is any mighty man delivered by much strength.

15, 16. The futility of reliance upon merely human resources.

16 A horse is counted but a vain thing to save a man : neither shall he deliver any man by his great strength.

17 Behold, the eye of the LORD is upon them that fear him : and upon them that put their trust in his mercy;

Ps. 34. 15; 1 S. Pet. 3. 12.

18 To deliver their soul from death : and to feed them in the time of dearth.

19 Our soul hath patiently tarried for the LORD : for he is our help, and our shield.

19–21. The response to the summons to praise and thanksgiving (vv. 1–3).

20 For our heart shall rejoice in him : because we have hoped in his holy Name.

Ps. 89. 16.

21 Let thy merciful kindness, O LORD, be upon us : like as we do put our trust in thee.

Hence, in *Te Deum*: 'O Lord, let thy mercy lighten upon us: as our trust is in thee.'

PSALM 34. *Benedicam Domino*

A celebration of God's moral government and gracious providence, especially as regards his protection of the righteous. Many references to Christ have been discerned in this psalm. Every mention of 'the poor,' 'the righteous,' 'the humble,' is applicable to him above all others. The psalm is also suitable on festivals of the holy Angels (cp. v. 7) and those of the Saints.

I WILL alway give thanks unto the LORD : his praise shall ever be in my mouth.

2 My soul shall make her boast in the LORD : the humble shall hear thereof, and be glad.

3 O praise the LORD with me : and let us magnify his Name together.

4 I sought the LORD, and he heard me : yea, he delivered me out of all my fear.

5 They had an eye unto him, and were lightened : and their faces were not ashamed.

A.R.V. They looked unto him, They: the experience of others agrees with that of the psalmist. The meaning is that all who look unto him are lightened, i.e. brightened and cheered with the divine light. Cp. Ps. 4. 7.

R.V. shall never be confounded.

6 Lo, the poor crieth, and the LORD heareth him : yea, and saveth him out of all his troubles.

7 The angel of the LORD tarrieth round about them that fear him : and delivereth them.

A.R.V. encampeth round about. Cp. 2 Kings 6. 17. The Angel of the LORD is the special representative of Jehovah; cp. Gen. 16. 7; Exod. 23. 20 ff.; etc. The title is mentioned in the Psalter only here and in 35. 5, 6, where he is the agent of divine wrath. In this verse we are led to think especially of the Angel of the Agony (*S. Luke* 22. 43).

G

8 O taste, and see, how gracious the LORD is : blessed is the man that trusteth in him.

Quoted by S. Peter (1 *S. Pet.* 2. 3), who applies 'the LORD' to our Lord Jesus Christ: 'if ye have tasted that the LORD is gracious.'

blessed . . . trusted: cp. Ps. 2. 12.

9 O fear the LORD, ye that are his saints : for they that fear him lack nothing.

10 The lions do lack, and suffer hunger : but they who seek the LORD shall want no manner of thing that is good.

11 Come, ye children, and hearken unto me : I will teach you the fear of the LORD.

ye children: an affectionate form of address, as of a teacher to his disciples; cp. Prov. 4. 11; 1 S. John 2. 1, 12; etc.

12 What man is he that lusteth to live : and would fain see good days?

lusteth: i.e. as *A.R.V. desireth life: and loveth many days, that he may see good?*

fain: i.e. gladly.

vv. 12–16 are cited in 1 S. Pet. 3. 10 ff.

13 Keep thy tongue from evil: and thy lips, that they speak no guile.

14 Eschew evil, and do good : seek peace, and ensue it.

Cp. Ps. 15. 3, 39. 1, 141. 3, etc.

no guile: cp. S. John 1. 47; Rev. 14. 5.

A.R.V. Depart from evil, . . . pursue it.

ensue: i.e. follow after.

Cp. Ps. 33. 17.

15 The eyes of the LORD are over the righteous : and his ears are open unto their prayers.

16 The countenance of the LORD is against them that do evil : to root out the remembrance of them from the earth.

17 The righteous cry, and the LORD heareth them : and delivereth them out of all their troubles.

18 The LORD is nigh unto them that are of a contrite heart : and will save such as be of an humble spirit.

19 Great are the troubles of the righteous : but the LORD delivereth him out of all.

20 He keepeth all his bones : so that not one of them is broken.

This figurative description of God's watchful care, together with the direction about the Paschal Lamb (*Exod.* 12. 46), is referred to by S. John as literally fulfilled in Christ's Passion: 'They brake not his legs ... that the scripture might be fulfilled, A bone of him shall not be broken' (*S. John* 19. 33, 36).

21 But misfortune shall slay the ungodly : and they that hate the righteous shall be desolate.

R.V. shall be condemned.
A.R.V. The LORD redeemeth

22 The LORD delivereth the souls of his servants : and all they that put their trust in him shall not be destitute.

R.V. condemned.

THE SEVENTH DAY

MORNING PRAYER

PSALM 35. *Judica, Domine*

This is a psalm of a warrior, perhaps David, to whom the title ascribes it. He appeals to Jehovah for help against active and malicious enemies. He calls upon the LORD in warlike phrase and imagery. Christians are wont to think of Christ as the speaker in this psalm, and of the enemies as his and their spiritual foes. We can make this psalm our own, in so far as we have the mind of Christ. The faithful warrior desires the overthrow of the enemies, even at any cost, in order that God's righteousness, impugned by their triumph, may be vindicated. Cp. v. 27. This is always the implication in those verses of the psalms which would otherwise appear to be merely vindictive. Pss. 34 and 35 form a pair and explain each other: God's destruction of his enemies is his deliverance of the righteous.

PLEAD thou my cause, O LORD, with them that strive with me : and fight thou against them that fight against me.

2 Lay hand upon shield and buckler : and stand up to help me.

buckler: i.e. a small shield.

3 Bring forth the spear, and stop the way against them that persecute me : say unto my soul, 'I am thy salvation.'

R.V.mg. the spear and the battle axe against
R.V. pursue me:

4 Let them be confounded, and put to shame, that seek after my soul : let them be turned back, and brought to confusion, that imagine mischief for me.

5 Let them be as the dust before the wind : and the angel of the LORD scattering them.

A.R.V. as chaff. Cf. Ps. 1. 5. Cf. Ps. 34. 7.

6 Let their way be dark and slippery : and let the angel of the LORD persecute them.

R.V. and the angel of the LORD pursuing them.
privily: i.e. secretly.
without a cause: cp. v. 19.

7 For they have privily laid their net to destroy me without a cause : yea, even without a cause have they made a pit for my soul.

8 Let a sudden destruction come upon him unawares, and his net, that he hath laid privily, catch himself : that he may fall into his own mischief.

him: the singular is used collectively, or some individual enemy is referred to.

9 And, my soul, be joyful in the LORD : it shall rejoice in his salvation.

A.R.V. And my soul shall be

10 All my bones shall say, 'LORD, who is like unto thee, who deliverest the poor from him that is too strong for him : yea, the poor, and him that is in misery from him that spoileth him?'

All my bones: i.e. the joy of my soul (v. 9) will throb through every member of my body; cp. Ps. 51. 8. We may see also a reference to Ps. 34. 20. With this verse cp. Ps. 34. 16, 17.
spoileth: i.e. despoileth.
Cp. S. Matt. 26. 59-61.

11 False witnesses did rise up: they laid to my charge things that I knew not.

12 They rewarded me evil for good : to the great discomfort of my soul.

Cp. Ps. 38, 20, 109. 4; Jer. 18. 20; S. John 10. 32.

13 Nevertheless, when they were sick, I put on sackcloth, and humbled my soul with fasting : and my prayer shall turn into mine own bosom.

He who prays for his enemies in their distress is not vindictive. And his prayer for them will bring him the blessings which he asked for them but they were unworthy to receive. Cp.S.Matt. 10. 13.

14 I behaved myself as though it had been my friend, or my brother : I went heavily, as one that mourneth for his mother.

15 But in mine adversity they rejoiced, and gathered themselves together : yea, the very abjects came together against me unawares, making mouths at me, and ceased not.

the very abjects: i.e. even the outcasts. The lowest of the rabble join the ranks of my persecutors. Cp. S. Matt. 27. 39.

mouths: the word 'mouths' has been substituted for 'mowes,'i.e. grimaces, which appeared in the earlier editions of the B.C.P.

A.R.V. against me, and I knew it not: they did tear me, and ceased not.

R.V. Like the profane mockers at feasts, they gnashed: i.e. like professional buffoons who earned their dinners by making sport for the guests.

16 With the flatterers were busy mockers : who gnashed upon me with their teeth.

17 LORD, how long wilt thou look upon this : O deliver my soul from the calamities which they bring on me, and my darling from the lions.

my darling: *A.R.V. mg. my only one*, i.e. my soul, or life, as the parallel clause shews; cp. Ps. 22. 20.

the lions: i.e. my savage assailants. Cp. 2 Tim. 4. 17.

Cp. Ps. 22. 25.

18 So will I give thee thanks in the great congregation : I will praise thee among much people.

19 O let not them that are mine enemies triumph over me ungodly : neither let them wink with their eyes that hate me without a cause.

A.R.V. wrongfully:

wink: i.e. make gestures to express their joy at my calamity.

hate me without a cause: these words were quoted by our Lord as fulfilled in his own case (*S. John* 15. 25). They occur also in Ps. 69. 4.

20 And why? their communing is not for peace : but they imagine deceitful words against them that are quiet in the land.

21 They gaped upon me with their mouths, and said : 'Fie on thee, fie on thee, we saw it with our eyes.'

A.R.V. Aha, aha, our eye hath seen it, i.e. thy misfortune. Cp. Ps. 22. 13; S. Matt. 27. 39 ff.

22 This thou hast seen, O LORD : hold not thy tongue then, go not far from me, O LORD.

23 Awake, and stand up to judge my quarrel : avenge thou my cause, my God, and my Lord.

As often in O.T. God is addressed in words suited to a man. Cp. Ps. 44. 23.

24 Judge me, O LORD my God, according to thy righteousness : and let them not triumph over me.

25 Let them not say in their hearts, 'There, there, so would we have it' : neither let them say, 'We have devoured him.'

26 Let them be put to confusion and shame together, that rejoice at my trouble : let them be clothed with rebuke and dishonour, that boast themselves against me.

27 Let them be glad and rejoice, that favour my righteous dealing : yea, let them say alway, 'Blessed be the LORD, who hath pleasure in the prosperity of his servant.'

28 As for my tongue, it shall be talking of thy righteousness : and of thy praise all the day long.

It is zeal for God's righteousness that is the root of his desires against his enemies.

PSALM 36.   *Dixit injustus*

The wickedness of the ungodly in contrast with the faithfulness and loving-kindness of the LORD.   Title: 'A psalm of David, the servant of the Lord.'

MY heart sheweth me the wickedness of the ungodly: that there is no fear of God before his eyes.

1–5. The wickedness of the ungodly.
Cited by S. Paul in Rom. 3. 18 as the climax in his description of the ungodly. To have no fear of God is the fundamental sin. Cp. Ps. 14. 1 ff.

2 For he flattereth himself in his own sight : until his abominable sin be found out.

R.V. that his iniquity shall not be found out and be hated.

3 The words of his mouth are unrighteous, and full of deceit : he hath left off to behave himself wisely, and to do good.

4 He imagineth mischief upon his bed, and hath set himself in no good way : neither doth he abhor any thing that is evil.

5 Thy mercy, O LORD, reacheth unto the heavens : and thy faithfulness unto the clouds.

5–9. The loving-kindness of the LORD, providing safety and satisfaction.
reacheth, etc.: i.e. beyond measure, infinite.

6 Thy righteousness standeth like the strong mountains : thy judgements are like the great deep.

R.V. is like the mountains of God, which God hath reared, and not man (cp. Ps. 104. 16), i.e. strong and permanent.
like the great deep: i.e. profound and all-pervading.

7 Thou, LORD, shalt save both man and beast; how excellent is thy mercy, O God : and the children of men shall put their trust under the shadow of thy wings.

A.R.V. O LORD, thou preservest
excellent: formerly meant excelling, surpassing; cp. Ps. 8. 1.
A.R.V. the children of men take refuge
the shadow: cp. Ps. 17. 8.

8 They shall be satisfied with the plenteousness of thy house : and thou shalt give them drink of thy pleasures, as out of the river.

The LORD is regarded as a most gracious host; cp. Ps. 23. 5, 65. 4, 107. 9.

A.R.V. thou shalt make them drink of the river of thy pleasures. Cp. Ps. 46. 4; Rev. 22. 1.

9 For with thee is the well of life : and in thy light shall we see light.

'The water that I shall give shall become in him a well of water springing up unto eternal life' (*S. John* 4. 14).

'In him was life, and the life was the light of men' (*S. John* 1. 4).

10 O continue forth thy lov-ing-kindness unto them that know thee : and thy righteous-ness unto them that are true of heart.

10–12. A prayer upon the meditation.

11 O let not the foot of pride come against me : and let not the hand of the ungodly cast me down.

12 There are they fallen, all that work wickedness : they are cast down, and shall not be able to stand.

R.V. drive me away: i.e. into exile from the LORD's land.

The vision of faith sees the wicked already overthrown, be-cause condemned by God.

EVENING PRAYER

PSALM 37. *Noli aemulari*

This psalm teaches that the apparent prosperity of the wicked should not make men lose faith in the righteous government of God. The beauty of patience is inculcated, and the picture of Christ's patience is suggested. It may be that the righteous are not angered against the prosperous evil-doers, but yet may be vexed at the apparent triumph of unrighteousness in defiance of God. The righteous do not wish evil to the ungodly, but they do desire the vindication of righteousness, and when it does not appear they are tempted to lose patience.

FRET not thyself because of the ungodly : neither be thou envious against the evil-doers.

2 For they shall soon be cut down like the grass : and be withered even as the green herb.

Cp. Ps. 90. 5–6.

3 Put thou thy trust in the
LORD, and be doing good : dwell
in the land, and verily thou shalt
be fed.

*A.V. so shalt thou dwell in the
land. R.V. Dwell in the land,
and follow after faithfulness.* To
dwell in the LORD's land, i.e.
Canaan, was a duty of the Israelite, with which his prosperity
was bound up; cp. vv. 9, 11, 22,
30, 35. Similarly now in the
communion of the Church there
is spiritual satisfaction for the
faithful Christian who can abide
therein patiently.

4 Delight thou in the LORD :
and he shall give thee thy heart's
desire.
5 Commit thy way unto the
LORD, and put thy trust in him :
and he shall bring it to pass.

put thy trust: as did our
Lord, who 'committed himself
to him that judgeth righteously'
(1 *S. Pet.* 2. 23).
Cp. Isa. 58. 8; Dan. 12. 3;
S. Matt. 13. 43.

6 He shall make thy righteousness as clear as the light :
and thy just dealing as the noon-
day.
7 Hold thee still in the LORD,
and abide patiently upon him :
but grieve not thyself at him
whose way doth prosper, against
the man that doeth after evil
counsels.
8 Leave off from wrath, and
let go displeasure : fret not thyself, else shalt thou be moved to
do evil.
9 Wicked doers shall be rooted out : and they that patiently
abide the LORD, those shall inherit the land.

still: i.e. tranquil. *A.R.V.
Rest in the LORD.* Cp. Ps. 62. 1.
abide upon: i.e. as *A.R.V.
wait for.* Cp. v. 9.
*A.R.V. because of the man who
bringeth wicked desires to pass.*

Cp. v. 1. Fretful zeal may become an occasion of sin.

This promise may not be fulfilled for many in this life, but
only in heaven, which is our
promised land (*Heb.* 11. 14).

10 Yet a little while, and the
ungodly shall be clean gone :
thou shalt look after his place,
and he shall be away.

*R.V. thou shalt diligently con-
sider his place, and he shall not
be.*

11 But the meek-spirited shall possess the earth : and shall be refreshed in the multitude of peace.

R.V. the meek shall inherit the land, i.e. Canaan. The words are quoted with a larger meaning by our Lord in the Sermon on the Mount (*S. Matt.* 5. 5).

12 The ungodly seeketh counsel against the just : and gnasheth upon him with his teeth.

13 The Lord shall laugh him to scorn : for he hath seen that his day is coming.

Cp. Ps. 2. 4.

his day: i.e. the day of retribution.

14 The ungodly have drawn out the sword, and have bent their bow : to cast down the poor and needy, and to slay such as are of a right conversation.

conversation: i.e. manner of life, behaviour. *R.V. such as be upright in the way*.

15 Their sword shall go through their own heart : and their bow shall be broken.

16 A small thing that the righteous hath : is better than great riches of the ungodly.

17 For the arms of the ungodly shall be broken : and the LORD upholdeth the righteous.

18 The LORD knoweth the days of the godly : and their inheritance shall endure for ever.

knoweth: i.e. regardeth with loving care; cp. Ps. 17; 31. 8.

inheritance: an inheritance, as it has since been revealed, 'that fadeth not away,' in the kingdom that shall have no end (1 *S. Pet.* 1. 4).

19 They shall not be confounded in the perilous time; and in the days of dearth they shall have enough.

20 As for the ungodly, they shall perish; and the enemies of the LORD shall consume as the fat of lambs : yea, even as the smoke, shall they consume away.

I.e. they shall consume away as utterly as a sacrificial victim that is burnt upon the altar. But R.V. has: *And the enemies of the LORD shall be as the excellency of the pastures; they shall consume; in the smoke shall they consume away.* By this the wicked are compared to grass, which is often used for fuel in Palestine; cp. S. Matt. 6. 30.

21 The ungodly borroweth, and payeth not again : but the righteous is merciful, and liberal.

The ungodly is driven by stress of poverty to borrow money, and cannot pay it back; but the righteous has enough not only for his own needs but also for those of others.

22 Such as are blessed of God shall possess the land : and they that are cursed of him shall be rooted out.

23 The LORD ordereth a good man's going : and maketh his way acceptable to himself.

ordereth: i.e. sets in order, directs; not, commandeth.

I.e. acceptable to the LORD.

24 Though he fall, he shall not be cast away : for the LORD upholdeth him with his hand.

25 I have been young, and now am old : and yet saw I never the righteous forsaken, nor his seed begging their bread.

26 The righteous is ever merciful, and lendeth : and his seed is blessed.

27 Flee from evil, and do the thing that is good : and dwell for evermore.

dwell: i.e. in the land; cp. v. 3.

28 For the LORD loveth the thing that is right : he forsaketh not his that be godly, but they are preserved for ever.

29 The unrighteous shall be punished : as for the seed of the ungodly, it shall be rooted out.

30 The righteous shall inherit the land : and dwell therein for ever.

31 The mouth of the righteous is exercised in wisdom : and his tongue will be talking of judgement.

is exercised in: R.V. talketh of

I.e. speaketh with discretion.

32 The law of his God is in his heart : and his goings shall not slide.

33 The ungodly seeth the righteous : and seeketh occasion to slay him.

34 The LORD will not leave him in his hand : nor condemn him when he is judged.

A.R.V. The wicked watcheth the

When he is judged adversely by the wicked, in whose power he is, the LORD will not condemn him, but will deliver him out of the hand of the wicked.

35 Hope thou in the LORD, and keep his way, and he shall promote thee, that thou shalt possess the land : when the ungodly shall perish, thou shalt see it.

36 I myself have seen the ungodly in great power : and flourishing like a green bay-tree.

37 I went by, and lo, he was gone : I sought him, but his place could no where be found.

A.R.V. but he could not be found.

A.R.V. Mark the perfect man, and behold the upright : for the latter end of that man is peace. Some prefer the *R.V.mg. for there is a reward* (or *future* or *posterity*) *for the man of peace*, meaning that the posterity of the man of peace shall be continued, while the posterity (the latter end, v. 39) of the wicked shall be cut off.

38 Keep innocency, and take heed unto the thing that is right : for that shall bring a man peace at the last.

39 As for the transgressors, they shall perish together : and the end of the ungodly is, that they shall be rooted out at the last.

R.V. The latter end of the wicked shall be cut off.

40 But the salvation of the righteous cometh of the LORD : who is also their strength in the time of trouble.

R.V. their strong hold.

41 And the LORD shall stand by them, and save them : he shall deliver them from the ungodly, and shall save them, because they put their trust in him.

R.V. because they have taken refuge in him, as in a strong hold.

THE EIGHTH DAY

MORNING PRAYER

PSALM 38.   *Domine, ne in furore*

The psalmist is passing through a period of acute suffering in soul and body. His sickness is aggravated by the insults of his enemies and the desertion of his friends. He turns to God as his only helper. The psalm is proper on Ash Wednesday. It is the third of the Penitential Psalms, and is used especially against the sin of Gluttony. Here, as in all the Penitential Psalms, we see and hear Christ crucified, suffering because of sin which he has taken upon himself. And we endeavour to recite the psalm with Christ's mind, thinking of our own sins and those of others for whom he suffered.

PUT me not to rebuke, O LORD, in thine anger : neither chasten me in thy heavy displeasure.

1–3. The psalmist regards his sickness as God's punishment for his sin.

Verse 1 is almost the same as Ps. 6. 1.

2 For thine arrows stick fast in me : and thy hand presseth me sore.

3 There is no health in my flesh, because of thy displeasure : neither is there any rest in my bones, by reason of my sin.

4 For my wickednesses are gone over my head : and are like a sore burden, too heavy for me to bear.

gone over: like a flood of water.

Cp. 'the burden of them is intolerable,' in the General Confession before Communion.

5 My wounds stink, and are corrupt: through my foolishness.

foolishness: thus he describes his sin which he now sees in its true light.

6 I am brought into so great trouble and misery : that I go mourning all the day long.

R.V. I am pained and bowed down greatly

7 My loins are filled with a sore disease : and there is no whole part in my body.

R.V. filled with burning

8 I am feeble, and sore smitten : I have roared for the very disquietness of my heart.

9 Lord, thou knowest all my desire : and my groaning is not hid from thee.

Cp. S. Matt. 6. 8: 'Your Father knoweth that ye have need of all these things, before ye ask him.'

10 My heart panteth, my strength hath failed me : and the sight of mine eyes is gone from me.

A.R.V. the light of. The eye discloses the state of the health; cp. Ps. 6. 7, 31. 10.

11 My lovers and my neighbours did stand looking upon my trouble : and my kinsmen stood afar off.

R.V. stand aloof from my plague
This verse and Ps. 88. 7 seem to have suggested S. Luke's wording: 'All his acquaintance stood afar off, seeing these things' (*S. Luke* 23. 49).

12 They also that sought after my life laid snares for me : and they that went about to do me evil talked of wickedness, and imagined deceit all the day long.

went about: i.e. endeavoured.

13 As for me, I was like a deaf man, and heard not : and as one that is dumb, who doth not open his mouth.

13–15. Cp. Isa. 53. 7; 1 S. Pet. 2. 23.

14 I became even as a man that heareth not : and in whose mouth are no reproofs.

15 For in thee, O LORD, have I put my trust : thou shalt answer for me, O Lord my God.

reproofs: i.e. disproofs, self-justifications, answering back.
Here occurs the change from the minor key to the major which is usual in the Penitential Psalms. There is ground for confidence in his distress, for God is with him.

16 I have required that they, even mine enemies, should not triumph over me : for when my foot slipped, they rejoiced greatly against me.

required: i.e. sought from God; not, demanded.

R.V. For I said, Lest they rejoice over me: They would see in the psalmist's misfortune a proof that God had condemned him.

17 And I, truly, am set in the plague : and my heaviness is ever in my sight.

R.V. For I am ready to halt; set: i.e. fixed.

18 For I will confess my wickedness : and be sorry for my sin.

Cp. Ps. 32. 6, 51. 3.

19 But mine enemies live, and are mighty : and they that hate me wrongfully are many in number.

A.R.V. Mine enemies are lively

20 They also that reward evil for good are against me : because I follow the thing that good is.

21 Forsake me not, O LORD my God : be not thou far from me.

22 Haste thee to help me : O Lord God of my salvation.

PSALM 39.   *Dixi, custodiam*

The psalmist, in trouble or sickness, and perplexed by the prosperity of the wicked, is confirmed in his trust in God by the consideration of the shortness and uncertainty of life, which makes this life's affairs of smaller significance. The psalm is appointed for use at burials.

I SAID, I will take heed to my ways : that I offend not in my tongue.

I.e. by complaining of my lot, and so murmuring against God.

2 I will keep my mouth as it were with a bridle : while the ungodly is in my sight.

I.e. while I see the ungodly prospering.

3 I held my tongue, and spake nothing : I kept silence, yea, even from good words : but it was pain and grief to me.

4 My heart was hot within me, and while I was thus musing the fire kindled : and at the last I spake with my tongue;

unable at last to suppress my pent-up feelings.

5 LORD, let me know mine end, and the number of my days : that I may be certified how long I have to live.

5 to end: The words of the psalmist.
R.V. let me know how frail I am.
Cp. Ps. 103. 15.

6 Behold, thou hast made my days as it were a span long : and mine age is even as nothing in respect of thee; and verily EVERY MAN LIVING IS ALTOGETHER VANITY.

R.V. every man at his best estate.
'vanity': i.e. emptiness, nothing, *Heb. a breath R.V. mg.* Cp. Ps. 62. 9, 78. 40, 144. 4; S. Jas. 4. 14.

7 For man walketh in a vain shadow, and disquieteth himself in vain : he heapeth up riches, and cannot tell who shall gather them.

Cp. Ps. 49. 17.

8 And now, Lord, what is my hope : truly my hope is even in thee.

9 Deliver me from all mine offences : and make me not a rebuke unto the foolish.

Man, in God's presence, has no need to concern himself about anything except his sinfulness. The 'foolish' are the ungodly (cp. Ps. 14. 1), who would interpret my sufferings as a proof of God's displeasure with me. *A.R.V. make me not the reproach of the foolish.*

10 I became dumb, and opened not my mouth : for it was thy doing.

11 Take thy plague away from me : I am even consumed by the means of thy heavy hand.

A.R.V. Remove thy stroke away from me. The word plague formerly had this meaning.

12 When thou with rebukes dost chasten man for sin, thou makest his beauty to consume away, like as it were a moth fretting a garment : EVERY MAN THEREFORE IS BUT VANITY.

I.e. by disease and decay; cp. Ps. 49. 19.

13 Hear my prayer, O LORD, and with thine ears consider my calling : hold not thy peace at my tears.

14 For I am a stranger with thee : and a sojourner, as all my fathers were.

'We are strangers before thee, and sojourners, as all our fathers were: our days on earth are as a shadow, and there is no remaining' (1 *Chron.* 29. 15). The words are applied in 1 S. Pet. 2. 11 to the condition of Christians in the world.

15 O spare me a little, that I may recover my strength : before I go hence, and be no more seen.

A.R.V. and be no more.

PSALM 40. *Expectans expectavi*

The psalmist records God's mercy in delivering him from some great trouble in the past, and proceeds to pray for release from present persecution and distress. Christians have learnt, from the Epistle to the Hebrews, to regard the psalm as a prayer of Christ in his passion, and a prayer of Christ's members in union with him. It is proper on Good Friday.

I WAITED patiently for the LORD : and he inclined unto me, and heard my calling.

2 He brought me also out of the horrible pit, out of the mire and clay : and set my feet upon the rock, and ordered my goings.

3 And he hath put a new song in my mouth : even a thanksgiving unto our God.

4 Many shall see it, and fear : and shall put their trust in the LORD.

H

'Jesus said, Father, I thank thee that thou hast heard me. And I knew that thou hearest me always' (*S. John* 11. 41).

A metaphorical description of a position of great danger and difficulty (*Ps.* 69. 2).

A.R.V. and established (i.e. made firm) *my goings.* Cp. Ps. 37. 23 and v. 6.

new: a fresh expression of gratitude; cp. Ps. 33. 3.

5 Blessed is the man that hath set his hope in the LORD : and turned not unto the proud, and to such as go about with lies.

A.R.V. *such as turn aside to lies,* i.e. to false gods and to courses opposed to truth. *R.V. mg.* *such as fall away treacherously.*

6 O LORD my God, great are the wondrous works which thou hast done, like as be also thy thoughts which are to us-ward : and yet there is no man that ordereth them unto thee.

ordereth: i.e. sets in order, directs. Man has no control over God's works and thoughts; his purposes of loving-kindness are free and unmerited. But *R.V. mg.* has *there is none to be compared to thee*; cp. Isa. 40. 14.

7 If I should declare them, and speak of them : they should be more than I am able to express.

8–10. God's goodness and greatness are acknowledged rather by obedience to his will than by sacrifice; cp. Ps. 51. 16, 17; 1 Sam. 15. 22. The passage is quoted in Heb. 10. 5–9 as finding its complete fulfilment in Christ, whose sacrifice of himself on the cross resulted from the surrender of his obedient will: 'When he cometh into the world he saith, Sacrifice and . . . I am come to do thy will, O God. . . . By which will we have been sanctified through the offering of the body of Jesus Christ once for all.'

8 Sacrifice and meat-offering thou wouldest not : but mine ears hast thou opened.

9 Burnt-offerings, and sacrifice for sin, hast thou not required : then said I, 'Lo, I come,

10 (In the volume of the book it is written of me), that I should fulfil thy will, O my God : I am content to do it; yea, thy law is within my heart.'

11 I have declared thy righteousness in the great congregation : lo, I will not refrain my lips, O LORD, and that thou knowest.

12 I have not hid thy righteousness within my heart : my talk hath been of thy truth, and of thy salvation.

R.V. *thou hast no delight in:* ears opened: i.e. thou hast given me the power of hearing thy commands and obeying them. The quotation in Heb. 10. 5 follows the Sept., *but a body didst thou prepare me*, with particular reference to the body of Christ Incarnate. The two renderings are not widely apart, since the body is the instrument through which obedience is put into action.

The psalmist's, and Christ's, proffer of obedient service to God.

The first clause of this verse is parenthetical, and refers to the Book of the Law in which man's duty was laid down. But we may apply the words also to the book of divine predestination.

R.V.mg. has: *In the roll of the book it is prescribed to me : I delight to do thy will, O my God.* Cp. S. Matt. 26. 24: 'The Son of Man goeth as it is written of him.'

thy law is within my heart : an earnest of the days of the New Covenant, when God's law would be written in the hearts of all his people; cp. Ps. 37. 32; Jer. 31. 33.

The great congregation now means to us the Church universal. As in Ps. 22. 25.

13 I have not kept back thy mercy and truth : from the great congregation.

---

14 Withdraw not thou thy mercy from me, O LORD : let thy loving-kindness and thy truth alway preserve.

15 For innumerable troubles are come about me; and my sins have taken such hold upon me that I am not able to look up : yea, they are more in number than the hairs of my head, and my heart hath failed me.

16 O LORD, let it be thy pleasure to deliver me : make haste, O LORD, to help me.

17 Let them be ashamed, and confounded together, that seek after my soul to destroy it : let them be driven backward, and put to rebuke, that wish me evil.

18 Let them be desolate, and rewarded with shame : that say unto me, 'Fie upon thee, fie upon thee.'

19 Let all those that seek thee be joyful and glad in thee : and let such as love thy salvation say alway, 'The LORD be praised.'

20 As for me, I am poor and needy : but the Lord careth for me.

21 Thou art my helper and redeemer : make no long tarrying, O my God.

14–21. A prayer for deliverance from the enemies. The deliverance of the faithful can only be by the destruction of the enemies.

These words also may be taken as words of Christ; for 'God made him to be sin for us, who knew no sin' (2 *Cor.* 5. 21), and he 'his own self bare our sins in his body upon the tree' (1 *S. Pet.* 2. 24).

16–21. These verses appear again, with slight variations, as Ps. 70.

R.V. Aha, Aha. Thus expressing delight at my misfortune.

A.R.V. my help and my deliverer:

EVENING PRAYER

PSALM 41. *Beatus qui intelligit*

The psalmist is lying upon a sick-bed, and is visited by pretended friends who long for his death. Even so Christ is the Poor Man, who for our sakes became poor, and yet in his Passion he was surrounded by ill-wishers. He asks for our sympathy. The blessed of the LORD are those who have consideration for the suffering Christ in his poverty and need, and in his poor and suffering members.

BLESSED is he that considereth the poor and needy : the LORD shall deliver him in the time of trouble.

1–3. He considers the blessings which belong to those who show compassion to the afflicted, a compassion which he has not experienced in his own illness; cp. vv. 5–9.

The blessings upon the considerate man are stated in the three clauses beginning with 'the LORD . . .'

2 The LORD preserve him, and keep him alive, that he may be blessed upon earth : and deliver not thou him into the will of his enemies.

R.V.mg. blessed in the land of promise; cp. Ps. 37. 3.

3 The LORD comfort him, when he lieth sick upon his bed : make thou all his bed in his sickness.

R.V. The LORD support him, thou: i.e. the LORD.

make his bed: the picture is of one who smoothes the pillow and gives other care to the patient. But *R.V.mg.* has: *thou turnest* or *changest* his bed of sickness into one of health.

4 I said, 'LORD, be merciful unto me : heal my soul, for I have sinned against thee.'

He acknowledges that not only his body but also his soul is sick. Perhaps he means that his sickness is the penalty of his sin; perhaps also he suggests that his sin was his own previous inconsiderateness to the sick and needy. The healing of the sick soul comes by divine forgiveness, as in the Sacrament of Unction.

5 Mine enemies speak evil of me : 'When shall he die, and his name perish?'

6 And if he come to see me, he speaketh vanity : and his heart conceiveth falsehood within himself, and when he cometh forth he telleth it.

vanity: i.e. falsehood. He pretends a sympathy which he does not really feel. Perhaps some special enemy is referred to; cp. v. 9.

his heart conceiveth: *A.R.V. his heart gathered iniquity to itself.*

cometh forth: i.e. he says in public the hypocrisies which he has devised in private.

7 All mine enemies whisper together against me: even against me do they imagine this evil.

8 'Let the sentence of guiltiness proceed against him : and now that he lieth, let him rise up no more.'

A.R.V. against me do they devise this hurt.

The words of the enemies: 'Let him die the death which his guilt deserves. But *A.R.V.* has: '*An evil disease,*' say they, '*cleaveth fast unto him.*'

lieth: i.e. on the sick-bed.

9 Yea, even mine own familiar friend, whom I trusted : who did also eat of my bread, hath laid great wait for me.

This verse is applied by our Lord to the treachery of Judas (*S. John* 13. 18).

A.R.V. hath lifted up his heel against me, to kick backwards at me: a metaphor of treacherous attack.

10 But be thou merciful unto me, O Lord : raise thou me up again, and I shall reward them.

11 By this I know thou favourest me : that mine enemy doth not triumph against me.

12 And when I am in my health, thou upholdest me : and shalt set me before thy face for ever.

A.R.V. that I may requite them.

this: i.e. the fact that the enemy does not prevail.

A.R.V. And as for me, thou upholdest me in mine integrity:

before thy face: cp. 1 S. John 3. 2; Rev. 22. 4.

13 Blessed be the Lord God of Israel : world without end. Amen.

This doxology is not suggested by the subject-matter of the psalm, but is added to mark the close of the First Book of the Psalter.

BOOK TWO

PSALM 42. *Quemadmodum*

Probably this and the next psalm, which are similar in subject and language and have common refrains, originally formed one psalm.

A Levite, in exile and surrounded by enemies, expresses his earnest longings for the worship of God in the Temple at Jerusalem from which he is debarred. The Christian expresses a similar longing for the presence of God, but does so with the joyful consciousness that his desire for God has been met by the opening to him of direct access to God through Christ, not only hereafter in the unveiled glory of the heavenly Jerusalem, but also now during his exile through the Blessed Sacrament of the Altar. We have 'boldness to enter into the holy place by the Blood of Jesus, by the way which he dedicated for us, a new and living way, through the veil . . . and, having a great priest over the house of God,' we 'draw near in fullness of faith' (*Heb.* 10. 19).

LIKE as the hart desireth the water-brooks : so longeth my soul after thee, O God.

2 My soul is athirst for God, even for the living God : when shall I come to appear before the presence of God?

Cp. Ps. 63. 2, 84. 2.

The living God: i.e. the Source of life, the 'fountain of living waters'; cp. Jer. 2. 13.

appear before God: the phrase is used of going up to the Temple at the festival-times; cp. Ps. 84. 7; Exod. 23. 17; Deut. 16. 16.

3 My tears have been my meat day and night : while THEY DAILY SAY UNTO ME, 'WHERE IS NOW THY GOD?'

4 Now when I think thereupon, I pour out my heart by myself : for I went with the multitude, and brought them forth into the house of God;

they: i.e. the heathen neighbours.

R.V. These things I remember, and pour out my soul within me, how I went . . . He comforts himself with the recollection of past days when he used to conduct the caravans of pilgrims to Jerusalem.

5 In the voice of praise and thanksgiving : among such as keep holy-day.

6 WHY ART THOU SO FULL OF HEAVINESS, O MY SOUL : AND WHY ART THOU SO DISQUIETED WITHIN ME?

7 PUT THY TRUST IN GOD : FOR I WILL YET GIVE HIM THANKS, FOR THE HELP OF HIS COUNTENANCE.

Our Lord's words in Gethsemane, 'My soul is exceeding sorrowful' (*S. Matt.* 26. 38), closely resembles the Sept. of this verse.

R.V.mg. who is the health of my countenance, and my God, as also in v. 15 and 43. 6. God's countenance means God as he shows himself in favour to mankind. Our countenance similarly means ourselves as we show ourselves to others.

---

8 My God, my soul is vexed within me : therefore will I remember thee concerning the land of Jordan, and the little hill of Hermon.

my soul, etc. These words, which occur also in Ps. 6. 3, as they appear in the Sept., were used by our Lord before his passion, 'Now is my soul troubled' (*S. John* 12. 27).
R.V. therefore do I remember thee from the land of Jordan, and the Hermons, from the hill Mizar. The psalmist's place of exile is the land of Jordan, i.e. the country east of Jordan in the vicinity of the range of Mt. Hermon, of which Mizar was probably one of the peaks (the word Mizar means 'little').

9 One deep calleth another, because of the noise of the waterpipes : all thy waves and storms are gone over me.

R.V. Deep calleth unto deep at the noise of thy water-spouts (*R.V.mg.* better, *cataracts*): *all thy waves and thy billows are gone over me.* The mountain torrents of the Jordan supply images to describe the flood of sorrows and trouble which God has allowed to overwhelm him.

10 The LORD hath granted his loving-kindness in the day-time: and in the night-season did I sing of him, and made my prayer unto the God of my life.

His reminiscence of the former time of happiness when the manifestation of the LORD'S loving-kindness ceased not day or night, and the song of praise was uninterrupted.

Here as elsewhere the 'night-season' may be interpreted as denoting the 'dark night of the soul': 'even in desolation did I sing to God.' Cp. Ps. 16. 8.

R.V. unto God my rock. Cp. Ps. 43. 11.

11 I WILL SAY UNTO THE GOD OF MY STRENGTH, 'WHY HAST THOU FORGOTTEN ME : WHY GO I THUS HEAVILY, WHILE THE ENEMY OPPRESSETH ME?'

12 My bones are smitten a-sunder as with a sword : while mine enemies that trouble me cast me in the teeth;

I.e. as A.R.V. reproach me.

13 Namely, while THEY SAY DAILY UNTO ME : 'WHERE IS NOW THY GOD?'

14 WHY ART THOU SO VEXED, O MY SOUL : AND WHY ART THOU SO DISQUIETED WITHIN ME?

15 O PUT THY TRUST IN GOD : FOR I WILL YET THANK HIM, WHICH IS THE HELP OF MY COUN-TENANCE, AND MY GOD.

A.R.V. the health of

PSALM 43. *Judica me, Deus*

See the Preface to Ps. 42. This psalm is used for the preparation at the altar at the beginning of Mass. Christ in his perfect humanity and priesthood is primarily the speaker.

GIVE sentence with me, O God, and defend my cause against the ungodly people : O deliver me from the deceitful and wicked man.

I.e. Judge me favourably.

I.e. heathen neighbours of the psalmist in his exile; and now all who oppose Christ the Priest.

2 FOR THOU ART THE GOD OF MY STRENGTH, WHY HAST THOU PUT ME FROM THEE : AND WHY GO I SO HEAVILY, WHILE THE ENEMY OPPRESSETH ME?

Ps. 42. 11.

3 O send out thy light and thy truth, that they may lead me : and bring me unto thy holy hill, and to thy dwelling.

Light and truth are described, by a bold figure, as God's messengers despatched to guide the psalmist to God's house. There may be also an allusion to the Urim and Thummim, which in the Sept. are rendered 'light' and truth.'

4 And that I may go unto the altar of God, even unto the God of my joy and gladness : and upon the harp will I give thanks unto thee, O God, my God.

5 WHY ART THOU SO HEAVY, O MY SOUL : AND WHY ART THOU SO DISQUIETED WITHIN ME?

6 O PUT THY TRUST IN GOD : FOR I WILL YET GIVE HIM THANKS, WHICH IS THE HELP OF MY COUNTENANCE, AND MY GOD.

A.R.V. the health

THE NINTH DAY

MORNING PRAYER

PSALM 44. *Deus, auribus*

An earnest appeal for divine succour on behalf of Israel which though faithful to Jehovah is hard pressed by foes. The Church, and in it first the Apostles and Martyrs, in conflict with the spirit of the world, cries out to God.

WE have heard with our ears, O God, our fathers have told us : what thou hast done in their time of old;

'O God, we have heard with our ears, and our fathers have told us, the noble works that thou didst in their days, and in the old time before them' (Litany); cp. Ps. 78. 3.

planted them: i.e. our fathers in the Promised Land.

2 How thou hast driven out the heathen with thy hand, and planted them in : how thou hast destroyed the nations, and cast them out.

cast them out: i.e. cast out the nations by the hand of our fathers who dispossessed them. But *R.V.* has: *thou didst spread them* (i.e. our fathers) *abroad.* Israel's increase is compared to the growth of a tree; cp. Ps. 80. 8-11.

3 For they gat not the land in possession through their own sword : neither was it their own arm that helped them;

4 But thy right hand, and thine arm, and the light of thy countenance: because thou hadst a favour unto them.

the light of thy countenance: a reminiscence of the priestly blessing (*Num.* 6. 25; *Ps.* 4. 6).

5 Thou art my King, O God : send help unto Jacob.

R.V. command deliverance for Jacob. As King issue thy command, and it must be obeyed.

6 Through thee will we overthrow our enemies : and in thy Name will we tread them under that rise up against us.

7 For I will not trust in my bow : it is not my sword that shall help me;

8 But it is thou that savest us from our enemies : and puttest them to confusion that hate us.

Deliverance comes from God alone. 'There is none other that fightest for us, but only thou, O God.'

9 We make our boast of God all day long : and will praise thy Name for ever.

———

10-17. Apparent change in God's attitude towards Israel. The Church always, even where most faithful, is fighting what seems to be a losing battle. This is a part of the mystery of the Cross.

Verse 10 is repeated almost verbally in Ps. 60. 10.

10 But now thou art far off, and puttest us to confusion : and goest not forth with our armies.

R.V. But now thou hast cast us off

There may be an allusion here to the practice in earlier times of carrying the ark, the symbol of God's presence, to the field of battle.

11 Thou makest us to turn our backs upon our enemies : so that they which hate us spoil our goods.

12 Thou lettest us be eaten up like sheep : and hast scattered us among the heathen.

spoil: i.e. despoil, loot.

A.R.V. Thou hast given us like sheep appointed for meat:

scattered us: i.e. by allowing us to be taken captive in war and sold into slavery.

13 Thou sellest thy people for nought : and takest no money for them.

So worthless are they. But *R.V. hast not increased thy wealth by their price.* I.e. thou hast gained nothing by abandoning the people—a bold expostulation to God!

14 Thou makest us to be rebuked of our neighbours : to be laughed to scorn, and had in derision of them that are round about us.

14-15. The surrounding nations mock Israel as a people deserted by its God. Cp. Ps. 42. 3.

This verse occurs again in Ps. 79. 4.

15 Thou makest us to be a by-word among the heathen : and that the people shake their heads at us.

R.V. peoples

16 My confusion is daily before me : and the shame of my face hath covered me;

17 For the voice of the slanderer and blasphemer : for the enemy and avenger.

avenger: i.e. revengeful (*Ps. 8. 2*).

———

18-22. The psalmist is not conscious of any national apostasy for which Israel deserves this chastisement. The Church's heroes likewise stand humbly but firmly in their integrity.

A.R.V. yet have we not forgotten thee, neither have we dealt falsely in thy covenant.

18 And though all this be come upon us, yet do we not forget thee : nor behave ourselves frowardly in thy covenant.

19 Our heart is not turned back : neither our steps gone out of thy way;

20 No, not when thou hast smitten us into the place of dragons : and covered us with the shadow of death.

R.V. That thou hast sore broken us in the place of jackals, i.e. brought us low, and made our land a wilderness, the haunt of wild beasts. Cp. *Jer.* 9. 11.

the shadow of death: i.e. deadly darkness (*Job* 3. 5; *Ps.* 23. 4).

21 If we have forgotten the Name of our God, and holden up our hands to any strange god : shall not God search it out? for he knoweth the very secrets of the heart.

22 For thy sakes also are we killed all the day long : and are counted as sheep appointed to be slain.

'Thou knowest, Lord, the secrets of our hearts' (Burial of the Dead, cp. *Heb.* 4. 13).

Applied by S. Paul to the condition of Christians in his time (*Rom.* 8. 36). See v. 12.

23-26. The Church cries for help.

23 Up, Lord, why sleepest thou? : awake, and be not absent from us for ever.

A.R.V. arise, cast us not off.

The sleep of God denotes any period of his apparent non-intervention.

24 Wherefore hidest thou thy face : and forgettest our misery and trouble?

25 For our soul is brought low, even unto the dust : our belly cleaveth unto the ground.

26 Arise, and help us : and deliver us for thy mercy's sake.

PSALM 45. *Eructavit cor meum*

A nuptial song composed to celebrate some royal marriage. It foreshadows the union between Christ, the divine Son of David, and his Bride the Church, through the Incarnation; cp. Eph. 5. 26; Rev. 21. 9. The Bride has also been understood to signify our Lady Saint Mary, who is the first representative of the Church of the redeemed, and the Queen of heaven. (Similarly the Woman in Rev. 12. 1, ff., is explained as meaning both the Church and the Blessed Virgin Mary; and Jerusalem the City of God is given the same double signification in many of the psalms, e.g. Ps. 87.) This psalm is proper at Christmas and on the feasts of S. Mary and of Dedication.

MY heart is inditing of a good matter : I speak of the things which I have made unto the King.

1-2. The psalmist's preface.

inditing: i.e. writing, cp. v. 2.

made: i.e. composed. The word 'poet' means 'maker.'

R.V. My heart overfloweth with a goodly matter: I speak the things which I have made touching the king.

In its Greek and Latin form, 'My heart hath uttered forth a good Word,' this verse was regarded as the saying of God the Father asserting that his Son, the Word of God, was of one substance with himself.

2 My tongue is the pen : of a ready writer.

---

3 Thou art fairer than the children of men : full of grace are thy lips, because God hath blessed thee for ever.

The psalmist addresses the royal bridegroom.

fairer: cp. Ps. 27. 4, 'To behold the fair beauty of the LORD'; Ps. 50. 2 'God appeared in perfect beauty'; Isa. 23. 17, 'Thine eyes shall see the King in his beauty'; and contrast Isa. 53. 2, 'There is no beauty that we should desire him.'

full of grace: cp. S. John 1. 14, 'full of grace and truth'; S. Luke 4. 22, 'the gracious words which proceeded out of his mouth.'

because: *A.R.V. therefore.* Cp. v. 8.

4 Gird thee with thy sword upon thy thigh, O thou most mighty : according to thy worship and renown.

R.V. Gird thy sword upon thy thigh, O mighty one, thy glory and majesty. 'gird' belongs to both clauses.

Cp. the picture of the Divine Conqueror in Rev. 21. 11 ff.

R.V. And in thy majesty ride on prosperously, because of truth and . . . A.R.V. omit 'the word of': the King is the champion of truth, meekness, and righteousness; cp. Ps. 85. 10, 'Mercy and truth are met together : righteousness and peace have kissed each other.'

5 Good luck have thou with thine honour : ride on, because of the word of truth, of meekness, and of righteousness; and thy right hand shall teach thee terrible things.

thy right hand, etc.: i.e. thy exploits in war shall be terrific.

6 Thy arrows are very sharp, and the people shall be subdued unto thee : even in the midst among the king's enemies.

A.R.V. the peoples fall under thee : they (i.e. thy arrows) *are in the heart of the king's enemies.*

7 Thy seat, O God, endureth for ever : the sceptre of thy kingdom is a right sceptre.

A.R.V. Thy throne,

The King is here called 'God,' as representing and deriving his authority from the Almighty. (Cp. *Exod.* 22. 28; *Ps.* 82. 6; for other instances where the title 'God' is assigned to earthly rulers.) 'For ever' claims the promise of permanency made to the throne of David (2 *Sam.* 7. 16, etc.). This was fulfilled only in Christ, of whom the whole passage must be spiritually interpreted, as it is in Heb. 1. 8, 9; where the word 'God' is used in its full meaning as ascribing Deity to Christ.

a right sceptre: *R.V. a sceptre of equity.*

8 Thou hast loved righteousness, and hated iniquity : wherefore God, even thy God, hath
anointed thee with the oil of
gladness above thy fellows.

anointed: cp. Ps. 2. 2; Acts
10. 38.

oil of gladness: the reference
is to the custom of anointing
guests on festive occasions (*Ps.
21. 6, 23. 5; S. Luke* 7. 46).

above thy fellows: i.e. other
monarchs; and, by application,
the Angels; cp. Heb. 1. 4.

Cp. 2 Cor. 2. 15, 'a sweet
savour of Christ.' *Cant.* 4. 14
ascribes these fragrant odours
to the bride.

9 All thy garments smell of
myrrh, aloes, and cassia : out of
the ivory palaces, whereby they
have made thee glad.

*R.V. out of ivory palaces
stringed instruments have made
thee glad.*

were : *R.V. are*

10 Kings' daughters were a-
mong thy honourable women :
upon thy right hand did stand
the queen in a vesture of gold,
wrought about with divers
colours.

*R.V. doth stand the queen in
gold of Ophir,* which was the
best gold.

thy right hand: cp. 1 Kings
2. 19.

the queen: i.e. the 'king's
daughter' of vv. 11, 14, mentioned here as being with the
king by anticipation; thus transition is made to vv. 11-16.
Mystically 'the queen' denotes
the Church Triumphant and
especially the Blessed Virgin
Mary.

11 Hearken, O daughter, and
consider, incline thine ear : forget also thine own people, and
thy father's house.

11-16. The psalmist addresses
the bride.

forget: the Church forgets
her former Judaism in Christianity, or, the members of the
Church forget their former
paganism and nationalism in
Catholicism. Cp. 2 Cor. 5. 17,
'If any man is in Christ, he is a
new creature: the old things are
passed away; behold, they are
become new.'

12 So shall the king have pleasure in thy beauty : for he is thy Lord God, and worship thou him.

A.R.V. for he is thy Lord (not LORD). Cp. Gen. 18. 12; 1 S. Pet. 3. 6, 'Sarah obeyed Abraham, calling him lord.' And so 'worship' here means primarily 'pay him respect,' cp. S. Luke 14. 10. The word 'God' was added because of the identification of the king-bridegroom with Christ; and in that case 'worship' will mean 'give him divine honours.'

the daughter: i.e. the people of Tyre; cp. 'the daughter of Sion' (*Ps.* 9. 14). Mentioned here as one of the rich tributary states.

13 And the daughter of Tyre shall be there with a gift : like as the rich also among the people shall make their supplication before thee.

A.R.V. even the rich among the people (i.e. among the Israelites as well as foreigners) *shall intreat thy favour,* i.e. as intercessor and mediator with the King.

14-16. The bridal procession is described.

14 The king's daughter is all glorious within : her clothing is of wrought gold.

glorious within: i.e. as *R.V. within the palace.* The inward and contemplative life of the Church.

raiment: the graces which adorn her, her active works, the merits of the martyrs and saints.

15 She shall be brought unto the king in raiment of needlework : the virgins that be her fellows shall bear her company, and shall be brought unto thee.

the virgins: particularly the religious virgins of the Church, the servants of Mary, in glory.

thee: a transition is made here, and the bridegroom is again addressed.

16 With joy and gladness shall they be brought : and shall enter into the king's palace.

I

17 Instead of thy fathers thou shalt have children : whom thou mayest make princes in all lands.

A.R.V. shalt make princes: the bishops in apostolic succession.

18 I will remember thy name from one generation to another : therefore shall the people give thanks unto thee, world without end.

A.R.V. I will make thy name to be remembered
R.V. the peoples

PSALM 46. *Deus noster refugium*

The safety of those who are under the protection of God. This psalm and the two following are hymns of triumph and thanksgiving celebrating some great deliverance of Jerusalem, the city of God (v. 4). Jerusalem may be interpreted as signifying the Church, and also S. Mary, as in Ps. 45; cp. v. 5 below. The main thought for Christians is that the Church is preserved safe amid all onslaughts. The psalm is proper on Epiphany, and Dedication, and Feasts of S. Mary.

GOD is our hope and strength : a very present help in trouble.

2 Therefore will we not fear, though the earth be moved : and though the hills be carried into the midst of the sea;

3 Though the waters thereof rage and swell : and though the mountains shake at the tempest of the same.

The meaning of these images is stated in v. 6.

4 The rivers of the flood thereof shall make glad the city of God : the holy place of the tabernacle of the most Highest.

The attacks upon the Church result only in its well-being and joy, being unable to shake her secure foundations. But better as *R.V. There is a river, the streams whereof* . . . i.e. Amid the turmoil of the hostile world, Sion, watered by the river of God's grace, enjoys peace and blessedness. Cp. Ps. 36. 8; 65. 9; Rev. 22. 1, 2; Isa. 8. 6; Ezek. 47. 1.
the holy place of the tabernacle: cp. Ps. 43. 3; 84. 1.

5 God is in the midst of her, therefore shall she not be removed : God shall help her, and that right early.

God, who at his Incarnation made his abode in S. Mary, is present in his Church. Cp. Rev. 12. 15, 16.

removed: *A.R.V. moved.*

and that right early: *R.V.mg. at the dawn of the morning.* The night of trial will be followed by the morning of deliverance; cp. Ps. 30. 3.

6 The heathen make much ado, and the kingdoms are moved : but God hath shewed his voice, and the earth shall melt away.

Cp. Ps. 2. 1, 5, 'Why do the heathen so furiously rage together . . . then shall he speak unto them in his wrath.'

R.V. The nations raged, the kingdoms were moved (unlike the city of God, v. 5): *he uttered his voice* (in thunder), *the earth melted.* Cp. Ps. 18. 13.

7 THE LORD OF HOSTS IS WITH US : THE GOD OF JACOB IS OUR REFUGE.

The LORD of the armies of heaven is in our midst. He is none other than the God who blessed Jacob with the blessings of his Covenant, after Jacob had struggled with him in prayer (*Gen.* 32. 26, 28, 30).

8 O come hither, and behold the works of the LORD : what destruction he hath brought upon the earth.

9 He maketh wars to cease in all the world : he breaketh the bow, and knappeth the spear in sunder, and burneth the chariots in the fire.

knappeth: i.e. snappeth.

10 'Be still then, and know that I am God : I will be exalted among the heathen, and I will be exalted in the earth.'

11 THE LORD OF HOSTS IS WITH US : THE GOD OF JACOB IS OUR REFUGE.

The LORD speaks.

EVENING PRAYER

PSALM 47.   *Omnes gentes, plaudite*

An anticipation of the universal acknowledgement of the sovereignty of Jehovah when 'the kingdom of the world is become the kingdom of our Lord and of his Christ' (*Rev.* 11. 15). Composed probably in celebration of some great victory of Israel over the heathen. This psalm is one of several 'missionary' psalms, exalting Christ's Kingship in his Church. Proper on Ascension Day and in Epiphanytide.

O CLAP your hands together, all ye people : O sing unto God with a voice of melody.

R.V. peoples
A.R.V. of triumph.

2 For the LORD is high, and to be feared : he is the great King upon all the earth.

3 He shall subdue the people under us : and the nations under our feet.

the people: *R.V. the peoples.*
This is being progressively fulfilled as the nations of the heathen are subjugated to Christ and his Church.

God will confirm his people Israel in the land which he has chosen for them, i.e. the earthly possession, pointing forward to that of the heavenly Canaan.

4 He shall choose out an heritage for us : even the worship of Jacob, whom he loved.

the worship of Jacob: *A.R.V. the excellency of Jacob,* i.e. Canaan, the land in which Israel glories, his heritage; cp. Gen. 35. 9-12 and Amos 6. 8.

5 God is gone up with a merry noise : and the LORD with the sound of the trump.

with a merry noise: *A.R.V. with a shout*: as a king returning to his city, cp. 2 Sam. 6. 15, God returns with triumph to his heavenly throne after delivering his people from their foes; in Christian eyes a prefiguration of Christ's Ascension after the redemption of the world. Cp. Ps. 68. 18, 'Thou art gone up on high, thou hast led captivity captive.'

6 O sing praises, sing praises unto our God : O sing praises, sing praises unto our King.

7 For God is the King of all the earth : sing ye praises with understanding.

8 God reigneth over the heathen : God sitteth upon his holy seat.

Cp. 1 Cor. 14. 15, 'I will sing with the understanding also.'

seat: *A.R.V. throne.*
The Session of Christ. Cp. Heb. 1. 3, 13. The Son 'when he had made purification of sins, sat down on the right hand of the Majesty on high. . . . Sit thou on my right hand, till I make thine enemies the footstool of thy feet.'

9 The princes of the people are joined unto the people of the God of Abraham : for God, which is very high exalted, doth defend the earth, as it were with a shield.

the God of Abraham: for the covenant was first made with Abraham (*Gen.* 17. 7).

R.V. The princes of the peoples are gathered together to be the people of the God of Abraham: for the shields of the earth belong unto God; he is greatly exalted. A vision of the world-wide extension of the kingdom of God on earth. The 'shields of the earth' are the princes, regarded as the defenders of their people. Cp. Ps. 72. 11, 'All kings shall fall down before him'; Rev. 21. 24, 'The kings of the earth do bring their glory into' the heavenly City.

PSALM 48. *Magnus Dominus*

The glorious beauty of Jerusalem, and the discomfiture of its foes by the hand of God. This is the third in this group of psalms, 46, 47, 48, applicable to the Church: it is proper on Whitsunday and Epiphanytide.

GREAT is the LORD, and highly to be praised : in the city of our God, even upon his holy hill.

The Church is the City of God (*Rev.* 21. 2).

2 The hill of Sion is a fair place, and the joy of the whole earth : upon the north side lieth the city of the great King; God is well known in her palaces as a sure refuge.

a fair place: *R.V. beautiful in elevation.* Cp. Ps. 50. 2, R.V., 'Zion the perfection of beauty.'

the joy: cp. Lam. 2. 15, 'Is this the city that men called, The joy of the whole earth?'

upon the north-side: so also the Church confronts the northern heathen, and the gospel at Mass is accordingly read at the north side of the altar.

the city: words used by our Lord, 'Swear not by Jerusalem, for it is the city of the great King' (*S. Matt.* 5. 34).

3 For lo, the kings of the earth : are gathered, and gone by together.

R.V. the kings assembled themselves, they passed by together. These kings are the princes opposing God and Israel (the Church).

passed by: i.e. marched along in battle array.

4 They marvelled to see such things : they were astonished, and suddenly cast down.

4-6. Description of the panic, flight, and ruin of the enemy.

R.V. They saw it (Sion), *then were they amazed : they were dismayed; they hasted away.*

5 Fear came there upon them and sorrow : as upon a woman in her travail.

Fear and sorrow came upon them violently, suddenly, and inevitably, as upon a travailing woman, and as on ships in a storm (v. 6).

6 Thou shalt break the ships of the sea : through the east wind.

A.R.V. Thou breaketh the ships of Tarshish, i.e. the ships of largest size, such as those that traded with Tarshish in Spain. The same almighty power which wrecks these ships (cp. 1 *Kings* 22. 48) has with similar destruction overthrown the hostile army.

The report of God's marvellous providence in the past has been confirmed by our own experience; cp. Ps. 44. 1.

7 Like as we have heard, so have we seen in the city of the LORD of hosts, in the city of our God : God upholdeth the same for ever.

8 We wait for thy lovingkindness, O God : in the midst of thy temple.

9 O God, according to thy Name, so is thy praise unto the world's end : thy right hand is full of righteousness.

R.V. We have thought on
Whither we went to offer our thanksgivings.

All men should praise thee for that which thou hast shewn thyself to be towards them.

10 Let the mount Sion rejoice, and the daughter of Judah be glad : because of thy judgements.

This verse occurs again almost without change in Ps. 97. 8.

daughter of Judah: i.e. Sion; but better as *R.V. daughters of Jerusalem*, i.e. the towns and villages around Sion (Jerusalem); cp. Num. 21. 25 mg.

11 Walk about Sion, and go round about her : and tell the towers thereof.

11-12. The siege being raised, the citizens are free to go forth and convince themselves that the walls and buildings of Jerusalem are still standing. So also the gates of hell shall not prevail against the Church (*S. Matt.* 16. 18).

tell: archaic for 'count.'

12 Mark well her bulwarks, set up her houses : that ye may tell them that come after.

A.R.V. consider her palaces:
The towers, bulwarks (battlements), palaces, invite various allegorization, if applied to the Church.

13 For this God is our God for ever and ever : he shall be our guide unto death.

PSALM 49. *Audite haec, omnes*

The transient prosperity of the wicked and the eternal blessedness of the righteous.

O HEAR ye this, all ye people : ponder it with your ears, all ye that dwell in the world;

2 High and low, rich and poor, one with another.

3 My mouth shall speak of wisdom : and my heart shall muse of understanding.

4 I will incline mine ear to the parable : and shew my dark speech upon the harp.

R.V. peoples:

parable: i.e. a poem conveying instruction; cp. Ps. 78. 2.

A.R.V. and open my dark saying.

The psalmist likens himself to a minstrel bending his ear over the harp until the full tide of inspiration comes to him.

5 Wherefore should I fear in the days of wickedness : and when the wickedness of my heels compasseth me round about?

days of wickedness, i.e. times when the wicked are prosperous and predominant.

R.V. when iniquity at my heels.
Iniquity is compared to a dog snapping at a traveller.

6 There be some that put their trust in their goods : and boast themselves in the multitude of their riches.

7 But no man may deliver his brother : nor make agreement unto God for him.

Cf. S. Mark 10.24, 'How hard is it for them that trust in riches to enter into the kingdom of God?'

A.R.V. None of them (i.e. the wicked rich) *can by any means redeem his brother, nor give to God a ransom for him.* Man, however wealthy, is impotent to deliver a fellow man from death when God demands his life.

8 (For it cost more to redeem their souls : so that he must let that alone for ever;)

R.V. (For the redemption of their soul (i.e. life) *is costly* (i.e. too costly for him to pay): *and must be let alone for ever).* Cf. S. Matt. 16. 26, 'What shall a man give in exchange for his soul (life)?' Christ is the one Redeemer of souls, who came to

9 Yea, though he live long : and see not the grave.

give his life a 'ransom for many' (*S. Mark* 8. 45). 'There was none other good enough to pay the price of sin.'

Verse 9 is in close connection with v. 7, v. 8 being parenthetical.

I.e. he could not redeem even if he had an endless life for the task. But, better as *R.V. That he* (i.e. the brother) *should still live alway, that he should not see corruption.*

10 For he seeth that wise men also die, and perish together : as well as the ignorant and foolish, and leave their riches for other.

However prudently they use their riches.

11 And yet they think that their houses shall continue for ever : and that their dwelling-places shall endure from one generation to another; and call the lands after their own names.

A.R.V. to others.

Cf. S. Luke 12. 15 ff., 'A man's life consisteth not in the abundance of things which he possesseth. . . . Soul, thou hast much goods laid up for many years. . . . Thou fool, this night thy soul shall be required of thee; then whose shall those things be which thou hast provided?'

after their own names: as if they expected to enjoy them for ever.

12 Nevertheless, man will not abide in honour : seeing he may be compared unto the beasts that perish; this is the way of them.

R.V. But man abideth not in honour: i.e. his splendour however great terminates in the grave. The emphatic word is 'abideth.'

13 This is their foolishness : and their posterity praise their saying.

R.V. This their way is their folly: yet after them men approve their sayings. I.e. and yet their foolish maxims find favour with subsequent generations.

14 They lie in the hell like sheep, death gnaweth upon them, and the righteous shall have domination over them in

R.V. They are appointed as a flock for Sheol; Death shall be their shepherd. This is the fate which awaits these rich fools.

the morning : their beauty shall consume in the sepulchre out of their dwelling.

Sheol and Death, personified, will tend and rule them.

in the morning: i.e. the morning of deliverance which succeeds the night of suffering; cp. Ps. 30. 5; 46. 5. From the Christian point of view the morning of the resurrection is signified; cp. Dan. 12. 2, 3; S. John 5. 28, 29.

R.V. and their beauty shall be for Sheol to consume, that there be no habitation for it. The unrighteous shall not be beautiful in the resurrection.

R.V. But God will redeem my soul from the power of Sheol. The psalmist's confident hope of immortal life with God. Cf. Ps. 16. 11, 'Thou shalt not leave my soul to Sheol: neither shalt thou suffer thy holy one to see corruption.'

15 But God hath delivered my soul from the place of hell : for he shall receive me.

receive me: 'receive' is the same word used in Gen. 5. 24 of Enoch, 'he was not; for God took him'; cp. Ps. 73. 23, R.V., 'receive me to glory.'

16 Be not thou afraid, though one be made rich : or if the glory of his house be increased;

17 For he shall carry nothing away with him when he dieth : neither shall his pomp follow him.

Cp. 1 Tim. 6. 7, 'We brought nothing into this world, and it is certain we can carry nothing out.'

For: *A.R.V. Though*

18 For while he lived, he counted himself an happy man : (and so long as thou doest well unto thyself, men will speak good of thee),

19 He shall follow the generation of his fathers : and shall never see light.

20 Man being in honour hath no understanding : but is compared unto the beasts that perish.

R.V. the light.
A.R.V. Man that is in honour, and understandeth not : is like the beasts that perish. Cp. v. 12.

THE TENTH DAY

MORNING PRAYER

PSALM 50. *Deus deorum*

God, in judgement upon his people, declares the character of the service which he requires of them. The duty of worship demands in the worshipper sincerity and righteousness. Cp. Isa. 1. 11-17. It has been revealed that the Judge is Jesus the Son of God made man (*S. John* 5. 26, 27). This psalm, which is proper in Advent, has been regarded as referring both to his first Advent and his second.

THE Lord, even the most mighty God, hath spoken : and called the world, from the rising up of the sun, unto the going down thereof.

1-6 The coming of the Judge. Note four steps: calling from heaven (v. 1); shining forth (v. 2); coming to earth (v. 3); calling from earth (v. 4).

called: the whole world, from east to west, cp. Ps. 113. 3, to witness his judgement.

R.V. Out of Zion, the perfection of beauty (cp. Ps. 48. 2), *God hath shone forth.*

2 Out of Sion hath God appeared : in perfect beauty.

3 Our God shall come, and shall not keep silence : there shall go before him a consuming fire, and a mighty tempest shall be stirred up round about him.

fire: cp. S. Matt. 3. 12; Heb. 12. 29.

tempest: cp. Ps. 18. 8; 21. 9.

R.V. He shall call to the heavens above. Heaven as well as earth (v. 1), is summoned as witness.

4 He shall call the heaven from above : and the earth, that he may judge his people.

The call of God.

Gather: 'Then shall he send forth his angels, and shall gather together his elect from the uttermost part of the earth' (*S. Mark* 13. 27). 'Where two or three are gathered together in my name, there am I in the midst of them' (*S. Matt.* 18. 20).

5 'Gather my saints together unto me : those that have made a covenant with me with sacrifice.'

my saints: i.e. favoured ones, cp. Ps. 4. 3. Here the word denotes the whole people of Israel, the covenanted nation (as described in the next clause); and, by application, the Church.

covenant with sacrifice: the primary reference is to Exod. 24. 7, 8; and the application to the Sacrifice of the new Covenant between God and man through Christ at Calvary and on the altar (*S. Matt.* 26. 28; *Heb.* 13. 10, 20).

6 (And the heaven shall declare his righteousness : for God is Judge himself.)

The heaven as witness will vouch the justice of God's sentence. (The verse is parenthetical.)

---

7 'Hear, O my people, and I will speak : I myself will testify against thee, O Israel; for I am God, even thy God.

The judgement opens. Cp. Micah 6. 1-8.

8 I will not reprove thee because of thy sacrifices, or for thy burnt - offerings : because they were not alway before me.

8-15 Condemnation pronounced against formalists.

R.V. and thy burnt-offerings are continually before me.

9 I will take no bullock out of thine house : nor he-goat out of thy folds.

10 For all the beasts of the forest are mine : and so are the cattle upon a thousand hills.

11 I know all the fowls upon the mountains : and the wild beasts of the field are in my sight.

12 If I be hungry, I will not tell thee : for the whole world is mine, and all that is therein.

13 Thinkest thou that I will eat bulls' flesh : and drink the blood of goats?

14 Offer unto God thanksgiving : and pay thy vows unto the most Highest.

God being spirit will not accept merely material sacrifices. He would be worshipped in spirit and in truth (*S. John* 4. 24), and with sincerity of thanksgiving and of supplication (v. 15).

thanksgiving: *R.V. the sacrifice of thanksgiving*. An application of this is obvious to the most Holy Eucharist, 'our sacrifice of praise and thanksgiving'; as the word 'Eucharist' means 'thanksgiving.' Cp. Heb. 13. 15, 'Through him let us offer up a sacrifice of praise to God continually, that is, the fruit of lips which make confession to his name.'

15 And call upon me in the time of trouble : so will I hear thee, and thou shalt praise me.'

A.R.V. deliver thee,

16 But unto the ungodly said God : 'Why dost thou preach my laws, and takest my covenant in thy mouth;

16 - 22. Condemnation pronounced against hypocrites.

in thy mouth: boasting of it; cp. Rom. 2. 17-24.
A.R.V. thou hatest instruction:

17 Whereas thou hatest to be reformed : and hast cast my words behind thee?
18 When thou sawest a thief, thou consentedst unto him : and hast been partaker with the adulterers.
19 Thou hast let thy mouth speak wickedness : and with thy tongue thou hast set forth deceit.
20 Thou satest, and spakest against thy brother : yea, and hast slandered thine own mother's son.

satest: taking your position with other slanderers; cp. Ps. 1. 1.

21 These things hast thou done, and I held my tongue, and thou thoughtest wickedly, that I am even such a one as thyself : but I will reprove thee, and set before thee the things that thou hast done.

God's non-interference was misunderstood as betokening acquiescence in sin.

22 O consider this, ye that forget God : lest I pluck you away, and there be none to deliver you.

A.R.V. lest I tear you in pieces,

23 Whoso offereth me thanks and praise, he honoureth me : and to him that ordereth his conversation right will I shew the salvation of God.'

R.V. Whoso offereth the sacrifice of thanksgiving; cp. v. 14.

This first clause is a summary of the teaching in vv. 8-15; and the second clause of that in vv. 16-22.

ordereth: i.e. sets in order, directs.

conversation: i.e. manner of life.

PSALM 51. *Miserere mei, Deus*

A psalm of David (title). David's expression of repentance and prayer for pardon for his sin. It has generally been regarded as the expansion of his confession, 'I have sinned against the Lord' (2 *Sam.* 12. 13). This is the fourth of the Penitential Psalms: against Lust. It is proper on Ash Wednesday in the Commination Service; and has been the most commonly used act of contrition among Christians. The major and minor keys alternate in it, according as the thought of the mercy of God or the sense of sinfulness predominate in the psalmist's mind.

HAVE mercy upon me, O God, after thy great goodness : according to the multitude of thy mercies do away mine offences.

The penitent comes to God, full of the thought of God's goodness, rather than of his wrath against sin, and of his own need of mercy as being an offender against God's goodness and personally unclean in God's sight. This is contrition.

after: i.e. as *A.R.V. according to.*

A.R.V. blot out my transgressions.

A.R.V. from mine iniquity:

In the Hebrew of vv. 1-2 three words are used, as in Ps. 32. 1-2, to express misdoing: (1) Breaking loose from God (transgression); (2) Perversion of soul (iniquity); (3) Falling short of

2 Wash me throughly from my wickedness : and cleanse me from my sin.

the mark (sin). Also the pardon of sin is described under two figures: (1) Blotting out, as from a book of remembrance; (2) Washing and cleansing from impurities.

Contrition leads to confession, and to an abiding compunction.

3 For I acknowledge my faults : and my sin is ever before me.

4 (Against thee only have I sinned, and done this evil in thy sight) : that thou mightest be justified in thy saying, and clear when thou art judged.

Against thee only: the aspect of his deed as a grievous wrong done to Uriah and Bathsheba is superseded in David's mind by the contemplation of it as a sin against God; as in 2 Sam. 12. 13, 'I have sinned against the Lord.' All sins against one's neighbour are primarily sins against God.

R.V. and done that which is evil that thou mightest, etc.: connects with v. 3. I acknowledge my sinfulness as justifying thy sentence against it, and clearing thee against any men who may presume to impugn thy righteousness. But better as *R.V.*, *that thou mayest be justified when thou speakest* (i.e. givest sentence), *and be clear when thou judgest.* God's righteousness was vindicated by his condemnation of David's sin. All true confession implies the acceptance of divine justice.

This verse is quoted in Rom. 3. 4, according to the Sept. P.B.V. 'when thou art judged,' comes from Vulg.

Behind actual sins lies original sin.

5 Behold, I was shapen in wickedness : and in sin hath my mother conceived me.

6 But lo, thou requirest truth in the inward parts : and shalt make me to understand wisdom secretly.

The God of truth enlightens the conscience.

secretly: *A.R.V. in the hidden part.*

7 Thou shalt purge me with hyssop, and I shall be clean : thou shalt wash me, and I shall be whiter than snow.

8 Thou shalt make me hear of joy and gladness : that the bones which thou hast broken may rejoice.

9 Turn thy face from my sins : and put out all my misdeeds.

10 Make me a clean heart, O God : and renew a right spirit within me.

11 Cast me not away from thy presence : and take not thy holy Spirit from me.

7-8. God's gladdening acceptance of the penitent.

Spiritual cleansing is expressed in the terms of the outward purifications required in the case of the leper and the unclean (*Lev.* 14. 4 ff.; *Num.* 19. 17 ff.). Cp. Isa. 1. 18, 'Though your sins be as scarlet, they shall be as white as snow'; and Heb. 9. 13-14; 12. 24; 1 S. Pet. 1. 2; 1 S. John 1. 7. Hyssop was a plant used for sprinkling.

The joy of absolution. Cp. S. Luke 15. 7, 'Joy shall be in heaven over one sinner that repenteth,' and 15. 32, 'make merry and be glad.'

that the bones, etc.: absolution effects complete restoration; cp. Isa. 38. 13; Ps. 35. 10; 38. 3.

9-12. Encouraged by these good hopes, the penitent begs for the bestowal upon him of God's mercies on sinners:cleansing from sin (v. 7), making glad (v. 8), not reckoning the sins, *A.R.V. blot out* (v. 9), restoring the sinner spiritually (v. 10), cancelling the spiritual penalties (v. 11), spiritual strengthening (v. 12).

Make me: *A.R.V. Create in me.* Cp. Ezek. 11. 19; Eph. 4. 23, 24.

a right spirit: *R.V.mg.a steadfast spirit.*

Cp. the versicle and response: 'O God, make clean our hearts within us. And take not thy Holy Spirit from us.'

Cp. Ps. 5. 10; S. Matt. 8. 12; 25. 41, etc.

Here the divine Spirit is meant, as in v. 10 the human

12 O give me the comfort of thy help again : and stablish me with thy free Spirit.

spirit. 'Holy Spirit' in O.T. occurs only here and in Isa. 63. 10, 11. Enlightened by the revelation by Christ of the most Holy Trinity, we can discern here a reference to the Third Person, which was not present in the mind of the psalmist.

R.V. Restore unto me the joy of thy salvation : and uphold me with a free (mg. willing) spirit, i.e. a (human) spirit willing to give itself freely to be led by God. P.B.V. 'Spirit' is understood as meaning the Holy Spirit.

13 Then shall I teach thy ways unto the wicked : and sinners shall be converted unto thee.

13-17. Some results of forgiveness : the conversion of others (v. 13), the greater glory of God (v. 14, 15), habitual compunction of the pardoned (v. 17).

sinners shall be converted: cp. S. Luke 22. 32; S. Jas. 5. 19, 20.

14 Deliver me from blood-guiltiness, O God, thou that art the God of my health : and my tongue shall sing of thy righteousness.

blood-guiltiness: David's sin had caused the shedding of Uriah's blood, and the sins of the world have caused the shedding of the precious Blood of Christ.

my health: i.e. welfare in general. *A.R.V. my salvation:*

thy righteousness: which is displayed as much in pardoning the penitent as in condemning the wicked. Cp. 1 S. John 1. 9, R.V., 'If we confess our sins, he is faithful and righteous to forgive us our sins.'

15 Thou shalt open my lips, O Lord; and my mouth shall shew thy praise.

A.R.V. O Lord, open thou my lips. Hence the versicle and response at the beginning of Morning and Evening Prayer.

K

16 For thou desirest no sacrifice, else would I give it thee : but thou delightest not in burnt-offerings.

17 The sacrifice of God is a troubled spirit : a broken and contrite heart, O God, shalt thou not despise.

18 O be favourable and gracious unto Sion : build thou the walls of Jerusalem.

19 Then shalt thou be pleased with the sacrifice of righteousness, with the burnt-offerings and oblations : then shall they offer young bullocks upon thine altar.

The Jewish sacrifices were not in themselves acceptable. Cp. Ps. 40. 8-10, 'Sacrifice thou wouldest not: but mine ears hast thou opened. Burnt-offerings hast thou not required: then said I, Lo, I come that I should fulfil thy will, O my God.'

A.R.V. The sacrifices of God are sacrifice of God: i.e. sacrifice acceptable to God.

a troubled spirit: *A.R.V. a broken spirit.* We discern the compunction of all penitents in the Sacred Heart of Jesus Victim for sinners. Cp. Ps. 69. 21, 'Thy rebuke hath broken my heart; I am full of heaviness.'

With this verse cp. Ps. 34. 18, 'The LORD is nigh unto them that are of a contrite heart: and will save such as be of an humble spirit.'

The penitent forgiven turns to intercession, and prays for blessing upon the Church. Many commentators have interpreted Sion as the Church on earth, and Jerusalem as the Church triumphant in heaven, here and in other psalms. God's favour upon the members of the Church militant means also the building of heavenly Jerusalem.

A.R.V. the sacrifices of righteousness, i.e. those which are offered in spiritual sincerity.

The frequent vision of the prophets of a reformed and acceptable worship in the restored Israel has been fulfilled in the Sacrifice of the Altar in the Church. Cp. Mal. 1. 11; 3. 3, 4.

then shall they offer: and no longer unacceptably, cp. v. 16.

PSALM 52. *Quid gloriaris?*

A bold denunciation of some man of wealth and power, who chiefly by his unscrupulous and slanderous tongue has become a centre of mischief. Tradition identifies him with Doeg the Edomite (1 *Sam.* 22. 9). Many have found that their own tongue has become a mischievous tyrant over themselves as well as over others.

WHY boasteth thou thyself, thou tyrant : that thou canst do mischief;

2 Whereas the goodness of God : endureth yet daily?

Cp. S. Jas. 3. 5, 'The tongue boasteth great things.' Ps. 12. 3, 4; 73. 8, 9.

The tyrant acts in contempt of the persistent goodness of God. God acts ever in goodness, the tyrant in malevolence.

3 Thy tongue imagineth wickedness : and with lies thou cuttest like a sharp razor.

Cp. Ps. 57. 4.

4 Thou hast loved unrighteousness more than goodness : and to talk of lies more than righteousness.

A.R.V. and lying rather than to speak righteousness.

5 Thou hast loved to speak all words that may do hurt : O thou false tongue.

6 Therefore shall God destroy thee for ever : he shall take thee, and pluck thee out of thy dwelling, and root thee out of the land of the living.

7 The righteous also shall see this, and fear : and shall laugh him to scorn;

The righteous shall fear, being awe-struck at the manifestation of the righteous judgement of God.

The words in which the righteous express their scorn.

8 'Lo, this is the man that took not God for his strength : but trusted unto the multitude of his riches, and strengthened himself in his wickedness.'

Cp. Ps. 49. 6.

9 As for me, I am like a green olive-tree in the house of God : my trust is in the tender mercy of God for ever and ever.

9-10. The psalmist speaks for himself.

As for me: compared with the rich tyrant whose doom is likened to an uprooted tree (v. 5). Cp. Ps. 92 11 ff.

my trust: i.e. I will take refuge in the mercy of God against the cruelty of the tyrant.

10 I will always give thanks unto thee for that thou hast done: and I will hope in thy Name, for thy saints like it well.

R.V. and I will wait on thy name, for it is good, in the presence of thy saints.

EVENING PRAYER

PSALM 53. *Dixit insipiens*

The depravity of the heathen world and its oppression of Israel (the Church). This psalm is another version of Ps. 14, which has been remodelled, cp. v. 6, so as to refer to some historical event, the destruction of the host of Sennacherib (2 *Kings* 19. 35), or some such triumph. According to the usage of this second book of the Psalms, 'God' is substituted for 'the LORD (Jehovah)' where that name occurs in Ps. 14.

THE foolish body hath said in his heart : 'There is no God.'

Folly is attributed in Holy Scripture to those who have forsaken the fear of God; cp. Ps. 74. 19, 23; 1 Sam. 13. 12, 13.

they: i.e. the fools.

Cp. Rom. 1. 28 ff.

2 Corrupt are they, and BE-COME ABOMINABLE IN THEIR WICKEDNESS : THERE IS NONE THAT DOETH GOOD.

3 God looked down from heaven upon the children of men : to see if there were any that would understand, and seek after God.

Cp. Ps. 11. 5; 102. 19; Gen. 11. 5; 18. 20.

4 But they are all gone out of the way, they are ALTOGETHER BECOME ABOMINABLE; THERE IS ALSO NONE THAT DOETH GOOD, NO NOT ONE.

5 'Are not they without understanding that work wickedness : eating up my people as if they would eat bread?' They have not called upon God.

6 They were afraid where no fear was : for God hath broken the bones of him that besieged thee; thou hast put them to confusion, because God hath despised them.

7 O that the salvation were given unto Israel out of Sion : O that the LORD would deliver his people out of captivity!

8 Then should Jacob rejoice : and Israel should be right glad.

God speaks.

they, the unbelieving fools, the foreign oppressors of Israel 'my people.'

where there was no reason to apprehend danger.

A.R.V. hath scattered round the walls of the city.

thee . . . thou: i.e. Israel.

This verse 6 was altered to suit the later occurrence. The parallel passage in Ps. 14. 5, 6 reads in R.V. 'There were they in great fear; for God is in the generation of the righteous. Ye put to shame the counsel of the poor, because (*mg. but*) the LORD is his refuge.'

A.R.V. When God bringeth back the captivity of his people, then shall Jacob . . . To 'bring back the captivity' is probably metaphorical for to 'restore to prosperity,' as in Job 42. 10.

'Sion' is usually interpreted as the Church on earth, where God dwells among men; cp. Ps. 3. 4. 'Jacob' also signifies the Church militant, and 'Israel' the Church triumphant in heaven prevailing with God; cp. Gen. 32. 28. So the Christian meaning of vv. 7-8 is not that salvation be given unto the Church on earth from God's dwelling-place in heaven; but that the total number of the saved may be brought into the Church above (Israel), as the contribution from the Church below (Sion); then should all the people of God, those from earth (Jacob) and those already in glory (Israel), rejoice together.

PSALM 54. *Deus, in nomine*

The psalmist, exposed to great danger from bitter foes, commends himself to the divine protection. This, the experience and the prayer pre-eminently of Christ in his Passion, is also those of each true follower of Christ in some measure. Christ is the speaker, and the members of his Church with him.

SAVE me, O God, for thy Name's sake : and avenge me in thy strength.

A.R.V. by thy name: cf. Ps. 52. 9.

A.R.V. and judge me, i.e. vindicate me.

2 Hear my prayer, O God : and hearken unto the words of my mouth.

3 For strangers are risen up against me : and tyrants, which have not God before their eyes, seek after my soul.

R.V. and violent men. We may think of devilish foes as well as human ones. And 'my soul' may be my physical life or my spiritual being: either may be the object of attack.

4 Behold, God is my helper : the Lord is with them that up-hold my soul.

R.V. the Lord is of them that uphold my soul. I.e. is my true upholder, according to a Hebrew idiom; cp. Ps. 118. 7; Judg. 11. 35.

R.V. shall require the evil

5 He shall reward evil unto mine enemies : destroy thou them in thy truth.

in thy truth: i.e. making true thy promise of deliverance. Cp. Ps. 89. 48.

R.V. With a freewill offering will I sacrifice unto thee,

6 An offering of a free heart will I give thee, and praise thy Name, O LORD : because it is so comfortable.

A.R.V. for it is good. To us the good and comfortable Name of the LORD is Jesus, God our Saviour. Cp. Isa. 40. 2; S. Matt. 1. 21.

As often in the psalms, the confidence of faith regards the deliverance prayed for as already accomplished.

7 For he hath delivered me out of all my trouble : and mine eye hath seen his desire upon mine enemies.

R.V. hath seen my desire. 'his' means 'its.'

The Christian may not desire

harm to his enemies as such, but only in so far as they are the enemies of Christ; and not for his own gratification, but for their ultimate benefit and for God's greater glory. Christ, the righteous King and Judge, is here the primary speaker, and in many such passages.

PSALM 55. *Exaudi, Deus*

The prayer of an inhabitant of Jerusalem persecuted by active enemies, one of whom was once a trusted friend. There are some foreshadowings of the Passion of Christ, who may be thought of as the speaker throughout.

HEAR my prayer, O God : and hide not thyself from my petition.

2 Take heed unto me, and hear me : how I mourn in my prayer, and am vexed.

3 The enemy crieth so, and the ungodly cometh on so fast : for they are minded to do me some mischief, so maliciously are they set against me.

4 My heart is disquieted within me : and the fear of death is fallen upon me.

5 Fearfulness and trembling are come upon me : and an horrible dread hath overwhelmed me.

6 And I said, 'O that I had wings like a dove : for then would I flee away, and be at rest.

1-8. Vexation of spirit.

R.V. I am restless in my complaint, and moan. Cp. S. John 12. 27, 'Now is my soul troubled; and what shall I say? Father, save me from this hour'; Heb. 5. 7, 'He offered up prayers and supplications with strong crying and tears.'

Cp. S. John 14. 30, 'The prince of this world cometh'; S. Luke 22. 53, 'This is your hour, and the power of darkness.'

Cp. S. Mark 14. 33, 'He began to be greatly amazed, and sore troubled. And he saith unto them, My soul is exceeding sorrowful even unto death.'

like a dove: cp. Hos. 11. 11, 'O that I were given means of

7 Lo, then would I get me away far off : and remain in the wilderness.

8 I would make haste to escape : because of the stormy wind and tempest.'

9 Destroy their tongues, O Lord, and divide them : for I have spied unrighteousness and strife in the city.
10 Day and night they go about within the walls thereof : mischief also and sorrow are in the midst of it.

11 Wickedness is therein : deceit and guile go not out of their streets.
12 For it is not an open enemy that hath done me this dishonour : for then I could have borne it.
13 Neither was it mine adversary that did magnify himself against me : for then peradventure I would have hid myself from him.

legitimate escape!' Cp. S. Matt. 17. 17, 'O faithless and perverse generation, how long shall I be with you?'; Phil. 1. 23, 'I am in a strait, having the desire to depart and be with Christ, which is far better'; 2 Cor. 5. 4, 'We that are in this tabernacle do groan, being burdened.'

R.V. *lodge*
in the wilderness: away from the noisy onslaughts of foes; cp. Ps. 31. 22.

9-16. The wickedness of the enemies.
divide: cp. Gen. 10. 25, 11. 9.

'They' may mean 'the enemy' and 'the ungodly' (v. 3); but some suppose 'they' to be 'violence' and 'strife' (v. 9) personified; and interpret in the same way 'iniquity,' 'mischief,' 'wickedness,' 'deceit,' and 'guile' in this and the next verse.
mischief: *R.V. iniquity*
sorrow: *R.V. mischief*

their streets: *A.R.V. her streets.*

14 But it was even thou, my companion : my guide, and mine own familiar friend.

R.V. thou, a man mine equal, my companion, and . . .

Cf. S. John 6. 71, 'Have not I chosen you twelve, and one of you is a devil?'; S. Matt. 26. 23, 'He that dippeth his hand with me in the dish, the same shall betray me'; S. Matt. 26. 50, 'Friend, wherefore art thou come?'

15 We took sweet counsel together : and walked in the house of God as friends.

as friends: *R.V. with the throng.*

Cp. note on Ps. 54. 7.

16 Let death come hastily upon them, and let them go quick into hell : for wickedness is in their dwellings, and among them.

R.V. go down alive into the pit (mg. Sheol). Cp. Num. 16. 33; Acts 1. 17.

17 As for me, I will call upon God : and the Lord shall save me.

17-25. Trust in God.

18 In the evening, and morning, and at noon-day will I pray, and that instantly : and he shall hear my voice.

I.e. all the day long. Evening is mentioned first, because the Hebrew day began at sunset. Many people have been guided by this verse to a habit of three times of prayer each day; as others by Ps. 119. 164, 'Seven times a day do I praise thee,' or by Ps. 119. 62, 'At midnight I will rise to give thanks unto thee,' etc.

R.V. will I complain and moan: cp. v. 2.

instantly: i.e. urgently.

19 It is he that hath delivered my soul in peace from the battle that was against me : for there were many with me.

hath delivered: the psalmist, with the assurance of faith, regards his deliverance as already effected.

R.V. many that strove with me.

20 Yea, even God, that endureth for ever, shall hear me,
and bring them down : for they
will not turn, nor fear God.

turn: i.e. turn away from sin.
But R.V. has: *the men who have
no changes, and who fear not God.*
'no changes,' i.e. of fortune.
Their prosperity has always been
ruffled, and therefore they think
themselves independent of God.

The perfidious friend (v. 14)
is again singled out.

covenant: i.e. of pledged friend-
ship.

21 He laid his hands upon
such as be at peace with him :
and he brake his covenant.

22 The words of his mouth
were softer than butter, having
war in his heart : his words were
smoother than oil, and yet be
they very swords.

23 O cast thy burden upon the
LORD, and he shall nourish thee:
and shall not suffer the righteous
to fall for ever.

24 And as for them : thou, O
God, shalt bring them into the
pit of destruction.

25 The blood-thirsty and deceitful men shall not live out
half their days : nevertheless, my
trust shall be in thee, O LORD.

A.R.V. drawn swords.
Cp. Ps. 37. 3-6; 1 S. Pet. 5. 7.
A.R.V. shall sustain thee:

THE ELEVENTH DAY

MORNING PRAYER

PSALM 56. *Miserere mei, Deus*

The psalmist, hard pressed by foes, is comforted by the assurance that God is with him. Such may not have been one's own personal experience; but we behold Christ in that suffering, and take the words of the psalm as spoken by him: also in Christ we become conscious of the onslaught of evil against the mystical Body of Christ of which we are members.

BE merciful unto me, O God, for man goeth about to devour me : he is daily fighting, and troubling me.

1-8. Perturbation mingled with confidence.

'man' here may be understood as meaning 'the world' which Christians have renounced, i.e. those who, not being ruled by Christian principles, tend to drag Christians down to their worldly level, and so, sometimes even unintentionally, lay wait for our souls.

goeth about: i.e. attempts.
daily: *R.V. all the day long*

2 Mine enemies are daily in hand to swallow me up : for they be many that fight against me, O thou most Highest.

daily: *R.V. all the day long*
are in hand: i.e. are exerting themselves.
R.V. that fight proudly against me.

3 Nevertheless, though I am sometime afraid : yet put I my trust in thee.

4 I will praise God, because of his word : I HAVE PUT MY TRUST IN GOD, AND WILL NOT FEAR WHAT FLESH CAN DO UNTO ME.

his word: i.e. of promise of protection. Some see here and in v. 10 a reference to God's Incarnate Word.
R.V. what can flesh do unto me? These words are repeated in v. 11 and Ps. 118. 6; Heb. 3. 6.

5 They daily mistake my words : all that they imagine is to do me evil.

R.V. All the day long they wrest my words :

6 They hold all together, and keep themselves close : and mark my steps, when they lay wait for my soul.

7 Shall they escape for their wickedness?: thou, O God, in thy displeasure shalt cast them down.

I.e. as *A.R.V. They gather themselves together, they hide themselves:*
when: *R.V. even as*

R.V. In anger cast down the peoples, O God. The psalmist looks beyond his enemies, and asks for the extirpation of the world's ungodliness.
tellest: i.e. countest.
flittings: i.e. as *A.R.V. wanderings.*
put my tears, etc.: i.e. treasure them like drops of precious wine.
A.R.V. are they (i.e. my tears) *not in thy book?* Cp. Mal. 3. 16.

8 Thou tellest my flittings; put my tears into thy bottle : are not these things noted in thy book?

_____

9 Whensoever I call upon thee, then shall mine enemies be put to flight : this I know; for God is on my side.

9-13. Confidence triumphant. Cp. S. John 11. 42.

10 In God's word will I rejoice : in the LORD's word will I comfort me.

11 YEA, IN GOD HAVE I PUT MY TRUST : I WILL NOT BE AFRAID WHAT MAN CAN DO UNTO ME.

R.V. what can man do unto me? The word 'man' here refers back to v. 1, and it explains 'flesh' in v. 4.

12 Unto thee, O God, will I pay my vows : unto thee will I give thanks.

R.V. I will render thank-offerings.
Deliverance is regarded as already effected.
This verse occurs again in Ps. 116. 8, 9.

13 For thou hast delivered my soul from death, and my feet from falling : that I may walk before God in the light of the living.

Psalm 57. *Miserere mei, Deus*

The same subject as in Ps. 56: an expression of faith in God in presence of malignant enemies. This psalm is proper in Eastertide, the refrain (vv. 6, 12) being interpreted of Christ's exaltation in his human nature, and v. 9 of his resurrection, vv. 1-7 will then be understood of his passion.

BE merciful unto me, O God, be merciful unto me, for my soul trusteth in thee : and under the shadow of thy wings shall be my refuge, until this tyranny be over-past.

2 I will call unto the most high God : even unto the God that shall perform the cause which I have in hand.

3 He shall send from heaven : and save me from the reproof of him that would eat me up.

4 God shall send forth his mercy and truth : my soul is among lions.

5 And I lie even among the children of men, that are set on fire : whose teeth are spears and arrows, and their tongue a sharp sword.

6 SET UP THYSELF, O GOD, ABOVE THE HEAVENS : AND THY GLORY ABOVE ALL THE EARTH.

1-7. A faithful call for deliverance.
R.V. my soul taketh refuge in thee: cp. Ps. 17. 8.
A.R.V. until these calamities

A.R.V. unto God that performeth all things for me.

reproof: i.e. as *A.V. reproach*, taunting me with the absence of succour from God.

mercy and truth: cp. Ps. 40. 11; 85. 10; 89. 14. See also S. John 1. 17.
lions: i.e. my fierce opponents (as in Ps. 58. 6).

set on fire: i.e. incensed against me.
Cp. Ps. 55. 21, 59. 7.

The manifestation of God's glory would involve the downfall of the wicked, the psalmist's foes among them, and the deliverance of those who trust in him.
Cp. S. Matt. 28. 18, 'All authority hath been given unto me in heaven and on earth.'

7 They have laid a net for my feet, and pressed down my soul : they have digged a pit before me, and are fallen into the midst of it themselves.

———

8 My heart is fixed, O God, my heart is fixed : I will sing, and give praise.

9 Awake up, my glory; awake, lute and harp : I myself will awake right early.

8-12. Thanks for deliverance. fixed: i.e. steadfast in faith.

glory: poetical for 'soul' as being man's noblest part (*Ps.* 7. 5; 16. 10; 30. 13).

R.V.mg. I will awake the dawn. My song shall arouse the morning from its slumber. Cp. S. Mark 16. 2, 'Very early in the morning.'

R.V. peoples: cp. Ps. 18. 50.

10 I will give thanks unto thee, O Lord, among the people : and I will sing unto thee among the nations.

11 For the greatness of thy mercy reacheth unto the heavens : and thy truth unto the clouds.

12 Set up thyself, O God, above the heavens : and thy glory above all the earth.

Verses 8-12 occur again almost unchanged in Ps. 108. 1-5.

PSALM 58.   *Si vere utique*

A denunciation of unrighteous judges. We may apply it especially to those who have condemned Christ and his faithful servants.

ARE your minds set upon righteousness, O ye congregation : and do ye judge the thing that is right, O ye sons of men?

R.V. Do ye indeed in silence speak righteousness, i.e. Do ye imagine that ye give sentence on the side of righteousness when, instead of denouncing wickedness, ye keep silence? A sarcastic address to certain judges, called 'sons of men,' not 'sons of God.'

A.R.V. Do ye judge uprightly,

2 Yea, ye imagine mischief in your heart upon the earth : and your hands deal with wickedness.

R.V. Yea, in heart ye work wickedness : ye weigh out the violence of your hands in the earth. Ye dispense violence instead of justice.

3 The ungodly are froward, even from their mother's womb : as soon as they are born, they go astray, and speak lies.

The ungodly: i.e. especially these unjust judges and those whom they favour.

froward: hostile and obstinate.

A.R.V. The wicked are estranged. The word found here in the Sept. is used by S. Paul in Eph. 4. 18, 'alienated from the life of God,' and in Col. 1. 21.

4 They are venomous as the poison of a serpent : even like the deaf adder that stoppeth her ears;

5 Which refuseth to hear the voice of the charmer : charm he never so wisely.

They are obstinate as well as wicked, for they shut their ears to good advisers. Cp. Acts 7. 57.

6 Break their teeth, O God, in their mouths; smite the jaw-bones of the lions, O LORD : let them fall away like water that runneth apace; and when they shoot their arrows let them be rooted out.

Stop their calumnies and slander.

R.V. when he (one of these wicked men) *aimeth his arrows, let them* (the arrows) *be as though they were cut off,* i.e. broken and rendered harmless.

7 Let them consume away like a snail, and be like the untimely fruit of a woman : and let them not see the sun.

As a snail dries up in time of drought.

R.V. that hath not seen the sun.

8 Or ever your pots be made hot with thorns : so let indignation vex him, even as a thing that is raw.

R.V. Before your pots can feel the thorns, he shall take them away with a whirlwind, the green and the burning alike. The illustration is suggested by the preparation of a meal in the desert. Before the cooking-pot has been heated by the fire just lit, a whirlwind arising sweeps away the thorns of which the fuel is composed. Thus, almost as soon as they are devised, the schemes of the wicked will be swept away by the wrath of God.

9 The righteous shall rejoice when he seeth the vengeance : he shall wash his footsteps in the blood of the ungodly.

10 So that a man shall say, 'Verily there is a reward for the righteous : doubtless there is a God that judgeth the earth.'

Metaphor founded on the savagery of ancient, and of some modern, warfare.

EVENING PRAYER

PSALM 59. *Eripe me de inimicis*

A prayer that God will frustrate the machinations of heathen enemies, who with malicious speech (vv. 7, 12) assail the faithful. It has become the prayer of Christians suffering at the hand of anti-Christian powers, as Christ himself suffered.

DELIVER me from mine enemies, O God : defend me from them that rise up against me.

2 O deliver me from the wicked doers : and save me from the blood-thirsty men.

3 For lo, they lie waiting for my soul : the mighty men are gathered against me, without any offence or fault of me, O LORD.

my soul: may mean either my physical life or my spiritual being.

without any offence: the innocence of Christ; cp. Ps. 7. 3-4; 35. 7, etc., and S. Luke 23. 4, 'Then said Pilate, I find no fault in this man.'

4 They run and prepare themselves without my fault : arise thou therefore to help me, and behold.

5 Stand up, O LORD God of Israel, to visit all the heathen : and be not merciful unto them that offend of malicious wickedness.

all the heathen: he prays that God's judgement may reach not only his own enemies, but also all the other enemies of God.

be not merciful: for divine mercy can find no scope in those in whom malice persists. As often a spiritual law is stated in terms of a prayer.

6 THEY GO TO AND FRO IN THE EVENING : THEY GRIN LIKE A DOG, AND RUN ABOUT THROUGH THE CITY.

7 Behold, they speak with their mouth, and swords are in their lips: 'for who doth hear?'

They are like savage dogs which prowl about Eastern towns in the evenings looking for food.
grin: i.e. snarl.
A.R.V. they belch out swords: cp. Ps. 57. 5.
A.R.V. for who, say they, doth hear? They imagine that God pays no heed (*Ps.* 10. 12, 14).

8 But thou, O LORD, shalt have them in derision : and thou shalt laugh all the heathen to scorn.

Cp. Ps. 2. 4, 'He that dwelleth in heaven shall laugh them to scorn: the Lord shall have them in derision.'
all the heathen: cp. v. 5.

9 MY STRENGTH WILL I A-SCRIBE UNTO THEE : FOR THOU ART THE GOD OF MY REFUGE.

10 GOD sheweth me his goodness plenteously : and God shall let me see my desire upon mine enemies.

R.V. O my strength, I will wait upon thee : for God is my high tower. Cp. v. 17.
A.R.V. The God of my mercy shall prevent me. prevent: i.e. go before. The theological term 'preventing grace' is derived from this passage in the Vulgate.

After three verses, 8-10, of faithful praise, which are to be resumed in vv. 16, 17, the strain of supplication is begun again here.

11 Slay them not, lest my people forget it : but scatter them abroad among the people, and put them down, O Lord, our defence.

Slay them not: cp. Judges 2. 3; but see v. 13.
A.R.V. scatter them by thy power, and bring them down, O Lord our shield.

12 For the sin of their mouth, and for the words of their lips, they shall be taken in their pride : and why? their preaching is of cursing and lies.

13 Consume them in thy wrath, consume them, that they may perish : and know that it is God that ruleth in Jacob, and unto the ends of the world.

14 AND IN THE EVENING THEY WILL RETURN : GRIN LIKE A DOG, AND WILL GO ABOUT THE CITY.

A.R.V. and for cursing and lying which they speak.
As always, concern for God's glory is paramount in the prayers for the exercise of God's wrath. The heathen also are to benefit by being punished; cp. Ps. 9. 20, etc.

L

15 They will run here and there for meat : and grudge if they be not satisfied.

16 As for me, I will sing of thy power, and will praise thy mercy betimes in the morning : for thou hast been my defence and refuge in the day of my trouble.

grudge: i.e. grumble. But R.V. has: *tarry all night*.

in the morning: Although his enemies tarry all night, seeking to make him their prey, he is confident that in the morning he will be able to sing of the power of God which has kept him safe; cp. Ps. 30. 5, The morning is especially the time for prayer, cp. Ps. 5. 3, 88. 13, 'Early in the morning our song shall rise to thee.' As spoken by Christ, the words refer to the resurrection-morning.

Cp. v. 9.

17 UNTO THEE, O MY STRENGTH, WILL I SING : FOR THOU, O GOD, ART MY REFUGE, and my merciful God.

PSALM 60.   *Deus, repulisti nos*

The historical reference given traditionally to this psalm is 2 Sam. 8. 5, 6, 14, David's wars with Syria and Edom. The application treats it as a 'missionary' psalm: the people of God, the Church, may be afflicted for a season; but God will bring them victoriously into possession of the heathen, and each land in succession will be subdued to Christ.

O GOD, thou hast cast us out, and scattered us abroad : thou hast also been displeased; O turn thee unto us again.

2 Thou hast moved the land, and divided it : heal the sores thereof, for it shaketh.

3 Thou hast shewed thy people heavy things : thou hast given us a drink of deadly wine.

1-3 These opening verses allude to some unrecorded disaster.

R.V. thou hast cast us off, thou hast broken us down : thou hast been angry; O restore us again.

R.V. Thou hast made the land to tremble; thou hast rent it: heal the breaches thereof. The metaphor is taken from the effect of an earthquake on land and buildings.

R.V. thou hast made us to drink the wine of staggering. Cp. Isa. 51. 17, R.V.

4 Thou hast given a token for such as fear thee : that they may triumph because of the truth.

A.R.V. given a banner to them that fear thee: that it may be displayed because (i.e. on behalf) of the truth. Two gifts of God to his people are contrasted in vv. 3, 4. Some see in the token or banner an allusion to the holy Cross.

A.R.V. That thy beloved (i.e. Israel) *may be delivered: save with thy right hand, and answer us.*

5 Therefore were thy beloved delivered : help me with thy right hand, and hear me.
6 God hath spoken in his holiness, 'I will rejoice, and divide Sichem : and mete out the valley of Succoth.

5-12 occur again, but with a triumphal preface, in Ps. 108. 7-13.

6-8. The words of God: as a victorious warrior he claims afresh the whole land of Canaan. The distribution of territory (divide, . . . mete: i.e. measure out) is the fullest proof of possession. Shechem and Succoth are mentioned in the history of Jacob (*Gen.* 33. 17, 18). Of the localities mentioned here, Shechem, Ephraim, and Judah represent the country west of Jordan, Succoth and Gilead (inhabited by the half-tribe of Manasseh) the country east of Jordan.

7 Gilead is mine, and Manasses is mine : Ephraim also is the strength of my head; Judah is my law-giver;

R.V. the defence of Ephraim was the strongest tribe.
R.V. is my sceptre. Judah was the royal tribe.
God will extend his conquests to the neighbouring nations. Cp. Acts 1. 8.

8 Moab is my wash-pot; over Edom will I cast out my shoe: Philistia, be thou glad of me.'

wash-pot: a contemptuous symbol of subjugation.
cast, etc.: an Eastern sign of taking forcible possession.
R.V. Philistia, shout thou because of me, i.e. acclaim my victory over thee.

9 Who will lead me into the strong city : who will bring me into Edom?

9-11. The words of the psalmist.

strong city: probably, Petra, the capital of Edom. It denotes whatever centre of heathenism is resisting the proclamation of the gospel.

R.V. cast us off? and thou goest not forth. Cp. Ps. 44. 10.

10 Hast not thou cast us out, O God : wilt not thou, O God, go out with our hosts?

11 O be thou our help in trouble : for vain is the help of man.

R.V. Give us help against the adversary:

12 Through God will we do great acts : for it is he that shall tread down our enemies.

PSALM 61. *Exaudi, Deus*

Composed by or in the name of David the king, v. 6, this psalm is an exile's prayer and aspiration in the hope of glory. Cp. Heb. 11. 16, 'They desire a better country, that is, a heavenly,' in which desire Christians make this psalm their own, in union with Christ.

HEAR my crying, O God : give ear unto my prayer.

2 From the ends of the earth will I call upon thee : when my heart is in heaviness.

I.e. however far away I may be from Jerusalem and the fruition of God's presence. And every place, though it be but across the Jordan, seems to the exile to be very far away. The prayerful aspiration for heaven is the exile's antidote for his heart's heaviness.

3 O set me up upon the rock that is higher than I : for thou hast been my hope, and a strong tower for me against the enemy.

A.R.V. Lead me to the rock that is too high for me: i.e. too high for me to attain to it unaided. The Rock is mount Sion, the shrine and symbol of the divine presence. God is often called a Rock in the psalms (18. 1, etc.). Also, as in 1 Cor. 10. 4, 'that Rock was Christ.'

my hope: *R.V. a refuge for me.*

4 I will dwell in thy tabernacle for ever : and my trust shall be under the covering of thy wings.

Cp. Prov. 18. 10, 'The Name of the LORD is a strong tower; the righteous runneth into it, and is safe.'

Cp. Ps. 15. 1; 27. 5.

R.V. *I will take refuge in the covert of thy wings.* An allusion to the Cherubim overshadowing the mercy-seat in the Holy of Holies(*Exod.* 25. 17 ff.; *Ps.* 17.8).

5 For thou, O Lord, hast heard my desires : and hast given an heritage unto those who fear thy Name.

A.R.V. *my vows:*
an heritage: i.e. the land of promise and Jerusalem with its temple. Those who were faithful to God and his servant David, i.e. to Christ, would be confirmed in possession of the heritage which was theirs (*Ps.* 16. 6).

6 Thou shalt grant the King a long life : that his years may endure throughout all generations.

David claims the divine promise to his dynasty (2 *Sam.* 7. 13, 16), which was eventually fulfilled in the everlasting kingdom of his divine Son. Cp. S. Luke 1. 32, 33; Ps. 21. 4. And, as for the King, so shall it be for each faithful servant of the King, in the heavenly Jerusalem (*Rev.* 22. 3-5).

7 He shall dwell before God for ever : O prepare thy loving mercy and faithfulness, that they may preserve him.

8 So will I alway sing praise unto thy Name : that I may daily perform my vows.

I.e. lest he should fail to attain to his hope.

The due fulfilment of any holy vows, baptismal, priestly, religious, etc., is closely bound up with the worship of God, both in this exile and in our heavenly home.

THE TWELFTH DAY
MORNING PRAYER
PSALM 62.   *Nonne Deo?*

The psalmist, persecuted and slandered by enemies, is contented to wait patiently for God's deliverance: the member of Christ likewise.

MY SOUL TRULY WAITETH STILL UPON GOD : FOR OF HIM COMETH MY SALVATION.

2 HE VERILY IS MY STRENGTH AND MY SALVATION : HE IS MY DEFENCE, SO THAT I SHALL NOT GREATLY FALL.

3 How long will ye imagine mischief against every man : ye shall be slain all the sort of you; yea, as a tottering wall shall ye be, and like a broken hedge.

still: i.e. quietly. *R.V.mg. is silent unto God.* Cp. 37. 7.

all the sort of you: i.e. all your company.

R.V. How long will ye set upon a man, that ye may slay him, all of you, like a bowing wall, like a tottering fence?

R.V. They only consult to thrust him down from his excellency:

4 Their device is only how to put him out whom God will exalt : their delight is in lies; they give good words with their mouth, but curse with their hearts.

5 Nevertheless, MY SOUL, WAIT THOU STILL UPON GOD : FOR MY HOPE IS IN HIM.

6 HE TRULY IS MY STRENGTH AND MY SALVATION : HE IS MY DEFENCE, SO THAT I SHALL NOT FALL.

7 In God is my health, and my glory : the rock of my might, and in God is my trust.

8 O put your trust in him alway, ye people : pour out your hearts before him, for God is our hope.

health: i.e. well-being.

A.R.V. my refuge.
ye people: i.e. ye faithful people of God.

pour out your hearts: in sincere and earnest prayer. Cp. Ps. 42. 4.

A.R.V. God is a refuge for us.

9 As for the children of men, they are but vanity : the children of men are deceitful upon the weights, they are altogether lighter than vanity itself.

the children of men: i.e. mankind apart from God. They are 'weighed in the balances, and found wanting' (*Dan.* 5. 27). *R.V. Surely men of low degree are vanity* (i.e. emptiness, nothingness, *R.V.mg. a breath), and men of high degree are a lie: in the balances they will go up.*

10 O trust not in wrong and robbery, give not yourselves unto vanity : if riches increase, set not your heart upon them.

11 God spake once, and twice I have also heard the same: that power belongeth unto God;

The divine voice has often revealed to him the double truth of the power and the mercy of God. Cp. Rom. 11. 22, 'Behold the goodness and severity of God.'

once and twice: a Hebrew idiom for 'many times'; cp. Job 33. 14; 40. 5.

12 And that thou, Lord, art merciful : for thou rewardest every man according to his work.

rewardest: i.e. either with the severity of thy power or with the mercy of thy love, according to each one's work. This verse is quoted and commented on by S. Paul in Rom. 2. 6 ff. Cp. 1 Cor. 3. 8.

PSALM 63. *Deus, Deus meus*

The morning prayer of an exile, which has been used in the morning prayers of the Church on earth. It speaks of a sense of communion with God, and longing for his presence.

O GOD, thou art my God : early will I seek thee.

my God: (1) the God of all is God of me; (2) he is God apart from my recognition of him, yet I have truly chosen and accepted him as my God; cp. S. Thomas's 'My Lord and my God' (*S. John* 20. 28), and our Lord's 'My God and your God' (*S. John* 20. 17).

early: (1) in the morning

prayer; (2) in youth, the morning of life's day; (3) awaking from the death of sin to the light of Christ (*Eph.* 5. 14); (4) in the eternal morning of the resurrection-life.

seek thee: 'and he that seeketh findeth' (*S. Matt.* 7. 8).

Ps. 42. 2, 84. 2.

my soul . . . my flesh: Man needed God present with him, both physically and spiritually, a longing which was satisfied first by the Incarnation.

dry land: the image is taken from some desert place in which the psalmist is; cp. Ps. 84. 6, 143. 6.

2 My soul thirsteth for thee, my flesh also longeth after thee : in a barren and dry land where no water is.

Thus: with such fervour.

in holiness: i.e. in thine holiness. *R.V. So have I looked upon thee in the sanctuary : to see thy power and glory.*

3 Thus have I looked for thee in holiness : that I might behold thy power and glory.

A.R.V. is better than life:

4 For thy loving-kindness is better than the life itself : my lips shall praise thee.

5 As long as I live will I magnify thee on this manner : and lift up my hands in thy Name.

As long as I live: (1) all my life long; (2) for all eternity.

lift up my hands, in the gesture of prayer: (*Ps.* 28. 2; 1 *Tim.*2. 8).

Ps. 36. 8.

6 My soul shall be satisfied, even as it were with marrow and fatness : when my mouth praiseth thee with joyful lips.

7 Have I not remembered thee in my bed : and thought upon thee when I was waking?

when I was waking: i.e. as *R.V. in the night watches*; referring to (1) those who are in bed at night sleeping or awake; (2) those who sleep in Christ and watch in purgatory for the resurrection.

8 Because thou hast been my helper : therefore under the shadow of thy wings will I rejoice.

9 My soul hangeth upon thee : thy right hand hath upholden me.

Ps. 17. 8.
A.R.V. My soul followeth hard after thee:

10 These also that seek the hurt of my soul : they shall go under the earth.

A.R.V. But those
A.R.V. shall go into the lower parts of the earth. S. Paul's expression in Eph. 4. 9 was probably suggested by this verse and Ps. 139. 14.

11 Let them fall upon the edge of the sword : that they may be a portion of foxes.

R.V. They shall be given over to the power of the sword:
foxes: *R.V.mg. jackals,* which feed on dead bodies.

12 But the king shall rejoice in God; all they also that swear by him shall be commended : for the mouth of them that speak lies shall be stopped.

the king: (1) David; (2) Christ; (3) those who reign with Christ.
by him: i.e. by God.
A.R.V. shall glory:
speak lies: the character especially of the devils our adversaries (*S. John* 8. 44).

PSALM 64. *Exaudi, Deus*

The psalmist is assailed by the mischievous plottings and malicious accusations of evil men, but confidently predicts their overthrow. This psalm is applicable to devilish as well as to human enemies, and to the Church's assailants as well as to personal foes.

HEAR my voice, O God, in my prayer : preserve my life from fear of the enemy.

2 Hide me from the gathering together of the froward : and from the insurrection of wicked doers;

R.V. from the secret counsel of evil-doers : from the tumult (i.e. open attacks) *of*

3 Who have whet their tongue like a sword : and shoot out their arrows, even bitter words;

Cp. Ps. 57. 4.
Cp. Ps. 11. 2.

4 That they may privily shoot at him that is perfect : suddenly do they hit him, and fear not.

A.R.V. shoot at him

5 They encourage themselves in mischief : and commune among themselves how they may lay snares, and say that no man shall see them.

6 They imagine wickedness, and practise it : that they keep secret among themselves, every man in the deep of his heart.

7 But God shall suddenly shoot at them with a swift arrow: that they shall be wounded.

Cp. vv. 3, 4.   The retribution which overtakes them is described in like terms to their offence. Cp. Obad. 15, 'As thou hast done, it shall be done unto thee.'

8 Yea, their own tongues shall make them fall : insomuch that whoso seeth them shall laugh them to scorn.

their own tongues: with which they have attacked. Their malicious schemes turn against themselves.

9 And all men that see it shall say, 'This hath God done' : for they shall perceive that it is his work.

R.V. And all men shall fear; and they shall declare the work of God: They shall fear, unlike the ungodly who 'fear not'(v. 4).

10 The righteous shall rejoice in the LORD, and put his trust in him : and all they that are true of heart shall be glad.

EVENING PRAYER

PSALM 65.   *Te decet hymnus*

A thanksgiving in prospect of an abundant harvest. God has satisfied man's needs, both spiritual and physical. The psalm is often used in services of thanksgiving: it occurs also in the Office of the Dead, because of vv. 2 and 4.

THOU, O God, art praised in Sion : and unto thee shall the vow be performed in Jerusalem.

1 - 4. The merciful lovingkindness of God to sinful mankind.

Sion . . . Jerusalem: may be applied to the Church on earth and in heaven.

2 Thou that hearest the prayer : unto thee shall all flesh come.

To hear prayer is an essential part of the character of God.

come: i.e. to worship and give thanks; cp. Ps. 84. 7. The application of the phrase to the dead is readily made; but the main thought is that all nations shall some day approach to God; cp. Ps. 86. 9; Rev. 21. 26. Meanwhile man in his pilgrimage aspires to attain to God in the heavenly Jerusalem.

3 My misdeeds prevail against me : O be thou merciful unto our sins.

my . . . our: The psalmist thinks first of his own sins, and then unites himself with others in the Church.

A.R.V. as for our transgressions, thou shalt purge them away. Sins while unpurged prevail against the worshippers, hindering their access to God.

4 Blessed is the man, whom thou choosest, and receivest unto thee : he shall dwell in thy court, and shall be satisfied with the pleasures of thy house, even of thy holy temple.

The privilege of the Israelite, inherited by the Christian, fulfilled perfectly for him in heaven. Cp. Ps. 33. 12.

satisfied: cp. Ps. 16. 12.

5 Thou shalt shew us wonderful things in thy righteousness, O God of our salvation : thou that art the hope of all the ends of the earth, and of them that remain in the broad sea.

5-14. The bountiful lovingkindness of God in nature.

R.V. By terrible things thou wilt answer us in righteousness, O God. The wonderful and terrible things are the great deeds of deliverance like the rescue from Egypt; cp. Ps. 106. 22; Deut. 10. 21.

A.R.V. and of them that are afar off upon the sea.

6 Who in his strength setteth fast the mountains : and is girded about with power.
7 Who stilleth the raging of the sea : and the noise of his waves, and the madness of the people.

Cp. S. Matt. 8. 27; Ps. 107. 28.

his: i.e. its.
R.V. peoples.

8 They also that dwell in the uttermost parts of the earth shall be afraid at thy tokens : thou that makest the outgoings of the morning and evening to praise thee.

A.R.V. are afraid
thy tokens: i.e. the evidences of thy power.
the outgoings, etc.: i.e. the extreme east and west whence the morning and evening seem to issue.

9 Thou visitest the earth, and blessest it : thou makest it very plenteous.
10 The river of God is full of water : thou preparest their corn, for so thou providest for the earth.

A.R.V. and waterest it:

The river of God: this primarily means the rain; but, as all the phrases of this psalm admit of mystical application, we may see here Christ making human nature (earth) fruitful by his grace in his sacrament (corn). Cp. Ps. 36. 8 ff.; 46. 4; Rev. 22. 1.

11 Thou waterest her furrows, thou sendest rain into the little valleys thereof : thou makest it soft with drops of rain, and blessest the increase of it.
12 Thou crownest the year with thy goodness : and thy clouds drop fatness.

R.V. settlest the ridges thereof.
The rain presses down the ridges between the furrows.

A.R.V. thy paths drop fatness, while thou ridest through the heavens: (*Ps. 18. 10; Deut. 33. 26*).
A.R.V. They drop. All the verbs here are in the present tense. He is describing the scene before his eyes.
dwellings: *A.R.V. pastures* of the wilderness, i.e. the uncultivated land.

13 They shall drop upon the dwellings of the wilderness : and the little hills shall rejoice on every side.

14 The folds shall be full of sheep : the valleys also shall stand so thick with corn, that they shall laugh and sing.

PSALM 66. *Jubilate Deo*

Another psalm of thanksgiving to God for national and personal mercies vouchsafed by him. It takes the form of a summons to the whole world to sing God's praises. It occurs in B.C.P. as an act of thanksgiving after a storm at sea.

O BE joyful in God, all ye lands : sing praises unto the honour of his Name, make his praise to be glorious.

2 Say unto God, 'O how wonderful art thou in thy works : through the greatness of thy power shall thine enemies be found liars unto thee.

A.R.V. how terrible

works: i.e. of deliverance, such as the rescue from Egypt, cp. v. 5 and Ps. 65. 5. Each Christian has been delivered from evil by the works of God, for which thanks should be given.

be found liars unto thee: i.e. their boasts of proud independence of God will be proved untrue, cp. Ps. 2. 2-4; but *A.R.V.* has: *shall submit themselves unto thee (yield feigned submission, R.V.mg.)*, being reduced to impotence. Cp. Ps. 18. 45; 86. 16.

An anticipation of the time when the rule of the God of Israel shall be universally accepted; cp. Ps. 65. 2.

3 For all the world shall worship thee : sing of thee, and praise thy Name.'

4 O come hither, and behold the works of God : how wonderful he is in his doing towards the children of men.

5 He turned the sea into dry land : so that they went through the water on foot; there did we rejoice thereof.

A.R.V. terrible

The passage of the Red Sea. One greatest deliverance is cited to illustrate all (*Exod.* 14. 21; *Ps.* 74. 14). *R.V. through the river*, i.e. the Jordan, into the promised land; or, the Red Sea again.

Some have seen in verses 4-6 a reference to the resurrection and exaltation of the Lord Christ.

6 He ruleth with his power for ever; his eyes behold the people : and such as will not believe shall not be able to exalt themselves.

A.R.V. the nations : let not the rebellious exalt themselves.

7 O praise our God, ye people : and make the voice of his praise to be heard;

8 Who holdeth our soul in life : and suffereth not our feet to slip.

9 For thou, O God, hast proved us : thou also hast tried us, like as silver is tried.

R.V. ye peoples:

9-11. By a succession of metaphors the recent danger and deliverance of Israel is described.

tried us: cp. Job 23. 10; Zech. 13. 9; Mal. 3. 3; 1 S. Pet. 1. 7; and 1 Cor. 3. 13.

These trials were fully experienced by Christ, and his martyrs and confessors, and in some degree all true Christians know them.

10 Thou broughtest us into the snare : and laidest trouble upon our loins.

11 Thou sufferedst men to ride over our heads : we went through fire and water, and thou broughtest us out into a wealthy place.

fire and water: these have been allegorized variously as meaning purgatorial and baptismal cleansing, fire of divine love and penitential tears, etc.; but the literal meaning is perhaps sufficient.

a wealthy place: i.e. a position of prosperity and well-being. *R.V.mg. into abundance.*

12 I will go into thine house with burnt-offerings : and will pay thee my vows, which I promised with my lips, and spake with my mouth, when I was in trouble.

Note the change to the singular which continues to the end of the psalm. The general thanksgiving becomes singular when God's general favours are individually appropriated. Personal experience calls out the expression of thankfulness.

pay vows: cp. Ps. 50. 14.

13 I will offer thee fat burntsacrifices, with the incense of rams : I will offer bullocks and goats.

14 O come hither, and hearken, all ye that fear God : and I will tell you what he hath done for my soul.

incense: here the smoke and sweet savour ascending from the sacrifice (*Gen.* 8. 21).

15 I called unto him with my mouth : and gave him praises with my tongue.

16 If I incline unto wickedness with mine heart : the Lord will not hear me.

17 But God hath heard me : and considered the voice of my prayer.

18 Praised be God who hath not cast out my prayer : nor turned his mercy from me.

PSALM 67. *Deus misereatur*

A harvest thanksgiving hymn, with prayer for the spreading of God's kingdom through the world. We hear the Church speaking in this 'missionary' psalm: in the Church shall all nations of the world be blessed, and there will be a spiritual harvest.

GOD be merciful unto us, and bless us : and shew us the light of his countenance, and be merciful unto us;

Words borrowed from the priestly blessing (*Num.* 6. 24 ff.), with 'God' (Elohim) substituted for 'LORD' (Jehovah) according to the usage in this book of the Psalter. Cp. Ps. 4. 6.

2 That thy way may be known upon earth : thy saving health among all nations.

thy way: this means the same as the parallel 'saving health,' i.e. God's purpose of blessing and salvation. His manifestation of his goodness to Israel (the Church) would lead the other nations to his allegiance. Cp. Ps. 98. 3; S. Luke 2. 30 ff.

3 LET THE PEOPLE PRAISE THEE, O GOD : YEA, LET ALL THE PEOPLE PRAISE THEE.

4 O let the nations rejoice and be glad : for thou shalt judge the folk righteously, and govern the nations upon earth.

R.V. Let the peoples . . . all the peoples
The converted nations will rejoice in the moral government of God.
R.V. judge the peoples with equity.

5 LET THE PEOPLE PRAISE THEE, O GOD : LET ALL THE PEOPLE PRAISE THEE.

R.V. peoples

6 Then shall the earth bring forth her increase : and God, even our own God, shall give us his blessing.

R.V. The earth hath yielded her increase: An abundant harvest has apparently been reaped, which is seen as a token of the favour and mercy of God. A mystic reference to Christ has been seen in 'thy way . . . thy saving health' (v. 2), the righteous Judge (v. 4), the increase of the earth (v. 6); and to the Holy Trinity in the triple repetition of 'God' in vv. 6, 7.

7 God shall bless us : and all the ends of the world shall fear him.

THE THIRTEENTH DAY

MORNING PRAYER

PSALM 68. *Exurgat Deus*

Probably written in Babylon towards the close of the exile, and in view of the restoration to the Holy Land, this psalm depicts the triumphal march of the God of Israel, the conqueror of the nations; symbolizing the progress of Christ the King in the Catholic Church throughout the world. It is proper in Ascensiontide, and on Whitsunday as the festival of the inauguration of the Church and of the outpouring of the gifts of the Spirit by the ascended Lord upon the Church, cp. v. 18.

LET God arise, and let his enemies be scattered : let them also that hate him flee before him.

The words appointed to be used whenever the ark set forward in the wilderness (*Num.* 10. 35); with the substitution of 'God' (Elohim) for 'LORD' (Jehovah), as in Ps. 67. 1. This prayer found its fulfilment in the resurrection of Christ.

The 'ungodly' are the heathen and all opponents of God and his people. It is always better, not only for the world's welfare and for God's glory, but also for God's enemies themselves, that they should be overthrown and

2 Like as the smoke vanisheth, so shalt thou drive them away : and like as wax melteth at the fire, so let the ungodly perish at the presence of God.

3 But let the righteous be glad, and rejoice before God : let them also be merry and joyful.

4 O sing unto God, and sing praises unto his Name : magnify him that rideth upon the heavens, as it were upon a horse; praise him in his name JAH, and rejoice before him.

5 He is a Father of the fatherless, and defendeth the cause of the widows : even God in his holy habitation.

6 He is the God that maketh men to be of one mind in an house, and bringeth the prisoners out of captivity : but letteth the runagates continue in scarceness.

punished, than that they should be left to maintain an apparently successful opposition to God and the Church.

the 'righteous': i.e. Israel in its ideal character, symbolizing the faithful Church.

Cp. v. 33 and Ps. 18. 10; but *R.V.* has: *cast up a highway for him that rideth through the deserts,* a figure taken from the elaborate preparations made for the progresses of Eastern kings; cp. Isa. 40. 3. *Sept.* and *Vulg.* read: *Make a road for him that ascendeth above the sunset,* i.e. his death, over which Christ rose by his resurrection.

JAH, contracted form of JEHOVAH. It appears in 'Hallelujah,' i.e. 'Praise ye JAH, the LORD.'

his holy habitation: i.e. heaven.

The Church was ordained by God to be the home of unity.

But *R.V.* has: *God maketh the solitary to dwell in a house.* Those who have been born in the separateness and captivity of sin are brought unto God's house, with the family of God, the Church.

runagates: i.e. runaways, renegrades. *R.V.* has: *But the rebellious dwell in a parched land,* as happened to the Israelites in the wilderness, and as happens to those who are without the grace of Christ. The rebellious are mentioned again in vv. 18, 21.

M

7 O God, when thou wentest forth before the people : when thou wentest through the wilderness.

8 The earth shook, and the heavens dropped at the presence of God : even as Sinai also was moved at the presence of God, who is the God of Israel.

9 Thou, O God, sentest a gracious rain upon thine inheritance : and refreshedst it when it was weary.

10 Thy congregation shall dwell therein : for thou, O God, hast of thy goodness prepared for the poor.

11 The Lord gave the word : great was the company of the preachers.

12 Kings with their armies did flee, and were discomfited : and they of the household divideth the spoil.

7-8. God's triumphal march from Egypt to Canaan. The language is borrowed from the song of Deborah (*Judges* 5. 4ff.).

The earthquake and rain that accompanied the giving of the Law (*Exod.* 19. 18; *Ps.* 77. 17ff.).

9-10. Israel in Canaan.

a gracious rain: i.e. of blessings, showers of divine grace.

thine inheritance: i.e. Canaan, allotted to God's people, symbolizing the Church.

R.V. Thy congregation dwelt

prepared,: i.e. made provision for.

11-16. The conquest of Canaan.

Verse 11 in P.B.V. speaks of the apostolic preaching of the gospel of Christ, and the 'word' is understood either as the Incarnate Word, or as Christ's committal of the Gospel to the Apostles.

But *R.V. The Lord giveth the word* (in the sense of 'He spake, and it was done,' *Ps.* 33. 9): *the women that publish the tidings* (of victory) *are a great host*. Cp. the action of Miriam (*Exod.* 15. 20), and of Deborah (*Judges* 5. 1 ff.; 1 *Sam.* 18. 6); and v. 25 below.

The Church militant, against Christ's enemies.

R.V. and she that tarrieth at home, i.e. the Church contemplative. The spoils are the souls captured from the devil; cp. S. Matt. 12. 29.

13 Though ye have lien among the pots, yet shall ye be as the wings of a dove : that is covered with silver wings, and her feathers like gold.

lien: i.e. lain.

The meaning is doubtful. In P.B.V. the degradation of servitude in Egypt and in sinfulness is contrasted with the splendour of the redeemed in Canaan and in the Church glorified. The dove with feathers glistening in the sunlight is an image of peace and prosperity.

But *R.V. Will ye lie among the sheepfolds, as the wings of a dove covered with silver, and her pinions with yellow gold?* which is an allusion to Deborah's reproach of Reuben for his supineness (*Judges* 5. 16).

14 When the Almighty scattered kings for their sakes : then were they as white as snow in Salmon.

'The Almighty' occurs in the Psalter only here and in 91. 1.

for their sake: i.e. for the sake of his faithful people.

R.V. it was as when it snoweth in Zalmon. The kings fleeing in confusion are compared to snowflakes falling on Zalmon, the 'dark' mountain, as its name imports. Cp. Judges 9. 48.

15 As the hill of Basan, so is God's hill : even an high hill, as the hill of Basan.

R.V. A mountain of God is the mountain of Bashan : an high mountain is the mountain of Bashan. And yet not there nor in any of the high mountains around did God choose to dwell, but in 'the mountain of the LORD's house,' the hill of Sion, in Jerusalem (*Isa.* 2. 2).

16 Why hop ye so, ye high hills? this is God's hill, in the which it pleaseth him to dwell : yea, the LORD will abide in it for ever.

this: i.e. Sion.

R.V. Why look ye askance, ye high mountains, at the mountain which God hath desired for his abode? The lofty range of Bashan looks, as it were, with envy on the lowly hill of Sion, symbolizing the humble Church, which God has honoured with his presence.

17 The chariots of God are twenty thousand, even thousands of angels : and the Lord is among them, as in the holy place of Sinai.

18 Thou art gone up on high, thou hast led captivity captive, and received gifts for men : yea, even for thine enemies, that the LORD God might dwell among them.

17-18. Christ's entrance in triumph into his sanctuary in Sion, heaven. Cp. Deut. 33. 2. In P.B.V. the angels are pictured driving the triumphal chariots of God. But *R.V.* has only: *even thousands upon thousands.*

As God was in Sinai, so is he now in Sion (the Church).

on high: i.e. to Mount Sion, signifying to heaven at his ascension. Cp. Ps. 7. 7; 47. 5.

R.V. led thy captivity, i.e. thy train of captives, the multitude of the redeemed; cp. Judges 5. 12.

received gifts for men: *R.V. received gifts among men,* i.e. tribute-offerings from subjected nations; cp. Ps. 110. 3. The P.B.V. 'for men' is illustrated by Acts 2. 23: The ascended Lord 'being by the right hand of God exalted, and having received of the Father the promise of the Holy Ghost, he hath poured forth this'; and by S. Paul who in Eph. 4. 8 applies the words of the psalm to our Lord's ascension and to the spiritual gifts of Pentecost. He alters 'received gifts among men' to 'gave gifts unto men.'

R.V. continues: *Yea, among the rebellious also,* a proof that even those who were opposed to his rule have yielded to him.

might dwell among them: the ascension of Christ means the presence of God among men. Note how often the presence is mentioned in this psalm: vv. 2, 8, 16, 17, 18.

19 Praised be the Lord daily :
even the God who helpeth us,
and poureth his benefits upon us.

From this verse onwards the
psalmist turns to the present and
the future; God is still and ever
will be the champion of his
people. Christ the King will
triumph.

*R.V. Blessed be the Lord, who
daily beareth our burden : even
the God who is our salvation.* Cp.
1 S. Pet. 2. 24.

20 He is our God, even the
God of whom cometh salvation :
GOD is the Lord, by whom we
escape death.

*R.V. God is unto us a God of
deliverances: and unto Jehovah
the Lord belong the issues* (i.e.
ways of escape) *from death.*

21 God shall wound the head
of his enemies : and the hairy
scalp of such a one as goeth on
still in his wickedness.

*R.V. But God shall smite
through the head.* The thick
head of hair, the hairy scalp, is a
token of youthful strength and
pride.

22 The Lord hath said, 'I will
bring my people again, as I did
from Basan : mine own will I
bring again, as I did sometime
from the deep of the sea.

I.e. I will deliver Israel (the
Church) as I delivered it of old
from the enemies in Basan (cp.
v. 15), and I will conduct him
safely as of old through the Red
Sea. But *R.V.* reads: *I will bring
again from Bashan, I will bring
them* (i.e. mine enemies, v. 21)
again from the depths of the sea,
i.e. no matter where they may
hide themselves, they will not
escape. Cf. Amos 9. 2 ff.

23 That thy foot may be
dipped in the blood of thine
enemies : and that the tongue of
thy dogs may be red through
the same.'

24 It is well seen, O God,
how thou goest : how thou, my
God and King, goest in the
sanctuary.

God's future victory in Christ
is described in imagery drawn
from the savage excesses of
warfare; as in Ps. 58. 9; cp.
Isa. 63. 2 ff.; Rev. 19. 13.

24-27. A prophetic vision of
the triumphal procession of
Israel's God and King, when his
enemies shall have been overthrown. Again we think of
Christ's victorious ascension and
session. Christ, 'when he had
offered one sacrifice for sins for
ever, sat down on the right hand

of God; from henceforth expecting till his enemies be made the footstool of his feet' (*Heb.* 10. 12, 13).

R.V. goest into the sanctuary.

R.V. in the midst of the damsels, who take part in the procession on either side of the singers and minstrels.

This verse may be regarded as the refrain of the processional hymn.

P.B.V. 'from the ground,' i.e. from the bottom of the heart, with full sincerity. But *R.V. Bless ye God in the congregations, even the Lord, ye that are of the fountain of Israel,* i.e. sprung from the patriarch Israel (ye that have received life from union with Christ); cp. S. John 4. 14.

25 The singers go before, the minstrels follow after : in the midst are the damsels playing with the timbrels.

26 'Give thanks, O Israel, unto God the Lord in the congregations : from the ground of the heart.'

27 There is little Benjamin their ruler, and the princes of Judah their counsel : the princes of Zabulon, and the princes of Nephthali.

The psalmist looks forward to the reunion of the nation (the Church). Benjamin and Judah represent the southern tribes; Zabulon and Naphthali are chosen to represent the northern tribes, probably because they are commended in the Song of Deborah (*Judges* 5. 18), which was evidently before the psalmist as he wrote. Benjamin is called 'little' as being the smallest tribe, and 'their ruler' perhaps because Saul the first king was a Benjamite; cp. 1 Sam. 9. 21.

their counsel: *R.V. and their council.*

28 Thy God hath sent forth strength for thee : stablish the thing, O God, that thou hast wrought in us.

28-35. The completed triumph of the God of Israel : the establishment of Christ's kingdom.

thy . . . thee: Israel is addressed.

in us: *R.V. for us.*

29 For thy temple's sake at Jerusalem : so shall kings bring presents unto thee.

R.V. Because of thy temple at Jerusalem kings shall . . . The re-establishment of the temple, the visible sign of God's presence, will attract the homage and tribute of Gentile princes; cp. Ps. 76. 11 f.

30 When the company of the spear-men, and the multitude of the mighty are scattered abroad among the beasts of the people, so that they humbly bring pieces of silver : and when he hath scattered the people that delight in war;

R.V. Rebuke the wild beast of the reeds (i.e. the crocodile, symbolizing Egypt, cp. Ps. 74. 14 f.), *the multitude of the bulls with the calves of the peoples* (i.e. the princes with the populace of the nations). *R.V.mg. every one submitting himself with pieces of silver.* The Gentiles will offer their riches to God, thus declaring their submission to him; cp. Ps. 72. 10 f.; Rev. 21. 24 ff.

Egypt: cp. Isa. 19. 19, 21.

shall come: i.e. to pay homage and present gifts.

Morians: i.e. the Moors, cp. Ps. 87. 4. *A.R.V. Ethiopia,* i.e. Abyssinia, cp. Acts 8. 31.

31 Then shall the princes come out of Egypt: the Morians' land shall soon stretch out her hands unto God.

32 Sing unto God, ye kingdoms of the earth : O sing praises unto the Lord;

All nations and kingdoms are to glorify God, uniting in the Catholic Church (*Rev.* 7. 9; 11. 15).

33 Who sitteth in the heavens over all from the beginning : lo, he doth send out his voice, yea, and that a mighty voice.

R.V. To him that rideth upon the heavens of heavens, which are of old. Cp. 18. 10; 104. 3. *Sept.* and *Vulg.: who hath ascended over the heaven of heavens to the east,* i.e. Christ, who came as the Dayspring from on high is returned to the throne of his glory; and the mighty voice will be that of Christ at his coming again. Thunder is symbolic of the utterance of God's supreme power.

34 Ascribe ye the power to God over Israel : his worship, and his strength is in the clouds.

R.V. Ascribe ye strength unto God : his excellency is over Israel (the Church), *and his strength is in the skies* (heaven).

35 O God, wonderful art thou in thy holy places : even the God of Israel, he will give strength and power unto his people; blessed be God.

R.V. giveth

EVENING PRAYER

PSALM 69. *Salvum me fac*

In this prayer of a servant of God deeply and undeservedly afflicted, whose sufferings pre-eminently prefigure those of Christ, we may hear Christ's words in his passion, as he suffers for his zeal and does penance for sins not his own. This psalm is quoted more frequently in the N.T. than any part of the O.T. except Ps. 22. It is proper for Good Friday and Passiontide.

SAVE me, O God : for the waters are come in, even unto my soul.

1-12. The desolation of the innocent Sin-bearer.

1-2. A figurative description of a state of deep calamity; cp. vv. 15-16.

2 I stick fast in the deep mire, where no ground is : I am come into deep waters, so that the floods run over me.

3 I am weary of crying; my throat is dry : my sight faileth for waiting so long upon my God.

4 They that hate me without a cause are more than the hairs of my head : they that are mine enemies, and would destroy me guiltless, are mighty.

Words applied by our Lord to his own case: 'This cometh to pass, that the word may be fulfilled that is written in their law, They hated me without a cause' (*S. John* 15. 25). The inoffensiveness of Christ is mentioned also in Ps. 35. 7, 19; 59. 3, 4; 109. 2; 119. 161.

5 I paid them the things that never took : God, thou knowest my simpleness, and my faults are not hid from thee.

A.R.V. I restored that which I took. Probably a proverbial way of saying, 'I am suffering for sins which I did not commit.'

my simpleness: *A.R.V. my foolishness*, i.e. sinfulness; cp. Ps. 38. 5.

my faults: *A.R.V.* *my sins.*
The psalmist, though wrongfully accused in the present instance, is conscious of other transgressions: Christ bears in his heart the sins of the world which he has taken upon himself.

He is suffering for the sake of God (v. 7), and therefore, if he be left unsuccoured, the faithful will be discouraged.

6 Let not them that trust in thee, O Lord GOD of hosts, be ashamed for my cause : let not those that seek thee be confounded through me, O Lord God of Israel.

7 And why? for thy sake have I suffered reproof : shame hath covered my face.

for my cause: i.e. because of me.

for thy sake: i.e. as standing for faith and righteousness according to thy will. Cp. Ps. 44. 22.

A.R.V. for thy sake I have borne reproach:

Cp. Ps. 31. 15, 38. 11; S. John 1. 11; S. Matt. 10. 36. Even my nearest relatives are turned against me.

8 I am become a stranger unto my brethren : even an alien unto my mother's children.

Words which occurred to the disciples when our Lord cleansed the temple (*S. John* 2. 17); taking 'of' as meaning 'for.'

9 For the zeal of thine house hath even eaten me : and the rebukes of them that rebuked thee are fallen upon me.

A.R.V. and the reproaches of them that reproach thee. Words applied by S. Paul to Christ. 'Christ pleased not himself; but, as it is written, The reproaches,' etc. (*Rom.* 15. 3). Cp. S. John 15. 24, 'Now have they both seen and hated both me and my Father.'

10 I wept, and chastened myself with fasting : and that was turned to my reproof.

10-12. The psalmist publicly mourned for the dishonour done to God and his house, but he met with only contempt and ridicule. Herein is the grief of the Sacred Heart of Jesus.

my reproof: *A.R.V. my reproach.*

11 I put on sack-cloth also : and they jested upon me.

12 They that sit in the gate speak against me : and the drunkards make songs upon me.

'the gate' of the city, the general place of concourse.

---

13 But, LORD, I make my prayer unto thee : in an acceptable time.

13-20. Christ's prayer to the Father in his passion.

in an acceptable time: cp. Isa. 49. 8; 2 Cor. 6. 2, 'In an acceptable time have I answered thee, and in a day of salvation have I helped thee.' The acceptable time was the time of the offering of Christ's sacrifice, accepted once for all for the sins of the world.

14 Hear me, O God, in the multitude of thy mercy : even in the truth of thy salvation.

15 Take me out of the mire, that I sink not : O let me be delivered from them that hate me, and out of the deep waters.

15-16. Cp. vv. 1-2.

16 Let not the water-flood drown me, neither let the deep swallow me up : and let not the pit shut her mouth upon me.

17 Hear me, O LORD, for thy loving-kindness is comfortable : turn thee unto me according to the multitude of thy mercies.

18 And hide not thy face from thy servant, for I am in trouble : O haste thee, and hear me.

19 Draw nigh unto my soul, and save it : O deliver me, because of mine enemies.

20 Thou hast known my reproof, my shame, and my dishonour : mine adversaries are all in thy sight.

R.V. Thou knowest my reproach,

21 Thy rebuke hath broken my heart; I am full of heaviness : I looked for some to have pity on me, but there was no man, neither found I any to comfort me.

22 They gave me gall to eat : and when I was thirsty, they gave me vinegar to drink.

23 Let their table be made a snare to take themselves withal : and let the things that should have been for their wealth be unto them an occasion of falling.

21-22. The crisis of the Passion.

A.R.V. Reproach (omit 'Thy') of man, not of God.

heaviness: cp. S. Mark 14. 33.

Cp. Ps. 142. 2 and Isa. 63. 3, 5, 'I looked, and there was none to help, and I wondered that there was none to uphold. . . . I have trodden the wine-press alone.'

Metaphorical language for the infliction of extreme suffering; cp. Jer. 23. 15. S. Matt. 27. 34 describes in these words a literal detail in our Lord's passion.

thirsty: cp. S. John 19. 28, 'Jesus, knowing that all things were now finished, that the scripture might be accomplished, saith, I thirst.'

23-29. The 'wrath of the Lamb.' With the denunciation in these verses, cp. Rev. 16. 16, 'They say to the mountains and to the rocks, Fall on us, and hide us from the face of him that sitteth on the throne, and from the wrath of the Lamb; for the great day of their wrath is come'; and see our Lord's words to the Daughters of Jerusalem (*S. Luke* 23. 30).

23-24 are freely quoted in Rom. 11. 9-10 of unbelieving Israel.

their table: in return for the table which they spread with gall and vinegar for me (v. 22).

wealth: i.e. well-being. Such is the lot of God's opponents; their good things received in a wrong spirit, and used wrongfully, induce transgression.

24 Let their eyes be blinded, that they see not : and ever bow thou down their backs.

25 Pour out thine indignation upon them : and let the wrathful displeasure take hold of them.

26 Let their habitation be void : and no man to dwell in their tents.

27 For they persecute him whom thou hast smitten : and they talk how they may vex them whom thou hast wounded.

28 Let them fall from one wickedness to another : and not come into thy righteousness.

29 Let them be wiped out of the book of the living : and not be written among the righteous.

Cp. S. Matt. 13. 13-16.

Quoted in Acts 1. 20 as forecasting the doom of Judas.

Cp. Isa. 53. 4, 5.

The doom of the impenitent.

I.e. may they die and thus cease to be enrolled as citizens of Israel, the righteous nation; cp. Ezek. 13. 9, 'neither shall they be written in the writing (*R.V.mg. register*) of the house of Israel.' *R.V.* has *blotted out of the book of life* which may suggest to us 'the Lamb's book of life' (*Exod.* 32. 32; *Phil.* 4. 3; *Rev.* 3. 5, 8, etc.).

30 As for me, when I am poor and in heaviness : thy help, O God, shall lift me up.

31 I will praise the Name of God with a song : and magnify it with thanksgiving.

32 This also shall please the LORD : better than a bullock that hath horns and hoofs.

33 The humble shall consider this, and be glad : seek ye after God, and your soul shall live.

30-37. Thanksgiving.

Cp. Ps. 50. 13, 14.
I.e. of full age, having horns, and clean, parting the hoofs (*Lev.* 11. 3).

R.V. ye that seek after God, let your heart live; cp. Ps. 22. 26.

34 For the LORD heareth the poor : and despiseth not his prisoners.

The 'poor' may remind us especially of Christ in his poverty; and the 'prisoners' of the Israelites in exile, or of those whom God has redeemed from the captivity of sin into his Church, or of the departed, the 'prisoners of hope' (*Zech.* 9. 12; 1 *S. Pet.* 3. 19).

35 Let heaven and earth praise him : the sea, and all that moveth therein.

36 For God will save Sion, and build the cities of Judah : that men may dwell there, and have it in possession.

37 The posterity also of his servants shall inherit it : and they that love his Name shall dwell therein.

The Church of the redeemed throughout the generations, in peace and security.

PSALM 70. *Deus in adjutorium*

A cry for help against malicious enemies. Christ is mystically the speaker. This psalm is a repetition, with a few variations, of Ps. 40. 16-21.

HASTE thee, O God, to deliver me : make haste to help me, O LORD.

This verse is more often recited in the Western Church than any other part of the O.T. The versicle and response, 'O God, make speed to save me. O Lord, make haste to help me' which begin the Offices of each of the canonical hours, and are retained in the plural in the P.B. Offices, are taken from this verse. The Church has thus provided that, protected by the shield of divine assistance, we may resist the enemy who opposes us when we are engaging in divine service.

2 Let them be ashamed and confounded that seek after my soul : let them be turned backward and put to confusion that wish me evil.

3 Let them for their reward be soon brought to shame : that cry over me, 'There, there.'

4 But let all those that seek thee be joyful and glad in thee : and let all such as delight in thy salvation say alway, 'The Lord be praised.'

5 As for me, I am poor and in misery : haste thee unto me, O God.

6 Thou art my helper, and my redeemer : O LORD, make no long tarrying.

A.R.V. that say, 'Aha, aha,' exulting in my misfortune.

Ps. 40. 20 ends: 'but the Lord careth for me.'
A.R.V. and my deliverer:

THE FOURTEENTH DAY

MORNING PRAYER

PSALM 71. *In te, Domine, speravi*

A prayer for aid in renewed trouble by one (perhaps a personification of Israel), who in a long life has known great suffering but has been upheld by faith in God. This psalm follows closely in thought upon Ps. 70, with more outspoken expression of trust in God. The voice of the Church is heard rather than that of Christ personally; also the words are directly applicable to individual Christians, especially the elderly: hence the psalm is appointed in the B.C.P. to be used in the Visitation of the Sick.

IN thee, O LORD, have I put my trust; let me never be put to confusion : but rid me, and deliver me, in thy righteousness; incline thine ear unto me, and save me.

1-2 are almost identical with Ps. 31. 1-4; cp. also Ps. 18. 1.

Cp. *Te Deum*: 'O LORD, in thee have I trusted: let me never be confounded.' Cp. also Isa. 50. 6.

rid me: i.e. set me free, rescue. Cp. Ps. 18. 49.

in thy righteousness : the righteous God is pledged to deliver his faithful servant.

Show thyself to be that which I know thou art.

2 Be thou my strong hold, whereunto I may alway resort : thou hast promised to help me, for thou art my house of defence, and my castle.

3 Deliver me, O my God, out of the hand of the ungodly : out of the hand of the unrighteous and cruel man.

4 For thou, O Lord GOD, art the thing that I long for : thou art my hope, even from my youth.

my hope: 'Christ Jesus our hope' (1 *Tim.* 1. 11; *Col.* 1. 27).

5 Through thee have I been holden up ever since I was born : thou art he that took me out of my mother's womb; my praise shall be always of thee.

Cp. Ps. 22. 10.

6 I am become as it were a monster unto many : but my sure trust is in thee.

a monster: *A.R.V. a wonder*, as having been signally preserved through many dangers. 'Monster' formerly meant 'prodigy.' Cp. 1 Cor. 4. 9, 'a spectacle unto men.'

7 O let my mouth be filled with thy praise : that I may sing of thy glory and honour all the day long.

all the day: cp. v. 22.

8 Cast me not away in the time of age : forsake me not when my strength faileth me.

9 For mine enemies speak against me, and they that lay wait for my soul take their counsel together saying: 'God hath forsaken him : persecute him, and take him, for there is none to deliver him.'

R.V. Pursue and take him,

10 Go not far from me, O God : my God, haste thee to help me.

Ps. 70. 1, 6.

11 Let them be confounded and perish that are against my soul : let them be covered with shame and dishonour that seek to do me evil.

Ps. 70. 4.

12 As for me, I will patiently abide alway : and will praise thee more and more.

13 My mouth shall daily speak of thy righteousness and salvation : for I know no end thereof.

14 I will go forth in the strength of the Lord GOD : and will make mention of thy righteousness only.

15 Thou, O God, hast taught me from my youth up until now : therefore will I tell of thy wondrous works.

16 Forsake me not, O God, in mine old age, when I am gray-headed : until I have shewed thy strength unto this generation, and thy power to all them that are yet for to come.

17 Thy righteousness, O God, is very high : and great things are they that thou hast done; O God, who is like unto thee?

18 O what great troubles and adversities hast thou shewed me, and yet didst thou turn and refresh me : yea, and broughtest me from the deep of the earth again.

19 Thou hast brought me to great honour : and comforted me on every side.

20 Therefore will I praise thee and thy faithfulness, O God, playing upon an instrument of music : unto thee will I sing upon the harp, O thou Holy One of Israel.

Cp. v. 22.

R.V. I will come with the mighty acts of the Lord God: bringing them as the subjects of my praises.

R.V. and hitherto have I declared thy wondrous works.

R.V. unto the next . . .
In ten verses of this psalm there is mention of proclaiming the righteousness of God.

broughtest me: as Christ was brought from hell at his resurrection. But R.V. in this verse has a change of 'me' to 'us.' *Thou, which hast shewed us many and sore troubles, shalt quicken us again, and shalt bring us up again from the depths of the earth.* The psalmist enlarges his view to take in the calamities of the nation. 'The deep of the earth' is figurative for a state of extreme calamity; cp. Ps. 130. 1.

R.V. Increase thou my greatness, and turn again, and comfort me.

20-22. The prayer is heard, and the Church is triumphant.

thou Holy One of Israel: this title is found again in the Psalter only in 78. 41 and 89. 19. It frequently occurs in Isaiah.

21 My lips will be fain when I sing unto thee : and so will my soul whom thou hast delivered.

22 My tongue also shall talk of thy righteousness all the day long : for they are confounded and brought unto shame that seek to do me evil.

fain: i.e. glad. *A.R.V. My lips shall greatly rejoice . . . A.R.V. hast redeemed.*

Cp. v. 7. Perhaps, all the long day of eternity.
Cp. v. 11 and Ps. 70. 2.

PSALM 72. *Deus, judicium*

The reign of the ideal King of Israel, righteous, peaceful, prosperous, beneficent: to be realized only in the kingdom of Christ. The psalm is traditionally ascribed to Solomon. It is proper on Epiphany and in the celebration of Christ as King. Cp. Isa. 9. 6 ff., 'His name shall be called the Prince of Peace. Of the increase of his government and of peace there shall be no end, upon the throne of David, and upon his kingdom, to establish it, and to uphold it with judgement and with righteousness from henceforth even for ever.'

GIVE the king thy judgements, O God : and thy righteousness unto the king's son.

1-2. Cp. 1 Chron. 22. 12, 'The LORD give thee discretion and understanding, and give thee charge concerning Israel, that so thou mayest keep the law of the LORD thy God.'

The 'king's son' is the same person as the 'king': he is descended from a king. Similarly Christ is both King and King's Son. He is King as eternal God; and King's Son in that his Godhead is derived from the Father. Also he is king's Son in that by his manhood he is descended from David.

Cp. S. John 5. 22, 'The Father hath committed all judgement unto the Son.'

2 Then shall he judge thy people according unto right : and defend the poor.

3 The mountains also shall bring peace : and the little hills righteousness unto the people.

The mountains and hills as the marked features of the scenery of Palestine are put for the whole land.

peace . . . righteousness: cp. Ps. 85. 10, 'Righteousness and peace have kissed each other.'

N

4 He shall keep the simple folk by their right : defend the children of the poor, and punish the wrong-doer.

5 They shall fear thee, as long as the sun and moon endureth : from one generation to another.

A.R.V. He shall judge the poor of the people, he shall save the children of the needy, and shall break in pieces the oppressor.

Either God is addressed, 'They, the poor people, shall fear thee because of the righteous government of thy vicegerent the King-Messiah'; or the King himself is addressed, in the same sense as v. 17.

He: i.e. the King.

    into a fleece of wool: the reference is to Gideon's fleece (*Judges* 6. 37). *A.R.V. upon the mown grass.* Cp. Deut. 33. 2. In either rendering the image is of gentle bountifulness. Cp. Isa. 65. 10. Early commentators apply it to the silence and secrecy of the coming of Christ into the world at his Incarnation, the fleece denoting the Blessed Virgin. Cp. the antiphon, 'When thou wast born of a Virgin ineffably, then were the Scriptures fulfilled; as the dew on the fleece didst thou descend to save mankind.'

6 He shall come down like the rain into a fleece of wool : even as the drops that water the earth.

7 In his time shall the righteous flourish : yea, and abundance of peace, so long as the moon endureth.

8 His dominion shall be also from the one sea to the other : and from the flood unto the world's end.

the flood: *R.V. the River*, i.e. Euphrates. This verse is a poetical version of Exod. 23. 31: 'I will set thy border from the Red Sea even unto the sea of the Philistines [the Mediterranean] and from the wilderness unto the River.' Cp. Ps. 80. 11, 89. 26; Zech. 9. 10; Ecclus. 44. 21. The bounds of Solomon's kingdom denote the spread of Christ's kingdom throughout the world.

9 They that dwell in the wilderness shall kneel before him : his enemies shall lick the dust.

10 The kings of Tharsis and of the isles shall give presents : the kings of Arabia and Saba shall bring gifts.

Cp. Isa. 60. 14.

Tharsis: i.e. Tartessus in Spain (1 *Kings* 10. 1). The 'isles': i.e. in the Mediterranean. Cp. Isa. 60. 9, 'the isles shall wait for thee, the ships of Tarshish first.' Arabia: *A.R.V. Sheba*, which is in Arabia. Saba: i.e. Meroe in Ethiopia. Cp. Isa. 43. 3; 45. 14.

We apply these words to the universality of Christ's kingdom typified first in the adoration of the Magi. Cp. also Rev. 7. 9.

11 All kings shall fall down before him : all nations shall do him service.

12 For he shall deliver the poor when he crieth : the needy also, and him that hath no helper.

13 He shall be favourable to the simple and needy : and shall preserve the souls of the poor.

14 He shall deliver their souls from falsehood and wrong : and dear shall their blood be in his sight.

R.V. He shall redeem their soul from oppression and violence:
dear: i.e. as *A.R.V. precious*. Cp. Ps. 116. 13, 'right dear in the sight of the LORD is the death of his saints.'

15 He shall live, and unto him shall be given of the gold of Arabia : prayer shall be made ever unto him, and daily shall he be praised.

R.V. And they shall live, i.e. the 'poor' of v. 14, who being preserved and enriched by the king's bounty offer him costly gifts.
Arabia: *A.R.V. Sheba*.
R.V. and men shall pray for him continually. Prayer is made for Christ when it is made for the Church his Body and for his cause on earth.

16 There shall be an heap of corn in the earth, high upon the hills : his fruit shall shake like Libanus, and shall be green in the city like grass upon the earth.

high upon the hills: so great will be the fertility of the land that the cornfields will reach even to the mountain-tops, and will be like the tree-clad slopes of Lebanon as they sway before the wind.

his fruit: i.e. its fruit.

A.R.V. and they of the city shall flourish like grass of the earth.

Cp. S. Luke 1. 31, 'Thou shalt call his name Jesus. He shall be great . . . he shall reign over the house of Jacob for ever; and of his kingdom there shall be no end.' Gen. 22. 18, 'And in thy seed shall all the nations of the earth be blessed.'

17 His Name shall endure for ever; his Name shall remain under the sun among the posterities : which shall be blessed through him; and all the heathen shall praise him.

18 Blessed be the LORD God, even the God of Israel : which only doeth wondrous things.

18-19. This doxology marks the conclusion of the second book of the Psalter. Each book so ends.

19 And blessed be the Name of his Majesty for ever : and all the earth shall be filled with his Majesty. Amen, Amen.

BOOK THREE

EVENING PRAYER

PSALM 73. *Quam bonus Israel!*

The difficulties of a righteous soul perplexed by the prosperity of the wicked. The psalmist, amid temptations to despair, is upheld by steadfast trust in God and confident hope of future glory with him.

TRULY God is loving unto Israel: even unto such as are of a clean heart.

1–11. The problem stated.

Israel: i.e. each 'Israelite indeed, in whom is no guile' (*S. John* 1. 47), as the next words indicate.

of a clean heart: *R.V. pure in heart.* Cp. Ps. 24. 4; S. Matt. 5. 8.

2 Nevertheless, my feet were almost gone : my treadings had well-nigh slipt.

3 And why? I was grieved at the wicked : I do also see the ungodly in such prosperity.

4 For they are in no peril of death : but are lusty and strong.

R.V. envious at the arrogant, when I saw . . .
A.R.V. For there are no bands (pangs, *mg.*) *in their death*: i.e. their death is easy, without pains, cp. Job 21. 13.

5 They come in no misfortune like other folk : neither are they plagued like other men.

6 And this is the cause that they are so holden with pride : and overwhelmed with cruelty.

7 Their eyes swell with fatness : and they do even what they lust.

R.V. Therefore pride is as a chain about their neck : violence covereth them as a garment.

lust: i.e. desire.
A.R.V. they have more than heart could wish. R.V. mg. the imaginations of their heart overflow, in arrogant words, as in the verses following.

8 They corrupt other, and speak of wicked blasphemy : their talking is against the most High.

9 For they stretch forth their mouth unto the heaven : and their tongue goeth through the world.

other: i.e. others.

R.V. They scoff, and in wickedness utter oppression: they speak loftily. Cp. 2 S. Pet. 2. 18.

I.e. speaking blasphemously, they rail against everything in heaven and on earth. But *R.V.* has: *They have set their mouth in the heavens,* i.e. they speak from heaven, as it were, with the authority of God. Cp. 2 Thess. 2. 4.

10 Therefore fall the people unto them : and thereout suck they no small advantage.

I.e. the wicked make profit of the quislings that flock to them. *R.V.mg. waters of a full cup are drained by them.* The quislings drink deep of the cup of sinful pleasures.

11 'Tush,' say they, 'how should God perceive it : is there knowledge in the most High?'

12 Lo, these are the ungodly, these prosper in the world, and these have riches in possession : and I said, 'Then have I cleansed my heart in vain, and washed mine hands in innocency.'

Tush: cp. Ps. 10. 6, 12, 14.

Cp. Mal. 3. 14.
Metaphor drawn from the ceremonial purifications of the Jewish Law; cp. Ps. 26. 6.

13 All the day long have I been punished : and chastened every morning.

14 Yea, and I had almost said even as they : but lo, then I would have condemned the generation of thy children.

I, unlike the wicked.

I almost assented to the arrogant assertions of the wicked, I almost took my side against God's righteous ones.

15 Then thought I to understand this : but it was too hard for me,

15–27. He finds two solutions of his problem: (1) the wicked shall not prosper for ever; the balance will eventually be reversed, 17–19; (2) the righteous have spiritual compensations in abundance; 22–25.

16 Until I went into the sanctuary of God : then understood I the end of these men;

the sanctuary: i.e. the Temple, but the phrase admits of many further applications. The main sense is that the soul's perplexities can be solved only by seeking the presence of God.

17 Namely, how thou dost set them in slippery places : and casteth them down, and destroyest them.

18 O how suddenly do they consume : perish, and come to a fearful end!

19 Yea, even like as a dream when one awaketh : so shalt thou make their image to vanish out of the city.

A.R.V. So, O Lord, when thou awakest: thou shalt despise their image, i.e. regard their existence as the mere vision of a dream.

20 Thus my heart was grieved : and it went even through my reins.

reins: i.e. kidneys, which were regarded as the seat of the emotions.

21 So foolish was I, and ignorant : even as it were a beast before thee.

22 Nevertheless, I am always by thee : for thou hast holden me by my right hand.

Cp. S. Luke 15. 31, 'Son, thou art ever with me.'

by my right hand: i.e. leading me as I walk.

23 Thou shalt guide me with thy counsel : and after that receive me with glory.

24 Whom have I in heaven but thee : and there is none upon earth that I desire in comparison of thee.

25 My flesh and my heart faileth': but God is the strength of my heart, and my portion for ever.

26 For lo, they that forsake thee shall perish : thou hast destroyed all them that commit fornication against thee.

Anticipation of a glorious hereafter.

Cp. Ps. 16. 2 R.V.; Phil. 3. 8.

fornication: i.e. by unfaithfulness to Jehovah. Israel is the spouse of God (*Isa.* 54. 5, 6).

27 But it is good for me to hold me fast by God, to put my trust in the Lord GOD : and to speak of all thy works in the gates of the daughter of Sion.

the gates: the public meeting-places in Jerusalem; in the congregations of the Church. The psalm, however, rightly ends at 'works': the rest is interpolated from Ps. 9. 14.

PSALM 74. *Ut quid, Deus?*

A lamentation for the desolation of the land and profanation of the sanctuary, with a cry to God for help. An intercession for the Church ever militant and persecuted. See also Ps. 44. 10 ff.; 79; 80, etc.

O GOD, wherefore art thou absent from us so long: why is thy wrath so hot against the sheep of thy pasture?

absent: by apparent non-intervention; cp. S. John 6. 17.

this phrase here for the first time in the Psalter; cp. Ps. 79. 13, 95. 7, 100. 3; Jer. 23. 1; Ezek. 34. 31.

2 O think upon thy congregation: whom thou hast purchased, and redeemed of old.

purchased and redeemed: from Egyptian bondage; cp. Exod. 15. 13, 16. Cp. Acts 20. 28, 'The Church of God, which he hath purchased with his own blood.'

3 Think upon the tribe of thine inheritance : and mount Sion, wherein thou hast dwelt.

All Israel, as distinguished from other nations, is reckoned as one 'tribe.'

wherein: cp. Ps. 9. 11.

4 Lift up thy feet, that thou mayest utterly destroy every enemy : which hath done evil in thy sanctuary.

Lift up thy feet: i.e. come with speed.

R.V. Lift up thy feet unto the perpetual ruins; all the evil that the enemy hath done in the sanctuary.

R.V. have roared . . .

5 Thine adversaries roar in the midst of thy congregations : and set up their banners for tokens.

banners: military standards or pagan emblems triumphantly carried into the Temple.

6 He that hewed timber afore out of the thick trees : was known to bring it to an excellent work.

The excellent wood-work of the artificers of the Temple, v. 6, is now wantonly destroyed, v. 7. But *R.V.* has: *They seemed as men that lifted up axes upon a thicket of trees.* In the havoc the enemy wrought in the Temple, they may be compared to wood-men hewing down a plantation of trees.

7 But now they break down all the carved work thereof : with axes and hammers.

R.V. And . . .

8 They have set fire upon thy holy places : and have defiled the dwelling-place of thy Name, even unto the ground.

R.V. set thy sanctuary on fire:

Cp. Ps. 26. 8.

9 Yea, they said in their hearts, 'Let us make havoc of them altogether': thus have they burnt up all the houses of God in the land.

houses: *A.R.V. synagogues,* places of worship other than the Temple.

10 We see not our tokens, there is not one prophet more : no, not one is there among us, that understandeth any more.

our tokens: i.e. the outward evidences of our religion, such as sabbath and sacrifice. The tokens of the enemy, v. 5, only are to be seen.

A.R.V. that knoweth how long this persecution and desolation will continue.

11 O God, how long shall the adversary do this dishonour : how long shall the enemy blaspheme thy Name, for ever?

12 Why withdrawest thou thy hand : why pluckest thou not thy right hand out of thy bosom to consume the enemy?

13 For God is my King of old : the help that is done upon earth he doeth it himself.

An act of faith.

For: *R.V. Yet*, notwithstanding his previous non-interven-tion, *God is my King of old: working salvation in the midst of the earth*, words which have been applied to the Incarnation of the Son of God in Mary's womb, to his death in Jerusalem, to his descent into Hades, etc.

14 Thou didst divide the sea through thy power : thou brakest the heads of the dragons in the waters.

God is mighty, and has shewed himself mighty in his former deliverance of his people, 14–16, and in the powers of nature, 17–18.

the sea: i.e. the Red Sea.

dragons: *R.V.mg. sea-monsters.* This word and 'Leviathan' in v. 15 signify the crocodile and symbolize Egypt, and by application all God's enemies. Cp. Job 41. 1, R.V.mg.; Ps. 68. 30; Isa. 27. 1.

15 Thou smotest the heads of Leviathan in pieces : and gavest him to be meat for the people in the wilderness.

The corpses of the Egyptians cast up on the shore of the Red Sea (*Exod.* 14. 30), became food for the wild beasts which are called *the people inhabiting the wilderness, A.R.V.* Cp. Isa. 23. 13. Or the 'people' may denote savage tribes, or the Ethiopians, *Vulg.* It does not mean the Israelites.

16 Thou broughtest out fountains and waters out of the hard rocks : thou driedst up mighty waters.

At Horeb (*Exod.* 17. 6), and at Kadesh (*Num.* 20. 6).

waters: of the Red Sea and the river Jordan.

17 The day is thine, and the night is thine : thou hast prepared the light and the sun.

18 Thou hast set all the borders of the earth : thou hast made summer and winter.

Thou hast fixed the boundaries of the nations; cp. Acts 17. 26.

19 Remember this, O LORD, how the enemy hath rebuked : and how the foolish people hath blasphemed thy Name.

A.R.V. hath reproached:
The foolish people are the heathen oppressors of Israel, senseless in their antagonism to God; cp. v. 23.

203

20 O deliver not the soul of thy turtle-dove unto the multitudes of the enemies : and forget not the congregations of the poor for ever.

The 'turtle-dove' and the 'poor' denote Israel, the beloved of God (*Cant.* 2. 14), and therefore the Church.

21 Look upon the covenant : for all the earth is full of darkness, and cruel habitations.

A.R.V. Have respect unto the covenant, remember the favour which thou hast promised to Israel.

A.R.V. the oppressed . . .

22 O let not the simple go away ashamed : but let the poor and needy give praise unto thy Name.

ashamed: because they received no answer to their prayer.

23 Arise, O God, maintain thine own cause : remember how the foolish man blasphemeth thee daily.

foolish man: i.e. the heathen oppressors, as in v. 19.

24 Forget not the voice of thine enemies : the presumption of them that hate thee increaseth ever more and more.

A.R.V. the tumult of those that rise up against thee ascendeth continually.

THE FIFTEENTH DAY

MORNING PRAYER

PSALM 75. *Confitebimur tibi*

God's righteous government of the world. A deliverance, such as that prayed for in Ps. 74, has come to pass. This psalm is a song of praise called forth by the manifestation of God's power and goodness delivering his people, perhaps the overthrow of Sennacherib (2 *Kings* 19. 35 f.). The passion and victory and judgement of Christ are foreshadowed.

UNTO thee, O God, do we give thanks : yea, unto thee do we give thanks.
2 Thy Name also is so nigh : and that do thy wondrous works declare.

God's Name means God himself as he causes himself to be known by mankind, his nature and qualities; cp. Exod. 34. 5-7; Ps. 76. 1.

God's nearness to his people has been manifested by his recent mercies vouchsafed to them. Cp. Ps. 34. 18, 'The Lord is nigh unto them that are of a contrite heart'; 145. 18, 'The Lord is nigh unto all them that call upon him.'

wondrous works: especially the resurrection and ascension of Christ.

3–6. Christ speaks.

3 'When I receive the congregation : I shall judge according unto right.

I.e., When I have gathered together the inhabitants of the earth to listen to my judgement; cp. Ps. 7. 7, 50. 5; Rev. 20. 12. But *R.V.* has: *When I shall find the set time*, i.e. the time ripe for my interposition.

4 The earth is weak, and all the inhabiters thereof : I bear up the pillars of it.

weak: *A.R.V. dissolved*, and undone in the judgement.

A.R.V. I have set up . . .

pillars: cp. 1 Sam. 2. 8, 'The pillars of the earth are the LORD's.' Some have applied the word to the Saints.

5 I said unto the fools, "Deal not so madly" : and to the ungodly, "Set not up your horn on high."

R.V. '*I said unto the arrogant, "Deal not arrogantly"* ': i.e. the arrogant are those who oppose God; cp. Ps. 14. 1; 74. 19; etc.

A.R.V. '*Lift not up the horn.*' The horn is the emblem of power, here with the additional sense of arrogancy. The metaphor is taken from animals who use their horns as weapons of offence; cp. Zech. 1. 21.

6 Set not up your horn on high : and speak not with a stiff neck.'

A.R.V. Lift not up . . .

I.e. speak not stubbornly; cp. Deut. 31. 27, 'I know thy rebellion and thy stiff neck.'

7–12. The psalmist comments upon Christ's words.

7 For promotion cometh neither from the east, nor from the west : nor yet from the south.

promotion: *R.V. lifting up*, i.e. exaltation, deliverance; cp. Gen. 40. 13; Ps. 3. 3; Jer. 52. 31. (The north is not mentioned, perhaps because the Assyrians came from the north. But perhaps the word rendered 'promotion' should be rendered 'mountains,' meaning those north of Palestine.) In any case, the sense is, there is no escape anywhere from the immanent judgement of God.

8 And why? God is the judge: he putteth down one, and setteth up another.

setteth: *R.V. lifteth.* Cp. Hannah's words (1 *Sam.* 2. 7) and S. Mary's, 'He hath put down the mighty from their seats: and hath exalted the humble and meek.'

9 For in the hand of the LORD there is a cup, and the wine is red : it is full mixed, and he poureth out of the same.

Cp. Ps. 60. 3, 'Thou hast given us a drink of deadly wine.' The cup is the cup of the LORD's wrath; cp. Isa. 51. 17, 'Jerusalem, which has drunk at the hand of the LORD the cup of his fury'; Rev. 14. 10, 'He shall drink of the wine of the wrath of God, which is prepared unmixed in the cup of his anger.' In the work of redemption Christ himself was first to drink it: cp. S. John 18. 11, 'The cup which my Father hath given me, shall I not drink it?' and S. Mark 10. 38, 'Are ye able to drink of the cup that I drink of?'

mixed: i.e. with spices to add to its bitterness.

red: *R.V. foameth.*

10 As for the dregs thereof : all the ungodly of the earth shall drink them, and suck them out.
11 But I will talk of the God of Jacob : and praise him for ever.
12 All the horns of the ungodly also will I break : and the horns of the righteous shall be exalted.

will I break: The psalmist, representing Israel the agent of God's judgement, prophesies the ultimate triumph of righteousness, echoing Christ's words, v. 5.

exalted: *R.V. lifted up.*

PSALM 76.   *Notus in Judaea*

No power can withstand the might of God. This psalm, a companion to the foregoing, is a hymn of thanksgiving for some national deliverance.

IN Jewry is God known : his Name is great in Israel.

A.R.V. In Judah. Judah and Israel denote the whole nation.

known: cp. Ps. 75. 2.

2 At Salem is his tabernacle : and his dwelling in Sion.

Cp. Ps. 74. 2. Salem, i.e. Jerusalem, and Sion its citadel: they are applied to heaven and to the Church.

tabernacle: *R.V.mg. covert*; cp. v. 4.

3 There brake he the arrows and the bow : the shield, the sword, and the battle.

There: marks out Jerusalem as the place where the victory was gained. So too the victory of the Son of God.

4 Thou art of more honour and might : than the hills of the robbers.

God's power has prevailed over the Assyrians, or other foes, who were like robbers issuing from mountain strongholds. But *R.V.* has: *Glorious art thou and excellent, from the mountains of prey,* i.e. God is compared to a lion going forth to destroy from his lair in Mount Sion; cp. v. 2; Isa. 14. 25.

5 The proud are robbed, they have slept their sleep : and all the men whose hands were mighty have found nothing.

A.R.V. The stouthearted enemies *are spoiled.* They have slept their sleep of death; cp. Jer. 51. 39.

A.R.V. none of the men of might have found their hands, the hands which they raised against Jerusalem are paralysed (*Isa.* 10. 10–14, 32).

6 At thy rebuke, O God of Jacob : both the chariot and horse are fallen.

A.R.V. are cast into a dead sleep.

7 Thou, even thou art to be feared : and who may stand in thy sight when thou art angry?

Cp. Ps. 2. 2; 130. 3.

8 Thou didst cause thy judgement to be heard from heaven: the earth trembled, and was still,

9 When God arose to judgement : and to help all the meek upon earth.

The applicability of 7–10 to Christ is obvious.

10 The fierceness of man shall turn to thy praise : and the fierceness of them shalt thou refrain.

R.V. The wrath of man shall praise thee: the residue of wrath shalt thou gird upon thee as an ornament. The thought is that God, far from being injured by man's wrath against him, will utilize that wrath to the utmost for his own honour; cp. Exod. 9. 16.

refrain: i.e. restrain, bridle.

11 Promise unto the LORD your God, and keep it, all ye that are round about him : bring presents unto him that ought to be feared.

round about him: i.e. not Israel alone, but also the neighbouring nations, shall do homage to God; cp. Ps. 89. 7.

12 He shall refrain the spirit of princes : and is wonderful among the kings of the earth.

PSALM 77. *Voce mea ad Dominum*

In a time of great national affliction, probably the Exile, the psalmist finds comfort by calling to mind God's dealings with Israel in the past, especially in the deliverance from Egypt. The psalm is a meditation, divided into Distress, Questioning, Answer, Remembrance; and is suitable to Christians in their times of public or private trouble.

I WILL cry unto God with my voice : even unto God will I cry with my voice, and he shall hearken unto me.

2 In the time of my trouble I sought the Lord : my sore ran, and ceased not in the nightseason; my soul refused comfort.

1–4. Distress.
The distress has not weakened faith.

Figurative for 'my distress found no relief.' *R.V.: my hand was stretched out* (in prayer) *in the night, and slacked not.*' For prayer in the night-time, cp. Ps. 42. 8; 63. 7.

3 When I am in heaviness, I will think upon God : when my heart is vexed, I will complain.

R.V. I remember God, and am disquieted: I complain, and my spirit is overwhelmed. I.e. even in prayer I find no relief.

4 Thou holdest mine eyes waking : I am so feeble that I cannot speak.

I.e. thou withholdest sleep from mine eyes.

feeble: *A.R.V. troubled.*

5 I have considered the days of old : and the years that are past.

5–9. Questioning.

6 I call to remembrance my song : and in the night I commune with mine own heart, and search out my spirits.

my song : which I sang in my former days of happiness.

A.R.V. and my spirit made diligent search.

Cp. Ps. 74. 1.

7 Will the Lord absent himself for ever : and will he be no more intreated?

intreated: i.e. moved by entreaties.

8 Is his mercy clean gone for ever : and is his promise come utterly to an end for evermore?

9 Hath God forgotten to be gracious : and will he shut up his kindness in displeasure?

will: *A.R.V. hath.*

10 And I said, 'It is mine own infirmity : but I will remember the years of the right hand of the most Highest.

10–12. The answer.

It is only my weakness that tempts me to lose faith in God and hinders my prayer. I will remember the years in the past when God's people were delivered by his right hand and stretched out arm. Cp. Deut. 4. 34; Ps. 17. 7; 20. 6, 'the wholesome strength of his right hand'; 74. 12.

As the LORD does not change, the recollection of his former mighty deliverance gives good hope in the present distress.

11 I remember the works of the LORD : and call to mind thy wonders of old time.

12 I will think also of all thy works : and my talking shall be of thy doings.'

13 Thy way, O God, is holy : who is so great a God as our God?

13–20. Remembrance.

A.R.V. Thy way, O God, is in the sanctuary: cp. Ps. 68. 24.

14 Thou art the God that doeth wonders : and hast declared thy power among the people.

15 Thou hast mightily delivered thy people : even the sons of Jacob and Joseph.

R.V. the peoples.

A.R.V. with thine arm redeemed thy people.

Joseph may stand here as representing the northern kingdom, as the father of Ephraim and Manasseh; or because Joseph is prominent in the history of Israel in Egypt.

16 The waters saw thee, O God, the waters saw thee, and were afraid : the depths also were troubled.

16–18 give a picture, developed from Exod. 14. 24 f., of the thunder-storm and earthquake which attended the passage of the Red Sea.

17 The clouds poured out waters, the air thundered : and thine arrows went abroad.

18 The voice of thy thunder was heard round about : the lightnings shone upon the ground; the earth was moved, and shook withal.

Cp. Ps. 18. 14.

We are reminded of a common application of vv. 16 ff. to God's work done through his apostles and evangelists by the hymn: 'Like clouds are they borne to do thy great will, And swift as the winds about the world go; All full of thy Godhead, while earth lieth still, They thunder, they lighten, the waters o'erflow.'

19 Thy way is in the sea, and thy paths in the great waters : and thy foot-steps are not known.

are: *R.V. were.* The waters flowed back, and no trace was left of God's route by which he had led his people.

20 Thou leddest thy people like sheep : by the hand of Moses and Aaron.

and perfectly by the hand of Christ, who is both our Lawgiver and our High-priest.

O

EVENING PRAYER

PSALM 78.   *Attendite, popule*

The past history of Israel, its record of continual rebellion against God and ingratitude for his mercies. Emphasis is laid upon the backsliding of Ephraim, representing the northern kingdom, as compared with Judah, the southern. The meditation is a warning to the generation for whom it was composed, and to all subsequent generations, whether of Jews or Christians: for, while God's goodness changes not, neither alas does the frailty and self-seeking of mankind. The history of Israel has been paralleled by that of the Church in this respect; cp. v. 2, note.

HEAR my law, O my people : incline your ears unto the words of my mouth.

'law' here means, as in R. V. mg. *teaching*.

2 I will open my mouth in a parable : I will declare hard sentences of old.

A.R.V. I will utter dark sayings of old. By 'parable' and 'dark sayings' is meant the history of Israel regarded as containing veiled lessons for posterity. What the psalmist-prophet says here about his mode of teaching is transferred by S. Matthew (13. 34 f.) to the method of Christ the great Prophet.

3 Which we have heard and known : and such as our fathers have told us;

4 That we should not hide them from the children of the generations to come : but to shew the honour of the LORD, his mighty and wonderful works which he hath done.

5 He made a covenant with Jacob : and gave Israel a law : which he commanded our forefathers to teach their children;

5–8. Cp. Deut. 4. 9; 6. 20 ff.

6 That their posterity might know it : and the children which were yet unborn;

7 To the intent that when they came up : they might shew their children the same;

8 That they might put their trust in God : and not to forget the works of God, but to keep his commandments;

A.R.V. set their hope in God: Hope trusts in God, Faith discerns the working of God, and Charity obeys God.

9 And not to be as their fore-fathers, a faithless and stubborn generation : a generation that set not their heart aright, and whose spirit cleaveth not steadfastly unto God;

10 Like as the children of Ephraim : who being harnessed, and carrying bows, turned themselves back in the day of battle.

A.R.V. was not steadfast with God.

'harnessed,' etc.: having both defensive armour and offensive weapons. The language is figurative. Ephraim though well equipped and pledged to God's service proved faithless and treacherous. Ephraim is singled out, though the reproach belongs to all Israel, v. 9, probably to point forward to its future rejection, v. 68.

11 They kept not the covenant of God : and would not walk in his law;

12 But forgat what he had done : and the wonderful works that he had shewed for them.

13 Marvellous things did he in the sight of our forefathers : in the land of Egypt : even in the field of Zoan.

A.R.V. their fathers,

Zoan, or (as in Sept.) Tanis, one of the cities of Egypt, cp. Num. 13. 22.

14 He divided the sea, and let them go through : he made the waters to stand on an heap.

15 In the day-time also he led them with a cloud : and all the night through with a light of fire.

16 He clave the hard rocks in the wilderness : and gave them drink thereof, as it had been out of the great depth.

Exod. 13. 21 f.

At Horeb, cp. Exod. 17. 6, where the same word for 'rocks' is found.

17 He brought waters out of the stony rock : so that it gushed out like the rivers.

At Kadesh, cp. Num. 20. 8, where the word used here for 'rock,' different from that in v. 16, appears.

These events admit of mystical interpretation, as for example: 'The water and the blood from thy riven side which flowed;' cp. 1 Cor. 10. 4, 'They drank of that spiritual rock that followed them; and that Rock was Christ.'

R.V. Yet went they on still to sin against him, to rebel against. . .

18 Yet for all this they sinned more against him : and provoked the most Highest in the wilderness.

19 They tempted God in their hearts : and required meat for their lust.

tempted: i.e. put to the test. They challenged God to shew his power (Deut. 6. 16; Ps. 95. 9, 106. 14).

required: i.e. asked for.
meat: i.e. food.
lust: i.e. strong desire.
Exod. 16. 2 f.; Num. 11. 4 ff.

A.R.V. Can God

20 They spake against God also, saying, 'Shall God prepare a table in the wilderness?

21 He smote the stony rock indeed, that the water gushed out, and the streams flowed withal : but can he give bread also, or provide flesh for his people?'

In the wilderness the manna was actually given before the water; but in the Christian application the order of this verse is followed, baptism preceding communion.

22 When the LORD heard this, he was wroth : so the fire was kindled in Jacob, and there came up heavy displeasure against Israel;

23 Because they believed not in God : and put not their trust in his help.

At Taberah (Num. 11. 1 ff.).

A.R.V. kindled against

24 So he commanded the clouds above : and opened the doors of heaven.

25 He rained down manna also upon them for to eat : and gave them food from heaven.

A.R.V. salvation.

R.V. Yet, i.e. notwithstanding their unbelief.

Cp. Mal. 3. 10.

and gave them, etc.: A.R.V. gave them of the corn of heaven (Exod. 16. 4; Ps. 105. 39; S. John 6. 31).

26 So man did eat angels' food : for he sent them meat enough.

27 He caused the east-wind to blow under heaven : and through his power he brought in the south-west wind.

28 He rained flesh upon them as thick as dust : and feathered fowls like as the sand of the sea.

29 He let it fall among their tents : even round about their habitation.

30 So they did eat, and were well filled; for he gave them their own desire : they were not disappointed of their lust.

31 But while the meat was yet in their mouths, the heavy wrath of God came upon them, and slew the wealthiest of them : yea, and smote down the chosen men that were in Israel.

32 But for all this they sinned yet more : and believed not his wondrous works.

33 Therefore their days did he consume in vanity : and their years in trouble.

34 When he slew them, they sought him : and turned them early, and inquired after God.

35 And they remembered that God was their strength : and that the high God was their redeemer.

angels' food : as being bread from heaven where the angels dwell. As applied to the Eucharist the phrase teaches that both the angels and mankind are made partakers of the divine nature, we by sacrament, they without.

meat: i.e. food. Sept. has here 'food for the journey.'

Num. 11. 31.

R.V. South wind. East wind and south wind: i.e. south-east wind.

lust: i.e. strong desire.

Num. 11. 33.

God punishes men sometimes by granting their requests.

the wealthiest : *A.R.V. the fattest*, the most vigorous.

R.V. the young men

A.R.V. they sinned still:

A reference to the apparently aimless forty-years' wandering in the desert (*Num.* 4. 28 ff.).

34–40. A picture of human inconstancy and divine forbearance. Man repents after punishment, and then falls again, and yet God's mercy is not exhausted.

36 Nevertheless, they did but flatter him with their mouth : and dissembled with him in their tongue.

Cp. S. Mark 7. 6.

37 For their heart was not whole with him : neither continued they steadfast in his covenant.

A.R.V. right. This verse is quoted in Acts 8. 21.

38 But he was so merciful, that he forgave their misdeeds : and destroyed them not.

39 Yea, many a time turned he his wrath away : and would not suffer his whole displeasure to arise.

40 For he considered that they were but flesh : and that they were even a wind that passeth away, and cometh not again.

Ps. 103. 14.

41 Many a time did they provoke him in the wilderness : and grieved him in the desert.

42 They turned back, and tempted God : and moved the Holy One in Israel.

tempted: cp. v. 19.
R.V. provoked the Holy One of Israel. Cp. Ps. 71. 20.
his hand: i.e. his might.

43 They thought not of his hand : and of the day when he delivered them from the hand of the enemy;

44 How he had wrought his miracles in Egypt : and his wonders in the field of Zoan.

R.V. how he set his signs . . .
Cp. Exod. 10. 1 f.; Ps. 105. 27.
Zoan: cp. v. 13.
Some of the ten plagues; cp. Exod. 7. 20 f.

45 He turned their waters into blood : so that they might not drink of the rivers.

46 He sent lice among them, and devoured them up : and frogs to destroy them.

R.V. swarms of flies (*Exod.* 8. 24). Frogs. (*Exod.* 8. 3 f.)

47 He gave their fruit unto the caterpillar : and their labour unto the grasshopper.

Exod. 10. 13 ff.

48 He destroyed their vines with hail-stones : and their mulberry-trees with the frost.

A.R.V. locust.
Exod. 9. 23 ff.
A.R.V. sycomore

49 He smote their cattle also with hail-stones : and their flocks with hot thunder-bolts.

50 He cast upon them the furiousness of his wrath, anger, displeasure, and trouble : and sent evil angels among them.

> evil angels: angels sent on a mission of destruction. *R.V. a band of angels of evil.*
> *R.V. a path to his anger,*

51 He made a way to his indignation, and spared not their soul from death : but gave their life over to the pestilence;

52 And smote all the first-born in Egypt : the most principal and mightiest in the dwellings of Ham.

> Exod. 12. 29.
> *A.R.V. the chief (R.V.mg. beginning) of their strength.* A phrase used of the first-born (*Gen.* 49. 3; *Deut.* 21. 17; *Ps.* 105. 35).
> Ham: i.e. Egypt. Ham was the father of Mizraim (Egypt) (*Gen.* 10. 6).

53 But as for his own people, he led them forth like sheep : and carried them in the wilderness like a flock.

> Ps. 77. 20.

54 He brought them out safely, that they should not fear : and overwhelmed their enemies with the sea.

55 And brought them within the borders of his sanctuary : even to his mountain which he purchased with his right hand.

> his sanctuary: Canaan, made holy by God's special presence.
> *R.V.mg. To this mountain-land,* i.e. Canaan.
> purchased: cp. Ps. 74. 2.

56 He cast out the heathen also before them : caused their land to be divided among them for an heritage, and made the tribes of Israel to dwell in their tents.

57 So they tempted, and displeased the most High God : and kept not his testimonies;

> So: *A.R.V. Yet,* even after the settlement in Canaan.
> tempted: cp. vv. 19. 42.
> displeased : *R.V. rebelled against.*

58 But turned their backs, and fell away like their forefathers : starting aside like a broken bow.

A.R.V. a deceitful bow. Cp. v. 10.

59 For they grieved him with their hill-altars : and provoked him to displeasure with their images.

A.R.V. their high places:
A.R.V. moved him to jealousy.
The LORD is a jealous God: i.e. all glory and worship are due to him alone.

60 When God heard this, he was wroth : and took sore displeasure at Israel.

61 So that he forsook the tabernacle in Silo : even the tent that he had pitched among men.

The Ark left Shiloh for ever when it was carried into battle against the Philistines (1 *Sam.* 4. 4); cp. Jer. 7. 12.

62 He delivered their power into captivity : and their beauty into the enemy's hand.

power . . . beauty: *A.R.V. his strength . . . his glory*, i.e. the Ark, as being the visible token of God's presence. Cp. Ps. 96. 6; 132. 8.

63 He gave his people over also unto the sword : and was wroth with his inheritance.

64 The fire consumed their young men : and their maidens were not given to marriage.

The fire: i.e. of war (*Num.* 21.28).
to: i.e. in. *R.V. had no marriage-song.*

65 Their priests were slain with the sword : and there were no widows to make lamentation.

A.R.V. their widows made no lamentation. War prevented the customary mourning for the dead.
A.R.V. Then

66 So the Lord awaked as one out of sleep : and like a giant refreshed with wine.

67 He smote his enemies in the hinder parts : and put them to a perpetual shame.

R.V. backward:

68 He refused the tabernacle of Joseph : and chose not the tribe of Ephraim;

tabernacle: i.e. tent.
Shiloh, the former place of the Ark, was situated in the tribe of Ephraim, the son of Joseph.

69 But chose the tribe of Judah : even the hill of Sion which he loved.

Ps. 87. 2.

70 And there he built his temple on high : and laid the foundation of it like the ground which he hath made continually.

A.R.V. established for ever.

71 He chose David also his servant : and took him away from the sheep-folds.

72 As he was following the ewes great with young ones he took him : that he might feed Jacob his people, and Israel his inheritance.

The shepherd of the sheep was made the shepherd of the Lord's flock (2 *Sam.* 5. 2; *Ps.* 79. 14, 80. 1).

73 So he fed them with a faithful and true heart : and ruled them prudently with all his power.

THE SIXTEENTH DAY

MORNING PRAYER

PSALM 79. *Deus, venerunt*

A prayer that God may turn away his anger from the land, now crushed under some great calamity. This psalm is a companion psalm to 74; cp. also 44. It may be made an intercession for the Church in whatever place she may be suffering profanation and persecution: 'Jerusalem' being interpreted as meaning the Church militant (instead of, as more commonly, 'Sion'). The voice of the Martyrs is heard, cp. v. 11.

O GOD, the heathen are come into thine inheritance : thy holy temple have they defiled, and made Jerusalem an heap of stones.

1–4. The complaint.
inheritance: i.e. Canaan, which God had chosen for his special abode (*Exod.* 15. 17; *Ps.* 78. 69).
stones: cp. Micah's prophecy (3. 12, and *Ps.* 74. 8).
2–3 are quoted in 1 Macc. 7. 17.

2 The dead bodies of thy servants have they given to be meat unto the fowls of the air : and the flesh of thy saints unto the beasts of the field.

saints: i.e. the people in covenanted relation to God; cp. Ps. 50. 5.

3 Their blood have they shed like water on every side of Jerusalem : and there was no man to bury them.

4 We are become an open shame to our enemies : a very scorn and derision unto them that are round about us.

A.R.V. We are become a reproach to our neighbours: cp. v. 13.

Cp. Ps. 44. 14.

very: i.e. veritable.

5 LORD, how long wilt thou be angry : shall thy jealousy burn like fire for ever?

5–14. The prayers: (a) Pity our misery: be not angry because of Israel's sins (5–9).

jealousy: cp. Ps. 78. 59.

6 Pour out thine indignation upon the heathen that have not known thee : and upon the kingdoms that have not called upon thy Name.

7 For they have devoured Jacob: and laid waste his dwelling-place.

Not for their heathen ignorance, but for their wilful outrage in their ignorance.

R.V. know thee not . . call not.

Vv. 6–7 appear also in Jer. 10. 25.

8 O remember not our old sins, but have mercy upon us, and that soon : for we are come to great misery.

R.V. Remember not against us the iniquities of our forefathers. Cp. Litany: 'Remember not, Lord, our offences, nor the offences of our forefathers.'

9 Help us, O God of our salvation, for the glory of thy Name : O deliver us, and be merciful unto our sins, for thy Name's sake.

Cp. Commination Service: 'Help us, O God, our Saviour, and for the glory of thy Name deliver us; be merciful to us sinners, for thy Name's sake.' Cp. also the Litany: 'O Lord, arise, help us, and deliver us, for thy Name's sake.'

10 Wherefore do the heathen say: 'Where is now their God?'

(b) Vindicate thy divine power in retribution and in deliverance (10–14).

A.R.V. Wherefore should . . .

This verse occurs again in Joel 2. 17; cp. Ps. 42. 2.

11 O let the vengeance of thy servants' blood that is shed : be openly shewed upon the heathen in our sight.

vengeance: i.e. as *A.R.V. revenging*. Let the retribution be clear for us to see now. This prayer is not vindictive; for it is not beneficial even to the enemies that their punishment be postponed.

With this verse cp. Rev. 6. 10, 'How long, O Lord, holy and true, dost thou not avenge our blood on them that dwell on the earth?' and S. Luke 18. 7, 'And shall not God avenge his own elect that cry to him? I tell you, he will avenge them speedily.'

12 O let the sorrowful sighing of the prisoners come before thee : according to the greatness of thy power, preserve thou those that are appointed to die.

I.e. Israelites in captivity and in danger of being executed. And the Christian martyrs. Cp. Ps. 102. 20; Zech. 9. 12; 1 S. Pet. 3. 19.

13 And for the blasphemy wherewith our neighbours have blasphemed thee : reward thou them, O Lord, seven-fold into their bosom.

A.R.V. their reproach . . . reproached thee:

into their bosom: a metaphor from the use of the folds of the cloak as a receptacle; cp. Isa. 65. 6; S. Luke 6. 38.

This prayer is interpreted by some as being a petition for the conversion of sinners by sending into their hearts the sevenfold gifts of the Spirit.

14 So we, that are thy people, and sheep of thy pasture, shall give thee thanks for ever : and will alway be shewing forth thy praise from generation to generation.

sheep: cp. Ps. 74. 1, etc.

PSALM 80.   *Qui regis Israel*

Another intercession for the Church. May the true Israel, vine of God's planting and culture, be restored to its former health and vigour.

HEAR, O thou Shepherd of Israel, thou that leadest Joseph as a sheep : shew thyself also, thou that sittest upon the cherubims.

Shepherd: cp. Ps. 23. 1; 100. 2, etc.

leadest: through the wilderness of this world; cp. Ps. 77. 20.

Joseph : (cp. Ps. 78. 67; 81. 5) here includes all Israel.

sheep: *A.R.V. flock.* Cp. Ezek. 34. 11 ff.

shew thyself : *A.R.V. shine forth.*

the cherubims: which overshadowed the mercy-seat of the Ark, the throne of God's glory. Cp. Ps. 99. 1, and Exod. 25. 22, 'There I will meet with thee, and I will commune with thee from above the mercy-seat, from between the two cherubim which are upon the ark of the testimony.'

2 Before Ephraim, Benjamin, and Manasses : stir up thy strength, and come, and help us.

In the order of the march through the wilderness these tribes came immediately after the Ark (*Num.* 2. 17 ff.).

3 TURN US AGAIN, O GOD : SHEW THE LIGHT OF THY COUNTENANCE, AND WE SHALL BE WHOLE.

R.V.mg. Restore us, i.e. restore the Church to its proper position of spiritual power. This can only come to pass by a spiritual turning or conversion of the Church.

A.R.V. cause thy face to shine, part of the priestly benediction (*Num.* 2. 17 ff.), cp. v. 1, *and we shall be saved.* 'Whole' means 'safe and sound'; cp. vv. 7, 19.

4 O LORD God of hosts : how long wilt thou be angry with thy people that prayeth?

I.e. as *A.R.V. against the prayer of thy people.*

5 Thou feedest them with the bread of tears : and givest them plenteousness of tears to drink.

6 Thou hast made us a very strife unto our neighbours : and our enemies laugh us to scorn.

7 TURN US AGAIN, THOU GOD OF HOSTS : SHEW THE LIGHT OF THY COUNTENANCE, AND WE SHALL BE WHOLE.

8 Thou hast brought a vine out of Egypt : thou hast cast out the heathen, and planted it.

9 Thou madest room for it : and when it had taken root it filled the land.

10 The hills were covered with the shadow of it : and the boughs thereof were like the goodly cedar-trees.

11 She stretched out her branches unto the sea : and her boughs unto the river.

12 Why hast thou then broken down her hedge : that all they that go by pluck off her grapes?

13 The wild boar out of the wood doth root it up : and the wild beasts of the field devour it.

Cp. Ps. 42. 3; 102. 9.

I.e. as *Vulg.*, *Thou hast brought us into actual strife with*

8–11. The extension of the Church.

a vine: cp. Isa. 5. 1, 7; Ecclus. 24. 17, etc. This image was used by our Lord about himself and the Church in S. John 15. 1 ff., 'I am the vine, ye are the branches,' etc.

out of Egypt: as Israel, so Christ himself (*S. Matt.* 2. 15); and his Church out of the bondage of sin.

10, 11. The ideal boundaries of the Promised Land are here mentioned, viz. the hill-country on the south, Lebanon with its cedars on the north, the Mediterranean Sea on the west, and the river Euphrates on the east. Similarly the Church extends to the furthest boundaries of the world.

12–16. The defacement of the Church. The details admit of various allegorical applications, on which devout Christians may exercise their minds.

14 Turn thee again, thou God of hosts, look down from heaven: behold, and visit this vine;

15 And the place of the vineyard that thy right hand hath planted : and the branch THAT THOU MADEST SO STRONG FOR THYSELF.

Turn thee again : to be compared with 'Turn us again' in the refrain.

A.R.V. And the stock, i.e. Israel, and the Church; also denoted by 'the branch.'

16 It is burnt with fire, and cut down : and they shall perish at the rebuke of thy countenance.

17 Let thy hand be upon the man of thy right hand : and upon the son of man, WHOM THOU MADEST SO STRONG FOR THINE OWN SELF.

Let thy protecting hand (cp. Ps. 89. 22) shield the man (Israel) established by thy loving power. Mystically we may regard 'the man of thy right hand' and 'the son of man' as denoting Christ and his members, the true vine of Israel.

18 And so will not we go back from thee : O let us live, and we shall call upon thy Name.

R.V. Quicken thou us, i.e. restore our life as a nation and a Church.

19 TURN US AGAIN, O LORD GOD OF HOSTS : SHEW THE LIGHT OF THY COUNTENANCE, AND WE SHALL BE WHOLE.

A third time the Church prays for conversion, sanctifying grace, and salvation.

PSALM 81. *Exultate Deo*

A song of praise for use on high festivals. The traditional New Year's Day psalm in Jewish worship.

SING we merrily unto God our strength : make a cheerful noise unto the God of Jacob.

2 Take the psalm, bring hither the tabret : the merry harp with the lute.

tabret: a wood-wind instrument. *R.V.mg. strike the timbrel,* or tambourine.

3 Blow up the trumpet in the new-moon : even in the time appointed, and upon our solemn feast-day.

According to ancient Jewish interpretation the new moon of the seventh month (Tisri) is meant. It was the civil New Year's Day, and was called 'the Feast of Trumpets.' For 'in the time appointed' *R.V.* has: *at the full moon*, which refers to another feast, the Feast of Tabernacles, beginning at the full moon on the 15th of Tisri. Trumpets were blown at all festivals (*Num.* 10. 10).

4 For this was made a statute for Israel : and a law of the God of Jacob.

5 This he ordained in Joseph for a testimony : when he came out of the land of Egypt, and had heard a strange language.

this: i.e. this observance of festivals.

Joseph: is here put for the whole people of Israel, as was 'Jacob' in v. 4. Joseph is mentioned because of the association of his name with Egypt.

he came out: i.e. Joseph or Israel at the Exodus; but *R.V.* has: *when he went over*, i.e. when God went out for judgement over Egypt (*Exod.* 11. 4).

a strange, i.e. foreign, language: either that of the Egyptians or of the Canaanitish tribes. But *R.V. where I heard a language that I knew not*, which means that the psalmist in this verse is speaking in the person of his nation. The language which Israel knew not was the fresh revelation made at the Exodus, poetically embodied in the words of God which follow.

6 'I eased his shoulder from the burden : and his hands were delivered from making the pots.

6–17. God speaks. A summary of the people's history in its relation to him: God's favour to them, his law of monolatry, their unfaithfulness and punishment, their failure to fulfil their vocation, involving loss of favour with God—all of which is applicable also to the Church and to individual Christians.

making the pots: *R.V. the basket*, used for carrying bricks.

7 Thou calledst upon me in troubles, and I delivered thee : and heard thee what time as the storm fell upon thee.

A.R.V. I answered thee in the secret place of thunder, i.e. at the law-giving on Mount Sinai (*Exod.* 19. 18 ff.).

8 I proved thee also : at the waters of strife.

A.R.V. of Meribah (Exod. 17. 7).

9 Hear, O my people, and I will assure thee, O Israel : if thou wilt hearken unto me.

10 There shall no strange god be in thee : neither shalt thou worship any other god.

11 I am the LORD thy God, who brought thee out of the land of Egypt : open thy mouth wide, and I shall fill it.

I.e. God would satisfy their utmost wants.

12 But my people would not hear my voice : and Israel would not obey me.

13 So I gave them up unto their own heart's lusts : and let them follow their own imaginations.

A.R.V. would none of me.
I.e. as in *R.V.*: *So I let them go after the stubbornness of their heart: that they might walk in their own counsels.*

14 O that my people would have hearkened unto me : for if Israel had walked in my ways,

15 I should soon have put down their enemies : and turned my hand against their adversaries.

16 The haters of the LORD should have been found liars : but their time should have endured for ever.

I.e. their arrogant boastings would have been proved false. But *R.V. should submit themselves unto him. R.V.mg. yield feigned obedience, Heb. lie;* i.e. pay the insincere allegiance of the vanquished (*Ps.* 18. 45; 66. 2).

their time: i.e. Israel's time of prosperity.

17 He should have fed them also with the finest wheat-flour : and with honey out of the stony rock should I have satisfied thee.'

Cp. 'corn of heaven' (*Ps.* 78. 25).

honey: cp. Ps. 19. 10.

This verse has usually been interpreted of the Blessed Sacrament. Cp. 1 Cor. 10. 4, 'That rock was Christ.'

EVENING PRAYER

PSALM 82. *Deus stetit*

God, the supreme Judge, pronounces judgement upon earthly judges, who misuse their high office, and are but mortal men.

GOD standeth in the congregation of princes : he is a Judge among gods.

standeth: to pronounce judgement, cp. Isa. 3. 13; Ps. 76. 9.

the congregation of princes: *R.V. of God.* Israel is 'the congregation of the LORD,' cp. Num. 27. 17; Josh. 22. 16.

gods (elohim): i.e. the judges of Israel, so called as being God's delegates, dispensing justice in his name. Cp. Exod. 21. 6.

2 'How long will ye give wrong judgement : and accept the persons of the ungodly?

2–7. God speaks.

I.e. yield to human respect, favouring the rich and powerful.

3 Defend the poor and fatherless : see that such as are in need and necessity have right.

4 Deliver the outcast and poor : save them from the hand of the ungodly.

5 They will not be learned nor understand, but walk on still in darkness : all the foundations of the earth are out of course.

they: i.e. those judges.

learned: i.e. taught, instructed.

Owing to their malpractices the moral government, upon which the well-being of the world is based, is upset. Cp. Ps. 11. 3.

P

6 I have said, "Ye are gods : and ye are all the children of the most Highest.

I have said: at the moment of your appointment as judges, which was a divine call.

Ye are gods: Cp. S. John 10. 34 ff., 'Jesus answered them, Is it not written in your law, I said, Ye are gods? If he called them gods, unto whom the word of God came . . ., say ye of him whom the Father sanctified and sent him into the world, Thou blasphemest; because I said, I am the Son of God?' Our Lord here suited his argument to those whom he addressed, who were not yet capable of accepting his divine Sonship on higher grounds or in the fullest sense. But the fact that God under the old covenant conferred on men who represented him the title of gods was a plain foreshadowing of the future union of God with man in the Person of Christ.

7 But ye shall die like men : and fall like one of the princes."'

Ye shall not escape the common lot of men and princes notwithstanding your exalted titles and position.

8 Arise, O God, and judge thou the earth : for thou shalt take all heathen to thine inheritance.

The psalmist prays that God himself may act as judge, and not of Israel alone, but of all nations. This prayer found its answer in Christ the Son of God incarnate, the just Judge; and will be perfectly fulfilled in the general judgement at the last day. 'The Father gave him authority to execute judgement, because he is the Son of Man' (S. *John* 5. 27).

all heathen: cp. Ps. 2. 8.

PSALM 83. *Deus, quis similis?*

An earnest appeal to God to succour his people who are threatened by a confederacy of enemies: as has often been the condition of the Church militant.

HOLD not thy tongue, O God, keep not still silence : refrain not thyself, O God.

Sept. and Vulg. prefix to this verse the words: 'O God, who will be like unto thee?' Cp. Exod. 15. 11 and Isa. 14. 14.

2 For lo, thine enemies make a murmuring : and they that hate thee have lift up their head.

thine enemies: Israel's, and the Church's enemies, are the enemies of God.

lift up: in self-assertion and arrogance.

3 They have imagined craftily against thy people : and taken counsel against thy secret ones.

A.R.V. hidden ones, i.e. those whom God hides in the shelter of his presence; cp. Ps. 17. 8; 27. 5; 31. 22.

4 They have said, 'Come, and let us root them out, that they be no more a people : and that the name of Israel may be no more in remembrance.'

5 For they have cast their heads together with one consent: and are confederate against thee;

6 The tabernacles of the Edomites, and the Ismaelites : the Moabites, and Hagarens.

R.V. tents of . . .
The nations mentioned in vv. 6–7 were all in or near Canaan. Similarly in many places and many ages the world-forces surrounding the Church have been her enemies.

Hagarens: or Hagrites, lived east of Jordan (1 *Chron.* 5. 10 ff).

Gebal: a tribe dwelling south of the Dead Sea.

7 Gebal, and Ammon, and Amalek : the Philistines, with them that dwell at Tyre.

8 Assur also is joined with them : and have holpen the children of Lot.

Assur: i.e. Assyria, evidently not yet risen to be a world-power.

holpen: i.e. helped.

children of Lot: i.e. the Moabites and Ammonites (*Gen.* 19. 30 ff.). Cp. 2 Chron. 20. 1.

9 But do thou to them as unto the Madianites : unto Sisera, and unto Jabin at the brook of Kison;

R.V. Midian, overthrown by Gideon (*Judges* 6 and 7).
Sisera: cp. Judges 4 and 5.

10 Who perished at Endor: and became as the dung of the earth.

Endor was near Taanach and Megiddo where Sisera was routed (*Joshua* 17. 11; *Judges* 5. 19).

11 Make them and their princes like Oreb and Zeb : yea, make all their princes like as Zeba and Salmana;

Princes of the Midianites who were slain after the battle (*Judges* 7. 25, 8. 21).

12 Who say, 'Let us take to ourselves : the houses of God in possession.'

Who: i.e. the present foes of Israel.
houses: *R.V.mg. pastures,* i.e. the lands which he had given to Israel.

13 O my God, make them like unto a wheel : and as the stubble before the wind.

R.V. the whirling dust:

14 Like as the fire that burneth up the wood : and as the flame that consumeth the mountains;

15 Persecute them even so with thy tempest : and make them afraid with thy storm.

R.V. So pursue them . . .

16 Make their faces ashamed, O LORD : that they may seek thy Name.

The defeat of Israel's enemies is prayed for as a means of bringing them to a knowledge of God.

17 Let them be confounded and vexed ever more and more : let them be put to shame, and perish.

18 And they shall know that thou, whose Name is JEHOVAH : art only the most Highest over all the earth.

R.V. That they may . . .

PSALM 84.   *Quam dilects!*

The pleasantness of God's House, and the happy lot of those who are privileged to worship in it. The aspiration of an exile or pilgrim. This psalm is of similar subject to that of Psalms 42, 43. It is appointed in the Latin Missal to be used in preparation for Mass and Holy Communion, with Pss. 85, 86, 116 vv. 10-16, 130. The words 'dwelling,' 'court,' 'house,' are applicable to the Church on earth, or to any particular sacred building, or to heaven.

O HOW amiable are thy dwellings : thou LORD of hosts!

amiable: i.e. lovable.

2 My soul hath a desire and longing to enter into the courts of the LORD : my heart and my flesh rejoice in the living God.

soul, heart, flesh: i.e. my whole being.

Cp. Ps. 63. 2 and Ps. 42. 2, 'My soul is athirst for God, even for the living God: when shall I come to appear before the presence of God?' The temple-courts are desired because of the presence of a living God, in whose life the worshipper can enjoy communion.

3 Yea, the sparrow hath found her an house, and the swallow a nest where she may lay her young : even thy altars, O LORD of hosts, my King and my God.

May I be as privileged as the birds which have free entry into the temple-courts! 'In Christ we have access in confidence through our faith in him' (*Eph.* 3. 12).

4 Blessed are they that dwell in thy house : they will be alway praising thee.

5 Blessed is the man whose strength is in thee : in whose heart are thy ways.

Peculiarly applicable to Religious, as is v. 5 to faithful workers in the world.

I.e. who meditates in his heart on thy commandments. *R.V. in whose heart are the highways to Zion*, i.e. whose heart is set on pilgrimage to Jerusalem, or, who finds in his own heart (even while in exile) means of approach to God's presence. *Sept.* and *Vulg.* have: *He has disposed ascensions in his heart*, i.e. prayers of aspiration towards God.

6 Who going through the vale of misery use it for a well : and the pools are filled with water.

the vale of misery: i.e. this present life of suffering and mortification in this world, often termed (from the Vulgate) 'this vale of tears'; with special reference here to places where there is a dearth of the Word and Sacraments of the Church.

R.V. Passing through the valley of Weeping (mg. balsam trees, Heb. Baca) they make it a place of springs; yea, the early rain covereth it with blessings. Such is the enthusiasm of the pilgrims that even the arid and barren regions through which they journey seem to them well-watered and fertile. (Balsam trees love a dry soil.) According to their faith they receive grace even without the ordinary means of grace.

7 They will go from strength to strength : and unto the God of gods appeareth every one of them in Sion.

Their strength instead of flagging on the long and hard journey will increase as they progress. 'They that wait upon the Lord shall renew their strength; they shall mount up with wings as eagles; they shall run, and not be weary' (*Isa.* 40. 31).

R.V. appeareth before God, which is a common phrase used of going up to the temple at the festivals; cp. Ps. 42. 2.

8 O Lord God of hosts, hear my prayer : hearken, O God of Jacob.

9 Behold, O God our defender : and look upon the face of thine Anointed.

Anointed: the term is used of a king, or a priest, or the Messiah who is both king and priest. It is through Christ alone that we can have access to God (*S. John* 14. 6; *Heb.* 6. 20).

10 For one day in thy courts : is better than a thousand.

a thousand: days spent anywhere else.

11 I had rather be a doorkeeper in the house of my God : than to dwell in the tents of ungodliness.

be a door-keeper: i.e. be in the lowliest position.

12 For the LORD God is a light and defence : the LORD will give grace and worship, and no good things shall he withhold from them that live a godly life.

R.V. a sun and a shield: Only here in the O.T. is God called a sun.

worship: i.e. as *A.R.V. glory.* Cp. S. Luke 14. 10.

13 O LORD God of hosts : blessed is the man that putteth his trust in thee.

PSALM 85. *Benedixisti, Domine*

A vision of the glorious indwelling of Christ in his Church, and of the reign of love and righteousness. The psalmist makes God's mercies to Israel in the past, vv. 1-3, the ground of prayer for renewed favours, vv. 4-8, and foreshadows the blessings that flow to mankind through the Incarnation, vv. 9-12. Proper on Christmas Day.

LORD, thou art become gracious unto thy land : thou hast turned away the captivity of Jacob.

A.R.V. thou hast been favourable

A.R.V. thou hast brought back

'To bring back the captivity' is a general phrase for 'to restore prosperity'; cp. Ps. 53. 7. But the restoration from captivity in Babylon is here probably referred to specially, symbolizing delivery from the bondage of sin.

2 Thou hast forgiven the offence of thy people : and covered all their sins.

Cp. Ps. 32. 1.

3 Thou hast taken away all thy displeasure : and turned thyself from thy wrathful indignation.

4 Turn us then, O God our Saviour : and let thine anger cease from us.

I.e. restore us to our former state of divine favour. This can only be through our moral conversion. Cp. Ps. 80. 3, 14. Note how often the thought of God's turning and man's turning occurs in this psalm also, vv. 1, 3, 4, 6, 8.

5 Wilt thou be displeased at us for ever : and wilt thou stretch out thy wrath from one generation to another?

6 Wilt thou not turn again, and quicken us : that thy people may rejoice in thee?

quicken: i.e. give life, revive our national life.

7 Shew us thy mercy, O LORD : and grant us thy salvation.

Cp. B.C.P. Morning and Evening Prayer: 'V. O Lord, shew thy mercy upon us. R. And grant us thy salvation.'

8 I will hearken what the LORD God will say concerning me : for he shall speak peace unto his people, and to his saints, that they turn not again.

concerning me: these words are not in A.R.V.

A.R.V. but let them not turn again to folly.

9 For his salvation is nigh them that fear him : that glory may dwell in our land.

Cp. Zech. 2. 5, 'I will be the glory in the midst of her': the glory of God's presence, manifested of old above the mercy-seat in the temple. The psalmist's hope was fulfilled, in a far higher sense, in the Incarnation. Cp. S. John 1. 14, 'We beheld his glory, glory as of the only-begotten from the Father.'

Ps. 40, 13; 89. 15.

Ps. 72. 3. Cp. Heb. 7. 2, 'Melchisedek, being first, by interpretation, King of righteousness, and then also King of Salem, which is, King of peace, . . . made like unto the Son of God.'

10 Mercy and truth are met together : righteousness and peace have kissed each other.

11 Truth shall flourish out of the earth : and righteousness hath looked down from heaven.

In the Incarnation there was fulfilled the prophecy in Isa. 45. 8, 'Drop down, ye heavens, from above, and let the skies pour down righteousness: let the earth open, that they may bring forth salvation.'

12 Yea, the LORD shall shew loving-kindness : and our land shall give her increase.

A.R.V. the LORD shall give that which is good: Temporal blessings will not be absent in the glorious future. Cp. Ps. 67. 8.

13 Righteousness shall go before him : and he shall direct his going in the way.

in the way: i.e. of righteousness. But *R.V.* has: *he shall make his footsteps a way to walk in.* Righteousness shall go before the LORD as his herald (first clause): and also follow him to point out his footsteps as the way his people should walk in. *A.V. he shall set us in the way of his steps.*

THE SEVENTEENTH DAY

MORNING PRAYER

PSALM 86.   *Inclina, Domine*

An expression of unwavering faith in God in time of deep trouble. The speaker is Christ, in his own human nature, and in his several members.

BOW down thine ear, O LORD, and hear me : for I am poor, and in misery.

2 Preserve thou my soul, for I am holy : my God, save thy servant that putteth his trust in thee.

A.R.V. I am poor and needy. Cp. Ps. 40. 20; 41. 1.

I am holy: this is true of Christ, and of each of us in Christ. *A.V.mg. I am one whom thou favourest.*

The second clause is a versicle and response in the B.C.P., Visitation of the Sick.

3 Be merciful unto me, O Lord : for I will call daily upon thee.

R.V. do call

4 Comfort the soul of thy servant : for unto thee, O Lord, do I lift up my soul.

Ps. 25. 1.

5 For thou, Lord, art good and gracious : and of great mercy unto all them that call upon thee.

gracious: *A.R.V. ready to forgive:*

6 Give ear, LORD, unto my prayer : and ponder the voice of my humble desires.

7 In the time of my trouble I will call upon thee : for thou hearest me.

8 Among the gods there is none like unto thee, O Lord : there is not one that can do as thou doest.

A.R.V. neither are there any works like unto thy works.

9 All nations whom thou hast made shall come and worship thee, O Lord : and shall glorify thy Name.

'Great and marvellous are thy works, O Lord, God, the Almighty . . . all the nations shall come and worship before thee' (*Rev.* 15. 3 f.). Cp. Ps. 22. 30; 65. 2; 66. 3; and 67.

10 For thou art great, and doest wondrous things : thou art God alone.

11 Teach me thy way, O LORD, and I will walk in thy truth : O knit my heart unto thee, that I may fear thy Name.

A.R.V. unite my heart to fear thy name. I.e. give my heart a single aim; may its affections and powers be directed solely unto thee. *Sept.* and *Vulg.*: *let my heart rejoice, that it may fear thy name.*

12 I will thank thee, O Lord my God, with all my heart : and will praise thy Name for evermore.

13 For great is thy mercy toward me : and thou hast delivered my soul from the nethermost hell.

R.V. from the lowest pit. R.V.mg. from Sheol beneath. The psalmist has been saved when in some great peril of death. Mystically, the verse speaks of our deliverance in the risen Christ from spiritual death.

14 O God, the proud are risen against me : and the congregations of naughty men have sought after my soul, and have not set thee before their eyes.

A.R.V. violent men . . .

15 But thou, O Lord God, art full of compassion and mercy : long - suffering, plenteous in goodness and truth.

long-suffering: *R.V. slow to anger.*

16 O turn thee then unto me, and have mercy upon me : give thy strength unto thy servant, and help the son of thine handmaid.

As spoken by Christ, the 'handmaid' is the Blessed Virgin Mary, and Christ is the 'servant,' cp. Acts 3. 13. As spoken by us, the 'son of thine handmaid' is a member of the Church, born in the Lord's house, by baptism, and one of the 'household of God,' cp. Eph. 2. 19; Ps. 116. 14.

17 Shew some token upon me for good, that they who hate me may see it, and be ashamed : because thou, LORD, hast holpen me, and comforted me.

PSALM 87.   *Fundamenta ejus*

The spreading of the knowledge of Jehovah among the nations around. A vision of the future catholicity of the Church, and of the extension of the citizenship of Sion, the city of God, to all nations. A 'missionary' psalm. Cp. Ps. 86. 9, 'All nations whom thou hast made shall come and worship thee, O Lord.' Heb. 12. 22 f., 'Ye are come unto mount Zion, and unto the city of the living God, the heavenly Jerusalem . . . and to the general assembly and church of the first-born, who are enrolled in heaven.' Eph. 2. 19 f., 'Ye [Gentiles] are no more strangers and foreigners, but fellow-citizens with the saints, and of the household of God.'

HER foundations are upon the holy hills : the LORD loveth the gates of Sion more than all the dwellings of Jacob.

Her: i.e. of Sion (the Church). *R.V. His* (i.e. the LORD's) *foundation is* . . . The LORD's foundation is the city which he hath founded, Sion, or the Church. Cp. S. Matt. 5. 14, The Church is the 'city that is set on a hill'; Heb. 11. 10, 'the city which hath the foundations, whose builder and maker is God.' The LORD loveth the Church above the Synagogue. The 'hills' present a picture of permanence and security; cp. Ps. 48. 1; 125. 2.

2 Very excellent things are spoken of thee : thou city of God.

A.R.V. Glorious things . . . 'Excellent' formerly meant 'excelling,' 'pre-eminent.'

city of God: cp. Ps. 46. 4; Rev. 3. 12, 'I will write upon him that overcometh the name of the city of my God, the new Jerusalem, which cometh down out of heaven from my God.'

3 'I will think upon Rahab and Babylon : with them that know me.

3–4. God speaks.

'I will think of Rahab and Babylon together with the nations that know me. I will consider them also as knowing me.' With the same meaning *R.V.* has: *I will make mention of Rahab and Babylon as among them that know me,* and acknowledge me as God; cp. Isa. 19. 19–25. The word 'Rahab' denotes Egypt. It means pride, or violence; and is used to designate some fierce monster, perhaps the crocodile, and this became a symbol of Egypt; cp. Ps. 89. 11; Isa. 30. 7; 51. 9.

4 Behold ye the Philistines also : and they of Tyre, with the Morians; lo, there was he born.'

the Morians: i.e. the Moors, cp. Ps. 68. 31. *R.V. Ethiopia.*

R.V. Behold Philistia, and Tyre, and Ethiopia; this one was born there. God points out, as it were, each nation successively as incorporated among the children of Sion, by regeneration 'born there,' i.e. in Sion (symbolizing the Church).

In the P.B.V. the word 'he' in 'He was born (vv. 4–6) is best taken as meaning a typical Gentile, born by nature a Philistine, etc. (v. 4); born by grace into the Church, and reported as being a son of Sion (v. 5); in the divine judgement reckoned as such (v. 6); and proclaiming that all his grace comes to him through the Church (v. 7).

5 And of Sion it shall be reported that he was born in her : and the most High shall stablish her.

R.V. Yea, of Zion it shall be said, 'This one and that one was born in her.' The psalmist speaks, repeating the divine utterance of vv. 3–4.

6 The LORD shall rehearse it when he writeth up the people : that he was born there.

R.V. The LORD shall count, when he writeth up the peoples, 'This one was born there.' When God registers the nations in his book, he will count them as citizens of Sion, equal in privilege to those who were originally 'born there.' Cp. S. Matt. 8. 11.

7 The singers also and trumpeters shall he rehearse: 'All my fresh springs shall be in thee.'

R.V. They that sing as well as they that dance shall say, 'All my fountains (of salvation and sanctification) are in thee (Sion).'

Cp. S. John 4. 10, 14, 'A well of water springing up unto eternal life'; Isa. 12. 3, 'With joy shall ye draw water out of the wells of salvation'; Jer. 17. 14, 'The LORD, the fountain of living waters.'

The verse gives a picture of rejoicing with which those who were heretofore aliens hail their inclusion in the spiritual privileges of Sion.

PSALM 88.   *Domine Deus*

The plaintive supplication of a sufferer in utter desolation and distress of mind conscious of the wrath of God. This is the saddest of all the psalms. The Sin-bearer is the speaker. The psalm is to be recited with him as the Psalm of the Dereliction: 'My God, my God, why hast thou forsaken me?' Proper on Good Friday.

O LORD God of my salvation, I have cried day and night before thee : O let my prayer enter into thy presence, incline thine ear unto my calling.

In the depth of his despondency the psalmist has still faith to address Jehovah as 'God of my salvation'; cp. our Lord's 'My God, my God' upon the Cross.

Cp. S. John 12. 27, 'Now is my soul troubled'; S. Matt. 26. 37, 'My soul is exceeding sorrowful even unto death.'

2 For my soul is full of trouble : and my life draweth nigh unto hell.

hell: *R.V. Sheol. A.V. the grave.*

3 I am counted as one of them that go down into the pit : and I have been even as a man that hath no strength.

the pit: cp. Ps. 28. 1 note.
I have been: *A.R.V. I am.*

4 Free among the dead, like unto them that are wounded, and lie in the grave : who are out of remembrance, and are cut away from thy hand.

Free: may be understood as, of his own free-will, or, free from corruption, or, not bound by the power of death, or, free from sin. But *R.V.* has: *Cast off.*

wounded; cp. Isa. 53. 5, 9.

A.R.V. whom thou remember-est no more, and they are cut off from thy hand. He regards the dead, to whom he compares himself, as separated from God, and forgotten by him. We apply the words to the spiritually dead.

The Descent into Hades.

5 Thou hast laid me in the lowest pit : in a place of darkness, and in the deep.

6 Thine indignation lieth hard upon me : and thou hast vexed me with all thy storms.

Cp. Isa. 53. 6, 'The LORD hath laid upon him the iniquity of us all.'

A.R.V. thy waves. Cp. v. 17 and Ps. 42. 9; 69. 1; etc. Sorrow and turmoil are often depicted as floods of water.

thy: as being permitted by God.

7 Thou hast put away mine acquaintance far from me : and made me to be abhorred of them.

8 I am so fast in prison : that I cannot get forth.

Cp. Ps. 38. 11; 69. 8, and S. Luke 23. 49, 'All his acquaintance stood afar off.' Fulfilled also as regards many of Christ's members, Martyrs, Religious, etc.

There is a barrier between him and his former friends. Some take vv. 7, 8 literally and suppose him to have been a leper under confinement.

R.V. Mine eye wasteth away. The dullness of the eye marks suffering (*Ps.* 6. 7; 31. 10; 38. 10).

9 My sight faileth for very trouble : LORD, I have called daily upon thee, I have stretched forth my hands unto thee.

10 Dost thou shew wonders among the dead : or shall the dead rise up again, and praise thee?

10–12. In the psalmist's mind the answer to these questions was—No, there is no hope for the physically or spiritually dead. But in the light of Christ's resurrection all mankind can now answer, Yes. Cp. 1 S. Pet. 1. 3, 'God hath begotten us unto a lively hope by the resurrection of Jesus Christ.'

11 Shall thy loving-kindness be shewed in the grave : or thy faithfulness in destruction?

12 Shall thy wondrous works be known in the dark : and thy righteousness in the land where all things are forgotten?

13 Unto thee have I cried, O LORD : and early shall my prayer come before thee.

Apart from Christ there can be no restoration of the souls dead in sin.

R.V. But unto thee. His only resource is prayer. His faith remains unshaken. This is the third outcry of his prayer: cp. vv. 1, 9.
The Dereliction.

14 LORD, why abhorrest thou my soul : and hidest thou thy face from me?

15 I am in misery, and like unto him that is at the point to die : even from my youth up thy terrors have I suffered with a troubled mind.

16 Thy wrathful displeasure goeth over me : and the fear of thee hath undone me.

17 They came round about me daily like water : and compassed me together on every side.

18 My lovers and friends hast thou put away from me : and hid mine acquaintance out of my sight.

troubled: cp. v. 2.

A.R.V. thy terrors have cut me off.

water: cp. v. 6.

Cp. v. 7.

EVENING PRAYER

PSALM 89. *Misericordias Domini*

This psalm supplies an answer to the preceding. It celebrates the loving-kindness, power, faithfulness, and the covenanted mercies, of the LORD, and prays that the promises made to David, but apparently in abeyance, may be fulfilled. Proper on Christmas Day and on all commemorations of the Incarnation: the Incarnation was the perfect fulfilment of the psalmist's desire.

MY song shall be alway of the loving-kindness of the LORD : with my mouth will I ever be shewing thy truth from one generation to another.

A.R.V. thy faithfulness ...

2 For I have said, 'Mercy shall be set up for ever : thy truth shalt thou stablish in the heavens.'

3 'I have made a covenant with my chosen : I have sworn unto David my servant;

4 "Thy seed will I stablish for ever : and set up thy throne from one generation to another." '

5 O LORD, the very heavens shall praise thy wondrous works: and thy truth in the congregation of the saints.

6 For who is he among the clouds : that shall be compared unto the LORD?

7 And what is he among the gods : that shall be like unto the LORD?

8 God is very greatly to be feared in the council of the saints : and to be had in reverence of all them that are round about him.

9 O LORD God of hosts, who is like unto thee? : thy truth, most mighty God, is on every side.

10 Thou rulest the raging of the sea : thou stillest the waves thereof when they arise.

11 Thou hast subdued Egypt, and destroyed it : thou hast scattered thine enemies abroad with a mighty arm.

12 The heavens are thine, the earth also is thine : thou hast laid the foundation of the round world, and all that therein is.

A.R.V. thy faithfulness . . .

3–4. God's words. They are a summary of his promises to David and his house given in 2 Sam. 7. 8 ff.
covenant: this key-word occurs also in vv. 29, 34, 38.

'And of his kingdom there shall be no end (*Creed*); cp. Ps. 110. 4; Isa. 9. 7; S. Luke 1. 33.

5–15. The greatness of the LORD.
A.R.V. thy faithfulness in the assembly of the holy ones, i.e. the angels.
Cp. Ps. 35. 10.
R.V. For who in the skies . . .

A.R.V. among the sons of the mighty (*R.V.mg. of God*), i.e. angels; cp. Ps. 29. 1.

R.V. holy ones, angels.

A.R.V. faithfulness . . .

Ps. 65. 7.

A.R.V. Rahab; cp. Ps. 87. 3.

R.V. the world, and the fulness thereof, thou hast founded them.

Q

13 Thou hast made the north and the south : Tabor and Hermon shall rejoice in thy Name.

Tabor and Hermon were conspicuous landmarks in the west and east of the Jordan; cp. Ps. 42. 8; 72. 3. I.e. 'thou hast made the whole land.' Tabor has been connected by tradition with the Lord's transfiguration, and Hermon with S. Peter's confession of faith (*S. Matt.* 16. 13 ff.).

14 Thou hast a mighty arm : strong is thy hand, and high is thy right hand.

15 Righteousness and equity are the habitation of thy seat : mercy and truth shall go before thy face.

Cp. v. 2 and Ps. 85. 10 ff.
R.V. the foundation of thy throne:

16 Blessed is the people, O LORD, that can rejoice in thee : they shall walk in the light of thy countenance.

16-36. The LORD's covenanted goodness to his people, and to king David: Messianic promises.
A.R.V. Blessed is the people that know the joyful (R.V.mg. trumpet) sound. An allusion to the blowing of trumpets which ushered in the festivals (*Num.* 10. 10).
light of thy countenance: cp. Ps. 4. 6.

17 Their delight shall be daily in thy Name : and in thy righteousness shall they make their boast.

R.V. in thy righteousness are they exalted.
Cp. 1 Cor. 1. 30, 'Christ Jesus was made unto us wisdom from God, and righteousness, and sanctification, and redemption.'

18 For thou art the glory of their strength: and in thy lovingkindness thou shalt lift up our horns.

19 For the LORD is our defence : the Holy One of Israel is our King.

I.e. thou shalt give us power and courage.
Holy One: cp. Ps. 71. 20; 78. 42.
King: the earthly monarch was but the vice-gerent of Jehovah the true King of Israel.

R.V. For our shield belongeth unto the LORD : *and our king to the Holy One of Israel.* The nation's shield is the king, and he himself is in the LORD's safe-keeping.

20 Thou spakest sometime in visions unto thy saints, and saidst : 'I have laid help upon one that is mighty; I have exalted one chosen out of the people.

20-36. A further unfolding of the promise given to the house of David (2 *Sam.* 7. 8 ff.).

sometime: i.e. formerly.

thy saints: i.e. Israel, for whose benefit the promise was made.

laid: i.e. bestowed (*Ps.* 21. 5).

David: and, for us, the Son of David. Cp. Acts 13. 22.

21 I have found David my servant : with my holy oil have I anointed him.

anointed: cp. vv. 37, 50; and S. Luke 4. 17, 'The Spirit of the Lord is upon me, because he hath anointed me'; Acts 10. 38, 'God anointed Jesus of Nazareth with the Holy Ghost and with power.' Kings and priests were anointed with oil.

22 My hand shall hold him fast : and my arm shall strengthen him.

23 The enemy shall not be able to do him violence : the son of wickedness shall not hurt him.

Cp. B.C.P., Visitation of the Sick: '*V.* Let the enemy have no advantage of him. *R.* Nor the wicked approach to hurt him.'

son of wickedness: a Hebraism for 'wicked person.'

24 I will smite down his foes before his face : and plague them that hate him.

25 My truth also and my mercy shall be with him : and in my Name shall his horn be exalted.

A.R.V. But my faithfulness . . .

26 I will set his dominion also in the sea : and his right hand in the floods.

the sea: i.e. the Mediterranean.

the floods: *R.V. on the rivers,* i.e. the Euphrates: the plural is poetic. Cp. Ps. 72. 8.

27 He shall call me, "Thou art my Father : my God, and my strong salvation."

Cp. 2 Sam. 7. 14, 'I will be his father, and he shall be my son'; Heb. 1. 5; Rom. 8. 15, 'Ye received the spirit of adoption, whereby we cry, Abba, Father.'

28 And I will make him my first-born: higher than the kings of the earth.

my first-born: this frequent title of Israel in the O.T. is here assigned to the Messianic King. It was completely fulfilled only in the divine Son of David. Cp. Exod. 4. 22, 'Israel is my son, my first-born'; Rom. 8. 29, 'his Son, the first-born among many brethren'; Col. 1. 15, 18, 'the first-born of all creation' . . . 'the first-born from the dead.'

higher than the kings: cp. Rev. 1. 5, 'the first-born of the dead, and the ruler of the kings of the earth'; Rev. 19. 16, 'King of kings and Lord of lords.'

29 My mercy will I keep for him for evermore : and my covenant shall stand fast with him.

30 His seed also will I make to endure for ever : and his throne as the days of heaven.

31 But if his children forsake my law : and walk not in my judgements;

32 If they break my statutes, and keep not my commandments : I will visit their offences with the rod, and their sin with scourges.

Cp. 2 Sam. 7. 14, 'I will be his father, and he shall be my son: if he commit iniquity, I will chasten him with the rod of men, and the stripes of the children of men; but my mercy shall not depart from him'; Heb. 12. 6, 'Whom the Lord loveth he chasteneth, and scourgeth every son whom he receiveth.'

Man's sin cannot make void the promise of God.

A.R.V. my faithfulness . . .

33 Nevertheless, my loving-kindness will I not utterly take from him : nor suffer my truth to fail.

34 My covenant will I not break, nor alter the thing that is gone out of my mouth : I have sworn once by my holiness, that I will not fail David.

sworn: cp. v. 3. Cp. Heb. 6. 13-20 and 7. 20.

once: i.e. once for all.

my holiness: cp. Ps. 60. 6. Cp. v. 4.

A.R.V. his throne . . .

35 His seed shall endure for ever : and his seat is like as the sun before me.

36 He shall stand fast for evermore as the moon : and as the faithful witness in heaven.'

A.R.V. It, i.e. his throne.

witness: i.e. the moon or, perhaps, the rain-bow. But *R.V.mg. and the witness in the sky is faithful,* i.e. God himself. Cp. Job 16. 19, 'My witness is in heaven, and he that voucheth for me is on high.'

---

37 But thou hast abhorred and forsaken thine Anointed : and art displeased with him.

37-50. The contrast between the calamities of the present, and the divinely promised blessings. This has come to pass, it is implied, through the failure of men to fulfil their part in the covenant.

abhorred: *R.V. But thou hast cast off and rejected . . .*

thine Anointed: i.e. the kings of David's line, the leaders of the Church.

R.V. Thou hast abhorred. The covenant-mercies are in abeyance.

38 Thou hast broken the covenant of thy servant : and cast his crown to the ground.

A.V. profaned his crown by casting it to the ground.

39 Thou hast overthrown all his hedges : and broken down his strong holds.

The kingdom is likened to a vineyard: cp. Ps. 80. 12 ff.; Isa. 5. 5.

40 All they that go by spoil him : and he is become a reproach to his neighbours.

41 Thou hast set up the right hand of his enemies : and made all his adversaries to rejoice.

42 Thou hast taken away the edge of his sword : and givest him not victory in the battle.

R.V. Thou turnest back . . .

43 Thou hast put out his glory : and cast his throne down to the ground.

44 The days of his youth hast thou shortened : and covered him with dishonour.

I.e. the monarchy of David is in a state of premature decay. These verses admit of being applied to Christ himself.
The confused phrase shows a troubled mind; cp. Ps. 13. 1; 79. 5.

45 LORD, how long wilt thou hide thyself, for ever : and shall thy wrath burn like fire?

46 O remember how short my time is : wherefore hast thou made all men for nought?

46, 47. He pleads the shortness of life as a reason that God's anger should speedily give way to mercy. He wishes to survive this time of trouble. Cp. 'Give peace in our time, O Lord.'

47 What man is he that liveth, and shall not see death: and shall he deliver his soul from the hand of hell?

R.V. Sheol?

48 Lord, where are thy old loving-kindnesses : which thou swarest unto David in thy truth?

R.V. faithfulness?
A.R.V. reproach

49 Remember, Lord, the rebuke that thy servants have: and how I do bear in my bosom the rebukes of many people;

50 Wherewith thine enemies have blasphemed thee, and slandered the footsteps of thine anointed:

R.V. the reproach of all the mighty peoples;
R.V. Wherewith thine enemies have reproached, O Lord, wherewith they have reproached the footsteps . . .
An ancient Jewish comment on this verse is, 'They have scoffed at the slowness of thy Messiah's footsteps'; and another, 'He delays so long, they say he will never come.' Cp. 2 S. Pet. 3. 3, 4.

Praised be the LORD for evermore. Amen, and Amen.

This doxology was added to mark the end of the Third Book of the Psalter.

BOOK FOUR

THE EIGHTEENTH DAY

MORNING PRAYER

PSALM 90. *Domine, refugium*

The transitoriness of man's life, and his dependence upon the eternal God. This psalm is appointed in B.C.P. for use at the Burial of the Dead. Its theme is summarized in our Lord's words: 'The night cometh, when no man can work' (*S. John* 9. 4).

LORD, thou hast been our refuge : from one generation to another.

2 Before the mountains were brought forth, or ever the earth and the world were made : thou art God from everlasting, and world without end.

A.R.V. our dwelling-place:

Cp. the Creed, 'Begotten of the Father before all worlds.'

the world: i.e. the habitable part of the earth.

thou art (present) from everlasting (past) and world without end (future) God.

3 Thou turnest man to destruction : again thou sayest, 'Come again, ye children of men.'

R.V.mg. to dust. Cp. Gen. 3. 19, 'Dust thou art, and unto dust shalt thou return.'

Come again: i.e. God calls a new generation to replace the old.

4 For a thousand years in thy sight are but as yesterday : seeing that is past as a watch in the night.

Cp. 2 S. Pet. 3. 8, 'One day is with the Lord as a thousand years, and a thousand years as one day.'

A.R.V. are but as yesterday when it is past, and as a watch . . .

a watch: the night was divided by the Israelites into three watches (*Judges* 7. 19).

5 As soon as thou scatterest them they are even as a sleep : and fade away suddenly like the grass.

A.R.V. Thou carriest them away as with a flood (i.e. a river); *they are as a sleep.* Cp. Job 20. 8, 'He shall fly away as a dream . . . as a vision of the night.'

6 In the morning it is green, and groweth up : but in the evening it is cut down, dried up, and withered.

7 For we consume away in thy displeasure : and are afraid at thy wrathful indignation.

8 Thou hast set our misdeeds before thee : and our secret sins in the light of thy countenance.

9 For when thou art angry all our days are gone : we bring our years to an end, as it were a tale that is told.

10 The days of our age are threescore years and ten; and though men be so strong that they come to fourscore years : yet is their strength then but labour and sorrow; so soon passeth it away, and we are gone.

11 But who regardeth the power of thy wrath : for even thereafter as a man feareth, so is thy displeasure.

12 So teach us to number our days : that we may apply our hearts unto wisdom.

Cp. Ps. 37. 2, 103. 15; Isa. 40. 6-8; 1 S. Pet. 1. 24; S. Jas. 1. 10; and S. Matt. 6. 30.

we: the psalmist changes to the first person, and records the experience of Israel in general.
One clause states the physical, and the other the spiritual, effect of sin.
set our misdeeds before thee: not turning from them (*Ps.* 51. 9); nor covering them (*Ps.* 32. 1).
secret sins: cp. Ps. 19. 12.
the light: cp. Ps. 4. 6; 89. 16.
A.R.V. For all our days are passed away in thy wrath:

R.V. their pride, i.e. what men glory in.

I.e. Our fears of the divine wrath against sinful mankind are justified. 'thereafter' means 'accordingly.'
R.V. Who knoweth the power of thine anger, and thy wrath according to the fear that is due unto thee?
i.e. Who considers aright the intensity of God's wrath against sin, so as to fear to offend him?
Cp. Ps. 39. 4 and the Commendatory Prayer in the Visitation of the Sick, B.C.P.: 'Teach us . . . so to number our days, that we may seriously apply our hearts to that holy and heavenly wisdom, whilst we live here, which may in the end bring us to life everlasting.'

13 Turn thee again, O LORD, at the last : and be gracious unto thy servants.

at the last: may be taken as meaning 'in the hour of our death.' But *R.V.* has: *Return, O LORD; how long?* i.e. how long shall thine anger persist? This question finds an answer in Mal. 3. 7, 'Return unto me, and I will return unto you, saith the Lord of hosts.'

A.R.V. and let it repent thee concerning thy servants. I.e. change from wrath to compassion towards them. Cp. Exod. 32. 12 and Ps. 135. 14.

14 O satisfy us with thy mercy, and that soon : so shall we rejoice and be glad all the days of our life.

R.V. O satisfy us in the morning with thy mercy: when the night of anger is over (*Ps.* 30. 5, 46. 5).

15 Comfort us again now after the time that thou hast plagued us : and for the years wherein we have suffered adversity.

A.R.V. according to the time, i.e. in proportion to.

May the chastisement of the past be compensated for by the joy of the days spent in God's favour!

16 Shew thy servants thy work : and their children thy glory.

May God's work and glory, i.e. his providential care for Israel, be visibly manifested to his servants and to their posterity! The pre-eminent 'work of God' is the salvation of man by which God is glorified; and for us 'This is the work of God, that ye believe on him whom he hath sent.' The glory comes after the work: the glory of God after the completed work of man's salvation by faith.

17 And the glorious Majesty of the LORD our God be upon us : prosper thou the work of our hands upon us, O prosper thou our handy-work.

A.R.V. And let the beauty . . . Cp. Ps. 27. 4.

May God render effectual man's feeble efforts to carry out his purposes!

PSALM 91.   *Qui habitat*

The peace and safety of him who commits himself to the care and protection of Almighty God. The psalm is suitable on all feasts of the holy Angels, and is used as an evening prayer in the Office of Compline.

WHOSO dwelleth under the defence of the most High : shall abide under the shadow of the Almighty.

A.R.V. in the secret place of . . . Cp. Ps. 32. 3.

the shadow: that protects. Cp. Isa. 25. 4, 'Thou hast been a shadow from the heat'; 32. 2, 'the shadow of a great rock in a weary land.'

A.R.V. my refuge and my fortress:

2 I will say unto the LORD, 'Thou art my hope, and my strong hold' : my God, in him will I trust.

3 For he shall deliver thee from the snare of the hunter : and from the noisome pestilence.

thee: i.e. who dwellest in the secret place of the most High (v. 1).

hunter: *A.R.V. fowler.* Cp. Ps. 124. 6.

God will deliver thee from the devil's snare and from the pestilence of sin.

I.e. as a bird protects its young; cp. S. Matt. 23. 37.

4 He shall defend thee under his wings, and thou shalt be safe under his feathers : his faithfulness and truth shall be thy shield and buckler.

5 Thou shalt not be afraid for any terror by night : nor for the arrow that flieth by day;

6 For the pestilence that walketh in darkness : nor for the sickness that destroyeth in the noonday.

7 A thousand shall fall beside thee, and ten thousand at thy right hand : but it shall not come nigh thee.

8 Yea, with thine eyes shalt thou behold : and see the reward of the ungodly.

5-6. These onslaughts by night and by day admit of various allegorization.

reward: i.e. retribution (*Ps.* 37. 35).

9 (For thou, LORD, art my hope) : thou hast set thine house of defence very high.

For thou, etc.: a parenthesis; the first 'thou' refers to the divine, the second to the human, person.

very high: i.e. high above all assault; but *R.V.* has: *For thou, O LORD, art my refuge! Thou hast made the most High thy habitation. R.V.mg. Because thou hast said, 'The LORD is my refuge'; thou hast made the most High thy habitation.*

10 There shall no evil happen unto thee : neither shall any plague come nigh thy dwelling.

11 For he shall give his angels charge over thee : to keep thee in all thy ways.

Cp. Ps. 34. 7, 'The angel of the LORD tarrieth round about them that fear him : and delivereth them'. Verses 11-12 were quoted by Satan in his temptation of our Lord, with the significant omission of the words 'in all thy ways.' God's providence is pledged to protect only those who continue in the ways appointed for them.

12 They shall bear thee in their hands : that thou hurt not thy foot against a stone.

13 Thou shalt go upon the lion and adder : the young lion and the dragon shalt thou tread under thy feet.

dragon: *R.V. serpent.* Cp. S. Luke 10. 19, 'I have given you authority to tread upon serpents and scorpions and over all the power of the enemy'; cp. Rom. 16. 20 and the Litany, 'beat down Satan under our feet.'

14 'Because he hath set his love upon me, therefore will I deliver him : I will set him up, because he hath known my Name.

14-16. God speaks, confirming his servant's words.
A.R.V. set him on high,
Cp. Ps. 9. 10; S. John 17. 26.

15 He shall call upon me, and I will hear him : yea, I am with him in trouble; I will deliver him, and bring him to honour.

16 With long life will I satisfy him : and shew him my salvation.'

In these three verses God gives seven precious promises to those who put their trust in him.

Cp. Ps. 21. 4; 1 S. John 5. 11.

PSALM 92. *Bonum est confiteri*

A psalm of thanksgiving for God's righteous government of the world. Its traditional title was 'A song for the Sabbath day'.

IT is a good thing to give thanks unto the LORD : and to sing praises unto thy Name, O most Highest;

2 To tell of thy loving-kindness in the morning : and of thy truth in the night-season;

Night and day: cp. Ps. 91. 5-6; 109. 147-148.

truth: i.e. as *A.R.V. faithfulness.*

3 Upon an instrument of ten strings, and upon the lute : upon a loud instrument, and upon the harp.

4 For thou, LORD, hast made me glad through thy works : and I will rejoice in giving praise for the operations of thy hands.

R.V. with a solemn sound upon the harp.

A.R.V. thy work, wrought by thee as moral Ruler of the world; cp. vv. 7-14. See also Ps. 90.16, 'Shew thy servants thy work : and their children thy glory.'

operations: i.e. as *A.R.V. works.*

Cp. Rom. 11. 33, 'O the depth of the riches both of the wisdom and the knowledge of God! how unsearchable are his judgements, and his ways past finding out!'

5 O LORD, how glorious are thy works : thy thoughts are very deep.

6 An unwise man doth not well consider this : and a fool doth not understand it.

A.R.V. A brutish . . .

7 When the ungodly are green as the grass, and when all the workers of wickedness do flourish : then shall they be destroyed for ever; but thou, Lord, art the most Highest for evermore.

A.R.V. it is that they shall. Cp. Exod. 9. 16; Rom. 9. 17.

R.V. on high for evermore, ruling over all. Cp. Ps. 93. 4.

8 For lo, thine enemies, O LORD, lo, thine enemies shall perish : and all the workers of wickedness shall be destroyed.

9 But mine horn shall be exalted like the horn of an unicorn : for I am anointed with fresh oil.

A.R.V. scattered.

R.V. mine horn hast thou . . .

The horn is an emblem of vigour; cp. Ps. 65. 5.

unicorn: *R.V. wild-ox.*

fresh oil: like a guest at a joyous banquet; cp. Ps. 23. 5.

10 Mine eye also shall see his lust of mine enemies : and mine ear shall hear his desire of the wicked that arise up against me.

R.V. hath seen my desire on . . .

his: archaic for 'its.'

R.V. mine ears have heard my desire . . .

11 The righteous shall flourish like a palm-tree : and shall spread abroad like a cedar in Libanus.

12 Such as are planted in the house of the LORD : shall flourish in the courts of the house of our God.

I.e. Lebanon.

The righteous are planted, as it were, in the precincts of God's house, and from its sacred soil draw vitality and fruitfulness. The verse is specially applicable to the saints in heaven, and furnishes also an ideal for Religious on earth.

13 They also shall bring forth more fruit in their age : and shall be fat and well-liking.

A.R.V. They shall still bring forth fruit in old age, a characteristic of the palm-tree.

well-liking: i.e. in good condition. *R.V. they shall be full of sap and green.*

14 That they may shew how true the LORD my strength is : and that there is no unrighteousness in him.

EVENING PRAYER

PSALM 93. *Dominus regnavit*

The throne of God is set up above the restless waves of the nations of the world. This is the first of a series of theocratic psalms celebrating God's kingly rule of the world. They continue, with the exception of Ps. 94, to Ps. 100. This is suitable as an act of worship to Christ the King.

THE LORD is King, and hath put on glorious apparel : the LORD hath put on his apparel, and girdeth himself with strength.

R.V. The LORD reigneth; he is apparelled with majesty:

The 'apparel' has been applied variously: to the glories of nature; to the incarnate body of the Son of God; to that body glorified at Christ's exaltation.

2 He hath made the round world so sure : that it cannot be moved.

A.R.V. The world also is stablished: i.e. God's rule has firmly established the moral and political order of the world: a prophetic vision. Cp. Ps. 46. 5, 96. 10, and S. Matt. 28. 18.

3 Ever since the world began hath thy seat been prepared : thou art from everlasting.

A.R.V. thy throne . . .

4 The floods are risen, O LORD, the floods have lift up their voice : the floods lift up their waves.

The floods, i.e. the rivers, and the sea (v. 5), symbolize the world-powers that aim at universal conquest. Cp. Jer. 46. 8, 'Egypt riseth up like the Nile, and his waters toss themselves like the rivers: and he saith, I will rise up, I will cover the earth,' and Ps. 98. 7 ff.

5 The waves of the sea are mighty, and rage horribly : but yet the LORD, who dwelleth on high, is mightier.

6 Thy testimonies, O LORD, are very sure : holiness becometh thine house for ever.

house : i.e. wherever God manifests his presence. Cp. Ps. 96. 9.

PSALM 94. *Deus ultionum*

A meditation of one who waits patiently upon God in a time of oppression and perversion of justice, made in alternating prayers, vv. 1–7, 12–13, 18–20, and reflections, vv. 8–11, 14–17.

O LORD God, to whom vengeance belongeth : thou God, to whom vengeance belongeth, shew thyself.

1-7. A prayer to God for his intervention.

Cp. Deut. 32. 35; Rom. 12. 19, 'Vengeance belongeth unto me, I will recompence, saith the Lord.'

shew thyself: *R.V. shine forth.* Cp. Ps. 50. 2.

2 Arise, thou Judge of the world : and reward the proud after their deserving.

Cp. Ps. 58. 11, 'Doubtless there is a God that judgeth the earth.' The title 'Judge of the world' is especially suitable to the Incarnate Son (*S. Matt.* 25. 32; *S. John* 5. 22).

R.V. render to the proud their desert.

3 How LONG shall the ungodly : HOW LONG shall the ungodly triumph?

how long: cp. Ps. 74. 11; 89. 45; and Rev. 6. 10, 'I saw under the altar the souls of them that had been slain for the word of God . . . saying, How long dost thou not judge and avenge our blood?'

4 How LONG shall all wicked doers speak so disdainfully : and make such proud boasting?

5 They smite down thy people, O LORD : and trouble thine heritage.

Two reasons for God's intervention: they are his people, his heritage (v. 5); they are helpless (v. 6).

6 They murder the widow, and the stranger : and put the fatherless to death.

The 'widow,' 'stranger,' 'fatherless,' types of the helpless. Cp. Ps. 146. 9, 'The LORD careth for the strangers; he defendeth the fatherless and widow.'

7 And yet they say, 'Tush, the LORD shall not see : neither shall the God of Jacob regard it.'

Tush : cp. Ps. 10. 12; 73. 11.

8 Take heed, ye unwise a-
mong the people : O ye fools,
when will ye understand?

8-11. A reflection addressed
to Israel, that we must believe
that the Creator is aware of men's
doings.

unwise: *A.R.V. brutish.*

the people: i.e. of Israel, some
of whom, when oppressed, apparently doubted the power of
God to protect them.

9 He that planted the ear,
shall he not hear : or he that
made the eye, shall he not see?
10 Or he that nurtureth the
heathen : it is he that teacheth
man knowledge, shall not he
punish?

*R.V. He that chastiseth (R.V.
mg. instructeth) the nations, shall
not he correct? even he that teacheth man knowledge?* God's edu-
cation and discipline reaches
beyond Israel to the heathen
nations; cp. Rom. 2. 14 ff.

Quoted by S. Paul in 1 Cor.
3. 20, with the substitution of
'the wise' for 'man' as more
suitable to his argument.

vain: i.e. empty as air (*Heb. a
breath*).

11 The LORD knoweth the
thoughts of man : that they are
but vain.

12 Blessed is the man whom
thou chasteneth, O LORD : and
teachest him in thy law;

12-13. An act of thanksgiving
to God for profitable chastisement. Israel has the special
blessing of receiving divine instruction from direct revelation
—'thy law.'

Cp. Heb. 12. 7, 11, 'If ye
endure chastening, God dealeth
with you as with sons . . . it
yieldeth the peaceable fruit of
righteousness.'

*A.R.V. That thou mayest give
him rest from the days of adversity:*

digged up: i.e. as *A.R.V. digged.* Cp. Ps. 55. 24.

13 That thou mayest give him
patience in time of adversity :
until the pit be digged up for the
ungodly.

14 For the LORD will not fail
his people : neither will he forsake his inheritance;

14 - 17. Confidence in the
LORD's vindication of the right.

fail: *A.R.V. cast off.*

This verse answers v. 5.

15 Until righteousness turn again unto judgement : all such as are true in heart shall follow it.

R.V. For judgement shall return unto righteousness, i.e. judgement, so long perverted, shall resume its true character of righteousness. The words in P.B.V. bear the same meaning. with: *A.R.V. for.*

The answer is: No one but the LORD. 'There is none other that fighteth for us, but only thou, O Lord.' Cp. v. 17.

16 Who will rise up with me against the wicked : or who will take my part against the evil-doers?

17 If the LORD had not helped me : it had not failed but my soul had been put to silence.

Cp. Ps. 124. 1 f.

R.V. my soul had soon dwelt in silence, i.e. in the silence of the grave; cp. Ps. 31. 19.

18 But when I said, 'My foot hath slipt' : thy mercy, O LORD, held me up.

19 In the multitude of the sorrows that I had in my heart : thy comforts have refreshed my soul.

18-20. Grateful recognition of divine help.

R.V. of my thoughts (R.V. mg. my doubts) within me:

20 Wilt thou have anything to do with the stool of wickedness : which imagineth mischief as a law?

R.V. Shall the throne of wickedness have fellowship with thee, which frameth mischief by statute? i.e. Shall the judgement seat, now become a throne of wickedness which perpetrates wrong under legal forms, claim for its acts the authority of God? P.B.V., where 'stool' means 'seat' or 'throne,' bears the same sense.

21 They gather them together against the soul of the righteous : and condemn the innocent blood.

21-23 repeats the reflections of 14-17.

I.e. pass sentence of death against the innocent; cp. S. Matt. 27. 4, 'I have sinned in that I have betrayed the innocent blood.'

22 But the LORD is my refuge: and my God is the strength of my confidence.

R

23 He shall recompense them their wickedness, and destroy them in their own malice : yea, the LORD our God shall destroy them.

THE NINETEENTH DAY

MORNING PRAYER

PSALM 95.   *Venite, exultemus*

A call to worship, vv. 1–7, with a warning against disobedience, vv. 8–11. This psalm has been used from very early times as an introduction to divine service at Mattins.

O COME, let us sing unto the LORD : let us heartily rejoice in the strength of our salvation.

1-5. A call to religious joy in the LORD, because of what he is in himself (v. 3), and because he is the Creator and Maintainer of the world (vv. 4-5).

A.R.V. the rock of our salvation, applicable especially to Christ.

2 Let us come before his presence with thanksgiving : and shew ourselves glad in him with psalms.

3 For the LORD is a great God: and a great King above all gods.

4 In his hand are all the corners of the earth : and the strength of the hills is his also.

R.V. are the deep places of the earth : and the heights of the mountains are . . .

5 The sea is his, and he made it : and his hands prepared the dry land.

6 O come, let us worship, and fall down : and kneel before the LORD our Maker;

6-7. The call reiterated as a summons to the outward expression of humble worship, because of what the LORD is towards us, our Maker and our God, and we towards him, the sheep of his pasture, and the people of (under) his guiding and protecting hand.

our Maker: Israel as the LORD'S people was especially his creation; cp. Ps. 100. 2; Deut. 32. 15; Isa. 44. 2.

7 For he is the Lord our God : and we are the people of his pasture, and the sheep of his hand.

8 To-day if ye will hear his voice, 'Harden not your hearts : as in the provocation, as in the day of temptation in the wilderness;

8-11. Quoted in Heb. 3. 7-11, 4.7, as a warning to Christians.

'Harden not' to the end of the psalm is the utterance of God's 'voice.' It is a warning by God against obstinate disobedience against his revealed will; though the people challenged God's intervention, and saw his works of deliverance (vv. 8-9).

R.V. To-day, Oh that ye would hear his voice! Harden not your heart, as at Meribah, as in the day of Massah in the wilderness; cp. Exod. 17.7; Num. 20. 13.

harden not: cp. Exod. 9. 34.

hearts: i.e. wills, not feelings.

tempted me: i.e. put me to the test, challenged me to be true to my promises.

A.R.V. saw my work. Cp. Ps. 90. 16; Num. 14. 22.

9 When your fathers tempted me : proved me, and saw my works.

The injury that sin does against God (v. 10a). Sin is errant will, a self-willed straying from God, brought about through ignorance (v. 10b). Sin inevitably receives the anger of God and the sentence of exclusion from heaven (v. 11).

10 Forty years long was I grieved with this generation, and said: "It is a people that do err in their hearts, for they have not known my ways";

this generation: *R.V. that generation.*

my ways: cp. Ps. 81. 14.

They 'knew not' God's 'ways' though they 'saw his work.' Ignorance about God is a disposing cause of sin.

11 Unto whom I sware in my wrath : that they should not enter into my rest.'

sware: therefore the wrath was sure and certain; cp. Heb. 6. 17.

my rest: i.e. Canaan; cp.

Deut. 12. 9, 'Ye are not as yet come unto the rest and the inheritance, which the LORD thy God giveth thee.' Mystically interpreted in Heb. 4. 9, 11 of the rest of heaven; 'there remaineth a rest for the people of God . . . let us therefore give diligence to enter into that rest, that no man fall after the same example of disobedience.'

PSALM 96. *Cantate Domino*

A vision of the universal reign of Christ: and therefore a 'missionary' psalm. It is found also in 1 Chron. 16. 23–33, combined with Ps. 105. 1–15 and 106. 1, 47, 48. It is suitable in Advent, and on all feasts of Christ our Lord.

O SING UNTO THE LORD a new song : SING UNTO THE LORD, all the whole earth.

new: i.e. as giving expression to the new aspirations awakened by the return from captivity; but for Christians the 'new song' is that of Christian worship celebrating the redemption by Christ the LORD; cp. Ps. 33. 3.

2 SING UNTO THE LORD, and praise his Name : be telling of his salvation from day to day.

The triple repetition of 'the LORD' in vv. 1-2 has been regarded as a foreshadowing of the doctrine of the most holy Trinity.

3 Declare his honour unto the heathen : and his wonders unto all people.

R.V. Declare his glory among the nations: his marvellous works among all the peoples.

4 For the LORD is great, and cannot worthily be praised : he is more to be feared than all gods.

5 As for all the gods of the heathen, they are but idols : but it is the LORD that made the heavens.

all gods: cp. Ps. 95. 3.

6 Glory and worship are before him : power and honour are in his sanctuary.

A.R.V. Honour and majesty
A.R.V. strength and beauty.
In Ps. 78. 62 these terms are applied to the Ark as the place where God manifested his glory.

7 Ascribe unto the LORD, O ye kindreds of the people : ascribe unto the LORD worship and power.

8 Ascribe unto the LORD the honour due unto his Name : bring presents, and come into his courts.

9 O worship the LORD in the beauty of holiness : let the whole earth stand in awe of him.

10 Tell it out among the heathen that the LORD is King : and that it is he who hath made the round world so fast that it cannot be moved; and how that he shall judge the people righteously.

11 Let the heavens rejoice, and let the earth be glad : let the sea make a noise, and all that therein is.

12 Let the field be joyful, and all that is in it : then shall all the trees of the wood rejoice before the LORD;

13 For he cometh, for he cometh to judge the earth : and with righteousness to judge the world, and the people with his truth.

R.V. peoples:
A.R.V. glory and strength.

Again 'the LORD' thrice repeated, but one 'Name.'
A.R.V. bring an offering, and . . .

R.V. mg. in holy array. Cp. Ps. 29. 2. The worshippers of God are to be vested in holiness as the priests in the Temple were arrayed in holy attire. Cp. Exod. 3. 5 and S. John 4. 24.

A.R.V. the LORD reigneth: This passage appears in the Old Latin version as '*The LORD hath reigned from the Tree,*' and is often so quoted by early Christian writers. This says truth, and makes the Messianic reference clear; but it is not the original text, and is not found in the Hebrew or any other version.

R.V. the world also is stablished that it cannot be moved, i.e. God has established the moral principles by which he judges the world. Cp. Ps. 93. 2.

R.V. he shall judge the peoples with equity.

11–12. Let all nature praise the coming of Christ its maker and ruler. The 'sea' may also symbolize the unruly heathen peoples, and the cultivated ground Israel and the Church.

Applied to the first and the second coming of Christ, and to every manifestation of divine judgement. Cp. Isa. 11. 4–5.

R.V. the peoples

PSALM 97. *Dominus regnavit*

Similar in subject and in use to the preceding psalm. The reign of the divine King and Judge will cover the earth with righteousness and gladness.

THE LORD is King, the earth may be glad thereof : yea, the multitude of the isles may be glad thereof.

A.R.V. The LORD *reigneth.* Cp. Ps. 96. 10.

thereof: i.e. because of that.

the isles: i.e. of the Mediterranean, including the coast-lands; i.e. the civilized world, but yet heathen.

2 Clouds and darkness are round about him : righteousness and judgement are the habitation of his seat.

Cp. Exod. 19. 16, 20. 21, 'the thick darkness where God was'; 1 Kings 8. 12, 'the LORD hath said that he would dwell in the thick darkness'; Lev. 16. 2, 'I will appear in the cloud upon the mercy-seat'; and Ps. 18. 11, 'He made darkness his hiding-place . . . and thick clouds to cover him.'

R.V. are the foundation of his throne. Cp. Ps. 89. 15.

3 There shall go a fire before him : and burn up his enemies on every side.

Cp. Exod. 19. 18; 2 Thess. 1. 8.

A thunder-storm is used as a symbol of divine power also in Ps. 17. 18, 18. 8–15, 21. 9, 50. 3, 68. 2.

shall go: *A.R.V. goeth.*

and burn up: *A.R.V. burneth up.*

shine: i.e. sheen, brightness.

4 His lightnings gave shine unto the world : the earth saw it, and was afraid.
5 The hills melted like wax at the presence of the LORD : at the presence of the Lord of the whole earth.

The 'hills' suggest 'every high thing that is exalted against the knowledge of God' (2 *Cor.* 10. 5).

6 The heavens have declared his righteousness : and all the people have seen his glory.

R.V. peoples

7 Confounded be all they that worship carved images, and that delight in vain gods : worship him, all ye gods.

R.V. Ashamed be
A.R.V. boast themselves of idols:

all ye gods: i.e. angels. Cp. Heb. 1. 6, 'When he bringeth in the first-begotten into the world, he saith, And let all the angels of God worship him.'

This verse occurs also in Ps. 48. 10.

the daughters of Judah: i.e. the towns and villages of Judah; cp. Num. 21. 25; Joshua 15. 45. Understand this as signifying 'the Church in every local part thereof.'

8 Sion heard of it, and rejoiced : and the daughters of Judah were glad, because of thy judgements, O LORD.

9 For thou, LORD, art higher than all that are in the earth : thou art exalted far above all gods.

Ps. 95. 3.

10 O ye that love the LORD, see that ye hate the thing which is evil : the LORD preserveth the souls of his saints; he shall deliver them from the hand of the ungodly.

saints: i.e. 'the elect people of God,' as often in the Psalter; cp. Ps. 30. 4.

shall deliver: *A.R.V. delivereth.*

Cp. Isa. 9. 2, 'The people that walked in darkness have seen a great light: they that dwelt in the land of the shadow of death, upon them hath the light shined'; Ps. 112. 4, 'Unto the godly there ariseth up light in the darkness'; Ps. 118. 27, 'God is the LORD who hath shewed us light.'

11 There is sprung up a light for the righteous : and joyful gladness for such as are true-hearted.

12 Rejoice in the LORD, ye righteous : and give thanks for a remembrance of his holiness.

R.V. give thanks to his holy name (Heb. memorial).

EVENING PRAYER

PSALM 98. *Cantate Domino*

A hymn of praise to the LORD God for deliverance and restoration from the power of the heathen; to Christ the Incarnate LORD for his mighty work of salvation; looking forward to the final and universal victory of righteousness. Hence used as an alternative for *Magnificat* at Evensong.

O SING unto the LORD a new song : for he hath done marvellous things.

2 With his own right hand, and with his holy arm : hath he gotten himself the victory.

3 The LORD declared his salvation : his righteousness hath he openly shewed in the sight of the heathen.

4 He hath remembered his mercy and truth toward the house of Israel : and all the ends of the world have seen the salvation of our God.

5 Shew yourselves joyful unto the LORD, all ye lands : sing, rejoice, and give thanks.
6 Praise the LORD upon the harp : sing to the harp with a psalm of thanksgiving.

The psalm begins and ends (vv. 8–10) like Ps. 96.

marvellous things: the Incarnation, Passion, Resurrection.

Cp. Isa. 59. 16, 'He wondered that there was no intercessor: therefore his own arm brought salvation unto him; and his righteousness, it upheld him'; *Magnificat*: 'He hath shewed strength with his arm.'

Cp. Isa. 49. 6 and 52. 10, 'The LORD hath made bare his holy arm in the eyes of all the nations; and all the ends of the earth shall see the salvation of our God'; *Nunc Dimittis*, 'Mine eyes have seen thy salvation, which thou hast prepared before the face of all peoples; a light to lighten the Gentiles.'

Cp. *Magnificat*: 'He remembering his mercy hath holpen his servant Israel, as he promised.'

truth: *R.V. faithfulness.*

all the ends: cp. S. Luke 3. 6; Ps. 22. 27.

7 With trumpets also and shawms : O shew yourselves joyful before the LORD the King.

shawms: reed instruments like clarionets; but *R.V.* has: *and sound of cornet.*

8 Let the sea make a noise, and all that therein is : the round world, and they that dwell therein.

9 Let the floods clap their hands, and let the hills be joyful together before the LORD : for he is come to judge the earth.

floods: i.e. rivers.

Applicable to the first or the second Advent.

10 With righteousness shall he judge the world : and the people with equity.

R.V. peoples

PSALM 99. *Dominus regnavit*

Proclamation of the reign of the thrice-holy God (vv. 3, 5, 9), the LORD, Ruler over all the peoples of the world. Let the whole world worship him! This is the last of the series of six Royal Psalms (93–99 except 94, terminating in Ps. 100 as a doxology), which proclaim the Kingship of Christ.

THE LORD is King, be the people never so impatient : he sitteth between the cherubims, be the earth never so unquiet.

R.V. The LORD reigneth (cp. Ps. 93. 1, 97. 1): *let the peoples tremble.*

impatient: i.e. even if the nations resent his rule.

between the cherubims: which were above the mercy-seat upon the Ark; cp. Ps. 80. 1. *A.V. dwelleth between . . . R.V. sitteth upon . . .;* which may also suggest the thought of the exaltation of the LORD Christ in heaven; cp. Ps. 18. 10.

A.R.V. let the earth be moved.

in Sion: i.e. in Jerusalem, and in the Church on earth.

2 The LORD is great in Sion : and high above all people.

R.V. all peoples.

3 They shall give thanks unto thy Name : which is great, wonderful, AND HOLY.

R.V. Let them praise thy great and terrible name: 'Holy is he.'

4 (The King's power loveth judgement); thou hast prepared equity : thou hast executed judgement and righteousness in Jacob.

5 O magnify the Lord our God : and fall down before his footstool, for HE IS HOLY.

The King: i.e. the LORD (v. 1).
A.R.V. thou dost establish

fall down: cp. Ps. 95. 6.

footstool: i.e. the Ark with its mercy-seat, shrine of the divine presence, cp. Ps. 132. 7 and 1 Chron. 28. 2, 'It was in my heart to build an house of rest for the Ark of the covenant of the LORD, and for the footstool of our God.' We readily apply it to our altars and tabernacles. The Fathers quoted Isa. 66. 1, 'Thus saith the LORD, The heaven is my throne, and the earth is my footstool,' and applied the word to the sacred humanity of Christ.
R.V. worship at his footstool: 'Holy is he.'

6 Moses and Aaron among his priests, and Samuel among such as call upon his Name : these called upon the LORD, and he heard them.

6–8. The example of holy heroes in the past is adduced for the encouragement and warning of Christ's worshippers. A legislator, a priest, and a prophet are mentioned. The word 'priest' is used loosely; but Moses did perform priestly functions (*Exod.* 24. 6 ff.).

7 He spake unto them out of the cloudy pillar : for they kept his testimonies, and the law that he gave them.

cloudy pillar: cp. Exod. 19. 9; Num. 12. 5. Mystically it is the Eternal Wisdom, who said, 'My throne is in a cloudy pillar' (*Ecclus.* 24. 4), who veiled himself in type and figure under the Law, and in his human nature under the Gospel, and gave his law of love.

them: i.e. the three of v. 6; or the people of Israel generally.

8 Thou heardest them, O LORD our God : thou forgavest them, O God, and punishedst their own inventions.

inventions: i.e. idolatrous or sinful practices; cp. Ps. 106. 29, 39; Eccles. 7. 29, 'God made man upright; but they have sought out many inventions.' Cp. *Magnificat*: 'He hath scattered the proud in the imagination of their heart.'

R.V. thou forgavest them, though thou tookest vengeance of their doings, i.e. not even the saints were exempted from God's holy severity against sin. Cp. Exod. 34. 7; Amos 3. 2. Punishment sometimes follows upon forgiveness.

9 O magnify the LORD our God, and worship him upon his holy hill : for the LORD our God IS HOLY.

his holy hill: Sion (v. 2), the Church. Cp. Dan. 2. 34 f.

PSALM 100. *Jubilate Deo*

An invitation to the whole world to unite in the worship of the LORD. A 'missionary' psalm.

O BE joyful in the LORD, all ye lands : serve the LORD with gladness, and come before his presence with a song.

2 Be ye sure that the LORD he is God : it is he that hath made us, and not we ourselves; we are his people, and the sheep of his pasture.

R.V. and we are his; Cp. Ps. 74. 1; 95. 7.

3 O go your way into his gates with thanksgiving, and into his courts with praise : be thankful unto him, and speak good of his Name.

his gates: i.e. of the Temple. *R.V.mg. with a thank-offering,*

4 For the LORD is gracious, his mercy is everlasting : and his truth endureth from generation to generation.

R.V. his faithfulness

Psalm 101. *Misericordiam et judicium*

'A Psalm of David' (title). A king's resolve to make himself, his court, and his kingdom meet for God's presence. Somewhat similar in theme to Pass. 15 and 24. Applicable to all the children of the King of kings.

MY song shall be of mercy and judgement : unto thee, O LORD, will I sing.

Mercy and judgement, united in God (*Exod.* 34. 7), 'keeping mercy for thousands, forgiving iniquity, will by no means clear the guilty,' should be united also in man (*S. Jas.* 2. 13), 'for judgement is without mercy to him that hath shewed no mercy: and mercy glorieth against judgement.'

A.R.V. I will behave myself wisely in a perfect way.

A.R.V. O when wilt thou come unto me? He yearns for the divine presence. Cp. Exod. 20. 24, 'in every place where I record my name I will come unto thee,' and S. John 14. 23, 'If a man love me, we will come unto him, and make our abode with him.'

in my house: i.e. in my private life, and not only when others witness my conduct.

2 O let me have understanding : in the way of godliness.

3 When wilt thou come unto me? : I will walk in my house with a perfect heart.

4 I will take no wicked things in hand; I hate the sins of unfaithfulness : there shall no such cleave unto me.

5 A froward heart shall depart from me : I will not know a wicked person.

froward: i.e. self-willed and obstinate.

6 Whoso privily slandereth his neighbour : him will I destroy.

7 Whoso hath also a proud look and high stomach : I will not suffer him.

A.R.V. an high look and a proud heart. P.B.V. 'stomach' is figurative for pride. Cp. Ps. 18. 27, 131. 7.

8 Mine eyes look upon such as are faithful in the land : that they may dwell with me.

9 Whoso leadeth a godly life : he shall be my servant.

10 There shall no deceitful person dwell in my house : he that telleth lies shall not tarry in my sight.

11 I shall soon destroy all the ungodly that are in the land : that I may root out all wicked doers from the city of the LORD.

R.V. Morning by morning will I destroy. An allusion to the custom of holding courts of justice in the morning; cp. Jer. 21. 13.

the city of the LORD: cp. Ps. 48. 1, 7, and Rev. 21. 27, 'There shall in no wise enter into it [the new Jerusalem] anything unclean, or he that maketh an abomination and a lie.'

THE TWENTIETH DAY

MORNING PRAYER

PSALM 102. *Domine, exaudi*

'A prayer of the afflicted, when he is overwhelmed, and poureth out his complaint before the LORD' (title). The afflicted one is some particular person, or the nation of Israel personified, or Christ our Lord, or the Church, or one member of it: under any of these interpretations, the psalm yields fruitful meaning. Under all of them the transitoriness of man is contrasted with the eternity of God. This is the fifth of the Penitential Psalms: against the sin of avarice. Proper on Ash Wednesday or in any penitential season. It was written perhaps towards the close of the Exile.

HEAR my prayer, O LORD : and let my crying come unto thee.

1–11. The transitoriness, desolation, and loneliness of sinful man.

The Church frequently uses this verse in the form: '*V.* O Lord, hear my prayer. *R.* And let my cry come unto thee.'

2 Hide not thy face from me in the time of my trouble : incline thine ear unto me when I call; O hear me, and that right soon.

3 For my days are consumed away like smoke : and my bones are burnt up as it were a firebrand.

4 My heart is smitten down, and withered like grass : so that I forget to eat my bread.

5 For the voice of my groaning : my bones will scarce cleave to my flesh.

6 I am become like a pelican in the wilderness : and like an owl that is in the desert.

7 I have watched, and am even as it were a sparrow : that sitteth alone upon the house-top.

8 Mine enemies revile me all the day long : and they that are mad upon me are sworn together against me.

9 For I have eaten ashes as it were bread : and mingled my drink with weeping;

10 And that because of thine indignation and wrath : for thou hast taken me up, and cast me down.

11 My days are gone like a shadow : and I am withered like grass.

———

Compunction.

so that: *R.V. because*
my bread : especially the Eucharistic Bread.
For: *A.R.V. By reason of*
I.e. bones and flesh hardly hold together. But *R.V.* has: *my bones cleave to my flesh*, i.e. my limbs are stiff and incapable of active motion; cp. Job 19. 20.
Our Lord has often been symbolized by the pelican, which, according to fable, feeds its young with blood from its own breast.
watched: i.e. spent sleepless nights.

upon: *A.R.V. against*
R.V. do curse by me. Their curses take the form, 'May God do unto thee as he has done unto this man.' Cp. Jer. 29. 22; Isa. 65. 25.
Penance. Cp. Ps. 42. 3, 80. 5.

He sees in his sufferings God's punishment for his sins. The metaphor is from a violent storm; cp. Job 30. 22.
A.R.V. My days are like a shadow that declineth: cp. Ps. 109. 22; 144. 4.

12 But thou, O LORD, shalt endure for ever : and thy remembrance throughout all generations.

12–28. The majesty, mercy, and eternity of God: the glorious future of the Church (Sion). The transition to the happier theme comes earlier here than in the other penitential psalms.

remembrance: *R.V. memorial,* i.e. the Name of Jehovah, the pledge of God's covenant with Israel (*Exod.* 3. 14, 15; *Ps.* 97. 12, 135. 13).

13 Thou shalt arise, and have mercy upon Sion : for it is time that thou have mercy upon her, yea, the time is come.

14 And why? thy servants think upon her stones : and it pitieth them to see her in the dust.

have mercy: i.e. restore her from her state of ruin.

A.R.V. take pleasure in
If Israelites in exile think piteously of the ruins of Jerusalem, how deep must be the compassion of God!

15 The heathen shall fear thy Name, O LORD : and all the kings of the earth thy majesty;

R.V. So the nations . . . The restoration of Jerusalem will bring about the conversion of the world. Cp. Ps. 138. 4 and Isa. 60. 3, 'All nations shall come to thy light, and kings to the brightness of thy rising.'

16 When the LORD shall build up Sion : and when his glory shall appear;

17 When he turneth him unto the prayer of the poor destitute : and despiseth not their desire.

18 This shall be written for them that come after : and the people which shall be born shall praise the LORD.

the poor destitute: i.e. exiled Israel.

R.V. and a people which shall be created shall praise the LORD; i.e. the generations to come; or, the people restored as by a second birth from exile. Cp. Ps. 22. 32.

Cp. Exod. 3. 7; Ps. 11. 4 f.

19 For he hath looked down from his sanctuary : out of the heaven did the LORD behold the earth;

20 That he might hear the mournings of such as are in captivity : and deliver the children appointed unto death;

A.R.V. loose those that are . . . Heb. the children of death, i.e. all, not only the youthful, who are condemned.   Apply to sinners.

21 That they may declare the Name of the LORD in Sion : and his worship at Jerusalem;

In the Church on earth and in heaven. 'Worship' here means, as *A.R.V.*, *praise.*
R.V. peoples

22 When the people are gathered together : and the kingdoms also, to serve the LORD.

23 He brought down my strength in my journey : and shortened my days.

23–24. From the glorious vision of the future, he returns for a moment to his own hapless condition.
journey: i.e. through life.
Whether his prayer for a longer life be granted or not, he finds comfort in the thought of the eternity and unchangeableness (v. 27) of God, which is the guarantee of the perpetuity of his people (v. 28). Cp. Ps. 90. 2.

24 But I said, 'O my God, take me not away in the midst of mine age' : as for thy years, they endure throughout all generations.

25–27. Quoted in Heb. 1. 10–12 as addressed to Christ.
Cp. Col. 1. 16–17.

25 Thou, Lord, in the beginning hast laid the foundation of the earth : and the heavens are the work of thy hands.
26 They shall perish, but thou shalt endure : they all shall wax old as doth a garment;

wax: i.e. grow.

27 And as a vesture shalt thou change them, and they shall be changed : but thou art the same, and thy years shall not fail.

Cp. Heb. 13. 8, 'Jesus Christ, the same, yesterday, to-day, and for ever.'

28 The children of thy servants shall continue : and their seed shall stand fast in thy sight.

Cp. Ps. 69. 37. And the Church, being united with Christ, shall continue for ever.

PSALM 103. *Benedic, anima mea*

The thanksgiving of a full heart to the merciful and loving LORD for spiritual and temporal benefits; calling upon the angels to join their praises, who are the strong and obedient ministers of the LORD's beneficent will. The psalm is suitable to all occasions of thanksgiving, especially on receiving absolution of sins, and on all feasts of the holy angels.

PRAISE THE LORD, O MY SOUL : and all that is within me praise his holy Name.

Verses 2, 22, and Ps 104. 1, 35.

2 PRAISE THE LORD, O MY SOUL : and forget not all his benefits;

Six benefits are stated, vv. 3–5.

3 Who forgiveth all thy sin : and healeth all thine infirmities;

4 Who saveth thy life from destruction : and crowneth thee with mercy and loving-kindness;

5 Who satisfieth thy mouth with good things : making thee young and lusty as an eagle.

satisfieth: cp. Ps. 107. 9, 'He satisfieth the empty soul : and filleth the hungry soul with goodness.

lusty: i.e. vigorous. An allusion to the long life of the eagle, and its retention of vigour to extreme old age. Cp. Isa. 40. 31, 'They that wait upon the LORD shall renew their strength; they shall mount up with wings like eagles.'

6 The LORD executeth righteousness and judgement : for all them that are oppressed with wrong.

7 He shewed his ways unto Moses : his works unto the children of Israel.

Moses' prayer was 'Shew me now thy ways, that I may know thee' (*Exod.* 33. 13).

8 The LORD is full of compassion and mercy : long-suffering, and of great goodness.

9 He will not alway be chiding : neither keepeth he his anger for ever.

So the LORD revealed himself to Moses (*Exod.* 34. 6). Cp. Ps. 86. 15.

Therefore the final rejection of any one will only be through his refusal of God's loving mercy.

S

10 He hath not dealt with us after our sins : nor rewarded us according to our wickednesses.

Cp. Litany: '*V.* O Lord, deal not with us after our sins. *R.* Neither reward us after our iniquities.' 'After' means 'according to.'

Cp. Ps. 36. 5 and Isa. 55. 9.

11 For look how high the heaven is in comparison of the earth : so great is his mercy also toward them that fear him.

12 Look how wide also the east is from the west : so far hath he set our sins from us.

13 Yea, like as a father pitieth his own children : even so is the LORD merciful unto them that fear him.

A.R.V. so the LORD *pitieth.* Cp. *Magnificat,* 'His mercy is on them that fear him, throughout all generations.'

Cp. Gen. 2. 7, 'The LORD God formed man of the dust of the ground'; cp. 3. 19; Eccles. 12. 7; 1 Cor. 15. 47; and Ps .78. 40, 104. 29.

Cp. Ps. 90. 5 f.

14 For he knoweth whereof we are made : he remembereth that we are but dust.

15 The days of man are but as grass : for he flourisheth as a flower of the field.

16 For as soon as the wind goeth over it, it is gone : and the place thereof shall know it no more.

17 But the merciful goodness of the LORD endureth for ever and ever upon them that fear him : and his righteousness upon children's children;

Cp. v. 11.

his righteousness: i.e. in observing his covenant; cp. v. 18.

18 Even upon such as keep his covenant : and think upon his commandments to do them.

Cp. Exod. 20. 6, 'Shewing mercy unto thousands, of them that love me and keep my commandments.'

---

19 The LORD hath prepared his seat in heaven : and his kingdom ruleth over all.

R.V. established his throne. Cp. Ps. 93. 3.

Cp. Ps. 47. 2.

20 O praise the LORD, ye angels of his, ye that excel in strength : ye that fulfil his commandment, and hearken unto the voice of his words.

21 O praise the LORD, all ye his hosts : ye servants of his that do his pleasure.

22 O speak good of the LORD, all ye works of his, in all places of his dominion : PRAISE THOU THE LORD, O MY SOUL.

He turns from the thought of God's mercies to frail mankind, to that of the angels, the ministers of his beneficence, strong and holy in contrast with weak and sinful man.

A.R.V. ye ministers. Cp. Heb. 1. 14, 'Are they not all ministering spirits, sent forth to do service?' And cp. Ps. 104. 4.

I.e. everywhere; cp. v. 19.

EVENING PRAYER

PSALM 104. *Benedic, anima mea*

A hymn of praise to the LORD as the Maker and Sustainer of the Universe. It treats of the work of creation (*Gen.* 1) as an ever-continuing operation. Proper on Whitsunday, as being the festival of the 'Giver of life.'

PRAISE THE LORD, O MY SOUL : O LORD my God, thou art become exceeding glorious; thou art clothed with majesty and honour.

Cp. Ps. 103. 1. thou art become: i.e. in the minds of those who come to know thee through the creation. The LORD manifests himself in nature. Cp. Ps. 19. 1, 'The heavens declare the glory of God,' and Ps. 93. 1, 'The LORD hath put on his apparel, and girded himself with strength.' The words here may also be applied to the exaltation in human nature of the LORD incarnate at his Ascension, through whom all things were made; cp. Ps. 8. 5 f.

2 Thou deckest thyself with light as it were with a garment : and spreadest out the heavens like a curtain.

light: the first day of creation (*Gen.* 1. 3–5). Light is described as the permanent apparel of the Deity. Cp. 1 Tim. 6. 16, 'dwelling in light unapproachable'; and contrast Ps. 97. 2, 'Clouds and darkness are round about him'; cp. Ps. 18. 11; 1 Kings 8.12.

spreadest out the heavens: the second day of creation (*Gen.* 1. 6–8). The heavens or 'firmament' are compared to a canopy extended over the earth.

3 Who layeth the beams of his chambers in the waters : and maketh the clouds his chariot, and walketh upon the wings of the wind.

the waters: i.e. above the firmament (*Gen.* 1. 7). God's chambers are regarded as resting upon the reservoir of waters, which are conceived as held aloft by the blue firmament or expanse of the sky.

wings of the wind: cp. Ps. 18. 10.

4 He maketh his angels spirits: and his ministers a flaming fire.

R.V.mg. maketh his angels winds. God arrays his messengers with the outward properties of fire and wind. *R.V. maketh winds his messengers*; cp. Ps. 148. 8, 'winds and storm fulfilling his word.' The verse is quoted in Heb. 1. 7.

Gen. 1. 1.

5 He laid the foundations of the earth : that it never should move at any time.

6 Thou coveredst it with the deep like as with a garment : the waters stand in the hills.

Thou coveredst: in the primeval chaos before the separation of the waters from the dry land (*Gen.* 1. 2).

A.R.V. the waters stood above the mountains.

7 At thy rebuke they flee : at the voice of thy thunder they are afraid.

7–10. The third day (*Gen.* 1. 9–10).

they: i.e. the primeval waters.

rebuke: cp. Ps. 106. 9.

A.R.V. they fled:

A.R.V. they hasted away.

8 They go up as high as the hills, and down to the valleys beneath : even unto the place which thou hast appointed for them.

R.V. They went up by the mountains, they went down by the valleys. A description of the rush and commotion of the waters as they fled at the rebuke of the Creator.
R.V. which thou hadst founded for them.

9 Thou hast set them their bounds which they shall not pass : neither turn again to cover the earth.

Cp. Gen. 9. 11–16; Job 38. 11; Jer. 5. 22.

10 He sendeth the springs into the rivers : which run among the hills.

A.R.V. into the valleys:
which: i.e. the springs.

11 All beasts of the field drink thereof : and the wild asses quench their thirst.

The sixth day (*Gen.* 1. 24–25).

12 Beside them shall the fowls of the air have their habitation : and sing among the branches.

The fifth day (*Gen.* 1. 20).
Omit 'shall' with R.V.

13 He watereth the hills from above : the earth is filled with the fruit of thy works.

A.R.V. from his chambers, i.e. those mentioned in v. 3. The reference is to the rain.
the fruit: i.e. the vegetable products, such as are mentioned in the following verses, which spring from God's works in nature (*Ps.* 65. 9–12).
14–16. The third day (*Gen.* 1. 11–13).

14 He bringeth forth grass for the cattle : and green herb for the service of men;
15 That he may bring food out of the earth, and wine that maketh glad the heart of man : and oil to make him a cheerful countenance, and bread to strengthen man's heart.

corn, wine, oil: cp. Ps. 4. 8; Zech. 9. 17. In their sacramental uses the Creator's purpose attains its highest fulfilment.

16 The trees of the LORD also are full of sap : even the cedars of Libanus which he hath planted;
17 Wherein the birds make their nests : and fir-trees are a dwelling for the stork.

The trees of the LORD: i.e. the forest trees, as contrasted with crops of human cultivation.
Libanus: i.e. Lebanon.

18 The high hills are a refuge for the wild goats : and so are the stony rocks for the conies.

conies: i.e. rabbits. The Hebrew word means marmots, or rock-badgers, cp. Lev. 11. 5 mg.

19 He appointed the moon for certain seasons : and the sun knoweth his going down.

19–23. The fourth and sixth days (*Gen*. 1. 14–19, 24–31).

A.R.V. the moon for seasons, i.e. to mark divisions of time (*Gen*. 1. 14). The moon is mentioned before the sun because according to Hebrew reckoning the night preceded the day; cp. Gen. 1. 5, 8.

20 Thou makest darkness that it may be night : wherein all the beasts of the forest do move.
21 The lions roaring after their prey : do seek their meat from God.
22 The sun ariseth, and they get them away together : and lay them down in their dens.
23 Man goeth forth to his work, and to his labour : until the evening.

A.R.V. creep forth.

Man alone of all the animals is called to conscious purposeful labour. Such is his dignity, to be a worker, even before the Fall. Cp. Gen. 2. 15 and 19.

Until the evening: also, until life's evening; cp. S. John 9. 4, 'The night cometh, when no man can work.'

24 O LORD, how manifold are thy works : in wisdom hast thou made them all; the earth is full of thy riches.

At this verse the meditation turns into direct prayer.

in wisdom: cp. Prov. 3. 19, 'The LORD by wisdom founded the earth; by understanding he established the heavens,' and 8. 22–31.

25–26. The fifth day (*Gen*. 1. 21).

25 So is the great and wide sea also : wherein are things creeping innumerable, both small and great beasts.

R.V. Yonder is the sea, great and wide:

26 There go the ships, and there is that leviathan : whom thou hast made to take his pastime therein.

leviathan: i.e. usually, the crocodile; cp. Job 41. 1; Ps. 74. 14. Here used in general for 'sea-monster.'

27 These wait all upon thee : that thou mayest give them meat in due season.

Ps. 145. 15.
meat: i.e. food.

28 When thou givest it them they gather it : and when thou openest thy hand they are filled with good.

29 When thou hidest thy face they are troubled : when thou takest away their breath they die, and are turned again to their dust.

hidest thy face: i.e. withdrawest thy sustaining providence. Cp. Ps. 30. 7.

30 When thou lettest thy breath go forth they shall be made : and thou shalt renew the face of the earth.

dust: cp. Ps. 103. 14.
A.R.V. Thou sendest forth thy spirit, they are created : and thou renewest . . . Life is ever being renewed by the Spirit of God. The creation is a continuous process. Cp. Gen. 1. 2, A.V., 'The Spirit of God moved upon the face of the waters'; 2. 7, 'The LORD God breathed into his nostrils the breath of life; Job 33. 4, 'The spirit of God hath made me, and the breath of the Almighty giveth me life.' The verse is applied to the Holy Ghost at Pentecost, and to spiritual regeneration by his power.

31 The glorious majesty of the LORD shall endure for ever : the LORD shall rejoice in his works.

Cp. Gen. 1. 31, 'God saw every thing that he had made, and, behold, it was very good.'

32 The earth shall tremble at the look of him : if he do but touch the hills, they shall smoke.

R.V. Who looketh on the earth, and it trembleth: he toucheth the mountains, and they smoke. Cp. Ps. 144. 5; Exod. 19. 18.

33 I will sing unto the LORD as long as I live : I will praise my God while I have my being.

34 And so shall my words please him : my joy shall be in the LORD.

A.R.V. my meditation

35 As for sinners, they shall be consumed out of the earth, and the ungodly shall come to an end: PRAISE THOU THE LORD, O MY SOUL, PRAISE THE LORD.

And so by the banishment of evil the original harmony of Creation will be restored.

Cp. v. 1.

The final words should be, as in *A.R.V. Praise ye the LORD. R.V.mg. Heb. Hallelujah.* Here Hallelujah occurs for the first time in the Psalter. From the Psalter it passed into Apocalypse, cp. Rev. 19. 1; and thence into the Christian Liturgy.

THE TWENTY-FIRST DAY

MORNING PRAYER

PSALM 105. *Confitemini Domino*

A thanksgiving for God's protecting care of his people in the olden time. Like Pss. 78 and 106 it narrates the early history of Israel. In reciting it we may think also of God's similar care of his Church through the ages. Verses 1–15 combined with Pss. 96 and 106. 1, 47, 48 are found also in 1 Chron. 16. 8–22.

O GIVE thanks unto the LORD, and call upon his Name : tell the people what things he hath done.

1–6. Introduction.

Cp. Isa. 12. 4, 'In that day ye shall say, Give thanks unto the LORD, call upon his name, declare his doings among the peoples.'

the people: *R.V. the peoples.*

2 O let your songs be of him, and praise him : and let your talking be of all his wondrous works.

3 Rejoice in his holy Name : let the heart of them rejoice that seek the LORD.

4 Seek the LORD and his strength : seek his face evermore.

Cp. Ps. 27. 9.

5 Remember the marvellous works that he hath done : his wonders, and the judgements of his mouth,

6 O ye seed of Abraham his servant : ye children of Jacob his chosen.

R.V. of Jacob, his chosen ones.

7 He is the LORD our God : his judgements are in all the world.

7–15. The Patriarchs.

He is 'our God' by covenant, but his rule extends over all nations.

Cp. v. 41, and *Benedictus*: 'to remember his holy covenant; to perform the oath which he sware to our forefather Abraham.'

8 He hath been alway mindful of his covenant and promise : that he made to a thousand generations;

a thousand: i.e. to all of the many (*Deut.* 7. 9).

Gen. 17. 2 ff.

9 Even the covenant that he made with Abraham : and the oath that he sware unto Isaac;

10 And appointed the same unto Jacob for a law : and to Israel for an everlasting testament;

11 Saying, 'Unto thee will I give the land of Canaan : the lot of your inheritance';

Gen. 26. 3.

A.R.V. And confirmed (*Gen.* 28. 13 ff., 35. 9 ff.).

testament: i.e. as *A.R.V. covenant.*

lot: *R.V.mg. cord,* or *line.* A land allotted to Israelites by measuring-line; cp. Ps. 16.7, 78. 56.

12 When there were yet but a few of them : and they strangers in the land;

13 What time as they went from one nation to another : from one kingdom to another people;

14 He suffered no man to do them wrong : but reproved even kings for their sakes;

15 'Touch not mine anointed: and do my prophets no harm.'

kings: as Pharaoh (*Gen.* 12. 17) and Abimelech (*Gen.* 20. 3).

Touch not: the expression is taken from Gen. 20. 6, 26. 11.

R.V. mine anointed ones. The patriarchs are so designated as

16 Moreover, he called for a dearth upon the land : and destroyed all the provision of bread.

consecrated to God. So are Christians; cp. 1 S. John 2. 27. Abraham is called a prophet in Gen. 20. 7.

16–21. Joseph.
Gen. 41. 54.
A.R.V. he brake the whole staff of bread. Bread is so called as being the chief support of life. Cp. Lev. 26. 26.

17 But he had sent a man before them : even Joseph, who was sold to be a bond-servant;

Gen. 45. 5; 50. 20.

18 Whose feet they hurt in the stocks : the iron entered into his soul;

A.R.V. they hurt with fetters: the iron, etc.: P.B.V. follows the Vulg., which here perhaps gives the meaning better than the more literal *R.V. He was laid in chains of iron. R.V.mg. Heb. his soul entered into iron.*

19 Until the time came that his cause was known : the word of the LORD tried him.

R.V. Until the time that his word came to pass: i.e. until his predictions had been verified; cp. Gen. 40. 20 ff.; 41. 53 ff.
the word of the LORD: cp. Ps. 33. 4, 6; 119. 50. Here the phrase probably means the will of God declared by the events of his history.

20 The king sent, and delivered him : the prince of the people let him go free.

Gen. 41. 14; Ps. 146. 7.
R.V. even the ruler of the peoples, and

21 He made him lord also of his house : and ruler of all his substance;

Gen. 41. 40.

22 That he might inform his princes after his will : and teach his senators wisdom.

A.R.V. To bind his princes at his pleasure: cp. Ps. 149. 8.
his princes: i.e. Pharaoh's.
his will: i.e. Joseph's.

23 Israel also came into Egypt : and Jacob was a stranger in the land of Ham.

23–35. Israel in Egypt.
Israel: i.e. Jacob; cp. Gen. 46. 6.
land of Ham: i.e. Egypt; cp. Ps. 78. 52.

24 And he increased his people exceedingly : and made them stronger than their enemies;

25 Whose heart turned so that they hated his people : and dealt untruly with his servants.

26 Then sent he Moses his servant : and Aaron whom he had chosen.

27 And these shewed his tokens among them : and wonders in the land of Ham.

28 He sent darkness, and it was dark : and they were not obedient unto his word.

he: i.e. the LORD.
Exod. 1. 7 ff.

R.V. They set among them his signs: cp. Exod. 10. 1–2; Ps. 78. 44.

Darkness, the ninth plague, is mentioned first, because after it 'the LORD gave the people favour in the sight of the Egyptians' (*Exod.* 11. 3).

they: i.e. the Egyptians. *R.V. and they* (i.e. Moses and Aaron) *rebelled not against his words.*

29 He turned their waters into blood : and slew their fish.

30 Their land brought forth frogs : yea, even in their kings' chambers.

31 He spake the word, and there came all manner of flies : and lice in all their quarters.

32 He gave them hail-stones for rain : and flames of fire in their land.

33 He smote their vines also and fig-trees : and destroyed the trees that were in their coasts.

34 He spake the word, and the grasshoppers came, and caterpillars innumerable : and did eat up all the grass in their land, and devoured the fruit of their ground.

35 He smote all the first-born in their land : even the chief of all their strength.

Exod. 7. 20.

R.V. swarmed with
Exod. 8. 3–6.

Exod. 8. 17, 24.

Exod. 9. 23–25.

R.V. their borders.
Exod. 10. 13–15.
R.V. locust came, and the canker-worm
The plagues of the boils and of the murrain are omitted.
Exod. 12. 29.
R.V.mg. beginning of . . . 'The beginning of his strength' is a phrase used of a man's first-born (*Deut.* 21. 17; *Gen.* 49. 3; *Ps.* 78. 52).

36 He brought them forth also with silver and gold : there was not one feeble person among their tribes.

37 Egypt was glad at their departing : for they were afraid of them.

38 He spread out a cloud to be a covering : and fire to give light in the night-season.

39 At their desire he brought quails : and he filled them with the bread of heaven.

40 He opened the rock of stone, and the waters flowed out : so that rivers ran in the dry places.

41 For why? he remembered his holy promise : and Abraham his servant.

42 And he brought forth his people with joy : and his chosen with gladness;

43 And gave them the lands of the heathen : and they took the labours of the people in possession;

44 That they might keep his statutes : and observe his laws.

36–44. The Exodus.
Exod. 12. 35–36.

R.V. *his tribes*, i.e. the LORD's.
Exod. 12. 33.

Exod. 13. 21, 14. 19. A covering: to screen them from their enemies.
Num. 11. 31.

the bread of heaven : i.e. the Manna. Cp. Exod. 16. 4; Ps. 78. 24, 25; S. John 6. 31.
At Horeb (*Exod.* 17. 6; *Ps.* 78. 16).
We Christians now know that these wonderful events were typical of the greater things of Christ: e.g. 'that rock was Christ' smitten for us (1 *Cor.* 10. 4).
Cp. vv. 8, 9.

R.V. *with singing.* An allusion to the song of triumph after the passage of the Red Sea (*Exod.* 15).

R.V. *peoples*

A.R.V. add *Praise ye the* LORD. *Heb. Hallelujah.*

EVENING PRAYER

PSALM 106. *Confitemini Domino*

The history of Israel—a record of unfaithfulness, which has been paralleled in the history of the Church, and in the experience of fallen men and women, in spite of the grace of God. The psalm was written probably towards the end of the Exile, cp. v. 45. It is similar in subject to Psalms 78 and 105.

O GIVE thanks unto the LORD, for he is gracious : and his mercy endureth for ever.

A.R.V. prefix *Praise ye the* LORD. *Heb. Hallelujah.*

This expression of thanksgiving, found in those psalms only which were written during or after the Exile, occurs first in Jer. 33. 11, 'Give thanks to the LORD of hosts, for the LORD is good, for his mercy endureth for ever.' Cp. 1 Chron. 16. 34, 41; Ps. 136, etc.

1–3. Introduction.

2 Who can express the noble acts of the LORD : or shew forth all his praise?

3 Blessed are they that alway keep judgement : and do righteousness.

4 Remember me, O Lord, according to the favour that thou bearest unto thy people : O visit me with thy salvation;

4–5. Personal. He prays that he personally may share in the blessed lot of his people. There is no salvation for him apart from the corporate felicity of God's chosen ones, in this world or the next.

5 That I may see the felicity of thy chosen : and rejoice in the gladness of thy people, and give thanks with thine inheritance.

6 We have sinned with our fathers : we have done amiss, and dealt wickedly.

6–12. The Passage of the Red Sea.

The words are taken from Solomon's prayer (1 *Kings* 8. 47; cp. *Dan.* 9. 5; *Baruch* 2. 12).

7 Our fathers regarded not thy wonders in Egypt, neither kept they thy great goodness in remembrance : but were disobedient at the sea, even at the Red Sea.

Cp. S. Mark 6. 52, 'They considered not the miracle of the loaves, for their heart was hardened'; S. John 12. 37, 'Though he had done so many signs before them, yet they believed not on him.'

8 Nevertheless, he helped them for his Name's sake : that he might make his power to be known.

Cp. Exod. 9. 16, 'For this cause I have raised thee [Pharaoh] up, for to shew in thee my power; and that my name may be declared throughout all the earth.' Cp. 2 Sam. 7. 23; Isa. 63. 12.

9 He rebuked the Red Sea also, and it was dried up : so he led them through the deep, as through a wilderness.

Cp. Ps. 18. 15; 104. 7.

Cp. Exod. 14. 21; Isa. 51. 10.

a wilderness: i.e. dry land.

10 And he saved them from the adversary's hand : and delivered them from the hand of the enemy.

A.R.V. and redeemed. Cp. Ps. 107. 2.

11 As for those that troubled them, the waters overwhelmed them : there was not one of them left.
12 Then believed they his words : and sang praise unto him.

Cp. Exod. 14. 31, 15. 1, 'Israel saw the great work which the LORD did upon the Egyptians, and the people feared the LORD, and they believed in the LORD, and in his servant Moses. Then sang Moses and the children of Israel this song unto the LORD.'

13 But within a while they forgat his works : and would not abide his counsel.

13–23. In the Wilderness : lust, rebellion, idolatry, discontent.

would not abide: i.e. as *A.R.V. waited not for his counsel,* i.e. for the working out of his plans. Cp. Ps. 107. 11.

14 But lust came upon them in the wilderness : and they tempted God in the desert.

Cp. Num. 11. 5.

tempted: i.e. tested, by questioning his power to provide them with food (*Deut.* 6. 16; cp. *Ps.* 78. 19–21; 1 *Cor.* 10. 9).

15 And he gave them their desire : and sent leanness withal into their soul.

By sending quails (*Num.* 11. 31–34).

and: *A.R.V. but.*

leanness: *Sept.* and *Vulg.* *satiety.*

withal: i.e. with the gratification of their desire.

A.R.V. They envied

saint: *R.V.mg. holy one.* The contention of Korah and his company was that all the congregation were holy (*Num.* 16. 3).

16 They angered Moses also in the tents : and Aaron the saint of the LORD.

17 So the earth opened, and swallowed up Dathan : and covered the congregation of Abiram.

Num. 16. 31–33.

18 And the fire was kindled in their company : the flame burnt up the ungodly.

Num. 16. 35.

19 They made a calf in Horeb : and worshipped the molten image.

Exod. 32. 4–6.

20 Thus they turned their glory : into the similitude of a calf that eateth hay.

glory: i.e. Jehovah; cp. Jer. 2. 11, 'My people have changed their glory for that which did not profit.' This passage is referred to in Rom. 1. 23, 'They changed the glory of the invisible God for the likeness of an image of beasts.'

21 And they forgat God their Saviour : who had done so great things in Egypt;

22 Wondrous works in the land of Ham : and fearful things by the Red Sea.

land of Ham: i.e. Egypt; cp. Ps. 105. 23.

23 So he said, he would have destroyed them, had not Moses his chosen stood before him in the gap : to turn away his wrathful indignation, lest he should destroy them.

Cp. Exod. 32. 10 ff.; Deut. 9. 25; Num. 14. 11 ff. Moses' intercession is compared to the action of a brave warrior who fills with his body the breach made in the city wall. Cp. Ezek. 22. 30.

24 Yea, they thought scorn of that pleasant land : and gave no credence unto his word;

The rebellion which followed the report of the spies (*Num.* 14).

25 But murmured in their tents : and hearkened not unto the voice of the LORD.

Deut. 1. 27.

26 Then lift he up his hand against them : to overthrow them in the wilderness;

I.e. then he took an oath. Cp. Exod. 6. 8; Ezek. 20. 23.

27 To cast out their seed among the nations : and to scatter them in the lands.

28 They joined themselves unto Baal-Peor : and ate the offerings of the dead.

Num. 25.
the dead: i.e. lifeless idols as contrasted with the living God. Cf. Isa. 8. 19.

29 Thus they provoked him to anger with their own inventions : and the plague was great among them.

inventions: cp. Ps. 99. 8; and vv. 38, 42. *R.V. doings.*

30 Then stood up Phinees and prayed : and so the plague ceased.

A.R.V. and executed judgement:
Phinehas was a true heir of Abraham's faith, who 'believed in the LORD; and he counted it to him for righteousness' (*Gen.* 15. 6). His reward was 'the covenant of an everlasting priesthood' (*Num.* 25. 13).

31 And that was counted unto him for righteousness : among all posterities for evermore.

32 They angered him also at the waters of strife : so that he punished Moses for their sakes;

R.V. of Meribah (*Num.* 20. 10–13).
A.R.V. it went ill with Moses

33 Because they provoked his spirit : so that he spake unadvisedly with his lips.

R.V. Because they (the Israelites) *were rebellious against his* (God's) *spirit, and* . . . Cp. Isa. 63. 10, 'They rebelled, and grieved his holy spirit.'
Judges 1. 21, 27 ff.

34 Neither destroyed they the heathen : as the LORD commanded them;

35 But were mingled among the heathen : and learned their works.

36 Insomuch that they worshipped their idols, which turned to their own decay : yea, they offered their sons and their daughters unto devils;

which turned: i.e. which caused their downfall. *R.V. which became a snare unto them.*
devils: *R.V. demons,* such as were believed to be in the idols, cp. 1 Cor. 10. 20 and Deut. 32. 17.

37 And shed innocent blood, even the blood of their sons and of their daughters : whom they offered unto the idols of Canaan; and the land was defiled with blood.

38 Thus were they stained with their own works : and went a whoring with their own inventions.

Ezek. 16. 20, 21, 20. 31.

Idolatry is spiritual fornication. Cp. Exod. 34. 15 f.; Judges 2. 17; Ps. 73. 26, and v. 29.
R.V. own doings.

39 Therefore was the wrath of the LORD kindled against his people : insomuch that he abhorred his own inheritance.

36–44. The wrath and the mercy of the LORD.
Cp. Judges 2. 14.

40 And he gave them over into the hand of the heathen : and they that hated them were lords over them.

41 Their enemies oppressed them : and had them in subjection.

42 Many a time did he deliver them : but they rebelled against him with their own inventions, and were brought down in their wickedness.

R.V. in their counsel, and

43 Nevertheless, when he saw their adversity : he heard their complaint.

43–44. The fulfilment of Solomon's prayer (1 *Kings* 8. 49 f.).

44 He thought upon his covenant, and pitieth them, according unto the multitude of his mercies : yea, he made all those that led them away captive to pity them.

Cp. Ps. 105. 8.
A.R.V. and repented. Cp. Judges 2. 17.

45 Deliver us, O LORD our God, and gather us from among the heathen : that we may give thanks unto thy holy Name, and make our boast of thy praise.

45. An exile's prayer. A prayer for the reunion of the Church.
Cp. 1 Chron. 16. 35 f.

T

46 Blessed be the LORD God of Israel from everlasting, and world without end : and let all the people say, Amen.

This doxology does not harmonize with the tone of the psalm. It was added to mark the conclusion of the Fourth Book of the Psalter.

A.R.V. add *Praise ye the LORD. Heb. Hallelujah.*

BOOK FIVE

THE TWENTY-SECOND DAY

MORNING PRAYER

PSALM 107. *Confitemini Domino*

A call to the lately returned exiles to thank God for answering their prayers and restoring them to their own land. So too we in our turn give thanks for having been brought out of sin and error into the state of salvation.

O GIVE thanks unto the LORD, for he is gracious : and his mercy endureth for ever.

2 Let them give thanks whom the LORD hath redeemed : and delivered from the hand of the enemy;

3 And gathered them out of the lands, from the east, and from the west : from the north, and from the south.

4 They went astray in the wilderness out of the way : and found no city to dwell in;

The liturgical doxology as in Ps. 106. 1.

redeemed: i.e. released from captivity. Cp. Isa. 62. 12, 'They shall call them . . . The redeemed of the LORD.' Cp. Ps. 106. 10; 1 S. Pet. 1. 18; and Isa. 35. 10.

This is the answer to the prayer in Ps. 106. 45, 'Gather us from among the heathen'; cp. Isa. 43. 5 f.; 59. 19 f. Exiles had returned, not only from Babylon, but from all countries where they were scattered. So too people out of every nation shall find their deliverance and safety in the Catholic Church. Cp. S. Matt. 8. 11, 'Many shall come from the east and the west, and shall sit down in the kingdom of heaven.'

Four pictures of human peril and divine deliverance in answer to prayer. 4–9, first picture. Travellers who lost their way in the desert: heathen lost outside the Church, not knowing where to look 'for the city which hath the foundations, whose builder and maker is God'; fainting for need of the truth and grace of God. Cp. Eccles. 10. 15, 'He knoweth not how to go to the city.'

city to dwell in: *R.V. city of habitation*, inhabited city. Cp. vv. 6, 19, 28.

5 Hungry and thirsty : their soul fainted in them.

6 So THEY CRIED UNTO THE LORD IN THEIR TROUBLE : AND HE DELIVERED THEM FROM THEIR DISTRESS.

7 He led them forth by the right way : that they might go to the city where they dwelt.

R.V. by a straight way. Cp. Ezra 8. 21.

A.R.V. a city of habitation; i.e. to the Church.

8 O THAT MEN WOULD THERE-FORE PRAISE THE LORD FOR HIS GOODNESS : AND DECLARE THE WONDERS THAT HE DOETH FOR THE CHILDREN OF MEN!

9 For he satisfieth the empty soul : and filleth the hungry soul with goodness.

satisfieth: cp. Ps. 103. 5.

empty: *A.R.V. longing*.

Quoted in the *Magnificat* in a spiritual sense, 'He hath filled the hungry with good things.' As when the heathen are brought in to become catechumens.

goodness: *R.V. good*. Cp. S. Matt. 5. 6.

10–16. Second picture. Prisoners in a dungeon: habitual sinners.

shadow of death: i.e. dark shadow; cp. Ps. 23. 4.

10 Such as sit in darkness, and in the shadow of death : being fast bound in misery and iron;

11 Because they rebelled against the words of the LORD : and lightly regarded the counsel of the most Highest;

Their suffering is the divinely sent punishment of sin; but their sin does not prevent them from praying.

counsel: cp. Ps. 106. 47.

12 He also brought down their heart through heaviness : they fell down, and there was none to help them.

A.R.V. with labour : i.e. the toil imposed on them as prisoners.

13 So WHEN THEY CRIED UNTO THE LORD IN THEIR TROUBLE : HE DELIVERED THEM OUT OF THEIR DISTRESS.

14 For he brought them out of darkness, and out of the shadow of death : and brake their bonds in sunder.

Cp. *Benedictus,* 'To give light to them that sit in darkness, and in the shadow of death.' As when sinners receive absolution.

15 O THAT MEN WOULD THEREFORE PRAISE THE LORD FOR HIS GOODNESS : AND DECLARE THE WONDERS THAT HE DOETH FOR THE CHILDREN OF MEN!

16 For he hath broken the gates of brass : and smitten the bars of iron in sunder.

Fulfilling the promise in Isa. 45. 2.

17 Foolish men are plagued for their offence : and because of their wickedness.

I.e. the bonds of sin.

17–22. Third picture. Sick persons, physically and spiritually.

Foolish: i.e. morally senseless, wicked; cp. Ps. 14. 1.

18 Their soul abhorred all manner of meat : and they were even hard at death's door.

meat: i.e. food in general.

abhorred: e.g. by lapse from sacraments.

19 So WHEN THEY CRIED UNTO THE LORD IN THEIR TROUBLE : HE DELIVERED THEM OUT OF THEIR DISTRESS.

20 He sent his word, and healed them : and they were saved from their destruction.

his word: spoken of here almost as God's personal messenger and agent. A forecast of the future revelation of the Incarnate Word. Ps. 147. 15, 'He sendeth forth his commandment upon earth: and his word runneth very swiftly; 18, 'He sendeth out his word.' And cp. S. Matt. 8. 8, 'Speak the word only, and my servant shall be healed.'

21 O THAT MEN WOULD THERE-
FORE PRAISE THE LORD FOR HIS
GOODNESS : AND DECLARE THE
WONDERS THAT HE DOETH FOR
THE CHILDREN OF MEN!

22 That they would offer unto
him the sacrifice of thanksgiving:
and tell out his works with gladness!

As when the lapsed return
thankfully to Mass and Holy
Communion.

sacrifice: *A.R.V.* *sacrifices*;
cp. Lev. 7. 11 ff.; Ps. 50. 14.

23 They that go down to the
sea in ships : and occupy their
business in great waters;

23-32. Fourth picture. Sea-
farers in a storm at sea: pilgrims to
their promised land, beset by the
turmoils and dangers of their way.

A.R.V. *do business.* 'Occupy'
means 'transact,' cp. Ezek. 27. 9;
S. Luke 19. 13.

24 These men see the works
of the LORD : and his wonders
in the deep.

25 For at his word the stormy
wind ariseth : which lifteth up
the waves thereof.

26 They are carried up to the
heaven, and down again to the
deep : their soul melteth away
because of the trouble.

27 They reel to and fro, and
stagger like a drunken man :
and are at their wits' end.

28 SO WHEN THEY CRY UNTO
THE LORD IN THEIR TROUBLE :
HE DELIVERETH THEM OUT OF
THEIR DISTRESS.

29 For he maketh the storm
to cease : so that the waves
thereof are still.

Cp. S. Matt. 8. 25, 'His disciples came to him, and awoke
him, saying, Lord, save us : we
perish.'

Cp. Ps. 65. 7 and S. Matt. 8. 26,
'He arose, and rebuked the winds
and the sea; and there was a
great calm.'

Cp. S. John 6. 21, 'And immediately the ship was at the land
whither they went.'

Christ is himself the harbour
of safety for all tempest-tossed
souls. He is both the pilot and
the haven.

30 Then are they glad, because they are at rest : and so he
bringeth them unto the haven
where they would be.

31 O THAT MEN WOULD THERE-
FORE PRAISE THE LORD FOR HIS
GOODNESS : AND DECLARE THE
WONDERS THAT HE DOETH FOR THE
CHILDREN OF MEN!

32 That they would exalt him
also in the congregation of the
people : and praise him in the
seat of the elders!

33 Who turneth the floods into a wilderness : and drieth up
the water-springs;

At public worship and in the
council of state.

33–43. Various illustrations of
God's providential government
of the world: God's spiritual
favours to the faithful ones. The
tenor of the verses is the same
as that of *Magnificat*: 'He hath
put down the mighty from their
seat : and hath exalted the
humble and meek.'

floods: *A.R.V. rivers.*

34 A fruitful land maketh he
barren : for the wickedness of
them that dwell therein.

35 Again, he maketh the
wilderness a standing water : and
water-springs of a dry ground.

36 And there he setteth the
hungry : that they may build
them a city to dwell in;

37 That they may sow their
land, and plant vineyards : to
yield them fruits of increase.

38 He blessed them, so that
they multiply exceedingly : and
suffereth not their cattle to
decrease.

R.V. of habitation; cp. v. 4.

39 And again, when they are
minished, and brought low :
through oppression, through any
plague or trouble;

40 Though he suffer them to
be evil intreated through tyrants:
and let them wander out of the
way in the wilderness;

minished: i.e. diminished.
*R.V. through oppression,
trouble, and sorrow.*
*R.V. He poureth contempt up-
on princes, and causeth them to
wander in the waste, where there
is no way.* A quotation from Job
12. 21, 24.

intreated: i.e. treated.

41 Yet helpeth he the poor
out of misery : and maketh him
households like a flock of sheep.

42 The righteous will consider this, and rejoice : and the
mouth of all wickedness shall be
stopped.

All wicked people will be put
to silence.

Cp. Hosea 14. 9, 'Who is wise,
and he shall understand these
things? prudent, and he shall
know them? for the ways of the
LORD are right, and the just shall
walk in them; but transgressors
shall fall therein.'

43 Whoso is wise will ponder
these things : and they shall
understand the loving-kindness
of the LORD.

PSALM 108.   *Paratum cor meum*

A triumphant celebration of God's subjugation of the nations to
himself, with an earnest prayer for help in some time of national
danger. This psalm is a combination of Ps. 57, 8-12 and Ps. 60.
5-12, and like the latter, it is a 'missionary' psalm treating of the
extension of the Church. Proper on Ascension Day, as the day
of the inauguration of Christ's triumph.

O GOD, my heart is ready,
my heart is ready : I will
sing, and give praise with the
best member that I have.

A.R.V. is fixed, i.e. steadfast
in faith.

A.R.V. even with my glory.
Both 'best member' and 'glory'
denote 'soul.' Cp. Ps. 7. 5, 16.
10, 30. 13.

2 Awake, thou lute and harp:
I myself will awake right early.

*R.V.mg. I will awake the
dawn*, i.e. my song shall arouse
the morning from its slumber.

3 I will give thanks unto thee,
O LORD, among the people : I
will sing praises unto thee
among the nations.

R.V. peoples

4 For thy mercy is greater
than the heavens : and thy truth
reacheth unto the clouds.

Cp. Ps. 103. 11.

5 Set up thyself, O God,
above the heavens : and thy
glory above all the earth.

6 That thy beloved may be delivered : let thy right hand save them, and hear thou me.

7 God hath spoken in his holiness : 'I will rejoice therefore, and divide Sichem, and mete out the valley of Succoth.

8 Gilead is mine, and Manasses is mine : Ephraim also is the strength of my head;

9 Judah is my law-giver, Moab is my wash-pot : over Edom will I cast out my shoe; upon Philistia will I triumph.'

10 Who will lead me into the strong city : and who will bring me into Edom?

thy beloved: i.e. Israel and the Church.

7–9. The words of God: as a victorious warrior he claims afresh the whole land of Canaan. The distribution of territory ('divide,' 'mete,' i.e. measure out) is the fullest proof of possession. Shechem and Succoth are mentioned in the history of Jacob (*Gen.* 33. 17 f.). Of the localities mentioned here, Shechem, Ephraim, and Judah represent the country west of Jordan, Succoth and Gilead (inhabited by the half-tribe of Manasseh) the country east of Jordan.

strength: *R.V. defence.* Ephraim was the most powerful tribe.

law-giver: *R.V. sceptre.* Judah was the royal tribe. (The clause should be part of v. 8.)

God will extend his conquests to the neighbouring nations: the Church will be catholic.

wash-pot: a contemptuous symbol of subjugation.

cast, etc.: an Eastern sign of taking forcible possession.

10–13. The words of the psalmist personifying Israel or Israel's leader in war. The voice of the Church.

the strong city: probably Petra, the capital of Edom, apparently at war with Israel. It stands for whatever may be the next sphere of the Church's missionary conquest.

11 Hast not thou forsaken us, O God : and wilt not thou, O God, go forth with our hosts?

R.V. Hast not thou cast us off, O God, and thou goest not forth

12 O help us against the enemy : for vain is the help of man.

13 Through God we shall do great acts : and it is he that shall tread down our enemies.

PSALM 109. *Deus, laudem*

The voice of the persecuted pleading to God for vengeance. The psalm is suitable to Passiontide. Christ is to be heard as the speaker throughout.

HOLD not thy tongue, O God of my praise : for the mouth of the ungodly, yea, the mouth of the deceitful is opened upon me.

1–4. The Passion of Christ.
of my praise: i.e. the object of my praise. Cp. Ps. 71. 5, 'My praise shall be always of thee.'

2 And they have spoken against me with false tongues : they compassed me about also with words of hatred, and fought against me without a cause.

Cp. S. Matt. 27. 59,'The whole council sought false witness against Jesus, to put him to death; but found none: yea, though many false witnesses came.'
without a cause: cp. Ps. 35. 19, 69. 4; and S. John 15. 25, 'They hated me without a cause.'

3 For the love that I had unto them, lo, they take now my contrary part : but I give myself unto prayer.

I.e. they take side against me.
Cp. Ps. 69. 13, 'I make my prayer unto thee in an acceptable time'; S. Luke 23. 34, 'Then said Jesus, Father, forgive them'; 1 S. Pet. 2. 23, 'He committed himself to him that judgeth righteously.'

4 Thus have they rewarded me evil for good : and hatred for my good will.

Cp. Ps. 35. 11, 'False witnesses did rise up . . . they rewarded me evil for good.'

5 Set thou an ungodly man to be ruler over him : and let Satan stand at his right hand.

5–19. Righteous vengeance of the divine Judge and Saviour. Cp. Ps. 35. 4–8, 69. 23–29.

over him: one persecutor is singled out as representative of all; with the prayer that he may be put on trial before an unrighteous judge with a prosecutor ready to accuse him, instead of a champion to defend him; cp. v. 30.

Satan: *R.V. an adversary*.

6 When sentence is given upon him, let him be condemned : and let his prayer be turned into sin.

turned: i.e. regarded by God as sinful; cp. Prov. 28. 9.

7 Let his days be few : and let another take his office.

Applied in Acts 1. 20 by S. Peter to the case of Judas Iscariot. These verses are an expansion of our Lord's words: 'Woe unto that man through whom the Son of Man is betrayed: good were it for that man if he had not been born' (*S.Mark* 14. 21). But not all the details are applicable to him personally. Here is laid down the doom of all those who have betrayed Christ and not repented.

8 Let his children be fatherless : and his wife a widow.

9 Let his children be vagabonds, and beg their bread : let them seek it also out of desolate places.

R.V.mg. far from their desolate places, i.e. far from their ruined homes from which they have been expelled.

10 Let the extortioner consume all that he hath : and let the stranger spoil his labour.

R.V. make spoil of

11 Let there be no man to pity him : nor to have compassion upon his fatherless children.

12 Let his posterity be destroyed : and in the next generation let his name be clean put out.

Let the evil influence have but a brief duration. Cp. Ps. 21. 10
his: *A.R.V. their*

13 Let the wickedness of his fathers be had in remembrance in the sight of the LORD : and let not the sin of his mother be done away.

Cp. Exod. 20. 5.

14 Let them alway be before the LORD : that he may root out the memorial of them from off the earth;

memorial: had formerly the meaning of, as in *A.R.V. memory.* Cp. Ps. 9. 6, 34. 16.

15 And that, because his mind was not to do good : but persecuted the poor, helpless man, that he might slay him that was vexed at the heart.

A.R.V. Because that he remembered not to shew mercy. His sin was wilful, permanent, and inhuman.
poor, helpless, vexed at heart (*A.R.V. broken in heart*): such as the psalmist was, i.e. Christ, and those who belong to Christ.

16 His delight was in cursing, and it shall happen unto him : he loved not blessing, therefore shall it be far from him.

shall happen: *R.V. came.*

R.V. and it was far from him.

17 He clothed himself with cursing, like as with a raiment : and it shall come into his bowels like water, and like oil into his bones.

R.V. and it came
Cursing became a positive refreshment to his evil nature.

18 Let it be unto him as the cloke that he hath upon him : and as the girdle that he is alway girded withal.

19 Let it thus happen from the LORD unto mine enemies : and to those that speak evil against my soul.

withal: i.e. with.
R.V. This is the reward of mine adversaries from the LORD: and of . . .

---

20 But deal thou with me, O Lord GOD, according unto thy Name : for sweet is thy mercy.

20–30, a personal petition for divine grace.
God is merciful, even though he takes vengeance upon sinners.

21 O deliver me, for I am helpless and poor : and my heart is wounded within me.

Cp. v. 15. The Sacred Heart of Jesus, broken and wounded by sinners.
Cp. Ps. 102. 11.

22 I go hence like the shadow that departeth : and am driven away as the grasshopper.
23 My knees are weak through fasting : my flesh is dried up for want of fatness.
24 I became also a reproach unto them : they that looked upon me shaked their heads.

R.V. I am become
R.V. when they see me, they shake. Cp. Ps. 22. 7 and S. Matt. 27. 39.

25 Help me, O LORD my God : O save me according to thy mercy;
26 And they shall know, how that this is thy hand : and that thou, LORD, hast done it.

how that: i.e. as *A.R.V. that.*

27 Though they curse, yet bless thou : and let them be confounded that rise up against me; but let thy servant rejoice.

R.V. when they arise, they shall be ashamed, but thy servant shall rejoice.

28 Let mine adversaries be clothed with shame : and let them cover themselves with their own confusion, as with a cloke.
29 As for me, I will give great thanks unto the LORD with my mouth : and praise him among the multitude;
30 For he shall stand at the right hand of the poor : to save his soul from unrighteous judges.

Mark the contrast between this verse and v. 5. The LORD stands at the right hand of the persecuted poor (v. 15), to protect him; but the adversary stands at the right hand of the persecutor to accuse him (v. 5).

THE TWENTY-THIRD DAY
MORNING PRAYER

PSALM 110. *Dixit Dominus*

A message from the LORD to the King Messiah, that the LORD appoints him to be his vice-gerent and priest, and promises him divine aid in war to gain the victory over his enemies.

This psalm is a dramatic lyric, written by some one who adopts the character of David; the person prophetically addressed by David as 'my lord' was meant to be understood as being the promised Messiah.

Our Lord cited the psalm (*S. Matt.* 22. 43-45), asking the Pharisees, 'How doth David in the Spirit call him lord, saying, "The LORD said unto my lord," ' etc. His argument requires that David is the speaker in v. 1, but not necessarily that David was the author of the psalm, as some have thought.

The psalm is frequently quoted in the N.T., and in each passage is treated as having reference to the kingship and priesthood of Christ, the son of David but greater than David. Cp. Heb. 5. 5 ff. where Ps. 2. 7 is quoted together with v. 4 of this psalm: 'Christ glorified not himself to be made a high priest, but he (was glorified by the LORD) that spake unto him, "Thou art my Son, this day have I begotten thee," as he saith also, "Thou art a priest for ever after the order of Melchisedek." '

The psalm is proper on Christmas Day and Ascension Day, and on all feasts of Christ, and those of the Saints who share his triumph, cp. v. 3.

THE LORD said unto my lord : 'Sit thou on my right hand, until I make thine enemies thy footstool.'

1–8. The prophet - psalmist announces the message of the LORD Jehovah to the king ('my lord,' adoni). Mystically interpreted: 'The Father said to the Incarnate Son.'

said: *R.V. saith.*

Sit thou on my right hand: as sharing my throne and wielding my authority. 'Sit' may also mark the completion of Christ's saving work: rest after struggle. The words are mystically applied in the N.T. to the exaltation of Christ consequent on his death. Cp. S. Matt. 26. 64, 'The Son of Man sitting on the right hand of power.' Acts 2. 34, 'David is not ascended into the heavens, but he said himself, The LORD said,' etc. Eph. 1. 20, 'God raised him from the dead, and made him to sit at his right hand in the heavenly places.' Cp. also Heb. 1. 13; 8. 1; 12. 2; Col. 3. 1; 1 S. Pet. 3. 22, etc. and the Creed, 'He sitteth on the right hand of the Father.'

until I make . . . thy footstool: i.e. in subjection under thy feet. Cp. Ps. 8. 6; 1 Cor. 15. 25; Eph. 1. 22; Heb. 2. 8, and 10. 13, 'He sat down on the right hand of God; from henceforth expecting till his enemies be made the footstool of his feet.'

2 The LORD shall send the rod of thy power out of Sion : 'Be thou ruler, even in the midst among thine enemies.'

The rod or sceptre is the symbol of power and rule. Cp. Isa. 2. 3, 'Out of Sion shall go forth the law, and the word of the LORD from Jerusalem.' The rod of Christ's power is especially his cross, from Calvary at Jerusalem, by which Christ's enemies are converted or subdued.

The word 'saying' is to be understood before 'Be thou ruler . . .' This is part of the LORD'S message.

among thine enemies: as even in the passion Christ reigned from the tree. Cp. Ps. 96. 10. So he reigns in Sion, his Church militant and persecuted.

3 In the day of thy power shall the people offer thee free-will offerings with an holy worship : the dew of thy birth is of the womb of the morning.

The psalmist's vision of the mustering of the king's army. *R.V. Thy people offer themselves willingly* (mg. *are free-will offerings*) *in the day of thy power* (mg. *army*).

with an holy worship: *R.V.*

in the beauties of holiness. R.V. mg. in holy attire. Cp. Ps. 29. 2; 96. 9; 1 Chron. 16. 29. The warriors of the priest-king are themselves priests.

With this picture cp. that of Rev. 19. 14 ff., 'The armies which are in heaven followed him upon white horses, clothed in fine linen, white and clean.'

the dew of thy birth is of the womb of the morning: i.e. thy generation is 'before all worlds,' before the light, before creation, from eternity; or, thy birth is from the immaculate womb of Mary, cp. Cant. 6. 10. Similarly in Sept. and Vulg. the verse is *With thee is the beginning* (or, *the dominion*) *in the day of thy power, in the splendours of thy saints; from the womb before the morning star have I begotten thee.* Cp. Ps. 2. 7. But *R.V.* has: *from the womb of the morning, thou hast the dew of youth,* i.e. thy youthful warriors. In their freshness and multitude they are like the dew, the offspring of the morning (cp. 1 *Sam.* 17. 11, 12); the reference then is to the army-muster.

4 The LORD sware, and will not repent : 'Thou art a priest for ever after the order of Melchisedek.'

The LORD'S message continued. The king is solemnly inaugurated as the eternal priest.

sware: cp. Ps. 132. 11; Heb. 7. 21.

repent: i.e. change his mind; cp. Num. 23. 19.

order: i.e. as *R.V.mg. manner.*

Melchisedek was a priest, not of the order of Aaron, as were the Jewish priests; he was both a king and a priest (*Gen.* 14. 18); and in the O.T. records he 'abides a priest continually,' as he appears there without any lineage of predecessors or successors. The words of the prophecy received their final and adequate fulfilment in Christ the divine king of David's line. Cp. Heb. 5. 5 f., 'Christ glorified not himself to be made a high priest, but he (God, glorified him) that spake unto him, Thou art a priest'; 7. 16, 'Who hath been made priest, after the power of an endless life, for it is witnessed of him, Thou art a priest for ever'; 7. 23, 'This man, because he continueth ever, hath an unchangeable priesthood.'

5 The Lord upon thy right hand : shall wound even kings in the day of his wrath.

5–7. The psalmist's forecast of the king's victory.

The Lord (Adonai): here denotes the LORD Jehovah. He stands at the king's right hand as his champion to defend and aid him in the battle. Cp. Ps. 16. 8; 109. 30. But in v. 1 the king is on God's right hand, not God on his. So some think that the psalmist may be understood as now addressing the Father, the LORD, at whose right hand is the Messiah-King, the Lord Christ, who is to subjugate all his foes (which interpretation, however, involves an awkward change in the meaning of 'thy').

the day of his wrath: cp. Ps. 2. 5, 12.

He: i.e. the king.

heathen: *R.V. nations.*

divers: different, various. *R.V. he shall strike through the head in many countries.*

6 He shall judge among the heathen; he shall fill the places with the dead bodies : and smite in sunder the heads over divers countries.

Mystically interpreted, this battle-scene represents Christ's

U

conquest of the world. Cp. Rev.
19. 11–16, 'In righteousness he
doth judge and make war. And
out of his mouth proceedeth a
sharp sword, that with it he
should smite the nations: and
he shall rule them with a rod of
iron: and he treadeth the wine-
press of the fierceness of the
wrath of Almighty God.'

7 He shall drink of the brook
in the way : therefore shall he
lift up his head.

I.e. 'faint, yet pursuing' (*Judges*
8. 4, 15. 8); he refreshes himself
and renews his vigour. This
may be applied to the Christian warrior also, renewing his
strength at the waters of life.
Mystically, our Lord stooped to
drink the waters of his passion,
cp. Ps. 69. 1; and was uplifted in
his resurrection and ascension.

PSALM 111.　*Confitebor tibi*

The character of God declared by his marvellous acts. The psalm
spiritually understood points forward to Christ as the Redeemer and
the Mediator of the New Covenant, and especially to the Blessed
Sacrament. This and the following psalm are similar in form and
contents. This celebrates the glory, the righteousness, and the
mercy of God; Ps. 112 sets forth the blessedness, the righteousnes,
and the beneficence of God's servants. Proper at Easter and in
Vespers of the Blessed Sacrament.

I WILL give thanks unto the
LORD with my whole heart :
secretly among the faithful, and
in the congregation.

A.R.V. prefix, *Praise ye the
LORD. Heb. Hallelujah.*
I.e. privately and publicly.
*R.V. in the council of the up-
right, and . . .*
congregation: cp. Ps. 22. 25.

2 The works of the LORD are
great : sought out of all them
that have pleasure therein.

The works of the LORD:
specially those wrought by him
for the benefit of Israel (v. 6).
sought out: i.e. studied and
pondered.
of: i.e. by.

3 His work is worthy to be praised, and had in honour : and HIS RIGHTEOUSNESS ENDURETH FOR EVER.

4 The merciful and gracious LORD hath so done his marvellous works : that they ought to be had in remembrance.

Cp. Ps. 112. 3, 9.

A.R.V. He hath made his wonderful works to be remembered: the LORD is gracious and full of compassion.

in remembrance: the reference is to the Passover, the memorial of God's deliverance of his people from Egypt.

meat: i.e. food; here in particular the Passover meal, or the manna, both of them types of the Christian Eucharist. Cp. Ps. 34. 9, 10.

covenant: cp. Ps. 105. 6. Still more will the LORD be mindful of the New Covenant (*S. Matt.* 26. 28).

5 He hath given meat unto them that fear him : he shall ever be mindful of his covenant.

6 He hath shewed his people the power of his works : that he may give them the heritage of the heathen.

7 The works of his hand are verity and judgement : all his commandments are true.

8 They stand fast for ever and ever : and are done in truth and equity.

9 He sent redemption unto his people : he hath commanded his covenant for ever; holy and reverend is his Name.

R.V. in giving, i.e. by the conquest of Canaan.

A.R.V. are sure.

redemption: i.e. release from the bondage of Egypt; and from the slavery of sin.

commanded: i.e. established.

holy Name: cp. Ps. 99. 3.

Cp. Prov. 9. 10.

10 The fear of the LORD is the beginning of wisdom : a good understanding have all they that do thereafter; the praise of it endureth for ever.

thereafter: i.e. according to it.

A.R.V. his praise.

Psalm 112. *Beatus vir*

The character of the servant of God: a companion psalm to the preceding. Cp. also Pss. 15 and 26.

BLESSED is the man that feareth the LORD : he hath great delight in his commandments.

A.R.V. prefix, *Praise ye the* LORD. *Heb. Hallelujah.*
Cp. Ps. 128. 1, 4.
Delight is the offspring of holy fear.

2 His seed shall be mighty upon earth : the generation of the faithful shall be blessed.
3 Riches and plenteousness shall be in his house : and HIS RIGHTEOUSNESS ENDURETH FOR EVER.

his righteousness : these words, repeated in v. 9, which in the preceding psalm are used of God, are here applied to the man who fears God. Man's righteousness is a copy of the divine, and comes to man by God's gift.
Cp. Ps. 97. 11.

4 Unto the godly there ariseth up light in the darkness : he is merciful, loving, and righteous.
5 A good man is merciful, and lendeth : and will guide his words with discretion.

R.V. Well is it with the man that dealeth graciously and lendeth: he shall maintain his cause in judgement. I.e. no accusation can overthrow him; cp. v. 6.

6 For he shall never be moved: and the righteous shall be had in everlasting remembrance.
7 He will not be afraid of any evil tidings : for his heart standeth fast, and believeth in the LORD.
8 His heart is established, and will not shrink : until he see his desire upon his enemies.
9 He hath dispersed abroad, and given to the poor : and HIS RIGHTEOUSNESS REMAINETH FOR EVER; his horn shall be exalted with honour.

His good name shall endure among men.

Cp. Ps. 54. 7.
Cp. 2 Cor. 9. 9, 'God is able to make all grace abound unto you; that ye may abound unto every good work: as it is written, He hath dispersed abroad,' etc.
his horn: there is a reward for the charitable.

10 The ungodly shall see it, and it shall grieve him : he shall gnash with his teeth, and consume away; the desire of the ungodly shall perish.

Note that this psalm ends, as it begins, like Ps. 1.

PSALM 113. *Laudate, pueri*

A hymn of praise to the mighty God who condescends to visit and exalt the lowly.

Pss. 113–118 constitute the 'Hallel,' or great Hallelujah, which was sung at all the great Jewish festivals. At the Passover Pss. 113–114 were sung before and Pss. 115–118 after the meal; cp. S. Matt. 26. 30. This psalm therefore is proper at Eastertide.

PRAISE the LORD, ye servants : O praise THE NAME OF THE LORD.

A.R.V. prefix, *Praise ye the LORD. Heb. Hallelujah.*

A.R.V. Praise, O ye servants of the LORD: i.e. the Israelites, as set apart for the service of God.

2 Blessed be THE NAME OF THE LORD : from this time forth for evermore.

'*V.* Blessed be the Name of the Lord. *R.* Henceforth, world without end' (Confirmation Service).

3 THE LORD'S NAME IS praised : from the rising up of the sun unto the going down of the same.

'*V.* Praise ye the Lord. *R.* The Lord's Name be praised' (Daily Offices).

'The Name of the LORD' thrice : Three Persons, One God.

from the rising, etc.: a foreshadowing of the universal acceptance of God's rule. His praise will not only be ceaseless, but also world-wide. Cp. Ps. 50. 1; Isa. 59. 19; and Mal. 1. 11, 'From the rising of the sun even unto the going down of the same my Name is great among the Gentiles; and in every place incense is offered for my Name, and a pure offering: for my Name is great among the Gentiles.'

4 The LORD is high above all heathen : and his glory above the heavens.

A.R.V. all nations:

5 Who is like unto the LORD our God, that hath his dwelling so high : and yet humbleth himself to behold the things that are in heaven and earth?

Who is like: cp. 35. 10; Ezek. 31. 2.

Cp. Isa. 57. 15, 'Thus saith the high and lofty One that inhabiteth eternity, whose name is Holy: I dwell in the high and holy place, with him also that is of a contrite and humble spirit.' Here only in Scripture is God said to humble himself; but cp. Phil. 2. 8.

6 He taketh up the simple out of the dust : and lifteth the poor out of the mire;

6–7. Metaphors for extreme poverty and degradation. The verses follow those of the Song of Hannah (1 *Sam*. 2. 8); cp. the *Magnificat* (*S. Luke* 1. 52).

mire: *A.R.V. dunghill*. The allusion is to the refuse-heaps, outside Eastern villages, the haunts of outcasts.

7 That he may set him with the princes : even with the princes of his people.

8 He maketh the barren woman to keep house : and to be a joyful mother of children.

Cp. 1 Sam. 2. 5. Besides the literal meaning, the psalmist probably has in view the state of Sion before and after her captivity; and the words are readily applied to the Catholic Church taking the place of the Jewish. Cp. Isa. 54. 1, quoted in Gal. 4. 27, 'The Jerusalem that is above is free, which is our mother. For it is written, Rejoice, thou barren that barest not; for more are the children of the desolate than of her which hath the husband.' Other applications have been made, to souls heretofore unfruitful in good works, but wedded to Christ by faith and repentance, and bringing forth abundant progeny; and to the virgins who in the Religious Life have spiritually many offspring.

EVENING PRAYER

PSALM 114. *In exitu Israel*

The awe and commotion of nature as it witnessed God's guidance of his people out of Egypt. Proper on Easter Day, the Church's celebration of a greater redemption than that of Israel from Egypt, and also on Sundays, the weekly memorial of the resurrection of the Lord.

WHEN Israel came out of Egypt : and the house of Jacob from among the strange people,

2 Judah was his sanctuary : and Israel his dominion.

strange: i.e. foreign.

his: i.e. God's.

was: *R.V. became.* At the Exodus the nation, designated here by its two historical divisions, was sanctified by God as his abode and kingdom. Exod. 19. 5–6, 'Ye shall be a peculiar treasure unto me from among all peoples: and ye shall be unto me a kingdom of priests, and an holy nation.' Cp. Ps. 59. 13, 78. 68. And similarly at our Lord's exodus, his resurrection and ascension, he led the way for the new chosen people out of the bondage of sin into his holy Church.

3 THE SEA SAW THAT, AND FLED : JORDAN WAS DRIVEN BACK.

sea: i.e. the Red Sea. Nature acknowledged the power of God at the passage of the Red Sea and of the river Jordan, and at the giving of the Law at Sinai.

4 THE MOUNTAINS SKIPPED LIKE RAMS : AND THE LITTLE HILLS LIKE YOUNG SHEEP.

5 What aileth thee, O THOU SEA, THAT THOU FLEDDEST : AND THOU JORDAN, THAT THOU WAST DRIVEN BACK?

6 YE MOUNTAINS, THAT YE SKIPPED LIKE RAMS : AND YE LITTLE HILLS, LIKE YOUNG SHEEP?

Cp. Exod. 19. 18, 'The whole mount quaked greatly,' at God's presence; cp. v. 7.

Symbolizing the overthrowing of the resistance of the powers of evil, at the preaching of the Gospel.

7 Tremble, thou earth, at the presence of the Lord : at the presence of the God of Jacob;

Gives the answer to the question in vv. 5–6, in the form of a command.
Cp. Ps. 18. 7–8.

8 Who turned the hard rock into a standing water : and the flint-stone into a springing well.

At Rephidim and Kadesh (*Exod.* 17. 6; *Num.* 20. 11); symbolizing the conversion of sinners and unbelievers.

PSALM 115.   *Non nobis, Domine*

A prayer to the living God to vindicate the honour of his name by succouring those who trust in him. In Sept. and Vulg. this psalm is joined to the preceding to make one psalm, 114 celebrating the true God, as compared with the idols of the false gods in 115. Pss. 115–118 were probably sung by our Lord and his apostles after the institution of the Blessed Sacrament; cp. Ps. 113 introd.

NOT unto us, O LORD, not unto us, but unto thy Name give the praise : for thy loving mercy, and for thy truth's sake.

1–2. A prayer for help.
the praise: *A.R.V. glory.* May God glorify, not us, but his own name by delivering his people, and thus silencing the taunts of their enemies. It is a prayer, not a thanksgiving. Cp. Isa. 48. 11, 'For my own sake will I do it; for how should my name be profaned? and my glory will I not give to another.'
Cp. Ps. 42. 3 and Exod. 32. 12.

2 Wherefore shall the heathen say : 'Where is now their God?'
3 As for our God, he is in heaven : he hath done whatsoever pleased him.

3–8. God is almighty: the idols cannot help.
God is almighty, i.e. his power is adequate to his good pleasure.
their: i.e. those of the heathen.
Cp. Isa. 44. 10–20.

4 Their idols are silver and gold : even the work of men's hands.
5 They have mouths, and speak not : eyes have they, and see not.
6 They have ears, and hear not : noses have they, and smell not,

7 They have hands, and handle not; feet have they, and walk not: neither speak they through their throat.

8 They that make them are like unto them : and so are all such as put their trust in them.

R.V. shall be like unto them, yea, every one that

One reason for the necessity of having a true faith is that people tend to become conformed to the objects of their worship.

9 But thou, house of Israel, TRUST THOU IN THE LORD : HE IS THEIR SUCCOUR AND DEFENCE.

9–11. Trust in the LORD for help.

The classifications 'Israel,' 'house of Aaron,' 'ye that fear the LORD' occur also in Ps. 118. 2–4, 136. 19.

9, 10, 11. *A.R.V. he is their help and their shield.* Probably the response of the choir; hence the change of person in 'their.' And v. 13 is the antiphonal response to v. 12, and vv. 16–18 to vv. 14–15.

10 Ye house of Aaron, PUT YOUR TRUST IN THE LORD : HE IS THEIR HELPER AND DEFENDER.

11 Ye that fear the LORD : PUT YOUR TRUST IN THE LORD: HE IS THEIR HELPER AND DEFENDER.

12 The LORD hath been mindful of us, and HE SHALL BLESS US : HE SHALL BLESS the house of Israel, HE SHALL BLESS the house of Aaron.

13 HE SHALL BLESS them that fear the LORD : both small and great.

14 The LORD shall increase you more and more : you and your children.

15 Ye are the blessed of the LORD : who made heaven and earth.

16 All the whole heavens are the LORD'S : the earth hath he given to the children of men.

12–18. The blessed of the LORD shall praise him here in this world and this life which he has given them.

17 The dead praise not thee, O LORD : neither all they that go down into silence.

The dead: this would be understood literally by the Jews; cp. Ps. 6. 5, 31. 19. Here, however, the reference may be to the idolaters, spiritually lifeless as their idols are physically, and so to all who are spiritually dead in sin.

18 But we will praise the LORD : from this time forth for evermore. Praise the LORD.

R.V. Praise ye the LORD. R.V. mg. Heb. Hallelujah.

THE TWENTY-FOURTH DAY

MORNING PRAYER

PSALM 116.   Dilexi, quoniam

A thanksgiving for recovery from an almost fatal sickness. The psalm is used in the Churching of Women, omitting vv. 13–15.

In Sept. and Vulg. it is divided after v. 9 to form two psalms. The first part has been interpreted mystically as an Easter psalm, the speaker being the Risen Lord; and the second part as being the words of the holy Martyrs. Cp. Ps. 16.

I AM well pleased : that the LORD hath heard the voice of my prayer;

1–9. God's help in trouble.
A.R.V. I love the LORD, because he hath heard my voice and my supplications. Cp. S. John 14. 31, 'that the world may know that I love the Father,' and 'offered up prayers and supplications . . . and having been heard' (Heb. 5. 7).
A.R.V. Because he hath

2 That he hath inclined his ear unto me : therefore WILL I CALL UPON HIM as long as I live.

Cp. S. John 11. 41, 'Father, I thank thee that thou hast heard me. And I knew that thou hearest me always.'

3 The snares of death compassed me round about : and the pains of hell gat hold upon me.

R.V. The cords. Death is compared to a hunter seeking his prey. Cp. Ps. 18. 3, 4.
hell: R.V. Sheol.

4 I shall find trouble and heaviness, and I WILL CALL UPON THE NAME OF THE LORD : O LORD, I beseech thee, deliver my soul.

A.R.V. I found
A.R.V. then called I
Cp. vv. 12, 15.

5 Gracious is the LORD, and righteous : yea, our God is merciful.

6 The LORD preserveth the simple : I was in misery, and he helped me.

simple: i.e. guileless, single-hearted (cp. *Ps.* 19. 7) ; referable to our Lord.

7 Turn again then unto thy rest, O my soul : for the LORD hath rewarded thee.

I.e. return to thy restful trust in God. Applicable also to the eternal rest; cp. Heb. 4. 9, 'There remaineth a sabbath rest for the people of God.' Cp. Rev. 14. 13.
A.R.V. hath dealt bountifully with.

8 And why? thou hast delivered my soul from death : mine eyes from tears, and my feet from falling.

8–9 are quoted, with slight changes, from Ps. 56. 13.
Cp. Ps. 16. 11, 86. 13.
Three characteristics of the beatific life: immortality, impassibility, inalienability.

9 I will walk before the LORD: in the land of the living.

10 I believed, and therefore will I speak; but I was sore troubled : I said in my haste, 'All men are liars.'

10–16. My thank-offering to God.
In all my tribulation I retained faith in God, and therefore will I speak in the confident tone of v. 9. 'Speak' refers to what precedes, not to what follows.
The passage is quoted from the Sept. in 2 Cor. 4. 13. S. Paul teaches that devout utterance is a necessary outcome of true belief. 'Having the same spirit of faith, according to that which is written, I believed, and therefore did I speak; we also believe, and therefore also we speak.'
all men are liars: i.e. my

troubles had led me to conclude that all human helpers were treacherous (cp. *Rom.* 3. 4), and thereby I was led to have recourse to God.

11 What reward shall I give unto the LORD : for all the benefits that he hath done unto me?

12 I will receive the cup of salvation : and CALL UPON THE NAME OF THE LORD.

the cup of salvation: i.e. the Paschal cup of wine; or the drink-offering which would accompany the 'sacrifice of thanksgiving' (v. 15). Another interpretation was, the cup of suffering or martyrdom, accepted in devotion to Christ, cp. S. Matt. 20. 22, 'the cup that I drink of.' Or we may see a mystic reference to the 'cup of blessing' (1 *Cor.* 10. 16), for our Lord sang these words after his institution of the Sacrament. They are spoken by the priest in the Latin rite before his communion. Cp. Ps. 16. 6, 'The LORD himself is the portion of my inheritance and of my cup.'

A.R.V. my vows unto the LORD, yea,

13 I WILL PAY MY VOWS NOW IN THE PRESENCE OF ALL HIS PEOPLE : right dear in the sight of the LORD is the death of his saints.

right dear: i.e. very costly, precious; cp. Ps. 72. 14, 'dear shall their blood be in his sight.' The LORD does not lightly suffer his elect to perish.

saints: i.e. his beloved and chosen ones; cp. Ps. 16. 11, 50. 5.

14 Behold, O LORD, how that I am thy servant : I am thy servant, and the son of thine handmaid; thou hast broken my bonds in sunder.

the son of thine handmaid: i.e. born in the LORD'S house, from my earliest years I am 'of the household of God' (*Eph.* 2. 19). Cp. Ps. 86. 16.

broken my bonds: i.e. the bonds of my great sickness; or, those of the bond-slave, cp. Gal. 4. 7, 'Thou art no longer a bond-

15 I will offer to thee the sacrifice of thanksgiving : and WILL CALL UPON THE NAME OF THE LORD.

servant, but a son; and if a son, then a heir.' Or it may be the bonds that held the martyr to this life in the flesh; or, as the verse is especially the prayer of Religious, the bonds that used to tie them to the world. In all these, the thought is of newly gained liberty in which to love God better.

For the 'sacrifice of thanksgiving' presented as an acknowledgement of blessings received; cp. Lev. 7. 11 ff. The Eucharist is our sacrifice of 'thanksgiving,' as the word signifies. Unite 'receive' (v. 12) with 'offer' here, and there is presented the double action of holy Mass. Cp. Ps. 50. 14.

16 I WILL PAY MY VOWS UNTO THE LORD, IN THE SIGHT OF ALL HIS PEOPLE : in the courts of the LORD's house, even in the midst of thee, O Jerusalem. Praise the LORD.

A.R.V. the presence of
The martyrs in heaven; as in v. 13 we see the martyrs on earth.
A.R.V. Praise ye the LORD.
R.V.mg. Heb. Hallelujah.

PSALM 117. *Laudate Dominum*

An invitation to all mankind to praise God for his mercies towards Israel, which were the pledge and earnest of the salvation of the whole world. A 'missionary' psalm, suitable at Epiphany, and as an act of Christian thanksgiving at any season.

O PRAISE the LORD, all ye heathen : praise him, all ye nations.

Quoted by S. Paul in Rom. 15. 11 as predictive of the calling of the Gentiles: 'I say that Christ hath been made a minister of the circumcision for the truth of God, that he might confirm the promises given unto the fathers, and that the Gentiles might glorify God for his mercy; as it is written, Praise the Lord, all ye Gentiles; and let all the peoples praise him.'

2 For his merciful kindness is ever more and more towards us : and the truth of the LORD endureth for ever. Praise the LORD.

R.V. For his mercy is great toward
Cp. Ps. 100. 5.
A.R.V. Praise ye the LORD. R.V.mg. Heb. Hallelujah.

PSALM 118. *Confitemini Domino*

A triumphant hymn of thanksgiving to God sung by worshippers in procession to the Temple. The last of the 'Hallel' psalms, cp. Ps. 113. Mystically, the risen Lord speaks in his glorified human nature, and his Church rejoices in union with him in the completed work of redemption. Proper on Easter Day and on Sundays.

O GIVE thanks unto the LORD, for HE IS GRACIOUS : because HIS MERCY ENDURETH FOR EVER.

2 Let Israel now confess that HE IS GRACIOUS : and that HIS MERCY ENDURETH FOR EVER.

3 Let the house of Aaron now confess : that HIS MERCY ENDUR-ETH FOR EVER.

4 Yea, let them now that fear the LORD confess : that HIS MER-CY ENDURETH FOR EVER.

5 I called upon the LORD in trouble : and the LORD heard me at large.

1–18. Sung by the procession. The liturgical doxology, as in Ps. 106. 1, 107. 1; cp. Jer. 33. 10 ff.; 2 Chron. 5. 13.
Cp. Ps. 115. 9–11; 135. 19–20.

I : the psalmist speaks in the name of his nation. Mystically, it is the voice of the Lord Christ in his passion and his exaltation, of his Church under persecution and in expansion, and of the Christian soul in purgation and in contemplation.
A.R.V. and set me in a large place, i.e. freed me from restrictions, and gave me liberty. The historical reference is to the release from the Babylonian captivity. Cp. Ps. 18. 19.

6 THE LORD IS ON MY SIDE : I will not fear what man doeth unto me.

From Ps. 66. 11; quoted in Heb. 13. 6 according to the Septuagint.
A.R.V. I will not fear: what can man do unto me?

7 THE LORD TAKETH MY PART with them that help me : therefore shall I see my desire upon mine enemies.

R.V. is on my side among, i.e. is my true upholder, according to a Hebrew idiom; cp. Ps. 54. 4; Judges 11. 35.

see my desire: cp. Ps. 54. 7.

8 IT IS BETTER TO TRUST IN THE LORD : than to put any confidence in man.

9 IT IS BETTER TO TRUST IN THE LORD : than to put any confidence in princes.

princes: i.e. the Persian kings and governors who frequently hindered the building of the Temple.

all nations: i.e. the neighbouring tribes who harassed the restored exiles.

10 All nations compassed me round about : but IN THE NAME OF THE LORD WILL I DESTROY THEM.

11 They kept me in on every side, they kept me in, I say, on every side : but IN THE NAME OF THE LORD WILL I DESTROY THEM.

12 They came about me like bees, and are extinct even as the fire among the thorns : for IN THE NAME OF THE LORD I WILL DESTROY THEM.

extinct : i.e. extinguished. *A.R.V. quenched.* Fire among thorns blazes up quickly, and as quickly dies out.

thou: i.e. the enemies are addressed as one individual.

13 Thou hast thrust sore at me, that I might fall : but the LORD was my help.

14 The LORD is my strength, and my song : and is become my salvation.

From the Song of Moses (*Exod.* 15. 2; cp. *Isa.* 12. 2). God's care of Israel does not belong only to the past. The glorious passage of Christ through death fulfilled the type of the passage of the Red Sea.

health: i.e. well-being. *A.R.V. salvation.*

15 The voice of joy and health is in the dwellings of the righteous; THE RIGHT HAND OF THE LORD BRINGETH MIGHTY THINGS TO PASS.

dwellings: *R.V. tents,* temporary lodgements on their journey home. This is one of the texts claimed by Religious for themselves specially.

A.R.V. the right hand of the LORD doeth valiantly; cp. Exod. 15. 6.

16 THE RIGHT HAND OF THE LORD hath the pre-eminence : THE RIGHT HAND OF THE LORD BRINGETH MIGHTY THINGS TO PASS.

17 I shall not die, but live : and declare the works of the LORD.

A.R.V. doeth valiantly.

17–18. Israel, chastened by suffering, will survive to proclaim the doings of the LORD throughout the world.

Cp. 2 Cor. 6. 9, 'As dying, and behold we live; as chastened, and not killed.'

Mystically, Christ is predicting his resurrection and its proclamation by the a p o s t l e s through the world.

18 The LORD hath chastened and corrected me : but he hath not given me over unto death.

19 Open me the gates of righteousness : that I may go into them, and give thanks unto the LORD.

Cp. Ps. 16. 11.

19. The challenge of the choir as the procession reaches the Temple gates. They are called 'gates of righteousness' because God is righteous, and because he looks for the same character in those who worship in his courts; cp. v. 20. Cp. Ps. 24. 7, 9; Isa. 26. 2. 'We have a strong city; salvation will God appoint for walls and bulwarks. Open ye the gates, that the righteous nation which keepeth truth may enter in.' Here we discern the voice of Christ at his ascension, and of the glorified martyrs and saints attaining their reward in him.

20 This is the gate of the LORD : the righteous shall enter into it.

20. The answer of the priests from within the Temple.

the gate: singular, not plural as in v. 19, for there is 'one Lord, one faith, one baptism' (*Eph.* 4. 5).

21 I will thank thee, for thou hast heard me : and art become my salvation.

22 The same stone which the builders refused : is become the head-stone in the corner.

23 This is the LORD's doing : and it is marvellous in our eyes.

24 This is the day which the LORD hath made : we will rejoice and be glad in it.

25 Help me now, O LORD : O LORD, send us now prosperity.

26 Blessed be he that cometh in the Name of the LORD : we have wished you good luck, ye that are of the house of the LORD.

27 God is the LORD who hath showed us light : (bind the sacrifice with cords, yea, even unto the horns of the altar).

21–25. Sung by the procession entering in.

Cp. v. 14.

22–23. Israel, rejected as of no account by the builders of the world's empires, has been chosen by God as the head-stone of his spiritual temple. This vision of the psalmist was actually fulfilled in Christ, the representative of Israel, and these words are applied by our Lord to himself; cp. S. Matt. 21. 42; and by S. Peter (*Acts* 4. 11); and by S. Paul (*Eph.* 2. 20), 'Christ Jesus himself being the chief corner stone.' Cp. also Isa. 28. 16; 1 S. Pet. 2. 6, 7. From this v. 22 the mystical interpretation of the whole psalm in reference to Christ is justified.

The LORD by his providence has enabled us pilgrims to keep this day of gladness. The verse is used as an Easter anthem, claiming the 'day' as the day of the resurrection of Christ.

A.R.V. Save now, we beseech thee. In Hebrew 'Hosanna,' with which and with the words of v. 26 the multitudes welcomed our Lord as the Messiah on Palm Sunday. Hence we sing at Mass, 'Blessed is he that cometh in the Name of the Lord; Hosanna in the highest.' Cp. S. Matt. 21. 9, 23. 39.

26. The greeting of the priests within the Temple.

A.R.V. we have blessed you out of the house of the LORD.

27–29. Sung by the procession.

light: cp. Ps. 18. 28; 97. 11; 1 S. Pet. 2. 9.

X

bind, etc.: as this seems to have formed no part of the sacrificial usage, the meaning probably is, may the victims be so numerous that they will fill the temple court up to the very horns of the altar: or, bind the festal victim with cords, and lead it unto the horns of the altar.

28 Thou art my God, and I will thank thee : thou art my God, and I will praise thee.

29 O give thanks unto the LORD, for HE IS GRACIOUS : and HIS MERCY ENDURETH FOR EVER.

Cp. v. 1.

EVENING PRAYER

PSALM 119

The praises of the law of God, sung by one who suffered for his adherence to it.

This is the most elaborate of the alphabetical or acrostic psalms. (Other examples are Pss. 9, 10, 25, 34, 37, 112, 145.) It is divided into twenty-two stanzas corresponding with the number of letters in the Hebrew alphabet. In each stanza all the verses begin with the same letter, as is indicated in A.R.V., beginning with Aleph in the first stanza and proceeding in regular order to Tau.

In every verse except two, 122 and 132, the law, which may be taken as meaning the whole of divine revelation, is referred to under that name or some equivalent one. The term 'word' often occurs, and sometimes admits of being applied to the Word Incarnate, e.g. 89 and 105.

This psalm has formed the basis of the regular recitation of the Psalter; according to many religious rules it has been recited daily. It is therefore peculiarly the psalm of Religious and of all those who follow the ordered ways of prayer. It has also been called 'the Psalm of the Saints,' because of the wealth of spiritual meaning that may be discerned in it by devout minds, far beyond what is suggested in this commentary. Each person who uses it needs to learn personally how to make it the vehicle of his or her own devotion.

The speaker in this psalm is one who stands fast in his own integrity and unimpaired righteousness. There is only one definite expression of faultiness (cp. the last verse), with which contrast the more frequent assertions of sinlessness, e.g. 97–124. But the consciousness of righteousness never becomes self-righteousness. The speaker is always conscious of his need of the divine help on which he relies. It is only because of God's grace that he stands fast.

The 'I' in this psalm is not to be taken as chiefly meaning the individual or the community that recites the psalm. But rather, they in their recitation are meditating on and expressing the perfect righteousness, first of Christ, secondly of the Church in its ideal state, the Church as it should be, and only thirdly of themselves, in so far as they are spiritually united with Christ in his Church.

Beati immaculati
The blessedness of unreserved obedience to God's law.

BLESSED are those that are undefiled in the way : and walk in the law of the LORD.

Beatitudes occur also at the beginning of Pss. 1, 32, 41, 112, 128.

undefiled: cp. Heb. 7. 26 where the word is applied to Christ.

way: i.e. the pilgrim's way to the Promised Land. Cp. Isa. 35. 8, 'An high way shall be there, and a way, and it shall be called The way of holiness; the unclean shall not pass over it.' S. John 14. 6, 'Jesus saith, I am the way, and the truth, and the life: no man cometh unto the Father, but by me.'

the law: especially the law of love to God and man; cp. Eph. 5. 2, 'Walk in love, even as Christ loved you.'

2 Blessed are they that keep his testimonies : and seek him with their whole heart.

Note the verbs 'walk . . . keep . . . seek,' implying progress, persevering loyalty, and personal zeal in seeking after union with God, without which obedience would be of little worth.

3 For they who do no wickedness : walk in his ways.

4 Thou hast charged : that we shall diligently keep thy commandments.

Deut. 4. 2.

5 O that my ways were made so direct : that I might keep thy statutes!

R.V. O that my ways were established to observe thy statutes! 'My ways' are to be the same as

6 So shall I not be confounded : while I have respect unto all thy commandments.

7 I will thank thee with an unfeigned heart : when I shall have learned the judgements of thy righteousness.

8 I will keep thy ceremonies : O forsake me not utterly.

'his ways' (v. 3). Cp. Jer. 10. 23, 'O Lord, I know that the way of man is not in himself: it is not in man that walketh to direct his steps.'

confounded: i.e. ashamed; cp. vv. 31, 80.

A.R.V. with uprightness of heart:
R.V. when I learn thy righteous judgements.
A.R.V. thy statutes:
His confidence of rectitude depends upon his faith in God, without whom he could do nothing.

In quo corriget?

The young man is safeguarded by adherence to God's word.

WHEREWITHAL shall a young man cleanse his way: even by ruling himself after thy word.

I.e. keep his way pure.
after: i.e. as *A.R.V. according to.*
thy word: i.e. God's revelation in general, or, the Word Incarnate.

10 With my whole heart have I sought thee : O let me not go wrong out of thy commandments.

11 Thy words have I hid within my heart : that I should not sin against thee.

12 Blessed art thou, O Lord : O teach me thy statutes.

13 With my lips have I been telling : of all the judgements of thy mouth.

14 I have had as great delight in the way of thy testimonies : as in all manner of riches.

A.R.V. O let me not wander from thy commandments.

R.V. Thy word have I laid up in . . . Cp. Ps. 37. 32.

This prayer occurs again in vv. 26, 33, 64, 68, 108, 124.
Cp. this telling with the silence in v. 11.

15 I will talk of thy commandments : and have respect unto thy ways.

16 My delight shall be in thy statutes : and I will not forget thy word.

A.R.V. I will meditate in

Retribue servo tuo

God's law gives comfort and strength amidst contempt and persecution.

O DO well unto thy servant : that I may live, and keep thy word.

R.V. that I may live; so will I observe thy word.
Cp. 2 Cor. 3. 14, 4. 28.

18 Open thou mine eyes : that I may see the wondrous things of thy law.

19 I am a stranger upon earth: O hide not thy commandments from me.

Cp. Ps. 39. 14; Lev. 25. 23; 2 Cor. 5. 6; Heb. 11. 13; 1 S. Pet. 2. 11.

hide not: i.e. let me not become unspiritual and unable to see. Cp. Isa. 6. 9.

20 My soul breaketh out for the very fervent desire : that it hath alway unto thy judgements.

A.R.V. breaketh for

21 Thou hast rebuked the proud : and cursed are they that do err from thy commandments.

22 O turn from me shame and rebuke : for I have kept thy testimonies.

Cp. Deut. 27. 26.

23 Princes also did sit and speak against me : but thy servant is occupied in thy statutes.

Princes: may include fellow-countrymen of high rank and power (cp. vv. 46, 161); but the Saints have found the word literally true.

sit: i.e. speaking with deliberation.

is occupied in: *A.R.V. did meditate in*

24 For thy testimonies are my delight : and my counsellors.

Adhaesit pavimento

God's word is the true consolation in affliction.

MY soul cleaveth to the dust : O quicken thou me, according to thy word.

dust: cp. Ps. 44. 25.

quicken me: this prayer occurs again in vv. 37, 40, 88, 107, 149, 154, 156, 159. I.e. revive my courage, give me new life.

according to thy word: again in vv. 28, 41, 58, 65, 76, 107, 169, 170.

I have laid open before God all the details of my life.

26 I have acknowledged my ways, and thou heardest me : O teach me thy statutes.

27 Make me to understand the way of thy commandments : and so shall I talk of thy wondrous works.

talk: *R.V. meditate.*

28 My soul melteth away for very heaviness : comfort thou me according to thy word.

comfort: i.e. as *A.R.V. strengthen.*

29 Take from me the way of lying : and cause thou me to make much of thy law.

lying: i.e. insincerity in serving God, contrasted with faithfulness (v. 30).

way: note in how many different connections this word occurs in this psalm.

30 I have chosen the way of truth : and thy judgements have I laid before me.

R.V. of faithfulness:

31 I have stuck unto thy testimonies : O Lord, confound me not.

32 I will run the way of thy commandments : when thou hast set my heart at liberty.

at liberty: free from entanglements of sin and error; cp. v. 45. *A.R.V. when thou shalt enlarge my heart,* i.e. set it free from care and trouble. Cp. 1 Kings 4. 29 and 2 Cor. 6. 11.

THE TWENTY-FIFTH DAY

MORNING PRAYER

Legem pone

Prayer for fuller knowledge of God's commandments, and for divine help to keep them.

TEACH me, O LORD, the way of thy statutes : and I shall keep it unto the end.

34 Give me understanding, and I shall keep thy law : yea, I shall keep it with my whole heart.

35 Make me to go in the path of thy commandments : for therein is my desire.

36 Incline my heart unto thy testimonies : and not to covetousness.

Cp. Jer. 6. 13; Col. 3. 5; and 1 S. John 2. 15, 'Love not the world, neither the things that are in the world.'

37 O turn away mine eyes, lest they behold vanity : and quicken thou me in thy way.

Cp. 1 S. John 2. 16, 'the lust of the eyes.'

vanity: i.e. falsehood, here that which is unreal and worthless, as opposed to God.

38 O stablish thy word in thy servant : that I may fear thee.

39 Take away the rebuke that I am afraid of : for thy judgements are good.

rebuke: *A.R.V. reproach*, i.e. of mine adversaries who scorn me for my loyalty to God's law, or perhaps for falling away from it. Cp. vv. 22, 23, 42.

40 Behold, my delight is in thy commandments : O quicken me in thy righteousness.

Et veniat super me

Trust in God's word gives courage to confess him before men.

LET thy loving mercy come also unto me, O LORD : even thy salvation, according unto thy word.

42 So shall I make answer unto my blasphemers : for my trust is in thy word.

So: i.e. by being able to appeal to manifest proofs of God's loving mercy, cp. v. 41.

my blasphemers: *A.R.V. him that reproacheth me* for my loyalty to God's law.

43 O take not the word of thy truth utterly out of my mouth : for my hope is in thy judgements.
44 So shall I alway keep thy law : yea, for ever and ever.
45 And I will walk at liberty : for I seek thy commandments.

True liberty is gained only by conformity to the law of God 'whose service is perfect freedom.' Cp. v. 32; S. Jas. 1. 25, 'the perfect law, the law of liberty.'
Cp. v. 23 and S. Matt. 10. 18.

46 I will speak of thy testimonies before kings : and will not be ashamed.
47 And my delight shall be in thy commandments : which I have loved.
48 My hands also will I lift up unto thy commandments, which I have loved : and my study shall be in thy statutes.

lift up hands: making a vow of obedience; cp. Gen. 14. 22 and Ps. 28. 2, 63. 5.

Memor esto servi tui

God's word is the source of comfort in trouble, and of joy in life's pilgrimage.

O THINK upon thy servant, as concerning thy word : wherein thou hast caused me to put my trust.

A.R.V. Remember the word unto thy servant:
thy word: i.e. thy co-eternal and incarnate Word, my Saviour. Other mentions of the 'word' of God are interpreted similarly.

50 The same is my comfort in my trouble : for thy word hath quickened me.

quickened: cp. v. 25 and Ps. 71. 18; and Heb. 4. 12, 'The word of God is quick' (*R.V. living*).

51 The proud have had me exceedingly in derision : yet have I not shrinked from thy law.

proud: cp. vv. 69, 78, 85, 122.

52 For I remembered thine everlasting judgements, O LORD: and received comfort.

A.R.V. thy judgements of old

53 I am horribly afraid : for the ungodly that forsake thy law.

R.V. Hot indignation hath taken hold of me, because of . . .
Cp. Ps. 39. 12.

54 Thy statutes have been my songs : in the house of my pilgrimage.

55 I have thought upon thy Name, O LORD, in the night-season : and have kept thy law.

Ps. 42. 8, 10.

56 This I had : because I kept thy commandments.

This: i.e. all the blessings enumerated in this stanza—comfort, zeal, courage, cheerfulness, recollection of God.

Portio mea, Domine

A declaration of earnestness and constancy in keeping God's law.

THOU art my portion, O LORD : I have promised to keep thy law.

Cp. Ps. 16. 6.
The promise of obedience follows and is dependent upon the realization of God as one's 'portion.'

58 I made my humble petition in thy presence with my whole heart : O be merciful unto me, according to thy word.

59 I called mine own ways to remembrance : and turned my feet unto thy testimonies.

60 I made haste, and prolonged not the time : to keep thy commandments.

I.e. as *A.R.V. and delayed not:*

61 The congregations of the ungodly have robbed me : but I have not forgotten thy law.

I.e. worldly associates.
R.V. The cords of the wicked have wrapped me round, as a hunter ensnares his prey. Cp. v. 110.

62 At midnight I will rise to give thanks unto thee : because of thy righteous judgements.

Literally fulfilled in some Religious Orders. Cp. v. 55 and Acts 16. 25.

63 I am a companion of all them that fear thee : and keep thy commandments.

64 The earth, O Lord, is full of thy mercy : O teach me thy statutes.

I.e. for I desire to know the statutes of the so merciful God.

Bonitatem fecisti

Devotion to God's law is taught in the school of adversity.

O LORD, thou hast dealt graciously with thy servant : according unto thy word.

66 O learn me true understanding and knowledge : for I have believed thy commandments.

I.e. O teach me

67 Before I was troubled, I went wrong : but now have I kept thy word.

Cp. vv. 71, 75.

68 Thou art good and gracious : O teach me thy statutes.

A.R.V. and doest good:

69 The proud have imagined a lie against me : but I will keep thy commandments with my whole heart.

A.R.V. have forged

70 Their heart is as fat as brawn : but my delight hath been in thy law.

brawn: A.R.V. grease; a figure of obduracy and insensibility.

71 It is good for me that I have been in trouble : that I may learn thy statutes.

72 The law of thy mouth is dearer unto me : than thousands of gold and silver.

v. 127 and Ps. 19. 10.

EVENING PRAYER

Manus tuae fecerunt me

God's word is pledged to revive and comfort those whom he afflicts.

THY hands have made me and fashioned me : O give me understanding, that I may learn thy commandments.

74 They that fear thee will be glad when they see me : because I have put my trust in thy word.

Cp. v. 63.

75 I know, O LORD, that thy judgements are right : and that thou of very faithfulness hast caused me to be troubled.

Cp. v. 65.

76 O let thy merciful kindness be my comfort : according to thy word unto thy servant.

Though God's chastisement is just and beneficial (v. 75), yet may its bitterness be tempered by his mercy, and his discipline be followed by his comforting!

77 O let thy loving mercies come unto me, that I may live : for thy law is my delight.

78 Let the proud be confounded, for they go wickedly about to destroy me : but I will be occupied in thy commandments.

go about: i.e. endeavour.
R.V. for they have overthrown me wrongfully (R.V.mg. with falsehood). A.V. for they have dealt perversely with me without a cause.
occupied: i.e. as *A.R.V. but I will meditate in.*

79 Let such as fear thee, and have known thy testimonies : be turned unto me.

R.V. Let those that fear thee turn unto me, and they shall know thy testimonies, from what they see is my experience; cp. v. 74.

80 O let my heart be sound in thy statutes : that I be not ashamed.

Cp. v. 6.

Defecit anima mea

God's word gives hope in days of gloom and persecution.

MY soul hath longed for thy salvation : and I have a good hope because of thy word.

A.R.V. My soul fainteth and: *A.R.V. but.*

82 Mine eyes long sore for thy word : saying, 'O when wilt thou comfort me?'

A.R.V. Mine eyes fail for . . . Cp. v. 123; Ps. 69. 3, 'my sight faileth me for waiting so long upon my God.

83 For I am become like a bottle in the smoke : yet do I not forget thy statutes.

bottle: i.e. as *R.V.mg. wine skin*, suspended from the rafters blackened and shrivelled by the smoke.

not forget: again in vv. 61, 93 176.

84 How many are the days of thy servant : when wilt thou be avenged of them that persecute me?

The sense of the shortness of life prompts the prayer for the speedy manifestation of God's righteous judgement. Cp. Ps 39. 5, 102. 13.

85 The proud have digged pits for me : which are not after thy law.

which: *R.V. who*, i.e. the proud.

after: i.e. according to.

86 All thy commandments are true : they persecute me falsely, O be thou my help.

true: *A.R.V. faithful.*

87 They had almost made an end of me upon earth : but I forsook not thy commandments.

88 O quicken me after thy loving-kindness : and so shall I keep the testimonies of thy mouth.

after: i.e. according to.

In aeternum, Domine

God's word is eternal, unchangeable, and unlimited in range.

O LORD, thy word : endureth for ever in heaven.

God's word may often be forgotten or disregarded on earth but it is eternally obeyed in heaven. The enduring word of the LORD is explained also by S. Peter as 'The word of good tidings that was preached unto you' (1 *S. Pet.* 1. 25). The Gospel remains on earth as in heaven. The verse speaks mystically of the eternal generation of the consubstantial Word of God; and to the exaltation of that Word made incarnate to the throne in heaven.

90 Thy truth also remaineth from one generation to another : thou hast laid the foundation of the earth, and it abideth.

A.R.V. Thy faithfulness
Cp. Ps. 148. 5, 6.

91 They continue this day according to thine ordinance : for all things serve thee.

They: i.e. 'heaven' (v. 89) and 'earth' (v. 90).
The 'laws of nature' are the expression of the Creator's will.

92 If my delight had not been in thy law : I should have perished in my trouble.

The comfort of God's unswerving law has sustained the psalmist in his affliction. He realized that even his trouble came to him under divine providence.
Cp. v. 83.

93 I will never forget thy commandments : for with them thou hast quickened me.

94 I am thine, O save me : for I have sought thy commandments.

I am thine: by nature and by grace, by creation and by redemption, by predestination and by adoption.

95 The ungodly laid wait for me to destroy me : but I will consider thy testimonies.

96 I see that all things come to an end : but thy commandment is exceeding broad.

A.R.V. I have seen the end of all perfection. All earthly things, however beautiful and perfect, are limited and transitory, but God's commandment, t h a t which his word reveals, has an infinite range. Our circumstances change, but we never pass outside the scope of the divine will.

Quomodo dilexi!

God's law imparts a higher than worldly wisdom.

O LORD, what love have I unto thy law : all the day long is my study in it.

98 Thou through thy commandments hast made me wiser than mine enemies : for they are ever with me.

wiser: i.e. the possessor of a better wisdom.
they: i.e. thy commandments.

99 I have more understanding than my teachers : for thy testimonies are my study.

A.R.V. than all my

100 I am wiser than the aged : because I keep my commandments.

101 I have refrained my feet from every evil way : that I may keep thy word.

102 I have not shrunk from thy judgements : for thou teachest me.

R.V. turned aside from

103 O how sweet are thy words unto my throat : yea, sweeter than honey unto my mouth.

Ps. 19. 10.

104 Through thy commandments I get understanding : therefore I hate all evil ways.

A.R.V. every false way, i.e. all insincerity in serving God; cp. vv. 29, 128, 163.

THE TWENTY-SIXTH DAY

MORNING PRAYER

Lucerna pedibus meis

God's word gives light and joy and strength in times of danger and sorrow.

THY word is a lantern unto my feet : and a light unto my paths.

Different applications of this verse are suggested by 2 S. Pet. 1. 19; S. John 1. 9; Rev. 22. 5.

106 I have sworn, and am steadfastly purposed : to keep thy righteous judgements.

Applicable to baptismal vows, to their renewal, and to religious profession of the counsels of poverty, chastity, and obedience.

107 I am troubled above measure : quicken me, O LORD, according to thy word.

Cp. v. 25.

108 Let the free-will offerings of my mouth please thee, O LORD : and teach me thy judgements.

I.e. my prayers and vows of obedience; cp. v. 106 and Ps. 19. 14, 50. 14; Hos. 14. 2. Perhaps also the round of ordered daily prayer willingly offered; or in particular devout exercises beyond those of obligation.

109 My soul is alway in my hand : yet do I not forget thy law.

I.e. my life is in constant jeopardy owing to the plots of enemies, whether human or devilish: cp. v. 110 and Judges 12. 3; 1 Sam. 19. 5. Some see here also the thought that my soul is continually being made an offering to God; cp. Ps. 25. 1, 'Unto thee lift I up my soul.'

110 The ungodly have laid a snare for me : but yet I swerved not from thy commandments.

Cp. Ps. 91. 3.

111 Thy testimonies have I claimed as mine heritage for ever : and why? they are the very joy of my heart.

Cp. v. 157.

God's law was the faithful Israelite's true inheritance, more permanent than the land of promise. The verse is applicable especially to the vocation of a Religious, with the following.

112 I have applied my heart to fulfil thy statutes alway : even unto the end.

Iniquos odio habui

The safety of those who keep God's commandments contrasted with the downfall of those who depart from them.

I HATE them that imagine evil things : but thy law do I love.

R.V. that are of a double mind, i.e. waver in their allegiance to God; cp. 1 Kings 18. 21; S. Jas. 1. 8.

114 Thou art my defence and shield : and my trust is in thy word.

A.R.V. my hiding place and . . . Cp. Ps. 32. 8.

my trust: cp. vv. 42, 74.

115 Away from me, ye wicked : I will keep the commandments of my God.

115–117 are especially applicable to Religious.

R.V. that I may keep

116 O stablish me according to thy word, that I may live : and let me not be disappointed of my hope.

Yet to keep God's commandments (v. 115) I need his assistance.

117 Hold thou me up, and I shall be safe : yea, my delight shall be ever in thy statutes.

A.R.V. be ashamed of

my delight: again in 14, 16, 24, 40, 47, 70, 77, 92, 122, 131, 143.

118 Thou hast trodden down all them that depart from thy statutes : for they imagine but deceit.

R.V. hast set at nought

119 Thou putteth away all the ungodly of the earth like dross : therefore I love thy testimonies.

dross: which the refiner separates from the pure ore; cp. Ezek. 22. 18; Zech. 13. 9; Mal. 3. 3.

120 My flesh trembleth for fear of thee : and I am afraid of thy judgements.

love (v. 119) and fear: cp. the Catechism, 'My duty towards God is to love him, to fear him.' It is only love perfected that 'casteth out fear' (1 *S. John* 4. 18).

Feci judicium

God's word, when despised by the world, becomes more precious to the righteous.

I DEAL with the thing that is lawful and right : O give me not over unto mine oppressors.

A.R.V. I have done judgement and justice:

122 Make thou thy servant to delight in that which is good : that the proud do me no wrong.

He cannot delight in good without divine assistance. But *A.R.V.* has: *Be surety for thy servant for good*, i.e. guarantee his welfare.

This verse and 132 are the only verses in this psalm which do not refer directly to God's law.

123 Mine eyes are wasted away with looking for thy health: and for the word of thy righteousness.

A.R.V. fail for thy salvation, cp. v. 82.

health: i.e. well-being.

124 O deal with thy servant according unto thy loving mercy: and teach me thy statutes.

125 I am thy servant, O grant me understanding : that I may know thy testimonies.

126 It is time for thee, LORD, to lay to thine hand : for they have destroyed thy law.

Cf. Ps. 102. 13.
I.e. as *A.R.V. to work.*

127 For I love thy commandments : above gold and precious
stone.

For: *A.R.V. Therefore.* Because evil men have abrogated
God's law (v. 126) it becomes
all the more precious to me.

128 Therefore hold I straight
all thy commandments : and all
false ways I utterly abhor.

hold straight: i.e. as *A.R.V.
esteem to be right.*

false ways: i.e. insincerity in
the service of God; cp. vv. 29,
104, 163.

Mirabilia

God's word enlightens the mind and preserves from evil those
who keep it.

THY testimonies are won-
derful : therefore doth my
soul keep them.

Cp. Rom. 11. 33.

130 When thy word goeth
forth : it giveth light and understanding unto the simple.

R.V. The opening (i.e. un-
veiling, cp. S. Luke 24. 32, 45)
*of thy words giveth light; it giveth
. . .* Mystically referable to the
Advent of 'The Word of God
proceeding forth.'

131 I opened my mouth, and
drew in my breath : for my delight was in thy commandments.

A.R.V. and panted, with eager
desire, *for I longed for . . .* Cp.
Ps. 81. 11.

132 O look thou upon me,
and be merciful unto me : as
thou usest to do unto those that
love thy Name.

Cp. v. 122.

133 Order my steps in thy
word : and so shall no wickedness have dominion over me.

Order: i.e. Set in order, direct.
A.R.V. and let not any

134 O deliver me from the
wrongful dealings of men : and
so shall I keep thy commandments.

135 Shew the light of thy
countenance upon thy servant :
and teach me thy statutes.

A part of the priestly blessing
(*Num.* 6. 25); cp. Ps. 31. 8.
A.R.V. Make thy face to shine.

136 Mine eyes gush out with
water : because men keep not
thy law.

men: *A.R.V. they,* meaning
'men,' as in v. 134; or 'mine
eyes.'

Y

Justus es, Domine

The righteousness, purity, and truth of God's law.

RIGHTEOUS art thou, O
LORD : and true is thy
judgement.

A.R.V. upright are thy judgements.

138 The testimonies that thou
hast commanded : are exceeding
righteous and true.

exceeding: i.e. exceedingly.

139 My zeal hath even consumed me : because mine enemies have forgotten thy words.

Cp. Ps. 69. 9; S. John 2. 17.

140 Thy word is tried to the
uttermost : and thy servant loveth it.

A.R.V. Thy word is very pure:
tried: i.e. refined, as metals
are in a furnace.

141 I am small, and of no
reputation : yet do I not forget
thy commandments.

142 Thy righteousness is an
everlasting righteousness : and
thy law is the truth.

143 Trouble and heaviness
have taken hold upon me : yet
is my delight in thy commandments.

144 The righteousness of thy
testimonies is everlasting : O
grant me understanding, and I
shall live.

EVENING PRAYER

Clamavi in toto corde meo

Earnest and constant prayer is needful for the due observance of
God's statutes.

I CALL with my whole heart :
hear me, O LORD, I will keep
thy statutes.

146 Yea, even unto thee do I
call : help me, and I shall keep
thy testimonies.

147 Early in the morning do
I cry unto thee : for in thy word
is my trust.

A.R.V. I prevented (i.e. anticipated) *the dawning of the
morning, and cried.* Cp. Ps. 5. 3;
63. 1.

148 Mine eyes prevent the night-watches : that I might be occupied in thy words.

R.V. prevented, anticipated. As by Compline, the Office 'before the ending of the day.' For night-prayers cp. v. 62 and Ps. 42. 10. The Israelites divided the night into three watches, cp. Judges 7. 19; 1 Sam. 11. 11; Lam. 2. 19; the Romans into four, cp. S. Mark 13. 35.

149 Hear my voice, O LORD, according unto thy loving-kindness : quicken me, according as thou art wont.

R.V. according to thy judgements. Cp. v. 156.

150 They draw nigh that of malice persecute me : and are far from thy law.

R.V. that follow after wickedness:

151 Be thou nigh at hand, O LORD : for all thy commandments are true.

When my enemies are nigh (v. 150) to assail me, be thou nigh to succour me. *R.V. Thou art nigh.*

152 As concerning thy testimonies, I have known long since: that thou hast grounded them for ever.

grounded: i.e. as *A.R.V. founded.* Cp. vv. 89, 160.

Vidi humilitatem

A prayer for grace to keep God's commandments.

O CONSIDER mine adversity, and deliver me : for I do not forget thy law.

154 Avenge thou my cause, and deliver me : quicken me, according to thy word.

A.R.V. Plead thou my cause, and redeem me:

155 Health is far from the ungodly : for they regard not thy statutes.

Health: i.e. well-being. *A.R.V. Salvation.*
regard: *A.R.V. seek.*

156 Great is thy mercy, O LORD : quicken me, as thou art wont.

A.R.V. according to thy judgements. Cp. v. 149.

157 Many there are that trouble me, and persecute me : yet do I not swerve from thy testimonies.

Cp. v. 110.

158 It grieveth me when I see the transgressors : because they keep not thy law.

159 Consider, O Lord, how I love thy commandments : O quicken me, according to thy loving-kindness.

160 Thy word is true from everlasting : all the judgements of thy righteousness endure for evermore.

Cp. v. 136.

R.V. The sum of thy word is truth: so the Incarnate Word said, 'I am the truth' (*S. John* 14. 6).

Principes persecuti sunt

The joy, peace, and hope of those who love God's commandments.

PRINCES have persecuted me without a cause : but my heart standeth in awe of thy word.

162 I am as glad of thy word : as one that findeth great spoils.

163 As for lies, I hate and abhor them : but thy law do I love.

164 Seven times a day do I praise thee : because of thy righteous judgements.

165 Great is the peace that they have who love thy law : and they are not offended at it.

166 Lord, I have looked for thy saving health : and done after thy commandments.

167 My soul hath kept thy testimonies : and loved them exceedingly.

168 I have kept thy commandments and testimonies : for all my ways are before thee.

Princes: perhaps Israelites of high rank and power; cp. v. 23.
without a cause: cp. Ps. 69. 4.

Seven times: i.e. constantly; cp. Prov. 24. 16. Seven Hours of prayer during the day-time are ordered in many Religious rules.

R.V. they have none occasion of stumbling. Cp. 1 S. John 2. 10.

A.R.V. thy salvation: cp. v. 174, and Gen. 49. 18; S. Luke 2. 30; Isa. 52. 10.
after: i.e. according to.

Supported by an approving conscience he fearlessly appeals to the all-seeing God in witness of his integrity.

Appropinquet deprecatio

The knowledge of God's commandments reveals to man his helplessness and need of succour.

LET my complaint come before thee, O LORD : give me understanding, according to thy word.

170 Let my supplication come before thee : deliver me, according to thy word.

171 My lips shall speak of thy praise : when thou hast taught me thy statutes.

172 Yea, my tongue shall sing of thy word : for all thy commandments are righteous.

173 Let thine hand help me : for I have chosen thy commandments.

174 I have longed for thy saving health, O LORD : and in thy law is my delight.

175 O let my soul live, and it shall praise thee : and thy judgements shall help me.

176 I have gone astray like a sheep that is lost : O seek thy servant, for I do not forget thy commandments.

A.R.V. my cry

R.V. for thou teachest

A.R.V. salvation,

Cp. General Confession, 'We have erred and strayed from thy ways like lost sheep.' Cp. Isa. 53. 6; Ezek. 34. 11; S. Matt. 18. 12; 1 S. Pet. 2. 25.

The psalm concludes with the only definite confession of failure and shortcoming; which, however, must be read into the former protestations of obedience to God's law; cp. vv. 110, 168, etc. The psalmist was not devoid of the spiritual dissatisfaction which compels us Christians to acknowledge that 'if we say that we have no sin, we deceive ourselves, and the truth is not in us' (1 *S. John* 1. 8); nor did he rely upon a sense of self-righteousness apart from the grace of God. But it remains true that many of the words of the psalm can find perfect application only to Christ himself.

THE TWENTY-SEVENTH DAY

MORNING PRAYER

PSALM 120.   *Ad Dominum*

The group of fifteen psalms, beginning with this Ps. 120, was compiled probably after the Exile, cp. Ps. 126. 1. They are entitled 'The Gradual Psalms.' The word 'Gradual' comes from the Latin word *gradus,* meaning 'steps.' Hence in A.V. they are termed 'Songs of Degrees,' i.e. of Steps; and in R.V. 'Songs of Ascents.' They were probably so called as forming a collection arranged for the use of returning exiles or of pilgrims ascending or 'going up' to keep the great festivals in the Temple at Jerusalem. Cp. Exod. 34. 24; 1 Kings 12. 27 f.; 2 Kings 20. 5 f.; Isa. 30. 29. The general application to be made when reciting them is to the Christians' pilgrimage in the Church militant here on earth towards the Temple of God in heaven, or to the spiritul ascents made by them towards union with God and his unveiled presence. It has been customary to recite the fifteen Gradual Psalms together in order, as an act of faith and devotion, in Lent and on other special occasions.

Ps. 120 is a prayer for deliverance from the intrigues of treacherous neighbours. The pilgrims consider their woeful condition living among the ungodly.

WHEN I was in trouble I called upon the LORD : and he heard me.

2 Deliver my soul, O LORD, from lying lips : and from a deceitful tongue.

As the LORD answered me when I prayed to him in a former time of distress, so now too will I pray to him to save me from my present enemies.

lying . . . deceitful: whether flattering, mocking, slandering, or tempting to some sin.

3 What reward shall be given or done unto thee, thou false tongue? : Even mighty and sharp arrows, with hot burning coals.

A.R.V. Sharp arrows of the mighty (i.e. Almighty God) *with coals of juniper.* A metaphorical description of God's punishment of the deceitful tongue. Juniper (*R.V.mg. broom*) was known as a fuel that retained heat for a long time. Cp. Ps. 140. 10.

4 Woe is me, that I am constrained to dwell with Mesech : and to have my habitation among the tents of Kedar.

Cp. S. Matt. 17. 17, 'How long shall I be with you? how long shall I bear with you?'

Mesech: a barbarous tribe living between the Black Sea and the Caspian. Kedar: a predatory horde of Arabians. These are put for all the rough and quarrelsome neighbours who troubled the exiles. Some interpret them as denoting the barbarian and the Mahomedan foes of the Church. Applicable also to spiritual foes.

5 My soul hath long dwelt among them : that are enemies unto peace.

The word 'peace' occurs again in the Gradual Psalms in v. 6 and Ps. 122. 6, 7, 8; 125. 5; 128. 7.

6 I labour for peace, but when I speak unto them thereof : they make them ready to battle.

The faithful must always in this life live in a state of war, suffering for their principles at the hands of those who would overthrow them; but in Christ they find peace now and hereafter.

PSALM 121. *Levavi oculos*

God is the keeper of his Church. The psalm perhaps suggests the picture of the pilgrims viewing from afar the hills about Jerusalem with Mt. Sion and Mt. Moriah.

I WILL lift up mine eyes unto the hills : from whence cometh my help.

Perhaps the 'holy hills' of Jerusalem; cp. Pss. 48. 1, 2; 87. 1; 125. 1. Hills suggest strength and stability, and these hills in particular were the site of God's temple, the source of spiritual aid. But R.V. gives the second clause as a question, as if the pilgrims thought of the hills of Palestine as a difficulty to be surmounted: *from whence shall my help come?* The answer is in v. 2. Cp. Jer. 2. 23, 'Truly in vain is the help that is looked for from the hills . . . truly in the

LORD our God is the salvation of Israel.'

Lift up: so Abraham (*Gen.* 22. 2, 4), 'Get thee into the land of Moriah. . . . Abraham lifted up his eyes, and saw the place afar off.'

2 My help cometh even from the LORD : who hath made heaven and earth.

Cp. Ps. 124. 7.

3 He will not suffer thy foot to be moved : and he that keepeth thee will not sleep.

The psalmist addresses himself, or another voice addresses him.

Cp. Ps. 66. 9, 'Who suffereth not our feet to slip.'

Cp. 1 Kings 18. 27; and S. Mark 4. 38.

4 Behold, he that keepeth Israel : shall neither slumber nor sleep.

5 The LORD himself is thy keeper : the LORD is thy defence upon thy right hand;

A.R.V. thy shade
upon thy right hand: the position of a protector. Cp. Ps. 16. 9, 109. 30. The metaphor in vv. 5–6 varies between shade and championship.

Cp. Isa. 49. 10; Rev. 7. 16.

6 So that the sun shall not burn thee by day : neither the moon by night.

7 The LORD shall preserve thee from all evil : yea, it is even he that shall keep thy soul.

8 The LORD shall preserve thy going out and thy coming in : from this time forth for evermore.

thy going out and thy coming in: i.e. all the occupations and interests of thy life. Cp. Deut. 28. 6; 1 Kings 4. 7; Acts 1. 21.

PSALM 122. *Laetatus sum*

The reverie and prayer of a pilgrim inspired by the prospect of visiting Jerusalem and the Temple. Jerusalem here foreshadows 'the holy city, new Jerusalem' (*Rev.* 2. 2), the Church triumphant.

I WAS glad when they said unto me : 'We will go into the house of the LORD.'

glad: cp. Ps. 27. 4.

they: undefined, may stand for those by whom each one severally has been led in the right way.

2 Our feet shall stand in thy gates : O Jerusalem.

R.V. are standing. R.V.mg. have stood. As in Heb. 12. 22, 'Ye are come unto mount Zion, and unto the city of the living God, the heavenly Jerusalem'; Phil. 3. 20, 'Our citizenship is in heaven.'

in thy gates: cp. Rev. 21. 25, 'The gates shall in no wise be shut.'

3 Jerusalem is built as a city : that is at unity in itself.

A.R.V. as a city that is compact together, i.e. restored from its ruins so that the buildings are joined closely one to another with no gaps between.

built: cp. Ps. 147. 2, 'The LORD doth build up Jerusalem: and gather together the outcasts of Israel.' The building is of living stones; cp. 1 S. Pet. 2. 5, 'Ye also, as living stones, are built up a spiritual house'; Eph. 4. 16, 'compacted by that which every joint supplieth.'

4 For thither the tribes go up, even the tribes of the LORD : to testify unto Israel, to give thanks unto the Name of the LORD.

A.R.V. Whither

He hopes for representatives of every tribe to take part, in spite of the dispersal of Israel. Or perhaps 'the tribes of the LORD' denote Gentiles; cp. Isa. 2. 3, 'Many peoples shall go and say, "Come ye, and let us go up to the mountain of the LORD, to the house of the God of Jacob"' ; and Zech. 8. 21.

to testify: i.e. to be a testimony of the unity of the nation and of its relation to Jehovah; or, of their union with the Chosen People in the worship of the true God.

5 For there is the seat of judgement : even the seat of the house of David.

R.V. For there are set thrones for judgement, the thrones of . . . Jerusalem was the location of the supreme court of justice, ideally administered by the king of David's line and the Aaronic priests; cp. Deut. 17. 8 ff. Cp. our Lord's words to his apostles, S. Matt. 18. 17, 'Tell it unto the church. . . . Whatsoever ye shall bind on earth shall be bound in heaven'; S. Luke 22. 30, 'Ye shall sit on thrones judging the twelve tribes of Israel.'

6 O pray for the peace of Jerusalem : They shall prosper that love thee.

Cp. Ps. 51. 18, 'O be favourable and gracious unto Sion: build thou the walls of Jerusalem.' Pray for the perfecting of the Church in peace and glory in heaven.

Our Lord's words, when he wept over Jerusalem, had probably a reference to this verse: S. Luke 19. 42, 'If thou hadst known the things which belong unto thy peace.'

7 Peace be within thy walls : and plenteousness within thy palaces.

6b–9 are the response to the request for prayer in v. 6a.

plenteousness: *A.R.V. prosperity.*

palaces: cp. Ps. 48. 12.

Note the alliteration in 'peace . . . plenteousness . . . palaces . . . prosperity' corresponding to a similar alliteration in the Hebrew.

8 For my brethren and companions' sakes : I will wish thee prosperity.

I.e. because I recognize all thy citizens as my brethren (the fellowship of the Communion of Saints); or, that all my exiled brethren may be received within thee (an intercession for the lapsed and scattered that they may return to the One Church).

A.R.V. I will now say, 'Peace be unto thee.'

9 Yea, because of the house of the LORD our God : I will seek to do thee good.

Jerusalem is dear to the exiles chiefly because it enshrines the Temple, where God dwells.

PSALM 123. *Ad te levavi oculos meos*

The eye of hope fixed patiently upon God in a time of desolation and contempt. Perhaps this psalm reflects the suffering to which the returning exiles were exposed by the ridicule and persecution of Samaritans and others.

UNTO thee lift I up mine eyes : O thou that dwellest in the heavens.

2 Behold, even as the eyes of servants look unto the hand of their masters, and as the eyes of a maiden unto the hand of her mistress : even so our eyes wait upon the LORD our God, until he have mercy upon us.

lift up: cp. Ps. 121. 1, there to the hills, here to God himself.

dwellest: cp. Ps. 2. 4.

The slave in utter dependence upon the master watches anxiously for the faintest expression of his will.

The 'hand' of the LORD upholds us (*Ps.* 37. 24); punishes us (*Ps.* 106. 26); receives us (*Ps.* 31. 6); supplies our need (*Ps.* 145. 16); directs us (*Ps.* 139. 9).

until: and not ceasing then; cp. Ps. 110. 1.

3 Have mercy upon us, O LORD, have mercy upon us : for we are utterly despised.

4 Our soul is filled with the scornful reproach of the wealthy; and with the despitefulness of the proud.

'Hear, O our God; for we are despised: and turn back their reproach upon their own head' (*Neh.* 4. 4; cp. 1 *Cor.* 4. 9 ff.).

wealthy: i.e. prosperous. *R.V. with the scorning of those that are at ease.*

proud: i.e. the contemners of God. Cp. Ps. 119. 51, 'The proud have had me exceedingly in derision.'

Psalm 124.   *Nisi quia Dominus*

'There is none other that fighteth for us, but only thou, O God.' This psalm, following the preceding, is a thanksgiving which suggests such a deliverance as that from the attack of Sanballat and his confederates on the rising walls of Jerusalem (*Neh.* 4. 7 ff.).

'IF the LORD himself had not been on our side,' now may Israel say : 'if the LORD himself had not been on our side, when men rose up against us;

2 They had swallowed us up quick : when they were so wrathfully displeased at us.

had: i.e. would have.
quick: i.e. as *R.V. alive.*

3 Yea, the waters had drowned us : and the stream had gone over our soul.

Cp. Ps. 32. 6; 69. 1, 2; 130. 1; and Isa. 43. 2.

4 The deep waters of the proud : had gone even over our soul.'

A metaphorical description of the enemies' insolence.
the proud: cp. Ps. 123. 4.

5 But praised be the LORD : who hath not given us over for a prey unto their teeth.

6 Our soul is escaped even as a bird out of the snare of the fowler : the snare is broken, and we are delivered.

Cp. Ps. 91. 3.
We have been delivered from Satan by our redemption through Christ's death, and cannot be again entangled except by our own consent.

7 Our help standeth in the Name of the LORD : who hath made heaven and earth.

Hence the versicle and response commonly used in Divine Service.

Psalm 125.   *Qui confidunt*

Trust in Jehovah, the protector of the Church, is the sure remedy against temptations to apostasy. The theme was probably suggested by the perils and temptations which beset the returning exiles.

THEY that put their trust in the LORD shall be even as the mount Sion : which may not be removed, but standeth fast for ever.

Cp. Ps. 93. 2; 104. 5. And cp. S. Matt. 16. 18, 'Upon this rock I will build my Church; and the gates of Hades shall not prevail against it.'

2 The hills stand about Jerusalem : even so standeth the LORD round about his people, from this time forth for evermore.

The hills which encompass Jerusalem are a symbol of Jehovah's guardianship of his people.

3 For the rod of the ungodly cometh not into the lot of the righteous : lest the righteous put their hand unto wickedness.

R.V. For the sceptre of wickedness (i.e. the rule of heathen tyranny) *shall not rest upon* (to remain upon it) *the lot of the righteous,* i.e. Canaan, the land allotted to Israel; and, by application, the Church, which may be chastised for its sins by being invaded, but will not be afflicted continually.

lest the righteous, etc.: i.e. lest Israel (the Church) by the continuance of oppression, in despair of divine succour, should join in the wickedness of the heathen, and become like them.

4 Do well, O LORD : unto those that are good and true of heart.

5 As for such as turn back unto their own wickedness : the LORD shall lead them forth with the evil-doers : but peace shall be upon Israel.

A.R.V. such as turn aside unto their crooked ways. Those who go astray by their own wilfulness shall be brought to the punishment awarded to sinners of evil life: apostasy is as culpable as immorality.

R.V. Peace be upon Israel. A prayer, not a statement. Cp. Ps. 122. 7; 128. 7.

EVENING PRAYER

PSALM 126. *In convertendo*

May the shallow streams of returned exiles become abundant rivers fertilizing the land! Having been delivered from the bondage of sin, the Church, if it faithfully endures, will attain to glory.

WHEN the LORD turned the captivity of Sion : then were we like unto them that dream.

Cp. Ps. 14. 7; and v. 5.

So strange was our change of lot, that we could hardly believe it real.

2 Then was our mouth filled with laughter : and our tongue with joy.

Cp. Isa. 35. 10, 'The ransomed of the LORD shall return, and come with singing unto Zion; and everlasting joy shall be upon their heads.'

3 Then said they among the heathen : 'The LORD hath done great things for them.'

4 Yea, the LORD hath done great things for us already : whereof we rejoice.

5 Turn our captivity, O LORD : as the rivers in the south.

Bring back the exiles in such crowds that they may be compared to the water channels of southern Palestine when the dry season has passed and they are filled with the autumnal rains. The word 'Negeb' translated 'the south' literally means 'the dry country'; cp. Gen. 12. 9 mg.; Judges 1. 15.

6 They that sow in tears: shall reap in joy.

Cp. Isa. 35. 10, 'They shall obtain joy and gladness, and sorrow and sighing shall flee away'; Jer. 31. 9–12; S. John 16. 20, 'Ye shall be sorrowful, but your sorrow shall be turned into joy.'

7 He that now goeth on his way weeping, and beareth forth good seed : shall doubtless come again with joy, and bring his sheaves with him.

beareth forth: i.e. from the storehouse to sow it.

Cp. Gal. 6. 9, 'In due season we shall reap, if we faint not.'

PSALM 127. *Nisi Dominus*

'Every good gift and every perfect boon is from above,' especially the gifts of sleep and strong children. God bestows upon the Church tranquillity, and gives her spiritual offspring. This psalm is used in its literal sense in the Churching of Women.

EXCEPT the LORD build the house : their labour is but lost that build it.

2 Except the LORD keep the city : the watchman waketh but in vain.

Cp. Ps. 121. 4, 'Behold, he that keepeth Israel shall neither slumber nor sleep.'

3 It is but lost labour that ye haste to rise up early, and so late take rest, and eat the bread of carefulness : for so he giveth his beloved sleep.

R.V. the bread of toil.

his beloved: i.e. faithful Israel; cp. Ps. 60. 5.

sleep: which is the gift of God, but is banished by care or toil. Cp. S. Mark 4. 27.

so: i.e. without anxiety on their part.

4 Lo, children and the fruit of the womb : are an heritage and gift that cometh of the LORD.

5 Like as the arrows in the hand of the giant : even so are the young children.

A.R.V. of a mighty man:

R.V. children of youth (i.e. of those who marry young), specially mentioned as likely to be vigorous in health, and to grow up to be the support and protection of their father's old age.

6 Happy is the man that hath his quiver full of them : they shall not be ashamed when they speak with their enemies in the gate.

they: i.e. the fathers of such offspring.

the gate: the place of judgement and public concourse (*Deut.* 21. 19; *Ps.* 69. 12). The father of stalwart sons has a guarantee that in suits with opponents and in business transactions he will be treated fairly.

PSALM 128. *Beati omnes*

The family happiness of the God-fearing man. The joy of the Church in her offspring. This psalm is used in the Marriage Service.

BLESSED are all they that fear the LORD : and walk in his ways.

2 For thou shalt eat the labours of thy hands : O well is thee, and happy shalt thou be.

Cp. Ps. 112. 1; 119. 1.

thou: a typical one of the 'all' is addressed.

shalt eat, etc.: not robbed of the fruits of thy labour by blight or the raids of enemies.

well is thee: archaic for 'well is it with thee.'

3 Thy wife shall be as the fruitful vine : upon the walls of thy house.

R.V. in the innermost parts of . . . i.e. in the women's apartments.

4 Thy children like the olive-branches : round about thy table.

5 Lo, thus shall the man be blessed : that feareth the LORD.

the man: applied especially to Christ himself. Christ and his members are the One Vine (*S. John* 15. 1). So too the Church is the Spouse of Christ (*Eph.* 5. 25 ff.); her members are his children round about the table of the LORD, i.e. the altar: they shall in their turn beget their spiritual offspring, i.e. the new converts brought into the Church.

6 The LORD from out of Sion shall so bless thee : that thou shalt see Jerusalem in prosperity all thy life long.

Cp. Ps. 20. 2; 135. 21.
The LORD, who dwelleth in Sion (the Church militant on earth) shall so bless thee whilst thou art still in it here, that thou shalt see the prosperity of Jerusalem (the Church triumphant in heaven) for all thy life long, thy eternal life.

PSALM 129.   *Saepe expugnaverunt*

Israel's (the Church's) history, a record of suffering and deliverance.

'MANY a time have they fought against me from my youth up' : may Israel now say;

A.R.V. afflicted me
Israel's youth was spent in Egyptian bondage: the Church's under persecution.

2 'Yea, many a time have they vexed me from my youth up : but they have not prevailed against me.

A.R.V. afflicted
Cp. 2 Cor. 4. 8, 9, 'We are pressed on every side, yet not straitened; smitten down, yet not destroyed.'

3 The plowers plowed upon my back : and made long furrows.

Metaphorical for savage maltreatment. Cp. Micah 3. 12, 'Therefore shall Zion for your sakes be plowed as a field.' The words have been understood mystically of our Lord's scourging.

A.R.V. cut asunder the cords of the wicked, the cords with which Israel was bound.

4 But the righteous LORD : hath hewn the snares of the ungodly in pieces.'

5 Let them be confounded and turned backward : as many as have evil will at Sion.

at: i.e. against. *R.V. all they that hate Sion.* Cp. Ps. 35. 4.

6 Let them be even as the grass growing upon the house-tops : which withereth afore it be plucked up;

house-tops: flat-roofed, lacking soil.

A.R.V. groweth. Cp. Ps. 37. 2.

7 Whereof the mower filleth not his hand : neither he that bindeth up the sheaves his bosom.

bosom: the fold of the robe was used as a receptacle; cp. S. Luke 6. 38.

A.R.V. Neither do they which go by say, 'The blessing of the LORD be upon you': 'We bless you in the Name of the LORD.' The latter clause may be the answer of the reapers to the salutations of the passers by. Cp. Ruth, 2. 4, 'Boaz came from Bethlehem, and said unto the reapers, "The LORD be with you." And they answered him, "The LORD bless thee."'

8 So that they who go by say not so much as, 'The LORD prosper you' : 'We wish you good luck in the Name of the LORD.'

Z

PSALM 130. *De profundis*

A cry from the waters of distress, for the pardon of God who is ready to forgive. The pilgrims' sense of unworthiness is mingled with faith and trust in the good God. The speaker is a pilgrim, speaking probably as representative of all Israel rather than in his own person alone.

This is the sixth of the Penitential Psalms, and is directed especially against Envy. The penitent from the depth of sinfulness looks to God's justice and mercy; his eyes are now set, not on earthly goods, but on God alone in whom is all plenteousness.

The psalm is also commonly used as a prayer for the departed; in which case the departed soul, or the whole company of the Holy Souls, is the speaker from the 'depths' of Purgatory, conscious of the guilt of past sins and also of God's merciful forgiveness, looking for deliverance from penance, and for the crown of the 'plenteous redemption' through Christ.

It is proper on Ash Wednesday and on other penitential occasions; and in Vespers of the Dead; and in the priest's preparation before Mass.

OUT of the deep have I called unto thee, O LORD : Lord, hear my voice.

2 O let thine ears consider well : the voice of my complaint.

3 If thou, LORD, wilt be extreme to mark what is done amiss : O Lord, who may abide it?

4 For there is mercy with thee : therefore shalt thou be feared.

the deep: a figure for deep trouble; cp. Ps. 69. 1–2. *A.R.V. Out of the depths*

A.R.V. my supplications.

A.R.V. who shall stand?

A.R.V. But there is forgiveness with thee : that thou mayest be feared. The knowledge that God is forgiving and the consciousness that sins have been forgiven call forth a final and reverent fear of God which is far different from slavish fear.

5 I look for the LORD; my soul doth wait for him : in his word is my trust.

6 My soul fleeth unto the Lord : before the morning watch, I say, before the morning watch.

The note of confidence usual in the Penitential Psalms is heard here.

R.V. looketh after

Cp. Ps. 5. 3; but *R.V.* has: *more than watchman look for the morning; yea, more than watchmen for the morning.*

7 O ISRAEL, 'TRUST IN THE LORD, for with the LORD there is mercy : and with him is plenteous redemption.

The speaker, representing Israel, here hears a voice encouraging him. Or, if speaking in his own person, he here turns to address his people. Cp. Ps. 131. 4.

8 And he shall redeem Israel : from all his sins.

Cp. Ps. 111. 9; and S. Matt. 1. 21, 'Thou shalt call his name JESUS, for it is he that shall save his people from their sins.'

PSALM 131. *Domine, non est*

The tranquillity of soul and contentment of mind that come from self-discipline and humility.

LORD, I am not high-minded : I have no proud looks.

2 I do not exercise myself in great matters : which are too high for me.

3 But I refrain my soul, and keep it low, like as a child that is weaned from his mother : yea, my soul is even as a weaned child.

Cp. Rom. 12. 16, 'Set not your mind on high things, but condescend to things that are lowly.'
R.V. Surely I have stilled and quieted my soul; like a weaned child with his mother, my soul is with me as a weaned child, who having learnt, as the soul should learn, from its troubles and disappointment, and having ceased to long fretfully for the breast, rests peacefully and contentedly in his mother's arms: not demanding the spiritual favours and encouragements bestowed on beginners.

4 O ISRAEL, TRUST IN THE LORD : from this time forth for evermore.

Cp. Ps. 130. 7.

THE TWENTY-EIGHTH DAY

MORNING PRAYER

PSALM 132. *Memento, Domine*

Israel restored from captivity prays that God will fulfil his promise to David. A thanksgiving for the restoration of the Temple. Proper on Christmas Day and other festivals of our Lord, and on the Feast of Dedication.

LORD, remember David: and all his trouble;

R.V. remember for (i.e. with respect to) *David all his affliction.* Cp. 1 Chron. 22. 14, 'Now, behold, in my affliction I have prepared for the house of the LORD.'

2 How he sware unto the LORD : and vowed a vow unto the Almighty God of Jacob;

R.V. unto the Mighty One of Jacob. Cp. v. 5 and Gen. 49. 24.

3 'I will not come within the tabernacle of mine house : nor climb up into my bed;

3–5. David's vow. Cp. 2 Sam. 7. 2; Hag. 1. 4. Even so David's Son ascended not up to his rest in his mansion in heaven until he had established the Church on earth.

tabernacle: i.e. tent.
climb: *A.R.V. go.*

4 I will not suffer mine eyes to sleep, nor mine eyelids to slumber : neither the temples of my head to take any rest,

5 Until I find out a place for the temple of the LORD : an habitation for the mighty God of Jacob.'

R.V. a place for the LORD, a tabernacle for the Mighty One of Jacob.

6 Lo, we heard of the same at Ephrata : and found it in the wood.

The people of David's time are here introduced as the speakers.

the same: i.e. the Ark, which is implied in v. 5, although not expressly mentioned until v. 8.

Ephrata is Bethlehem; cp. Gen. 35. 19.

in the wood: *R.V. in the field of the wood. R.V.mg. Jaar.* Jaar is probably a contracted form of Kirjathjearim, the 'city of the woods,' where the Ark lay many years before its removal to Sion. Cp. 1 Sam. 7. 1–2. It seems to have been a daughter-town to Bethlehem; cp. 1 Chron. 2. 19, 50; 4. 4.

Later, in the Ark of his human nature, God was found in Ephrata. Cp. Micah 5. 2 and S. Matt. 2. 6, 'Thou Bethlehem . . . out of thee shall come forth a Governor, which shall be shepherd of my people Israel.'

7 We will go into his tabernacle : and fall low on our knees before his footstool.

'tabernacle' denotes the same as 'footstool'; for which Sept. and Vulg. read: *the place where his feet have stood;* i.e. all his earthly shrines, from the scene of the first visit (*S. Luke* 2. 15), through all pilgrimages, to the last shrine of Eucharistic adoration. Cp. Ps. 5. 7; 99. 5.

8 Arise, O LORD, into thy resting-place : thou, and the ark of thy strength.

Suggested by the prayer appointed to be used on behalf of Israel in the wilderness, when the Ark set forward 'to seek out a resting-place for them.' Cp. Num. 10. 33, 35; Ps. 68. 1; 78. 62; and 2 Chron. 6. 41 f., Solomon's prayer: 'Arise, O LORD God, into thy resting-place, thou, and the ark of thy strength: let thy priests be clothed with salvation, and let thy saints rejoice in goodness. O LORD God, turn not away the face of thine anointed: remember the mercies of David thy servant.'

9 Let thy priests be clothed with righteousness : and let thy saints sing with joyfulness.

Cp. the common '*V*. Endue thy ministers with righteousness. *R*. And make thy chosen people joyful.'

This prayer is answered in v. 17.

10 For thy servant David's sake : turn not away the presence of thine anointed.

I.e. reject not the prayer of thine anointed king or priest. Answered in v. 18.

---

11 The Lord hath made a faithful oath unto David : and he shall not shrink from it;

11–19. The Lord's answer to the prayer of v. 1. The oath found fulfilment chiefly in Christ and the Church. Cp. Acts 2. 30.

12 'Of the fruit of thy body : shall I set upon thy seat.

12–13. A summary of the divine promise recorded in 2 Sam. 7. 12 ff. Cp. Ps. 89. 3–4, 20 ff., 34.

seat: *A.R.V. throne.*

13 If thy children will keep my covenant, and my testimonies that I shall learn them : their children also shall sit upon thy seat for evermore.'

learn: i.e. teach.

seat: *A.R.V. throne.*
Cp. Ps. 78. 69.

14 (For the Lord hath chosen Sion to be an habitation for himself : he hath longed for her.)

15 'This shall be my rest for ever : here will I dwell, for I have a delight therein.

R.V. resting-place, as in v. 8.
Cp. S. Matt. 28. 20, 'I am with you alway,' in Sion (the Church).

16 I will bless her victuals with increase : and will satisfy her poor with bread.

Sacramental sustenance in the Church for the spiritually hungry.

17 I will deck her priests with health : and her saints shall rejoice and sing.

R.V. Her priests also will I clothe with salvation:
health: i.e. well-being.
saints: i.e. the elect people of God, as in v. 9.

18 There shall I make the horn of David to flourish : I have ordained a lantern for mine Anointed.

the horn: interpreted of Christ by Zacharias in S. Luke 1. 68 f., 'The Lord hath raised up a horn of salvation for us in the house of his servant David.'
to flourish: *A.R.V. to bud.*
a lantern: the lighted lamp in a house is a symbol of the continued life and prosperity of the family; cp. Ps. 18. 28; 1 Kings 11. 36; 15. 4, etc.
mine Anointed: the Messiah.

19 As for his enemies, I shall clothe them with shame : but upon himself shall his crown flourish.'

crown: the Hebrew word denotes not only the kingly crown, but also the high-priestly mitre. The King Messiah of David's line should also be high priest.

PSALM 133. *Ecce, quam bonum!*

An exhortation to brotherly fellowship among the people of God; between pilgrims arriving and the residents in Jerusalem; and in the Communion of the Saints.

BEHOLD, how good and joyful a thing it is : brethren, to dwell together in unity!

2 It is like the precious ointment upon the head, that ran down unto the beard : even unto Aaron's beard, and went down to the skirts of his clothing;

A.R.V. for brethren to dwell

ointment: *R.V. oil.*
skirts: *R.V.mg. collar.*
Aaron represents Israel, the priestly nation; and the consecrating oil which spread from his head to his beard and raiment symbolizes the unity of the people. Cp. Exod. 29. 7. From Christ, our High Priest and Head, grace spread through the Church, his Body, whereby the unity is maintained which calls for brotherly love among the members. Cp. 1 Cor. 12. 12 f.; and 1 S. John 2. 20, 'Ye have an unction from the Holy One.'

3 Like as the dew of Hermon : which fell upon the hill of Sion.

R.V. that cometh down upon

Hermon in the north, abundant in dew, fertilizes, in the thought of the psalmist, the aridity of Sion in the south—another symbol of the unity and interdependence of the Israelites. Also, Hermon stands for our Lord, and Sion for the Church on earth. Also, Hermon, outside the boundary of the Holy Land, may symbolize the

Gentile Church and Sion the Jewish, cp. Eph. 2. 15; and similarly in these times the Church in 'missionary' lands reviving the Church at home.

4 For there the LORD promised his blessing : and life for evermore.

there: i.e. in Sion, the religious centre and meeting-place of the people: the Church militant.

PSALM 134. *Ecce nunc*

The congregation of pilgrims meet the priests and Levites who are conducting the night-service in the Temple, and receive their blessing. This psalm has been placed at the end of these Songs of Ascent, that they may conclude with a benediction. The pilgrimage has reached its goal. The psalm has been used in Compline in all parts of the Church.

BEHOLD now, PRAISE THE LORD : ALL YE SERVANTS OF THE LORD;

2 YE THAT by night STAND IN THE HOUSE OF THE LORD : EVEN IN THE COURTS OF THE HOUSE OF OUR GOD.

1–3. The greeting to the Temple ministrants. Cp. Ps. 135. 1-2.

To 'stand before the LORD' is the usual expression for the service of the priests and Levites; cp. Deut. 10. 8.

by night: cp. Lev. 8. 35; 1 Chron. 9. 33.

The latter clause is not in A.R.V.; Vulg. here copies from Ps. 135. 2.

3 Lift up your hands in the sanctuary : and praise the LORD.

4 The LORD that made heaven and earth : give thee blessing out of Sion.

The attitude of prayer; cp. Ps. 28. 2; 63. 5; 1 Tim. 2. 8.

4. The counter-greeting of the night-watch.

thee: the singular is used because the words are taken from the priestly blessing (*Num.* 6. 24); or perhaps because vv. 1–3 are supposed to be said by a single voice.

PSALM 135. *Laudate Nomen*

A thanksgiving to the God of Israel, the only true God, for his preservation of his people. This psalm, with Ps. 136, which is closely connected with it, was probably composed for liturgical use in the second Temple; cp. Ezra 3. 10.

O PRAISE THE LORD, laud ye the Name of the LORD: praise it, O YE SERVANTS OF THE LORD;

2 YE THAT STAND IN THE HOUSE OF THE LORD : IN THE COURTS OF THE HOUSE OF OUR GOD.

3 O PRAISE THE LORD, for the LORD is gracious : O sing praises unto his Name, for it is lovely.

4 For why? the LORD hath chosen Jacob unto himself : and Israel for his own possession.

1–2. Cp. Ps. 134. 1–2.
O praise the LORD: *R.V.mg. Heb. Hallelujah.*

Note three triplets of 'the LORD' in vv. 1–6.
lovely: *A.R.V. pleasant*, cp. Ps. 27. 2; 90. 17; 147. 1.
Three reasons for praising the LORD: his favours bestowed (v. 4), his essential pre-eminence (v. 5), his almighty power (v. 6).
A.R.V. for his peculiar treasure; cp. Exod. 19. 5; Deut. 7. 6; applied to the Church in Tit. 2. 14; 1 S. Pet. 2. 9, R.V., 'Ye are a people for God's own possession (A.V. a peculiar people).'

5 For I know that the LORD is great : and that our LORD is above all gods.

all gods: i.e. all false gods, thought of as demons; or, all angels; cp. Ps. 138. 1.
Cp. Ps. 115. 3.

6 Whatsoever the LORD pleased, that did he in heaven, and in earth : and in the sea, and in all deep places.

7 He bringeth forth the clouds from the ends of the world : and sendeth forth lightnings with the rain, bringing the winds out of his treasures.

7. A quotation from Jer. 10. 13.
A.R.V. He causeth the vapours to ascend from
from the ends: i.e. from the horizon where they seem to gather.
treasures: *A.R.V. treasuries.*

8 He smote the first-born of Egypt : both of man and beast.

9 He hath sent tokens and wonders into the midst of thee, O thou land of Egypt : upon Pharaoh, and all his servants.

10 He smote divers nations : and slew mighty kings;

Cp. Exod. 12. 29.

divers: i.e. various.

Similarly God has smitten many of those who have opposed Christ and his Church. Pharaoh may be taken as standing for the 'world,' Sihon for the devil, Og for the 'flesh,' and the seven nations of Canaan for the seven deadly sins.

Cp. Num. 21. 21 ff.

11 Sehon king of the Amorites, and Og the king of Basan : and all the kingdoms of Canaan;

12 And gave their land to be an heritage : even an heritage unto Israel his people.

13 Thy Name, O LORD, endureth for ever : so doth thy memorial, O LORD, from one generation to another.

Threefold 'LORD' in 13–14.

Omit, with A.R.V., 'so doth.' The LORD'S Name is his memorial, because it brings to mind his nature and operations; cp. Exod. 3. 15.

14 For the LORD will avenge his people : and be gracious unto his servants.

14. A quotation from Deut. 32. 36.

For: i.e. thus does he prove that the memorial of his Name endures for ever.

avenge: i.e. vindicate, cp. Ps. 54. 1.

A.R.V. and repent himself concerning his servants. I.e. change from wrath to compassion towards them; cp. Ps. 90. 13.

15 As for the images of the heathen, they are but silver and gold : the work of men's hands.

15–20. Taken from Ps. 115. 4–11.

However costly their material, they are merely of human workmanship.

16 They have mouths, and speak not : eyes have they, but they see not.

17 They have ears, and yet they hear not : neither is there any breath in their mouths.

18 They that make them are like unto them : and so are all they that put their trust in them.

R.V. shall be like unto them; yea, everyone that trusteth in them.

19–20. Cp. Ps. 115. 9–11 and 118. 2–4.

Note 'LORD' six times.

19 PRAISE THE LORD, ye house of Israel : PRAISE THE LORD, ye house of Aaron.

20 PRAISE THE LORD, ye house of Levi : ye that fear the LORD, PRAISE THE LORD.

21 Praised be the LORD out of Sion : who dwelleth at Jerusalem.

out of Sion: cp. Ps. 128. 6. The Church on earth is to offer praise to God in heaven.

A.R.V. add *Praise ye the LORD. R.V.mg. Heb. Hallelujah.*

EVENING PRAYER

PSALM 136. *Confitemini*

Closely connected with Ps. 135, this is a psalm of praise for the mercy of the LORD manifested in nature, and in the past history of his people.

O GIVE THANKS UNTO the LORD, for he is gracious : and HIS MERCY ENDURETH FOR EVER.

Cp. 1 Chron. 16. 41.

2 O GIVE THANKS UNTO the God of all gods : FOR HIS MERCY ENDURETH FOR EVER.

In vv. 1–3 there is a triple forecasting of the Blessed Trinity, under the titles Jehovah, Elohim, Adonai.

3 O THANK the Lord of all lords : FOR HIS MERCY ENDURETH FOR EVER.

4 Who only doeth great wonders : FOR HIS MERCY ENDURETH FOR EVER.

Cp. in the Daily Office, B.C.P., 'Who alone workest great marvels.'

5 Who by his excellent wisdom made the heavens : FOR HIS MERCY ENDURETH FOR EVER.

excellent: i.e. pre-eminent, excelling; cp. Ps. 8. 1.

Cp. Ps. 33. 6, 'By the word

of the LORD were the heavens made : and all the hosts of them by the breath of his mouth.' Cp. Prov. 3. 19; Jer. 10. 12; 51. 15. The Wisdom denotes the Second Person of the Blessed Trinity, 'by whom all things were made,' the Word of God. Cp. Ps. 24. 2.

6 Who laid out the earth above the waters : FOR HIS MERCY ENDURETH FOR EVER.

7 Who hath made great lights: FOR HIS MERCY ENDURETH FOR EVER;

7–9. Cp. Gen. 1. 14–18.

8 The sun to rule the day : for his mercy endureth for ever;

9 The moon and the stars to govern the night : FOR HIS MERCY ENDURETH FOR EVER.

A.R.V. to rule by night:

10 Who smote Egypt with their first-born : FOR HIS MERCY ENDURETH FOR EVER;

10–22. A repetition, with additions, of Ps. 135. 8–12. In such words as these Christians can celebrate every mighty deliverance of his Church by God, and every vindication of right over wrong, especially at the resurrection of Christ.

11 And brought out Israel from among them : FOR HIS MERCY ENDURETH FOR EVER;

12 With a mighty hand, and stretched out arm : FOR HIS MERCY ENDURETH FOR EVER.

13 Who divided the Red Sea in two parts : FOR HIS MERCY ENDURETH FOR EVER;

R.V. in sunder: P.B.V. is a printer's error for 'into parts,' as in A.V.

14 And made Israel to go through the midst of it : FOR HIS MERCY ENDURETH FOR EVER.

15 But as for Pharaoh and his host, he overthrew them in the Red Sea : FOR HIS MERCY ENDURETH FOR EVER.

16 Who led his people through the wilderness : FOR HIS MERCY ENDURETH FOR EVER.

17 Who smote great kings : FOR HIS MERCY ENDURETH FOR EVER;

18 Yea, and slew mighty kings : FOR HIS MERCY ENDURETH FOR EVER;

19 Sehon king of the Amorites : FOR HIS MERCY ENDURETH FOR EVER;

20 And Og the king of Basan : FOR HIS MERCY ENDURETH FOR EVER;

21 And gave away their land for an heritage : FOR HIS MERCY ENDURETH FOR EVER;

22 Even for an heritage unto Israel his servant : FOR HIS MERCY ENDURETH FOR EVER.

23 Who remembered us when we were in trouble : FOR HIS MERCY ENDURETH FOR EVER.

24 And hath delivered us from our enemies : FOR HIS MERCY ENDURETH FOR EVER.

25 Who giveth food to all flesh : FOR HIS MERCY ENDURETH FOR EVER.

26 O GIVE THANKS UNTO the God of heaven : FOR HIS MERCY ENDURETH FOR EVER.

27 O give thanks unto the Lord of lords : FOR HIS MERCY ENDURETH FOR EVER.

remembered: cp. Exod. 2. 24. *A.R.V.* remembered us in our *low estate:* i.e. in our exile.

Cp. Ps. 104. 27, 145. 15, especially the sacramental food, the crowning instance of God's power and mercy.

The title 'the God of heaven' occurs here only in the Psalter; cp. Ezra 1. 2; Dan. 2. 18; Rev. 11. 13.

This verse is not in A.R.V.; it was added in Vulg., repeating v. 3.

PSALM 137. *Super flumina*

A picture of Israel's despondency in the land of exile: probably written shortly after the return. Applications are to the Church mourning in her exile in this vale of tears, especially when under the dominion of heathen or Moslem rulers; and to sinners banished from the communion of the Church under penance, while vexed by the worldly.

BY the waters of Babylon we sat down and wept : when we remembered thee, O Sion.

A.R.V. By the rivers . . . Jews had places of prayer by the riverside; cp. Acts 16. 13.

Babylon: denotes the 'world,' as being then the capital; so Rome is called Babylon in 1 S. Pet. 5. 13; Rev. 17. 5; etc.

Sion: denotes the Church militant usually, the Church in bondage. But some take 'Sion' here in the same sense as 'Jerusalem' (v. 5).

harps: cp. harps being used (*Rev.* 5. 8; 14. 2; 15. 2).

trees: *A.R.V. willows.*

2 As for our harps, we hanged them up : upon the trees that are therein.

3 For they that led us away captive required of us then a song, and melody, in our heaviness : 'Sing us one of the songs of Sion.'

required: i.e. asked.

A.R.V. and they that wasted us required of us mirth, saying:

'Alleluia our transgressions make us for a while give o'er.'

strange: i.e. foreign.

Jerusalem: the Church triumphant; cp. Gal. 4. 26.

cunning: i.e. skill, in harping.

4 How shall we sing the LORD'S song: in a strange land?

5 If I forget thee, O Jerusalem: let my right hand forget her cunning.

6 If I do not remember thee, let my tongue cleave to the roof of my mouth : yea, if I prefer not Jerusalem in my mirth.

cleave: losing its power of song.

A.R.V. above my chief joy.

R.V. Remember, O LORD, against the children of Edom the day of Jerusalem; i.e. requite them for their savage exultation on the day of its fall. Cp. Obad. 10 ff. P.B.V. may mean: 'in the day of the manifestation of the

7 Remember the children of Edom, O LORD, in the day of Jerusalem: how they said, 'Down with it, down with it, even to the ground.'

8 O daughter of Babylon, wasted with misery : yea, happy shall he be that rewardeth thee, as thou hast served us.

9 Blessed shall he be that taketh thy children : and throweth them against the stones.

triumph of Jerusalem, at Christ's Second Coming.' Edom denotes all those who consent with the Church's persecutors.

I.e. Babylon itself, personified; cp. Ps. 9. 14.

wasted with misery: *R.V. that art to be destroyed.*

rewardeth: cp. Ps. 28. 4.

As Babylon symbolizes the world opposed to God, cp. Rev. 18. 2. ff., so her children may be mystically understood to mean evil thoughts, which must be broken against the Rock which is Christ, cp. 1 Cor. 10. 4; S. Matt 21. 44, before they gain strength. Or, the children are the world-leaders, who need to be broken on the rock of faith in Christ.

the stones: *R.V. the rock.*

For a Christian version of the thought of vv. 8–9, see Rev. 18. 2–6.

PSALM 138.   *Confitebor tibi*

An expression of Israel's gratitude to Jehovah for past mercies, and of confidence in him for future support. The psalmist speaks in the name of the people.

I WILL give thanks unto thee, O Lord, with my whole heart : even before the gods will I sing praise unto thee.

2 I will worship toward thy holy temple, and praise thy Name, because of thy loving-kindness and truth : for thou hast magnified thy Name, and thy word, above all things.

before the gods: In defiance of the imaginary gods of the heathen, I shall adore and praise Jehovah alone. Cp. Ps. 95. 3; 96. 5. But Sept. and Vulg. read: *before the angels.*

toward: cp. Ps. 28. 2; Dan. 6. 10.

A.R.V. magnified thy word above all thy name. By the fulfilment of his word of promise God has surpassed even the manifestation of his goodness which his name Jehovah implied. Cp. Exod. 34. 6, 7.

3 When I called upon thee, thou heardest me : and en-duedst my soul with much strength.

4 All the kings of the earth shall praise thee, O Lord : for they have heard the words of thy mouth.

enduedst: i.e. endowedst.

Cp. Ps. 102. 15.
In the psalmist's prophetic vision, the knowledge of God's ways and words has already reached and won over the world's kings.
in: *R.V. of.*
that: *A.R.V. for.*

5 Yea, they shall sing in the ways of the Lord : that great is the glory of the Lord.

6 For though the Lord be high, yet hath he respect unto the lowly : as for the proud, he beholdeth them afar off.

Cp. Ps. 113. 5.

I.e. he excludeth them from his fellowship.

7 Though I walk in the midst of trouble, yet shalt thou refresh me : thou shalt stretch forth thy hand upon the furiousness of mine enemies, and thy right hand shall save me.

8 The Lord shall make good his loving-kindness toward me : yea, thy mercy, O Lord, endur-eth for ever; despise not then the works of thine own hands.

A.R.V. The Lord will perfect that which concerneth me: Cp. Phil. 1. 6, 'He which began a good work in you will perfect it until the day of Jesus Christ.'
despise: *A.R.V. forsake.*
I.e. the works of mercy which thou hast hitherto wrought for thy people. Or, this people whom thou didst create; cp. Ps. 100. 2.

THE TWENTY-NINTH DAY

MORNING PRAYER

PSALM 139. *Domine, probasti*

The praises of God omniscient and omnipresent. In many of the verses an application to Christ as the speaker may readily be made. Proper on Feasts of the Apostles, cp. v. 17.

LORD, thou hast searched me out, and known me : thou knowest my down-sitting, and mine up - rising ; thou understandest my thoughts long before.

2 Thou art about my path, and about my bed : and spiest out all my ways.

3 For lo, there is not a word in my tongue : but thou, O LORD, knowest it altogether.

4 Thou hast fashioned me behind and before : and laid thine hand upon me.

5 Such knowledge is too wonderful and excellent for me : I cannot attain unto it.

6 Whither shall I go then from thy Spirit : or whither shall I go then from thy presence?

1–6. God's omniscience.

The verse can be applied to our Lord's life of trial, his passion, and his resurrection.

long before: i.e. before I think them. *A.R.V. afar off*, i.e. without nearer scrutiny.

path . . . bed: i.e. all my actions and restings, my life and death.

A.R.V. and art acquainted with all my ways.

Cp. Heb. 4. 12, 'All things are naked and laid open before the eyes of him with whom we have to do.'

but: i.e. except. There is no word which thou knowest not. Cp. Ps. 19. 3.

A.R.V. Thou hast beset . . . God's presence is around me. 'In him we live and move and have our being' (*Acts* 17. 28).

laid thine hand: i.e. to direct my actions; cp. Ps. 89. 21.

Cp. Rom. 11. 33, 'O the depth of the riches both of the wisdom and the knowledge of God! how unsearchable are his judgements, and his ways past tracing out!'

excellent: i.e. surpassing.

6–11. God's omnipresence.

Cp. Jer. 23. 24, 'Can any hide himself in secret places that I shall not see him? saith the LORD. Do not I fill heaven and earth?'

2A

7 If I climb up into heaven, thou art there : if I go down to hell, thou art there also.

8 If I take the wings of the morning : and remain in the uttermost parts of the sea;

A.R.V. If I ascend up
R.V. if I make my bed in Sheol. Cp. Amos 9. 2–4.

I.e. if I should fly from east to west with the speed of the sun's morning beams.

the sea: i.e. the west, the Mediterranean Sea being the western boundary of Palestine.

9 Even there also shall thy hand lead me : and thy right hand shall hold me.

10 If I say, 'Peradventure the darkness shall cover me' : then shall my night be turned to day.

11 Yea, the darkness is no darkness with thee, but the night is as clear as the day : the darkness and light to thee are both alike.

12 For my reins are thine : thou hast covered me in my mother's womb.

R.V. 'and the light about me shall be night';
Yea: *R.V. Even*

12–16. God my Maker knows me.

For: i.e. Thou knowest me, for thou hast made me.

reins: i.e. kidneys, regarded as the seat of the emotions; cp. Ps. 7. 10; 16. 8. Put here for the whole inner man; as is 'frame' in v. 14 for the outer form.

13 I will give thanks unto thee, for I am fearfully and wonderfully made : marvellous are thy works, and that my soul knoweth right well.

14 My bones are not hid from thee : though I be made secretly, and fashioned beneath in the earth.

R.V. My frame was not hidden from thee, when I was made in secret, and curiously (i.e. with care) *wrought in the lowest parts of the earth,* i.e. a region as dark and full of mystery as Sheol. Cp. Ps. 63. 10 and Eph. 4. 9.

15 Thine eyes did see my substance, yet being imperfect : and in thy book were all my members written;

book: cp. Ps. 40. 10; 56. 8.

16 Which day by day were fashioned : when as yet there was none of them.

17 How dear are thy counsels unto me, O God : O how great is the sum of them!

17–24. Various prayers upon the preceding meditation.

A.R.V. How precious also are thy thoughts unto me:

Vulgate and other versions read: *Thy friends are exceedingly honoured by me, O God : their principality is strengthened.* And the friends are understood to be the Apostles; cp. S. John 15. 13–15, 'Ye are my friends,' etc.

tell: i.e. as *A.R.V. count.*

than the sand: cp. Gen. 22. 27. God's loving thoughts are more numerous than I can reckon. Or, the Apostles and Saints are a 'great multitude which no man can number' (*Rev.* 7. 9).

18 If I tell them, they are more in number than the sand : when I wake up I am present with thee.

when I wake up : apply to the Resurrection of Christ. The clause is the Introit of the Mass of Easter.

present: *A.R.V. still.* Cp. Ps. 16. 9, 12.

Cp. Ps. 6. 8. The wicked hinder God's plans, and persecute God's friends.

19 Wilt thou not slay the wicked, O God : depart from me, ye blood-thirsty men.

20 For they speak unrighteously against thee : and thine enemies take thy Name in vain.

21 Do not I hate them, O LORD, that hate thee : and am I not grieved with those that rise up against thee?

22 Yea, I hate them right sore : even as though they were mine enemies.

A.R.V. I hate them with perfect hatred:

23 Try me, O God, and seek the ground of my heart : prove me, and examine my thoughts.

A.R.V. and know my heart:

ground: i.e. the deepest of my thoughts. Search me thoroughly, and purify me from whatever secret evil thou dost find in me.

24 Look well if there be any way of wickedness in me : and lead me in the way everlasting.

I would not be as the wicked, cp. v. 19.

I.e. the way of holiness and everlasting life.

PSALM 140. *Eripe me, Domine*

A prayer for deliverance from violent and crafty foes. Christ speaks in his Saints. Pss. 140, 141, 142, and 143 are similar in subject.

DELIVER me, O LORD, from the evil man : and preserve me from the wicked man;

A.R.V. the violent man;

2 Who imagine mischief in their hearts : and stir up strife all the day long.

3 They have sharpened their tongues like a serpent : adders' poison is under their lips.

Quoted in Rom. 3. 13; cp. Ps. 14. 5.

4 Keep me, O LORD, from the hands of the ungodly : preserve me from the wicked men, who are purposed to overthrow my goings.

A.R.V. violent

5 The proud have laid a snare for me, and spread a net abroad with cords : yea, and set traps in my way.

abroad: *A.R.V. by the way;* but not on it, cp. Isa. 35. 8.

6 I said unto the LORD, 'Thou art my God : hear the voice of my prayers, O LORD.'

7 O Lord God, thou strength of my health : thou hast covered my head in the day of battle.

A.R.V. of my salvation:
covered: as with a helmet of salvation; cp. Isa. 59. 17; Eph. 6. 17.
the day of battle: when the ungodly assailed me.

8 Let not the ungodly have his desire, O LORD : let not his mischievous imagination prosper, lest they be too proud.

9 Let the mischief of their own lips fall upon the head of them : that compass me about.

10 Let hot burning coals fall upon them : let them be cast into the fire, and into the pit, that they never rise up again.

11 A man full of words shall not prosper upon the earth : evil shall hunt the wicked person to overthrow him.

12 Sure I am that the LORD will avenge the poor : and maintain the cause of the helpless.

13 The righteous also shall give thanks unto thy Name : and the just shall continue in thy sight.

Cp. Ps. 11. 7; 18. 13.

A.R.V. deep pits. R.V.mg. floods.

R.V. An evil speaker shall not be established in the earth: A.R.V. the violent man

A.R.V. the upright shall dwell in thy presence. Cp. Ps. 11. 8.

PSALM 141. *Domine, clamavi*

A prayer for self-restraint and a spiritual mind by one who is exposed to bitter persecution, and who perhaps was absent from Jerusalem or otherwise debarred from taking part in the daily sacrifice, cp. v. 2. An evening psalm.

L ORD, I call upon thee, haste thee unto me : and consider my voice when I cry unto thee.

2 Let my prayer be set forth in thy sight as the incense : and let the lifting up of my hands be an evening sacrifice.

incense: cp. Exod. 30. 6–8; Rev. 5. 8, 'golden bowls full of incense, which are the prayers of the saints'; Rev. 8. 3–4, 'the smoke of the incense with the prayers of the saints went up before God.'

lifting up: the gesture of prayer; cp. Ps. 28. 2; 63. 5; 1 Tim. 2. 8.

A.R.V. be as the evening sacrifice; cp. Exod. 29. 38–42. The lamb sacrificed in the evening typifies Christ dying on the Cross with arms uplifted, the true sacrifice, at the ninth hour.

Cp. Ps. 15. 3; 34. 13; 39. 1.

3 Set a watch, O LORD, before my mouth : and keep the door of my lips.

4 O let not mine heart be inclined to any evil thing : let me not be occupied in ungodly works with the men that work wickedness, lest I eat of such things as please them.

5 Let the righteous rather smite me friendly : and reprove me.

lest I eat, etc.: *A.R.V. and let me not eat of their dainties*, i.e. let me not conform to their luxurious and sensual habits.

5–6. 'their' in v. 6 refers to the wicked. The general sense of the verses is 'Faithful are the wounds of a friend : but the kisses of an enemy are deceitful' (*Prov.* 27. 6). But *R.V.* has: *Let the righteous smite me, it shall be a kindness; and let him reprove me, it shall be as oil upon the head; let not my head refuse it.* I.e. the chastisement and reproof of the good will be taken by me in friendly part and welcomed.

6 But let not their precious balms break my head : yea, I will pray yet against their wickedness.

7 Let their judges be overthrown in stony places : that they may hear my words, for they are sweet.

R.V. for even in their wickedness shall my prayer continue.

R.V. Their judges are thrown down by the sides of the rock; and they shall . . . The psalmist is assured that the judges, i.e. the leaders of the wicked, will meet with condign punishment; or, will be brought up against the rock which is Christ, cp. Ps. 137. 9.

they may hear: i.e. the wicked, the followers of the 'judges,' will then appreciate and welcome his advice.

8 Our bones lie scattered before the pit : like as when one breaketh and heweth wood upon the earth.

The bones of the slaughtered servants of God are compared to the chips scattered by a woodcutter. But 'wood' is not in the original. *R.V.* reads, *As when one ploweth and cleaveth the earth, our bones are scattered at the grave's mouth* (*R.V.mg. at the mouth of Sheol*). Cp. Ps. 79. 1–3.

9 But mine eyes look unto thee, O Lord GOD : in thee is my trust, O cast not out my soul.

10 Keep me from the snare that they have laid for me : and from the traps of the wicked doers.

11 Let the ungodly fall into their own nets together : and let me ever escape them.

EVENING PRAYER

PSALM 142. *Voce mea ad Dominum*

A cry to God for succour by one who is persecuted and abandoned by earthly helpers. Christ is the speaker, and his Passion may be seen foreshadowed in the successive verses: 3a, Christ in his agony; 3b, betrayed by Judas; 4, deserted by the disciples; 5, arrested by his enemies; 6, his faith in the Father; 7, he humbled himself and became obedient unto death; 8, overwhelmed by the powers of evil, 'himself he cannot save'; 9a, his resurrection; and 9b, the fellowship of the Church.

I CRIED unto the LORD with my voice : yea, even unto the LORD did I make my supplication.

2 I poured out my complaints before him : and shewed him of my trouble.

3 When my spirit was in heaviness thou knewest my path : in the way wherein I walked have they privily laid a snare for me.

4 I looked also upon my right hand : and saw that there was no man that would know me.

right hand: where I would naturally expect a protector to stand (*Ps.* 16. 9; 109. 30; 121. 5). Cp. Ps. 31. 13; Isa. 63. 5.

5 I had no place to flee unto : and no man cared for my soul.

6 I cried unto thee, O LORD, and said: 'Thou art my hope, and my portion in the land of the living.'

A.R.V. my refuge,

7 Consider my complaint : for I am brought very low.

8 O deliver me from my persecutors : for they are too strong for me.

9 Bring my soul out of prison, that I may give thanks unto thy Name : which things if thou wilt grant me, then shall the righteous resort unto my company.

prison: probably figurative for deep distress. Cp. Ps. 143. 11. As spoken by Christ, the prison is that of the dead; cp. 1 S. Pet. 3. 19.

A.R.V. . . . thy name : the righteous shall compass me about; for thou shalt deal bountifully with me. Those who have hitherto held back (vv. 4–5), will gather round me.

PSALM 143. *Domine, exaudi*

A servant of the LORD appeals to him for succour in a dark day of persecution and calamity. We may hear the voice of the Church speaking to the Lord Christ. This is the last of the seven Penitential Psalms: against the sin of Sloth. Proper on Ash Wednesday, and as an act of penitence at any time.

HEAR my prayer, O LORD, and consider my desire : hearken unto me for thy truth and righteousness' sake.

A.R.V. in thy faithfulness answer me, and in thy righteousness. Cp. 1 S. John 1. 9, 'He is faithful and righteous to forgive us our sins.'

2 And enter not into judgement with thy servant : for in thy sight shall no man living be justified.

Cp. Rom. 3. 20, 'By the works of the law shall no flesh be justified in his sight'; Gal. 2. 16, 'A man is not justified save through faith in Jesus Christ.'

3 For the enemy hath persecuted my soul; he hath smitten my life down to the ground : he hath laid me in the darkness, as the men that have been long dead.

A figurative expression of a state of deep affliction.

4 Therefore is my spirit vexed within me : and my heart within me is desolate.

5 Yet do I remember the time past; I muse upon all thy works : yea, I exercise myself in the works of thy hands.

vexed: *A.R.V. overwhelmed.* Cp. Ps. 77. 3.

The contemplation of God's former mercies is my consolation in my present troubles; cp. Ps. 77. 5, 11, 12.
A.R.V. I remember the days of old; I meditate on all thy doings: I muse on the work of thy hands.
Cp. Ps. 42. 2; 63. 2.

6 I stretch forth my hands unto thee : my soul gaspeth unto thee as a thirsty land.

7 Hear me, O LORD, and that soon, for my spirit waxeth faint : hide not thy face from me, lest I be like unto them that go down into the pit.

8 O let me hear thy loving-kindness betimes in the morning, for in thee is my trust : shew thou me the way that I should walk in, for I lift up my soul unto thee.

9 Deliver me, O LORD, from mine enemies : for I flee unto thee to hide me.

10 Teach me to do the thing that pleaseth thee, for thou art my God : let thy loving Spirit lead me forth into the land of righteousness.

11 Quicken me, O LORD, for thy Name's sake : and for thy righteousness' sake bring my soul out of trouble.

waxeth: i.e. groweth.

Cp. Ps. 28. 1.
The usual change to hopefulness begins here.
the morning: of deliverance which will succeed the night of suffering; cp. Ps. 49. 14; 90. 14. Especially the early morn of Christ's resurrection.

R.V. thy spirit is good; lead me in the land of uprightness.

Quicken: i.e. give life.
Cp. Eph. 2. 4, 'God, being rich in mercy, for the great love wherewith he loved us, even when we were dead through our trespasses, quickened us together with Christ (by grace have ye been saved).'
This is best understood of spiritual enemies.
vex: *A.R.V. afflict.*

12 And of thy goodness slay mine enemies : and destroy all them that vex my soul; for I am thy servant.

2B

THE THIRTIETH DAY
MORNING PRAYER

PSALM 144. *Benedictus Dominus*

Some ruler of Israel is represented as interceding for the nation which is oppressed by foreign enemies, but yet looks forward to a golden age of peace and plenty. The psalm is mainly a compilation from earlier ones. We hear Christ speaking in his Body the Church.

BLESSED be the LORD my strength : who teacheth my hands to war, and my fingers to fight.

2 My hope and my fortress, my castle and deliverer, my defender in whom I trust : who subdueth my people unto me.

1–2. Taken from Ps. 18. 1, 34, 48.

A.R.V. the LORD *my rock:*

A.R.V. My loving-kindness and

my people: i.e. Israel submissive to its ruler through divine appointment. Ps. 18. 48 has 'peoples,' i.e. the heathen nations. As spoken by Christ, the reference is to converts in his kingdom.

Suggested by Ps. 8. 4.

3 LORD, what is man, that thou hast such respect unto him: or the son of man, that thou so regardest him?

4 Man is like a thing of nought : his time passeth away like a shadow.

5 Bow thy heavens, O LORD, and come down : touch the mountains, and they shall smoke.

R.V.mg. like a breath; cp. Ps. 39. 6, 12.

Cp. Ps. 102. 11.

Come in thy almighty power to the rescue of frail mankind.

5–7. Cp. Ps. 18. 9, 14, 16, 45; 104. 32.

6 Cast forth thy lightning, and tear them : shoot out thine arrows, and consume them.

7 Send down thine hand from above : DELIVER ME, and take me out of the great waters, FROM THE HAND OF STRANGE CHILDREN;

8 WHOSE MOUTH TALKETH OF VANITY : AND THEIR RIGHT HAND IS A RIGHT HAND OF WICKEDNESS.

A.R.V. and scatter them, i.e. the enemies of Israel.

R.V. of strangers, i.e. foreigners.

A.R.V. speaketh vanity, i.e. falsehood; cp. Ps. 12. 2; 41. 6.

The right hand was uplifted in taking an oath; cp. Ps. 106. 26.

A.R.V. of falsehood.

9 I will sing a new song unto thee, O God : and sing praises unto thee upon a ten-stringed lute.

Cp. Ps. 33. 2–3. The new song of Christian grace, mingled with the ten-stringed lute of the moral law of the Old Testament.

Cp. Ps. 18. 51.

10 Thou hast given victory unto kings : and hast delivered David thy servant from the peril of the sword.

11 Save me, and DELIVER ME FROM THE HAND OF STRANGE CHILDREN : WHOSE MOUTH TALKETH OF VANITY, AND THEIR RIGHT HAND IS A RIGHT HAND OF INIQUITY.

R.V. strangers, i.e. foreigners.
A.R.V. mouth speaketh vanity, i.e. falsehood.
A.R.V. of falsehood.

12 That our sons may grow up as the young plants : and that our daughters may be as the polished corners of the temple.

R.V. as corner stones hewn after the fashion of a palace. The 'corners' of reception rooms in Eastern palaces are ornamented with carved work coloured and gilded.

13 That our garners may be full and plenteous with all manner of store : that our sheep may bring forth thousands and ten thousands in our streets.

14 That our oxen may be strong to labour, that there be no decay : no leading into captivity, and no complaining in our streets.

R.V. fields.
R.V. When our oxen are well-laden with the produce of our fields, *when there is no breaking in* of foreign enemies, *and no going forth* either into exile (as A.V.), or to attack besiegers, *and no outcry in our streets.*

Cp. Ps. 33. 12; 89. 16; 146. 4.

15 Happy are the people that are in such a case : yea, blessed are the people who have the LORD for their God.

Blessedness consists not in temporal prosperity and peace, but in having the true religion.

PSALM 145. *Exaltabo te, Deus*

A hymn of praise to God, the universal King, all-bountiful and all-merciful. Proper on Whitsunday, the feast of the Lifegiver.

I WILL magnify thee, O God, my King : and I will PRAISE THY NAME FOR EVER AND EVER.

2 Every day will I give thanks unto thee : and PRAISE THY NAME FOR EVER AND EVER.

3 Great is the LORD, and marvellous worthy to be praised : there is no end of his greatness.

marvellous: an adverb, marvellously; as in Ps. 31. 23.

4 One generation shall praise thy works unto another : and declare thy power.

5 As for me, I will be talking of thy worship : thy glory, thy praise, and wondrous works;

A.R.V. thy mighty acts.
R.V. I will meditate
worship: i.e. as *R.V. honour.*

6 So that men shall speak of the might of thy marvellous acts: and I will also tell of thy greatness.

7 The memorial of thine abundant kindness shall be shewed : and men shall sing of thy righteousness.

R.V. They shall utter the memory of thy great goodness, and shall sing

8 The LORD is gracious and merciful : long-suffering, and of great goodness.

So God revealed himself to Moses (*Exod.* 34. 6; cp. *Ps.* 103. 8).

9 The LORD is loving unto every man : and his mercy is over all his works.

A.R.V. is good to all, not to man only, but to all his creatures.

10 All thy works praise thee, O LORD : and thy saints give thanks unto thee.

R.V. shall give thanks unto … God's works 'praise' him, for 'they continue according to thine ordinance: for all things serve thee' (*Ps.* 119. 91).

thy saints: i.e. thine elect people.

11 They shew the glory of thy kingdom : and talk of thy power ;

A.R.V. shall speak of

12 That thy power, thy glory, and mightiness of thy kingdom : might be known unto men.

13 Thy kingdom is an everlasting kingdom : and thy dominion endureth throughout all ages.

14 The LORD upholdeth all such as fall : and lifteth up all those that are down.

15 The eyes of all wait upon thee, O LORD : and thou givest them their meat in due season.

16 Thou openest thy hand : and fillest all things living with plenteousness.

17 The LORD is righteous in all his ways : and holy in all his works.

18 The LORD is nigh unto all them that call upon him : yea, all such as call upon him faithfully.

19 He will fulfil the desire of them that fear him : he also will hear their cry, and will help them.

20 The LORD preserveth all them that love him : but scattereth abroad all the ungodly.

21 My mouth shall speak the praise of the LORD : and let all flesh GIVE THANKS UNTO HIS HOLY NAME FOR EVER AND EVER.

A verse is added, here by Sept. and Vulg., etc.: *The LORD is faithful in all his words : and holy in all his works.* Cp. v. 17. Cp. Dan. 4. 3; S. Luke 1. 33.

The LORD declareth his almighty power most chiefly by shewing mercy and pity. Cp. Litany, 'That it may please thee to raise up them that fall.'
15–16. Commonly used in the Blessing of the Table. Cp. S. John 6. 14.
meat: i.e. food in general, the Eucharist in particular.

A.R.V. and satisfiest the desire of every living thing.

R.V. and gracious

A.R.V. all the wicked will he destroy.

A.R.V. bless his

PSALM 146. *Lauda, anima mea*

Praise to the LORD, the One true Helper of mankind. This psalm is the first of a series of Hallelujah Psalms with which the Psalter closes. They were written probably after the return from the Exile. This psalm is also used in the Office of the Dead.

PRAISE the LORD, O my soul; while I live will I praise the LORD : yea, as long as I have any being, I will sing praises unto my God.

2 O put not your trust in princes, nor in any child of man : for there is no help in them.

A.R.V. prefix *Praise ye the LORD. R.V.mg. Heb. Hallelujah.*

princes: probably the Persian kings and governors; cp. Ps. 118. 9.

any child of man: i.e. any person.

'Dust thou art, and unto dust shalt thou return' (*Gen.* 3. 19; cp. *Ps.* 104. 29; *Eccles.* 12. 7).

3 For when the breath of man goeth forth he shall turn again to his earth : and then all his thoughts perish.

4 Blessed is he that hath the God of Jacob for his help : and whose hope is in the LORD his God;

5 Who made heaven and earth, the sea, and all that therein is : who keepeth his promise for ever;

From the Fourth Commandment (*Exod.* 20. 11).

his promise: i.e. his covenant promise made with Jacob and the people. But *A.R.V.* has: *who keepeth truth*; cp. Ps. 117. 2.

6 Who helpeth them to right that suffer wrong : who feedeth the hungry.

7 The LORD looseth men out of prison : the LORD giveth sight to the blind.

Metaphors for deliverance from sins and spiritual evil; cp. Isa. 42. 7; 61. 1. Cp. also S. Matt. 11. 5. The former may have been suggested by the release from captivity; it has been applied to the deliverance of holy souls from purgatory. The latter is applied to the conversion of unbelievers and sinners.

8 The LORD helpeth them that are fallen : the LORD careth for the righteous;

R.V. The LORD raiseth up them that are bowed down; the LORD loveth the righteous; cp. Ps. 145. 14.

9 The LORD careth for the strangers; he defendeth the fatherless and widows : as for the way of the ungodly, he turneth it upside down.

strangers ... fatherless ... widow: types of the helpless; cp. Ps. 94. 6.

10 The LORD thy God, O Sion, shall be King for evermore : and throughout all generations.

Sion: the Church militant.

A.R.V. add *Praise ye the LORD. R.V.mg. Heb. Hallelujah.*

EVENING PRAYER

PSALM 147. *Laudate Dominum*

Thanksgiving to Jehovah, the Lord of Creation, the Restorer of Jerusalem, the Builder of the Catholic Church. The psalm was perhaps written in celebration of the dedication of the wall of Jerusalem after the return; cp. Neh. 12. 27 ff. The application of it to the Church is readily made, especially in the second part.

O PRAISE the LORD, for it is a good thing to sing praises unto our God : yea, a joyful and pleasant thing it is to be thankful.

A.R.V. prefix *Praise ye the LORD. R.V.mg. Heb. Hallelujah.*

2 The LORD doth build up Jerusalem : and gather together the out-casts of Israel.

build up: by restoring the walls and houses, and repopulating the city.

out-casts: those that had been exiles.

This verse has been applied to the gradual building of 'Jerusalem above' with living stones, and gathering into their true home in heaven the pilgrims released from the Babylon of this sinful world.

Prophesied of the Messiah, cp. Isa. 61. 1 ff.

A.R.V. and bindeth up their wounds.

3 He healeth those that are broken in heart : and giveth medicine to heal their sickness.

4 He telleth the number of the stars : and calleth them all by their names.

telleth: i.e. counteth.

He who knows every star will assuredly be acquainted with the case of each of his people, cp. Isa. 40. 26–28, however many they may be, cp. Gen. 15. 5. 'Stars' may also remind us of those who were leading lights in the Church, cp. Rev. 1. 19; Dan. 12. 3.

calleth; cp. S. John 10. 3, 'He calleth his own sheep by name.'

5 Great is our Lord, and great is his power : yea, and his wisdom is infinite.

6 The LORD setteth up the meek : and bringeth the ungodly down to the ground.

7 O sing unto the LORD with thanksgiving : sing praises upon the harp unto our God;

8 Who covereth the heaven with clouds, and prepareth rain for the earth : and maketh the grass to grow upon the mountains, and herb for the use of man:

The apostles and evangelists are as clouds storing the water of divine grace and truth to discharge them upon the world. 'Like clouds are they borne to do thy great will.'

9 Who giveth fodder unto the cattle : and feedeth the young ravens that call upon him.

10 He hath no pleasure in the strength of an horse : neither delighteth he in any man's legs.

Cp. Job 38. 41; S. Luke 12. 24. 10–11. Cp. Ps. 33. 15–17. God does not look with approval on those who rely on their own strength and resources.

11 But the LORD's delight is in them that fear him : and put their trust in his mercy.

———

12 Praise the LORD, O Jerusalem : praise thy God, O Sion.

In Sept. and Vulg. a new psalm begins here.

Jerusalem: i.e. 'Jerusalem above which is free, and the

mother of us all' (*Gal.* 4. 26), the Church triumphant in heaven.

Sion: i.e. 'Mount Sion, the Church of the first-born which are written in heaven' (*Heb.* 12. 22), the Church militant here in earth.

13 For he hath made fast the bars of thy gates : and hath blessed thy children within thee.

Probably there is a reference to the setting up of the gates of restored Jerusalem (*Neh.* 3. 3, 6, etc.). The 'bars' of the Church's gates are her great teachers and dogmas.

within thee: but not strayers from thy communion. Salvation is within the Church. Cp. Rev. 22. 14, 'Blessed are they that . . . may enter in by the gates into the city.'

14 He maketh peace in thy borders : and filleth thee with the flour of wheat.

peace in thy borders: so that no enemy assails thy frontiers. In the communion of the Church in heaven God gives peace, and also on earth we have peace with God, cp. Rom. 5. 1, through Jesus Christ. But on earth the Church has not perfect peace from outward assault or inward strife. Also this clause is a prophecy of the re-union of Christendom, the dissenting sects being the 'borders' of the Church.

filleth with the flour of wheat: *A.R.V. with the finest of the wheat.* I.e. the Eucharistic Bread, the sacrament of peace and unity.

15 He sendeth forth his commandment upon earth : and his word runneth very swiftly.

15–16. Cp. Isa. 55. 10–11; Ps. 107. 20.

swiftly: in accomplishing the errand on which it is sent.

Mystically, the 'commandment' is the new law of Christ's kingdom; and the 'word' is the

Word Incarnate, which 're-joiceth as a giant to run his course' (*Ps.* 19. 5), and is swiftly proclaimed throughout the world; cp. Acts 10. 36, 'The word which God sent, preaching peace by Jesus Christ, he is Lord of all, that word ye know, which was published,' etc.

16 He giveth snow like wool : and scattereth the hoar-frost like ashes.

The gospel of the Word directs the Church (v. 15); disciplines it (vv. 16–17); inducing penitence (v. 18).

I.e. hail like crumbs of bread.

17 He casteth forth his ice like morsels : who is able to abide his frost?
18 He sendeth out his word, and melteth them : he bloweth with his wind, and the waters flow.

The snow, frost, and hail, melted by the warm wind, flow away as water. By the operation of the Word of God, and the Wind of the Spirit, the waters of penitence are caused to flow. Cp. Ps. 33. 6; S. John 3. 8.

19 He sheweth his word unto Jacob : his statutes and ordin-ances unto Israel.

He who rules all nature by his word has specially privileged Israel, in giving it his written word. Cp. Rom. 3. 1, 'What advantage, then, hath the Jew? Much every way: first of all, that they were intrusted with the oracles of God.'

Two stages of receptivity and response, in relation to divine grace and truth in the Church, are marked by 'Jacob' under discipline, and 'Israel' prevailing with God; cp. Gen. 32. 28.

20 He hath not dealt so with any nation : neither have the heathen knowledge of his laws.

Cp. Deut. 4. 32-34. Still more favourably has he now dealt with the Church.

A.R.V. add *Praise ye the* LORD. *R.V.mg.Heb.Hallelujah.*

PSALM 148. *Laudate Dominum*

A call to heaven and earth to join with Israel in the praise of God.
The *Benedicite*, the apocryphal addition to Dan. 3, is an expansion
of this psalm. This psalm has often been recited together with 149
and 150 as one psalm, in the Church's worship.

O PRAISE the LORD of hea-ven : PRAISE HIM in the
height.

A.R.V. prefix *Praise ye the
LORD. R.V.mg. Heb. Hallelujah.*
1–6. Heaven invited to praise
God.
*A.R.V. praise the LORD from
the heavens.*

2 PRAISE HIM, all ye angels of
his : PRAISE HIM, all his host.
3 PRAISE HIM, sun and moon :
PRAISE HIM, all ye stars and light.
4 PRAISE HIM, all ye heavens :
and ye waters that are above the
heavens.

A.R.V. ye heavens of heavens,
i.e. ye highest heavens.
waters above the firmament:
cf. Gen. 1. 7; Ps. 104. 3.

5 Let them PRAISE THE NAME
OF THE LORD : for he spake the
word, and they were made; he
commanded, and they were
created.

spake the word: i.e. of creation; cp. Ps. 33. 9. Or we may
understand that God spake the
word when he said, 'Thou art
my Son,' in the eternal generation of the Son; and through that
Son, who is the Word of God,
all things were made. Cp. Col.
1. 16.

6 He hath made them fast for
ever and ever : he hath given
them a law which shall not be
broken.

*A.R.V. He hath established
them.* Cp. Ps. 119. 90, 91,
'Thou hast laid the foundation
of the earth, and it abideth.
They continue this day according to thine ordinance; for all
things serve thee.'
7–13. Earth is invited to praise
God.

7 Praise the LORD upon earth:
ye dragons, and all deeps;

*A.R.V. Praise the LORD from
the earth:*
dragons: *R.V.mg. sea-monsters.* Cp. Gen. 1. 21.

8 Fire and hail, snow and vapour : wind and storm, fulfilling his word;

9 Mountains and all hills : fruitful trees and all cedars;

10 Beasts and all cattle : worms and feathered fowls;

11 Kings of the earth and all people : princes and all judges of the world;

12 Young men and maidens, old men and children, PRAISE THE NAME OF THE LORD : for his Name only is excellent, and his praise above heaven and earth.

13 He shall exalt the horn of his people; all his saints shall praise him : even the children of Israel, even the people that serveth him.

Fire: i.e. lightning.

worms: *A.R.V. creeping things.*
11–12. Man mentioned last as the climax of creation.
people: *R.V. peoples.*
Cp. v. 5.
excellent: *R.V. exalted.* Cp. Phil. 2. 9, 'the Name which is above every name; that in the name of Jesus every knee should bow, of things in heaven and things on earth.'
R.V. And he hath lifted up the horn of his people, the praise of all his saints (i.e. the exaltation of his people is the special theme of their praise); *even of the children of Israel, a people near unto him.* (Cp. *Ps.* 145. 18 and *Deut.* 4. 7, 'What great nation is there, that hath a god so nigh unto them, as the LORD our God is whensoever we call upon him?')
A.R.V. add *Praise ye the LORD. Heb. Hallelujah.*

PSALM 149. *Cantate Domino*

Israel restored from Babylon, and new born as a nation, rejoices in its divine King; and exults in the prospect of future victories over the nations. The psalm, spiritually understood, foreshadows the conquest of the world by Christ and his Church. Proper on the Feast of All Saints.

O SING unto the LORD a new song : let the congregation of saints praise him.

A.R.V. prefix *Praise ye the LORD. R.V.mg. Heb. Hallelujah.*
a new song: the new epoch of joy and hope calls for a new expression of thanksgiving; cp. Ps. 33. 3, 96. 1, 98. 1; Rev. 5. 9, 14. 3. For us the new song is the worship of the Lamb of God.

2 Let Israel rejoice in him that made him : and let the children of Sion be joyful in their King.

The Church's duty of religious joy and joyous religion. Cp. Isa. 51. 3, 'The LORD hath comforted Zion . . . joy and gladness shall be found therein, and the voice of melody.'

that made him: i.e. made him a nation, and has now revived the national life. Cp. Ps. 95. 6; 100. 2.

children of Sion: the members of the Church, the same as the 'saints' in v. 1, the elect people of God, including pre-eminently but not exclusively the great Saints.

3 Let them PRAISE HIS NAME in the dance : let them sing praises unto him with tabret and harp.

Cp. Ps. 148. 5, 12.

Co-ordinated and rhythmic worship symbolizes the unity and order of the Church.

tabret: *A.R.V. timbrel,* or tambourine.

4 For the LORD hath pleasure in his people : and helpeth the meek-hearted.

hath pleasure: cp. Ps. 147. 11.

A.R.V. He will beautify the meek with salvation. Cp. Isa. 61. 3, 'To comfort all that mourn in Zion, to give unto them a garland for ashes, the oil of joy for mourning, the garment of praise for the spirit of heaviness.'

5 Let the saints be joyful with glory : let them rejoice in their beds.

R.V. sing for joy upon their beds. I.e. let their rejoicing be in private as well as in public (v. 3). Cp. Ps. 4. 4; 63. 7. Applied to the joy of the Holy Souls, and to the final consummation of bliss of the Saints in heaven, resting from their labours.

6 Let the praises of God be in their mouth : and a two-edged sword in their hands;

The saints worship and fight.

a two-edged sword: Christ came to send 'not peace, but a sword' (*S. Matt.* 10. 34); 'the sword of the Spirit, which is the word of God' (*Eph.* 6. 18); 'the word of God is sharper than any two-edged sword' (*Heb.* 4. 12); out of the mouth of the glorified Christ 'proceedeth a sharp two-edged sword' (*Rev.* 1. 16); that 'with it he should smite the nations' (*Rev.* 19. 15); while 'the armies which are in heaven' follow him to the conquest of the world. Some have thought the two edges refer to the Old and New Testaments, the Law and the Gospel.

7 To be avenged of the heathen : and to rebuke the people;

R.V. To execute vengeance upon the nations: and punishments upon the peoples. Cp. 2 Cor. 10. 4–5, 'The weapons of our warfare are not of the flesh, but mighty before God to the casting down imaginations, and every high thing that is exalted against the knowledge of God, and bringing every thought into captivity to the obedience of Christ.'

I.e. restrained by Christian faith and law.

8 To bind their kings in chains : and their nobles with links of iron;

9 That they may be avenged of them as it is written : Such honour have all his saints.

A.R.V. To execute upon them the judgement written, i.e. to carry into effect the divine will recorded in Holy Writ, that all kingdoms shall become subject to the Lord Christ. Cp. Isa. 41. 15, 16; 65. 6; Micah 4. 13; Joel 3. 12; and Rev. 11. 15, 'The kingdoms of this world are become the kingdoms of our Lord, and of his Christ; and he shall reign for ever and ever.'

Such honour: *A.R.V. This honour*, i.e. the honour of being God's agents in subjecting the world to Christ belongs to all the faithful members of his Church.

A.R.V. add *Praise ye the* Lord. *R.V.mg. Heb. Hallelujah.*

Psalm 150. *Laudate Dominum*

The closing Hallelujah. A call to the universal praise of the Lord God. As each of the Books of the Psalter ends with a doxology, so the concluding psalm of the last Book is solely a doxology.

O PRAISE God in his holiness : praise him in the firmament of his power.

A.R.V. prefix *Praise ye the* Lord. *R.V.mg. Heb. Hallelujah.*

holiness: *A.R.V. sanctuary,* i.e. the Church on earth.

The 'firmament' or sky which testifies to God's power, i.e. heaven. Cp. Ps. 68. 34.

2 Praise him in his noble acts: praise him according to his excellent greatness.

3 Praise him in the sound of the trumpet : praise him upon the lute and harp.

4 Praise him in the cymbals and dances : praise him upon the strings and pipe.

5 Praise him upon the well-tuned cymbals : praise him upon the loud cymbals.

6 Let every thing that hath breath : praise the Lord.

in: *A.R.V. for* his work, and also for himself.

excellent: cp. Ps. 148. 12.

Let every instrument of man be used to make its contribution to the praise of God.

cymbals: *A.R.V. timbrel,* tambourine.

A.R.V. add *Praise ye the* Lord. *R.V.mg. Heb. Hallelujah.*